Roslyn Fuller
Principles of Digital Democracy

Democracy in Times of Upheaval

Series Editor
Matt Qvortrup, Coventry University

Volume 8

Roslyn Fuller

Principles of Digital Democracy

Theory and Case Studies

DE GRUYTER

ISBN 978-3-11-079439-7
e-ISBN (PDF) 978-3-11-079446-5
e-ISBN (EPUB) 978-3-11-079454-0
ISSN 2701-147X
e-ISSN 2701-1488

Library of Congress Control Number: 2023939317

Bibliographic information published by the Deutsche Nationalbibliothek
The Deutsche Nationalbibliothek lists this publication in the Deutsche Nationalbibliografie;
detailed bibliographic data are available on the internet at http://dnb.dnb.de.

© 2023 Walter de Gruyter GmbH, Berlin/Boston
Cover image: ihsanyildizli / E+ / Getty Images
Printing and binding: CPI books GmbH, Leck

www.degruyter.com

Overview

Contents

Chapter 5
Communication —— 168

List of Figures

https://doi.org/10.1515/9783110794465-001

List of Tables

https://doi.org/10.1515/9783110794465-002

About the Author and the Series Editor

About the author

Dr. Roslyn Fuller is the Managing Director of the Solonian Democracy Institute, an Irish think tank focussed on researching alternative democratic practices. An international jurist by training (PhD International Law, Trinity College, Dublin), her research combines insights from ancient Athenian democracy with modern methods of digital, distributed decision-making. The author of several books including *Beasts and Gods: How Democracy Changed Its Meaning and Lost Its Purpose* (Zed Books, 2015) and *In Defence of Democracy* (Polity, 2019), she advocates for a principles-based understanding of democracy that cherishes wide and deep democratic participation not tied to specific outcomes. Dr. Fuller also regularly contributes to broadcast and print media, including *The Nation*, *The LA Review of Books* and *The Financial Times*.

About the series editor

Dr. Matt Qvortrup is Professor of Political Science at Coventry University. A political scientist, his research centers on the tension between political actors being driven by emotion and driven by rational argument. Author of many books on referendums and democracy, the new edition of Qvortrup's *Death by a Thousand Cuts* (DeGruyter 2023) pioneers interdisciplinary research in Neuropolitics and shows how political debates can be analysed using insights from fMRI-scans, history, and philosophy. Matt is also editor of *European Political Science Review*.

https://doi.org/10.1515/9783110794465-003

Introduction

It is customary to begin books about democracy with an inspiring tale about a grassroots event where people were really 'heard' and 'change was in the air'. Micro-vignettes of 'ordinary' people seemingly on the cusp of profound transformation feature prominently, because that (you will be reminded) is what it is all about – the people, *people like you*.

But it is not the purpose of this book to make you feel all giddy and inspired. That kind of fluff is not what makes the world go round and it is certainly not going to help you make a digital democracy that works.

The purpose of this book is to examine the underlying principles of digital democracy. It is a guide, an overview and a correction to the many misconceptions that proliferate in this understudied area. In particular, its aim is to bridge the gap between the often overlooked theory of democracy and its practice in real life. This bridge is vital – one can only hope to implement something well if one has a crystal-clear idea of what that something is.

Shockingly, most analyses of digital democracy fail to define both democracy and digital technology. This means that they fail to define the very thing they are seeking to achieve, relying instead on a fuzzy apprehension that democracy is 'good' and will somehow 'happen' with enough 'involvement' from 'ordinary people'. Nothing could be further from the truth and this wishful thinking is muddied still further by the many self-declared 'experts' operating in this field and offering unexamined tips, tricks and magic formulas for implementing these poorly defined, often extremely partisan, visions of 'digital democracy'. These fads, like all fads, come and go for the simple reason that they do not work.

This book does not have magic formulas. There are no magic formulas for politics, just as there are no magic formulas for life. Politics, like life in general, is far too complicated for such things. Instead, this book contains principles that can be used as a guide for designing processes that must be rigorously executed. These principles are based on, and tested against, hard data wherever possible. The aim is to help you, the reader, realize why what you do may be productive or counterproductive to the goals you are trying to reach, and to help you to create a system in your own mind for reaching those goals, which may change, develop or need to adapt to circumstances. This book can be read front-to-back, but the subject matter is dense and therefore it is also intended to serve as a reference work that systematizes knowledge in one place, and that you can return to if a particular challenge arises. While some of the ideas presented here have their roots in complex theory, the key to success remains repetition and practical implementation.

https://doi.org/10.1515/9783110794465-004

Despite the fact that this is an under-researched area, there is still more information available on digital democracy than could ever be included in one book. I have tried to avoid repeating what others have already said, and instead, wherever possible, have referenced further reading.

In addition, a work like this which takes account of the newest developments in practice must rely on practitioners to provide insights and data. The following people have been kind enough to share difficult-to-find papers, data, or their own experiences with me, and to frequently provide confirmation of me nit-picking the details: Róbert Bjarnason of Citizens Foundation; Davide Casaleggio of Rousseau; Eiríkur Búi Halldórsson of the City of Reykjavik; Lori Britt of James Madison University; Inete Ielīte of the Women's NGO Cooperation Network in Latvia; John Richardson of Ethelo; Mihkel Solvak of the University of Tartu; William Arhip-Paterson on participatory budgeting in Paris; Robert Krimmer on internet voting in Estonia; David Duenas-Cid, Fellow at Gdansk University; Vito Crimi, former Senator for the Five Star Movement; Ali Stoddart of the Participation and Communities Team at the Scottish Parliament; Sarah Brown of the City of Prince George; Michael Neblo of Ohio State University; William R. Nylen of Stetson University; and Stéphan De Loof of FrancoSud, as well as many others who wished to retain their privacy. In addition, I would like to thank the many organizations who have shared data for the Solonian Democracy Institute's Digital Democracy Report over the years, including: SkyVote, PlaceSpeak, VoxVote, Civocracy, CitizenLab, Slido, Ethelo, Every Voice Engaged, PolCo, Polys, Voatz, Manabalss, Rousseau, Rahvaalgatus, Democracy.Space, First Root, Aula, Novoville, Delib, Electis, Discuto and many more. I have often been relentless in pursuing this information, conducting factchecks and asking questions, so your patience as well as your generosity with your time has been appreciated. Of course, much as I am grateful for this assistance, the *interpretation* of this data is all my own, and the majority of the data included in this book was also obtained via my own independent research. I have tried to make the origin of data as clear as possible in the references.

Finally, I would like to thank Anthony Mason for working with me on commissioning this book, Michaela Göbels for guiding me through the publication process and, most of all, Matt Qvortrup of Coventry University for inviting me to contribute to the *Democracy in Times of Upheaval* series. It was in a time of upheaval that democracy was first introduced in ancient Athens and it was in a time of upheaval that it was (temporarily) overthrown. Times of upheaval are moments of opportunity and threat alike – how democracies evolve and whether they survive, depends on how we respond to these crises.

Chapter 1
What is Digital Democracy?

As the power of monarchs waned in the 18th and 19th centuries, philosophers began to contemplate how political life could be organized in a new, more literate, rational and free society. Many of these thinkers are familiar to us from school: Rousseau, Mill, Locke, Hobbes, Marx, Bukanin, Toqueville, Montesquieu, Paine, and Burke, to name but a few. This stage of theorizing and clarifying was necessary, because in order to achieve a goal, you must first have a clear idea of what that goal is.

Like these thinkers, we are also coming to terms with a world that has *physically* changed and for this reason I will also outline a brief theory of digital democracy. This theory will then be expanded upon and elucidated throughout the book using concrete examples.

Democracy means 'people power', that is, that the people of a nation or other polity have the *power* to govern their own affairs. This is different than just having the *right* to do so. In a democracy, this right has been realized, and one does not just have the right to govern oneself in an abstract sense, but the power to actually do so in the real world. This necessitates that the institutions to channel that power exist and can be made use of.

The term 'digital' simply describes the method used for communication, in this case binary code. Anything that is expressed in 0s and 1s (or 'on' and 'off') is 'digital', as opposed to communication transmitted by waves (e.g. radio, simply speaking), which is analogue. Like its forerunner, Morse code, digital communication can send encoded messages long distances, enabling (unlike Morse code) quick, multi-way, extremely flexible communication.[1]

Thus, digital democracy can be defined as **self-government enabled by instantaneous, peer-to-peer digital communication.**

This is a much more focused definition than is commonly used. Digital democracy is often defined more colloquially as any 'involvement', 'participation' or 'engagement' that makes use of computers. These terms are so beloved precisely because they are so flexible. One can be 'involved' in a decision simply by eavesdropping on a conversation and offering unsolicited advice. One can be 'en-

---

1 This and a few other passages were originally published (sometimes in slightly altered form) in the short contribution that served as the starting point for this book: Roslyn Fuller, 'Digital Democracy: Past, Present and Future' in Matt Qvortrup and Daniela Vancic (eds) *Complementary Democracy: The Art of Deliberative Listening* (De Gruyter 2022) 115–133.

https://doi.org/10.1515/9783110794465-005

gaged' simply by one's employer asking one's opinion (which they may or may not ignore). One can 'participate' in a bank robbery by being the hapless cashier who stuffs cash in a bag on the order of the robber.

Wide definitions are impossible to measure and easy to abuse. They can encapsulate almost anything, including many of the things we would think of as the furthest possible from democracy. Moreover, such wide definitions are not self-sustaining. Efforts at 'participation', 'engagement' and 'involvement' continuously run out of steam, fall into disuse and are abandoned. But democracy (despite being a lot of work) is self-sustaining, because it builds its own institutions and capital. Power, like gravity, is a self-maximizing force.

Without a focused definition, such as the one outlined above, one quickly becomes lost, distracted by the many other worthy goals and ideas that exist.

This focused definition of democracy, that has power at its centre, in turn demands that the following **Four Elements** be fulfilled:

1. the institutions of government must be constructed in such a manner that the polity's members can exercise their power on a free and equal basis without having to obtain permission to participate

2. no subset of the population may possess inherent privileges that can over-ride these decisions or prevent this exercise in power from occurring

3. each member's vote carries equal weight, which as a corollary necessitates majority rule (unless agreed otherwise)

4. the people, as the ultimate decision-making power, are accountable for the nation's policies and ultimately bear the benefits and consequences thereof

From these elements we can extrapolate further information about what democracy is and is not. We can thereby refine our meaning and give it contours that differentiate it from other understandings of 'democracy'.

10 Core Aspects of Democracy

1. Democracy is a **decision-making process**, not a debating society. Power cannot be exercised in the absence of decisions. If there is no decision-point, there is no democracy. This is why social media is not any form of democracy, digital or otherwise. Although talking, debating, deliberating and otherwise communicating can elucidate options and help people to form their opinions, discus-

sion does not in itself confer power, nor does it allow for majority will to be accurately measured. People may communicate about politics over social media, but political decision-making does not happen on social media. It happens in the institutions of government.

2. Democracy is the **rule of law.** Because there is no superior or external law-giver and all are equal, the highest authority in a democracy is the collectively decided-upon law. As the Swiss Enlightenment thinker Rousseau put it: 'only when the laws govern, does the public interest govern... The undertakings that bind us to the social body are obligatory only because they go both ways; and their nature is such that in fulfilling them we can't work for others without working for ourselves.' In ancient times, Greek writers also sometimes used the term 'isonomia' (legal equality) to refer to early Athenian democracy, and the Athenians themselves frequently appealed to 'the law' as the ruler of Athens.

3. Democracy is a set of **institutions**, not a particular ideology. These institutions serve the purpose of providing a venue for participation, scrutinizing proposals, voting on them and overseeing implementation. As such, democracy is a kind of scientific method for politics, and a way of making the unknown known. It is *not* merely a method of ratifying what is *already* known. As a corollary this means that democracy is not a wish-list or particular agenda. Democracy is not liberalism, conservatism, communism, capitalism or any other ism. Equally, democracy is not prosperity, or the position a society accords women. One can measure a society on whether it has achieved these goals as well, but it is important to keep those things *separate* and not call them all 'democracy'. Mangling various aims together causes confusion and makes it difficult to achieve anything. These goals may at times be *similar*, but they are not *identical.*

4. Democracy is **accountability.** This cannot be stressed enough, as democracy is commonly perceived as an *abdication* of responsibility and a form of government in which citizens are, like children, permitted to make demands without bearing the consequences of those demands. Nothing could be further from the truth. In order to achieve accountability, all situations in which it is unclear who is responsible for a choice, policy or other action must be stringently avoided.

5. Democracy is a method of **scrutinizing** far more than it is a method of inducing 'creativity or 'innovation'. Ideas are very easy to come by and most ideas

are bad ideas. Democracy is a method of winnowing out the few good ones over long periods of time. As this implies, democracy is – contrary to what is so often said – *not* a form of government that simply caters to the average. Instead, it demands excellence and provides institutions to achieve that excellence through rigorous scrutiny.

6. Democracy is **emancipatory.** This shares a root with the word 'manumission', the ancient practice of granting a slave freedom. This is the opposite of technocracy or 'good governance'. No one knows if a slave is going to have a good life when they are freed, but having a good life or a safe life or a rich life is not the *point* of emancipation. When we insist that it is right to free slaves because some of them went on to have very inspirational or productive lives we are falling into the trap of technocratic justification. Instead, we should focus on what gives a slave-holder the right to enslave people (nothing). Democracy (freedom from political slavery) also needs no technocratic justification. This is important, because democracy is not a panacea for social issues, just as emancipation is not a panacea for every issue a former slave will face. We may resolve social issues via democratic means, just as a former slave may improve their life via their own choices, but this still depends on our choices, rather than occurring automatically – this is the *point* of freedom.

7. Democracy may be satisfying and avoid suffering, but it is **not** necessarily **fun** in the conventional sense of the word. By insisting that democracy be fun, we are actually devaluing it. It is important. That is enough.

8. Democracy demands **clarity**, which necessitates eliminating distortions. This is a very important point we will return to throughout this book. Clarity necessitates that questions and decision-points are formulated in such a way as to present obviously delineated alternatives. Democracy also necessitates honest communication. Whenever we obfuscate or dissemble, we are doing a disservice to democracy, because this clouds the issues at stake.

9. Democracy is **fluid.** In a democracy, a person may find themselves in the minority on one issue and the majority on another. Democracy does not demand loyal partisanship to achieve its goals. Indeed, sustained partisanship has a profoundly negative impact on democracy.

10. Democracy is **not** primarily about **trusting** 'decision-makers'. A key error many people make about democracy is the idea that it functions well when people *trust* others to make decisions *for them*. This is the opposite of a

well-functioning democracy. In a democracy, the people hold power. There is no need for them to trust anyone, which is a good thing, because it is very difficult to assess anyone's trustworthiness accurately.

The above points are all very different than what we commonly accept as 'democracy' today. If you ask most people today, they will tell you that democracy is all about talking, trusting leaders, innovation, taking sides, good governance and having fun. Then they bemoan that it doesn't work. This is because the characteristics they like to believe in are not suitable to achieving the goal they desire.

In addition to these social misunderstandings about what democracy should be, we also suffer confusion due to the imperfect historical development of modern 'democracy' which has evolved in ways that create numerous logical tensions. Our current institutions of representative democracy were not designed to accurately measure, implement and reassess majority will in an iterative process. Our present institutions of government (elections, representative chambers) were mainly created by people who had rather dim views of the general population, often believing them to be ignorant and lacking self-control. For these reasons they intentionally created a system loosely based not on Greek democracy, but on Roman Republicanism. Republican government was an improvement on aristocratic rule, but it intentionally creates bottlenecks at key points, ensuring that power is ultimately exercised by a few of the most eminent citizens, who are judged to have the greatest stake in public affairs.[2]

The choice to institute republicanism over democracy (people power) cannot, however, be solely attributed to the personal preferences of 18th century Western elites. The fact is that at the time, physical constraints did not allow many other options for a government that depended, if only partly and imperfectly, on popular will. Even those political philosophers who perceived the shortcomings of representative republican government had to admit that true democracy would be impossible to exercise over the vast distances of modern states.

'If we take the term in the strict sense, there never has been a real democracy, and there never will be,' wrote Rousseau, 'It is unimaginable that the people should remain continually assembled to devote their time to public affairs, and it is clear that they cannot set up commissions for that purpose without the form of administration being changed'.[3]

---

2 For more details, see Roslyn Fuller, *Beasts and Gods: How Democracy Changed Its Meaning and Lost Its Purpose* (Zed/Bloomsbury 2015).
3 Jean-Jacques Rousseau, *The Social Contract and Discourses* (G.D.H. Cole tr, E.P. Dutton & Co 1913) Ch. IV.

Over 150 years later, Robert Michels wrote in his early 20th-century analysis of political parties:

> Even if we imagined the means of communication to become much better than those which now exist, how would it be possible to assemble such a multitude in a given place, at a stated time, and with the frequency demanded by the exigencies of party life? In addition must be considered the physiological impossibility even for the most powerful orator of making himself heard by a crowd of ten thousand persons.[4]

The fraught question of how to combine popular rule with a vast territorial government also prompted a debate in early America.

However, due to the impossibility of exercising a full democracy over large areas there never really was much of a contest about which form modern government should take. If anything that even approximated self-rule was going to be implemented, it would have to be representative, and it would have to take a lot of short-cuts. The only alternative to this would be to live in smaller, weaker States – a risky strategy in a world where one had to compete with larger, more powerful empires. All of the most celebrated changes to democracy and communication since this time (such as extending the franchise) have merely optimized this system of representative government, making it more efficient and inclusive, but without changing its fundamental nature as a relatively controlled form of government where a few people wield power.

Despite these shortcomings, Republicanism worked as a system of government for a long time (just as it did in ancient Rome). However, two crucial changes have now occurred – the first psychological, the second physical.

Around the time of the Second World War, Western government started to be routinely and vigorously referred to as 'democracy' in opposition to 'totalitarianism' in Germany, Japan, and later, the Soviet Union. The average person began to understand their role in politics differently, not merely as someone who would deferentially vote for a more capable but distant ruler who would exercise power on their behalf, but as someone who could also be mobilized to take part in politics directly. Unlike the learned opinion of previous generations which had seen democracy at least partly as a threat, common opinion now saw democracy as a good thing and as a key differentiator between free and unfree peoples. The psychological acceptance of a democracy in which every citizen could participate in politics equally now existed, but it still was not physically possible to achieve outside of small areas.

---

4 Robert Michels, *Political Parties: A Sociological Study of the Oligarchical Tendency of Modern Democracy* (Verlag Werner Klinkhardt 1911) 22.

The internet changed this, because it eliminated *physical* (rather than man-made) constraints on our activities. This is why the internet is so significant, and why it is one of the most contested and controversial inventions of history. Things that were once accepted as immutable limits to human interaction, have lost some of their power, some of their relevance, some of their *meaning*.

The internet does this by affecting three key factors:

1. Frequency (it enables continuous **presence**)
2. Transparency (which enables **structure**)
3. Peer-to-peer communication (**horizontality**, which reduces control)

As we have seen, in the past it was impossible for citizens of very large states to be continuously (or even regularly) *present* in decision-making forums. This difficulty has vanished. We now carry an access key to virtually any place on earth in our pocket. The physical limits that dictated delegation in so many areas, including politics, are gone.

Digitalization also enables immediate and unlimited transparency. This makes it possible to follow processes and create structure around public decision-making. It reduces the bottlenecks created by waiting for information (which may never come) and dealing with edited and contested information. This makes it much harder to break rules or to engage in many forms of manipulation that often undermine democracy.

Most famously of all, digital democracy has enabled mass peer-to-peer communication. This has, again, the potential to reduce bottlenecks as citizens can communicate with each other on public matters directly, rather than having to pass through another authority.

Like everything in life, these developments are not purely positive – if they were, we could sit back and enjoy them rather than analysing them in detail. But they are so profound that despite being largely procedural in nature, they have the potential to qualitatively change how we have been practicing democracy.

In particular, this allows us to better *fulfill* the democratic mission of achieving 'people power' by using these advantages to their fullest extent to create those characteristics of democracy mentioned above (e.g. institutions that fluidly channel majority decision-making). And although it is important to be grounded in theory to understand why this is happening and the full extent of the change, none of this is purely theoretical. In many ways, and in many nations, digital democracy is already happening.

1.1 Current Examples of Digital Democracy in Practice

Generally speaking, democracy consists of five stages: Ideation (coming up with proposals); Deliberation and Debate (examining those proposals); Decision-Making (measuring support via a vote); Implementation; and Re-Evaluation. Some digital tools focus on only one aspect of this process, but these steps can also be consolidated into a single end-to-end procedure. This section will briefly describe several modes of participation that are currently in use before moving to a consideration of how they fit in to the theory of digital democracy outlined above.

1.1.1 Pure Voting Applications (Decision-Making)

Pure voting applications are usually intended to replace paper ballot voting in elections. Therefore, they tend to mirror the electoral system precisely with no possibility for online debate among participants and with an emphasis on guaranteeing secret, anonymous voting. The most enduring online voting system in the world today is **Estonia's i-voting system**, which has enabled online voting since 2005 and now extends to local, national and European elections. While i-voting has sometimes faced criticism from abroad, as well as local legal challenges, it has thus far weathered these trials with more than half of Estonian voters now casting their ballots online.

Estonian i-voting has recently been joined by similar models in other nations. **Voatz**, a private online voting provider, has been used by several municipalities in US elections, while **Polys**, an online voting system developed by internet security giant Kaspersky, was used by Russia's Yabloko party to facilitate voting in primaries, as well as in Russia's 2021 parliamentary elections. These systems and many like them have proven quite popular where they are used (almost two million Muscovites voted online in the 2021 elections).[5]

Such systems can also be used for referendums. A cosmonaut cast his ballot on Russia's 2020 constitutional referendums from the International Space Station,[6]

---

5 'Moscow Voters Debate: Did Blockchain-Based Online Voting Undermine the Opposition?' *Current Time* (24 September 2021) <https://en.currenttime.tv/a/moscow-voters-debate-did-blockchain-based-online-voting-undermine-russia-s-opposition-/31476383.html> accessed 1 February 2023.

6 AFP, 'Cosmonaut Votes on Putin's Reforms from ISS' *The Moscow Times* (30 June 2020) <www.themoscowtimes.com/2020/06/30/russian-cosmonaut-votes-on-putins-reforms-from-iss-a70742> accessed 1 February 2023.

while several Swiss cantons have experimented with multiple online voting systems for referendums.[7]

1.1.2 Petition (Ideation)

Petitioning is another example of a traditional offline mode of participation that has moved online virtually unchanged. Petitioning could include gathering signatures to initiate a referendum, or directly petitioning parliament or another authority to pass, amend or repeal a law, take another measure, or change a policy. Several online petition vehicles have been launched with varying degrees of success, whereby some of the most enduring and impactful have been in Latvia and Estonia.

For example, **Manabalss** in Latvia is an online petitioning site, whereby petitions that receive more than 10,000 signatures must be voted on in parliament (as opposed to merely discussed or answered). In a country with ca. 1.5 million registered voters this is a relatively low bar (less than 1% of the voting population must sign the petition). In addition, petitioners are provided with support to craft their proposals into working legislation (reducing the risk that they are rejected on technicalities) and are allowed to call witnesses in the parliament to support their proposals. Manabalss is a separate institution not run by the government, and is financed by micro-payments. Participants can sign into the system using their bank identity. Similarly, Rahvaalgatus.ee in Estonia uses a low bar to petitioning (1,000 signatures for a discussion in parliament) as well as continuous follow-ups on the fate of proposals.[8] Between 2014 and 2021, 95 initiatives processed via **Rahvaalgatus** were presented to the Parliament.[9]

Because the petition process in Estonia and Latvia is connected to representative democracy (as opposed to direct democracy) the connection between petition and action is not always clear-cut. At times, petitions that receive low levels of signatures are adopted by authorities, presumably because the content accords with the governmental programme. Because the signature barrier is low, there is no compelling case as to why any particular petition should be adopted into law

---

7 Uwe Serdült, Micha Germann, Fernando Mendez, Alicia Portenier and Christoph Wellig, 'Fifteen Years of Internet Voting in Switzerland: History, Governance and Use' in Luis Teran and Andreas Meier (eds), *Second International Conference on eDemocracy & eGovernment (ICEDEG)* (2015).

8 Roslyn Fuller, *2022 Digital Democracy Report* (Solonian Democracy Institute 2022) 52.

9 'E-Governance Factsheet' (*E-Governance Academy*) <https://e-estonia.com/wp-content/uploads/e-governance-factsheet-aug2022.pdf>.

based on this criterium alone.[10] However, the follow-through is still impressive. Successful petitions are often either debated in parliament or passed to the subject matter committee or department responsible, just as other draft legislation would be. These bodies tend to deal with the matter thoroughly and in technical detail, making them very different from other petition mechanisms, like the European Citizens Initiative or former White House petition site, where petitioners simply receive a formal answer from the executive.

Perhaps the most interesting example of digital democracy in this regard is online signature collection for petitions that are intended to trigger referendums. In Switzerland, California, Italy and Taiwan (among others), referendums can be triggered this way *offline*, although it can be costly to collect signatures in the allotted timeframe. Online signature collection *could* help prevent initiatives tilting towards the well-financed interests and lobby groups that have an advantage when only offline collection is allowed. While all of these jurisdictions have flirted with online signature collection, Italy is thus far the only one to have allowed citizens to submit their signatures digitally, using a private platform to do so. This process started in 2021 during the Covid pandemic.[11]

1.1.3 Participatory Budgeting (Ideation/Debate/Decision-Making)

Participatory budgeting was first conceived of as an offline form of participation that allowed residents to allocate public funds for various purposes in their municipality. Its first use was in Porto Alegre, Brazil in 1989. Since then, participatory budgeting (or PB as it is often known) has been championed by both the World

---

10 For past and current Latvian petitions see: <https://manabalss.lv/page/progress>.

11 Federico Berti Arnoaldi Veli, 'Digital Signature for Referendums: Italy in Pole Position in Europe' (*Cloud Signature Consortium*, 31 August 2021) <https://cloudsignatureconsortium.org/digital-signature-for-referendums-italy-in-pole-position-in-europe/>; Daniela Vancic, 'First Ever Online Collection of Signatures sets Italy Up for Referendum on Euthanasia' (*Democracy International*, 10 September 2021) <https://www.democracy.community/stories/first-ever-online-collection-signatures-sets-italy-referendum-euthanasia>; 'Referendum cannabis, in tres giorni 333mila sottoscrizioni. E da oggi si può firmare anche senza identità digitale: ecco come' *Il Fatto Quotidiano* (14 September 2021) <https://www.ilfattoquotidiano.it/2021/09/14/referendum-cannabis-in-tre-giorni-333mila-sotto scrizioni-e-da-oggi-si-puo-firmare-anche-senza-identita-digitale-ecco-come/6320391/>; Viola Stefanello, 'Italy Gets Closer to Referendum Decriminalizing Cannabis' *EurActiv* (17 September 2021) <https://www.euractiv.com/section/politics/short_news/italy-gets-closer-to-referendum-decriminalis ing-cannabis/>.

Bank and the United Nations,[12] and partly as a result of those official endorsements, has grown exponentially, with more than 11,000 instances of PB around the world,[13] 5,000 of them in Europe alone.[14] Some of these uses (as in Brazil) have been far-reaching in their powers with a considerable budget available to participants.[15] Others, particularly those in Western nations, tend to focus on discretionary spending items of more limited importance, such as arts or recreational projects. Although it started offline, participatory budgeting lends itself well to online conversion or hybrid online/offline models.

PB generally involves participants initiating proposals for public spending (e.g. improving street lighting or building a childcare centre), and then voting on a number of these proposals. Arranging these proposals online (where they can be supplemented by videos, photos and other information) can help participants make comparative decisions. This also allows a greater number of people to vote than would likely otherwise be the case, and, where comments are allowed, lets them make the case for a project to other voters.

Participatory budgeting also serves the purpose of educating participants about costs and planning, often by allocating each of them a fixed amount of money that they can 'spend' on projects that have been costed in a way that is visible to the public. It is this explicitly budgetary focus of PB that distinguishes it from other forms of decision-making that may be purely ideological (e.g. voting on moral issues, such as abortion, stem cell research, or same-sex marriage).

One of the most long-running examples of online participatory budgeting is Better Reykjavik in Iceland, which has been in use since 2010.[16] South Dublin Coun-

---

12 Yuan Li, Yanjun Zhu and Catherine Owen, 'Participatory Budgeting and the Party: Generating 'Citizens Orderly Participation' through Party-Building in Shanghai' (2022) Journal of Chinese Governance 56, 60.

13 'Building Trust and Breaking Down Complexity: The Past, Present and Future of Participatory Budgeting: Interview with Tarson Nuñez' (*Solonian Democracy Institute*, 24 November 2021) <www.solonian-institute.com/post/building-trust-breaking-down-complexity-the-past-present-future-of-participatory-budgeting>.

14 Atlas Mundial dos Orçamentos Participativos (*OFICINA*) <http://www.oficina.org.pt/atlas.html>.

15 See Brian Wampler 'Citizen Participation and Participatory Institutions in Brazil' in *The People Shall Govern: Public Participation Beyond Slogans, Deliberations of the International Conference on Public Participation 2012* (Gauteng Legislature 2012) 88–108.

16 The platform can be viewed here: <https://betrireykjavik.is/domain/1/communities> while more information on its creators, Citizens Foundation is available here: <www.citizens.is/>.

ty Council in Ireland and the City of Paris have also run multi-year online or online/offline PB processes.[17]

1.1.4 Planning (Debate)

Due to its complexity, planning is an activity that can benefit from a structured online process. Traditionally, planning consultations have taken place at community centres in the evening or with plans displayed in libraries or council buildings. However, time-strapped constituents may struggle to attend in-person meetings, and the results of the meetings are often indeterminate to the participants, if not the planners. From the point of view of the participant, the face-to-face process can also seem unstructured.

Digital technology is now an essential tool for design planning and it is often easier to convey the content of a plan via technological options like video animation, 3-D renderings, or virtual reality experiences. Such technology can even allow participants to experimentally try their hand at design. Online planning allows participants to attend more flexibly and for organizers to present a more structured overview of the process than is often possible at walk-in sessions. Canadian software Ethelo (which can be used for many purposes) as well as American provider PolCo have often been involved in local planning on issues from aquatic complexes to community centres.[18] Ethelo, in particular, has the ability to allow participants to design a community centre, park or other local amenity subject to built-in constraints (such as total cost, building footprint, etc).

1.1.5 Consultation (Debate)

Some nations require authorities to conduct public consultations on a variety of issues from building to arts initiatives. Consultations are generally non-binding, but they also notoriously suffer from being ill-advertised and often lack transparency. The average person frequently does not even know that a consultation was

---

17 The South Dublin County Council site can be viewed here: <https://haveyoursay.southdublin.ie/>, while information on the Paris participatory budget can be viewed here: <https://budgetparticipatif.paris.fr/>.

18 Information obtained from interviews with platform providers, as well as usage in combination with local bodies.

held, and even people who do know are rarely informed as to what the outcome was or how public participation affected that outcome.[19]

Many nations hold online consultations, but Taiwan's have been particularly innovative over the past few years under the influence of Digital Minister Audrey Tang. In the past, these have included consultations on such topics as regulating Uber and financial services, and they have focused heavily on encouraging participants to build a consensus across multiple different aspects of regulation.

Perhaps even more interesting, however, were Taiwan's snap consultations on public health measures at the beginning of the COVID-19 pandemic. Some of these consultations utilized Slido, a simple software primarily used by corporations to facilitate crowd engagement at business events.[20] By allowing people to participate on Slido, the Taiwanese government was able to get an instant idea of where citizens stood on coronavirus measures – unlike most nations which were forced to act in a vacuum as to what their citizens' preferred course of action was. This example shows how digital tools can be flexibly deployed to gain public input even in difficult, crisis scenarios.

Online consultation can also help to prepare the way for further steps in the democratic process. For example, Common Ground for Action (a joint initiative of Every Voice Engaged and the Kettering Foundation) provides facilitated online deliberation for small groups. One of the key advantages of such consultations is that they can quickly identify the points on which there is agreement or disagreement as the functionality of the software allows the starting position of each participant to be visualized and recorded. This can save time compared to offline deliberations where participants may take a long while to realize what they already agree on and on which additional reflection is thus not necessarily a high priority. Allocating time to deliberating the remaining points of disagreement can clarify the concerns underlying that disagreement, potentially pointing out issues that can be addressed or amendments that can be made to proposals. This initiative can also scale to accommodate many parallel groups deliberating the same issue simultaneously.[21]

---

19 In this book, I will use the term 'consultation' in a wide sense to include all forms of engagement where the public is asked to give input in a non-binding manner while the decision-making authority lies elsewhere.

20 Information obtained through interviews with providers.

21 Interview with Lori Britt, Professor, School of Communication, James Madison University (11 March 2022).

1.1.6 Decision-Making within Associations, Parties, Unions and Cooperatives

Collective decision-making takes place not just in state elections, but within parties, unions, trade associations and other bodies.

For example, the Five Star Movement in Italy (M5S) used the online voting tool Rousseau for a number of years. This tool allowed party members to vote on policy (for example, on whether to form a coalition with another party), and to interact with representatives on legislation at all levels of government.[22] Having been the largest single party in the Italian parliament and part of Italy's coalition government for several years,[23] M5S represents one of the most successful examples of digital democracy implemented on a large scale. M5S also used Rousseau to select candidates to run for general election. By 2012, over 30,000 people were taking part in candidate selection, casting 95,000 online votes between them.[24] Following a schism in the party in 2021, partly centred on the movement's use of Rousseau, as well as its stipulation that elected representatives be limited to two terms in office, the Five Star Movement has fared less well in polls, but still uses SkyVote, a different Italian software, to facilitate member voting.

Other examples of intra-party voting include the Icelandic Pirate Party, which runs an online policy and development site for members,[25] the British Conservative Party, which allowed online voting to select the party leader in 2022, as well as numerous parties in France. For example, le Pôle écologiste (a small voting alliance) used Neovote to choose their candidate for the 2022 Presidential election, and the Union pour un Mouvement Populaire (France's previous centre-right party) used e-voting to select its party leader in 2012, as well as its candidate for the 2014 Paris mayoral elections.[26]

The Spanish party Podemos also uses digital tools internally. While Podemos' online internal democracy has been less utilized than the Five Star process, it did

---

22 For more details on the Rousseau software see: Fuller, *SDI Digital Democracy Report* 42.

23 Jane McIntosh 'Who are Italy's Two Leading Populist Parties: Five Star Movement and the League?' *Deutsche Welle* (6 March 2018) <https://www.dw.com/en/who-are-italys-two-leading-populist-parties-five-star-movement-and-the-league/a-42838238>.

24 Eric Turner, 'The 5 Star Movement and its Discontents: A Tale of Blogging, Comedy, Electoral Success and Tensions' (2013) 5(2) Interface: A Journal for and about Social Movements 178, 187–188.

25 'Issues to Discuss' (*Piratar Kosningakerfi*) <https://x.piratar.is/polity/1/topics/> accessed 22 March 2023.

26 Maddalena Landi, '6 Candidates Elected in Digital Primaries' (*Democracy Technologies*, 29 August 2022) <https://democracy-technologies.org/voting/6-candidates-elected-in-digital-primaries/> accessed 17 March 2023; Susan Collard and Elodie Fabre, 'Electronic Voting in the French Legislative Elections of 2012' in Dimitrios Zississ and Dimitrios Lekkas (eds) *Design, Development and Use of Secure Electronic Voting Systems* (IGI Global 2014) 176, 194.

contribute to one very notable vote: whether party leader Pablo Iglesias and his partner should lose their positions for buying a pricey home felt to contravene the party's social direction.[27] While the couple survived the membership vote, it demonstrates that some forms of digital participation can be used by party membership to call leaders to account in ways that were previously impractical.

This same logic can be applied to other member-based organizations, such as unions, co-operatives, and even corporate shareholders to further economic democracy. While applications can facilitate straight electoral voting that mimics the ballot box experience, they can also be combined with video conferencing and enhanced functionality, such as the ability of members to upload and review documents, or to propose an amendment to a motion during a meeting. This can facilitate further activities, such as party conferences, where participants generally propose amendments to motions and comment as well as vote on policy. To give just one example, the Conservative Party of Denmark used Assembly Voting to hold its party conference online during the Covid pandemic in September 2020.[28] Some professional organizations (often numbering tens or even hundreds of thousands of members) have also used software like SkyVote and Assembly Voting to facilitate the election of board members and to enable long-distance decision-making.[29]

Such tools can also be used to enhance other aspects of the process. After all, candidates running for electoral office within professional associations generally do not have the resources to mount offline campaigns. In the past, members might receive information about candidates in a membership magazine with a ballot at the back that they could cut out and mail in. Moving these processes online can make them less onerous, allowing online nomination and an area for candidates to present themselves and their policies to the wider membership via text or video presentation.[30]

---

27 'Spain's Far-Left Leader Wins Confidence Vote After Luxury Home Purchase' *RTE* (28 May 2018).

28 'Flexible Conference System: From Hybrid Model to 100% Digital Party Congress' (*Assembly Voting*, 22 May 2021) <https://assemblyvoting.com/customer-stories/flexible-conference-system-from-hybrid-model-to-100-digital-party-congress/>.

29 Interview with association officials (2022); 'How the Danish Society of Engineers Navigates Complex Elections with Assembly Voting' (*Assembly Voting*, 20 May 2022) <https://assemblyvoting.com/customer-stories/how-the-danish-society-of-engineers-navigates-complex-elections-with-assembly-voting/>.

30 'Assembly Pre-Election' (*Assembly Voting*) <https://assemblyvoting.com/products/pre-election/>.

While digital technology enables many modalities of participation, their connection to democracy depends on how they are used, and it is very important to always keep this in mind. As we saw above, if it is to be democratic, this participation needs to be structured and avoid being an end unto itself or simply a catch-all for various other goals.

1.2 Democratic Potential of Practical Applications

This section will demonstrate how democratic potential can be assessed using three different scales:

1. Arnstein's Ladder of Participation
2. Wide and Deep
3. Fuller Democracy

Arnstein's Ladder of Participation (see Fig. 1.1) was developed by American public administrator Sherry Arnstein to quantify the empowerment of community groups.[31] The higher the rung occupied on the ladder, the better the quality of participation.

Wide and Deep (see Fig. 1.2) is a very simple test I learned from long-time practitioner of participatory democracy Paul Vittles. This is a simple x/y axis that measures the breadth of participation (how many people can and do participate) as well as the depth of that participation.[32]

The third measurement system of my own design 'Fuller Democracy' is an end-to-end system of direct democracy that allows people to be in control of the political process at all stages.[33] The prime purpose of Fuller Democracy is to prevent elite capture of the political decision-making process, and it utilizes certain principles to realize this goal.

These principles are informed by the core definition of democracy presented above, which provides a yardstick for assessing when and to what extent democracy has been realized. While it is a more complex measurement system, it also

---

31 'Climbing the Ladder: A Look at Sherry R. Arnstein' (*AACOM*) <https://www.aacom.org/become-a-doctor/financial-aid-and-scholarships/sherry-r-arnstein-minority-scholarship/sherry-arnstein-biography>.

32 Paul Vittles, 'Let's Think Deeply about Citizens' Assemblies and Citizens' Juries' (*Medium*, 15 November 2020) <https://paulvittles.medium.com/lets-think-deeply-about-citizens-assemblies-citizens-juries-2038daa37b8d>.

33 More details on this in Roslyn Fuller, *In Defence of Democracy* (Polity 2019).

provides more guidance around the concrete implementation of digital democracy tools.

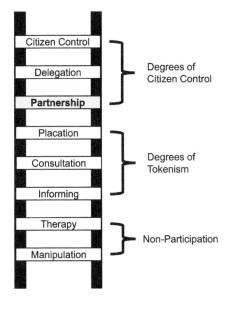

Fig. 1.1: Arnstein's Ladder
Source: Sherry Arnstein, 'A Ladder of Citizen Participation' (1969) 35 (4) Journal of the American Planning Association 216–224.

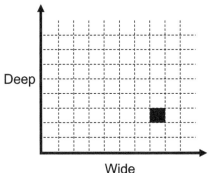

Fig. 1.2: Wide & Deep.

10 Principles of Fuller Democracy

1. **Channel – Don't Control**
   Political power flows continuously in any society, just as value flows continuously in an effective economy. Any attempt to constrain this flow inevitably leads to corruption, as it provides those wishing to engage in malpractice with a set of variables small enough to effectively manipulate. Instead,

power needs to be channelled through institutions which are open to all citizens, thus increasing the number of variables involved in any decision to the point where it is impossible for any person or subset of people to manipulate the outcome. Only this (rather than ever-increasing regulation) can effectively counteract corruption (we will return to this in detail in Chapter 7).

2. **Include Humans, Exclude Non-Humans**
To ensure equality, a democracy needs to exclude direct participation from non-human entities to the greatest extent possible. This is well understood (if poorly practiced) when it comes to businesses influencing politics, but is equally true for seemingly altruistic actors such as NGOs. Involving even grassroots, member-owned NGOs in decision-making leads to such members having twice the influence (once as a member and once as a citizen). In reality, this is compounded by the fact that most NGOs are not member-driven, but funded disproportionally by wealthy individuals, essentially buying themselves influence via their largesse.

3. **Avoid the Iron Law of Oligarchy**
The Iron Law of Oligarchy, expounded by sociologist Robert Michels, shows that any organization, however democratic in its origin, becomes oligarchic over time as power is delegated to functionaries of the organization. These functionaries then inevitably seek to retain and increase this power. To evade this mechanic, democracy should be as direct as possible, removing static, unchanging intermediaries wherever possible.

4. **Collective Action Does Not Necessitate Being a Collective**
Pirate crews traditionally worked together on an event-by-event basis (e.g. a particular raid or for a particular time) without permanently sacrificing their individual freedom. Perhaps because of this, many pirates also practiced rough forms of democracy with charters outlining the specific terms and rights governing cooperation.[34] This illustrates a way of preserving both freedom and equality, and that is to work together as much as you need to, but not more. For democracy this means that issue-based, rather than party-based voting is preferable. This allows people to wield power together on an issue without being tied to an organization or 'package of issues' such as a party political platform. This approach combines the advantages of acting collectively while avoiding

---

[34] See e.g. Gary Chartier, 'Pirate Constitutions and Workplace Democracy' (2010) 18 Annual Review of Law and Ethics 449–467.

extreme partisanship. Paradoxically, issue-based voting often allows for the maximum consensus to be reached on a wider range of issues.

This point deserves special mention because the demand for excessive agreement and group cohesion is one of the more common pitfalls that those who champion democracy fall into, and it prevents one of the more useful attributes of democracy from being harnessed – the so-called **Wisdom of the Crowd.**

The Wisdom of the Crowd is a long-established concept, thoroughly documented for the layperson by journalist James Surowiecki in his best-selling book.[35] The example Surowiecki uses to illustrate this concept is a fairground competition in which members of the general public attempt to guess the yield of an ox once butchered and dressed. Another example of the same type of game, possibly closer to the experience of modern readers, is guessing the number of jellybeans packed into a large jar. In both of these cases, the winner is the person whose guess is closest to the actual results. However, as some savvy observers noted, if you calculate the average of all the guesses in such games it is often *even more accurate* than the winning guess.

This interesting piece of math has been appropriated into political theory to mean that if a diverse group of people deliberate together, striving for consensus, the results of their cogitations will also be more likely to produce 'correct' policy precisely because they come at the problem from different angles. However, the Wisdom of the Crowd only works when each person makes their guess *in ignorance* of all the other guesses (indeed, in these sorts of games, players are generally required to write down their guess rather than announce it). The moment people start influencing each other (especially with the object of reaching consensus) the entire mathematical operation ceases to exist and the situation devolves into the *opposite* of the Wisdom of the Crowd: groupthink.

The operation, of necessity, also only works for simple, verifiable questions, such as the quantity of an item, rather than political questions which involve conflicting interests and moral choices. These are a matter of deliberate *choice* rather than guessing 'the truth'. We can open a jar of jellybeans and count them, but we will never 'find out' if a pro-choice or pro-life stance on abortion is definitively 'better'.

This is an extremely important point that we will return to many times throughout this work as it has a major impact of how we conceive of democracy and how communication should be structured.

---

35 James Surowiecki, *The Wisdom of Crowds* (Anchor Books 2005).

5. **Over-Alignment (Agreement on Cause is not Necessary to Agree on Action)**

   Similarly, democracy is often misunderstood to mean that all people need to hold the same views in order to agree on an action. This, again, is incorrect and *causes* rather than resolves political turmoil. If, for example, the recommended action is to lower carbon emissions, then it is irrelevant whether everyone believes in man-made climate change or the inevitable rising of sea levels. Some people might just want cleaner air, others might agree that rising temperatures need to be tackled regardless of cause, while remaining agnostic on whether that cause is human activity. If people vote for the same action for different reasons, then this means that democracy is working, not that it is broken. Forcing everyone to be ideologically, or even scientifically, aligned is counter-productive and *prevents* compromise and consensus on action.

6. **Disagreement is Democratic – Sabotage is Not**

   Once a democratic decision has been made, the losing side should be able to express their disagreement. In fact, it is important that other opinions are maintained, because if the majority decision does not work out, these alternative options may very well be needed. That being said, the losing side needs to accept their loss and cannot resort to sabotaging the implementation of the winning decision. Not only is this undemocratic, it reduces the likelihood that the losing side will be listened to later, even if the winning policy does not work out as planned.

   People often confuse a willingness to accept that a democratic decision has been made with the conviction that that decision is right. These are two completely different things. There is absolutely no need to believe that a decision is the correct or best decision in order to know that it was made in accordance with the rules for making decisions. At the same time, it is unproductive to sabotage decisions that have been made in accordance with the rules simply because one disagrees with the outcome.

   Life teaches all lessons. If, in fact, the winning side has made a poor decision, they *will* realise this in time, once they fail to get what they thought would be the results of that decision. And if the winning side *does* get what they wanted, then the decision was obviously not wrong for them.

7. **Don't Eliminate or Ignore Evil – Harness it**

   Political science often takes insufficient account of the many important insights into human behaviour that have been discovered via modern psychiatry. While psychiatry does not show that the 'crooked timber of humanity' is wholly irrational or hopeless, it does help us understand pathological character traits, such as those associated with narcissism, Machiavellianism and psychopathy. While these traits are harmful, in the sense that they often cause suffering to the person exhibiting them and to others, they can be managed and contained. Unfortunately, in democracy studies, there is often a tendency to either deny that harmful behaviour exists (and thus to fail to account for it when designing a system) or to feel so overwhelmed by it as to seek to impose excessive controls. However, it is possible to harness the destructive, even pathological, tendencies of some individuals in ways that don't infringe on freedom, and we will return to this point in detail in Chapter 5.

8. **Don't Ask if You Don't Want an Answer**
Any form of democracy where people either decide or give input directly rather than elect representatives is only sustainable if the outcome is respected. This is obvious for binding decisions such as referenda, but is equally valid for consultative forms of participation such as public consultations or participatory budgeting. Organizers should only ask for input they are prepared to translate into action. In electoral systems, the electorate is often condemned for political apathy or lack of participation, when in fact it is often the lack of follow-through on campaign promises on the part of the elected that creates this apathy in the first place. The lack of follow-through is probably the single biggest failing in democratic activity today (and Chapter 8 is entirely devoted to this issue).

9. **Experts are Judged on their Track Record, not their Qualifications**
A common criticism of the electorate is that people don't trust experts. This misunderstands the concept of trust: If experts make predictions about the future or the merits of a policy and these predictions turn out to be accurate, the experts who made them generally gain the justified confidence of others. This is very different than expecting people to blindly trust, or even worse, to trust despite numerous previous promises and forecasts having turned out to be incorrect. Assessing experts' abilities and thus the level of trust they seem to have earned, requires people to be able to monitor those experts *over time*, rather than engage in detached one-off exercises where this monitoring cannot occur.

10. **Democracy is Government of the Middle-Class**
The middle class – those people who work for a living, but are able to meet their own needs – is essential to democracy. Political equality requires a certain level of economic equality, as this prevents people from manipulating others into a situation of dependency that allows them to bypass the democratic institutions. It is thus in the interests of the middle-class, and of democrats, to ensure that the poor can become wealthier and that the rich do not become

too wealthy. When this fails, and the rich become richer while the poor become poorer, democracy starts to morph into oligarchy.

As Rousseau put it:

> If the object is to give the State consistency, bring the two extremes as near to each other as possible; allow neither rich men nor beggars. These two estates, which are naturally inseparable, are equally fatal to the common good; from the one come the friends of tyranny, and from the other tyrants. It is always between them that public liberty is put up to auction; the one buys, and the other sells.[36]

This book will deal with how to implement these general rules in more concrete detail. Almost every issue with democracy and public participation comes back to one of these things and if we assess them on a scale (see Fig. 1.3) we can get a good idea of how democratic any particular application is.

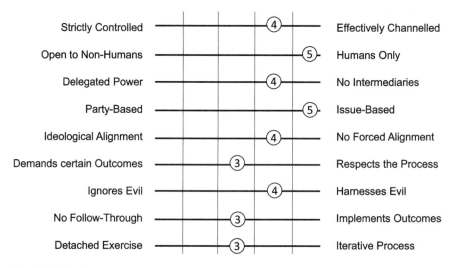

Fig. 1.3: Fuller Democracy.

If we look at the applications we spoke about previously, we can see that much depends on how we use them.

Let's take voting, for example, and compare elections to referendums.

---

36 Rousseau, *The Social Contract,* Chapter XI.

These assessment aids reveal why voting is the most important component of democracy.

The participation reach is very wide (everyone can take part and digital voting can scale up to include everyone in a nation), but it is not very deep. When citizens vote in elections (see Fig. 1.4) they delegate power. However, under these conditions, as has been noted, 'The people are a sovereign whose vocabulary is limited to two words, "Yes" and "No"'.[37] If we imagine a king or queen only able to utter the words 'yes' or 'no', it is obvious that that person would be excessively dependent on their advisors. The same is true here. Because such procedures do not involve citizens in the preparatory steps of the process, they are dependent on whoever pre-selects the options.

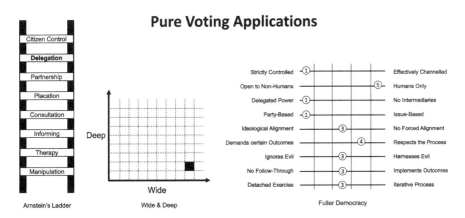

Fig. 1.4: Democratic Potential of Pure Voting Applications.

When voting occurs in a binding referendum, especially if we imagine one triggered by petition, these considerations change (see Fig. 1.5).

---

37 E.E. Schattschneider, *Party Government: American Government in Action* (Taylor & Francis Group 2004) 52.

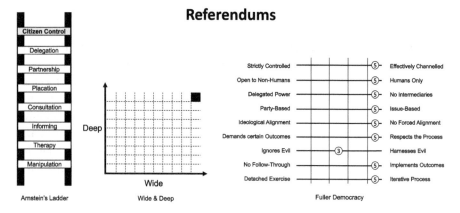

Fig. 1.5: Democratic Potential of Referendums.

The potential of other forms of participation is even more variable. The democratic potential of participatory budgeting is particularly difficult to assess, as its concrete usage has differed substantially from place to place and time to time (see Fig. 1.6).

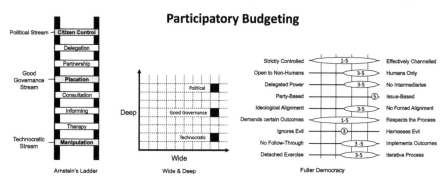

Fig. 1.6: Democratic Potential of Participatory Budgeting.

According to some of the most prolific writers on this subject, there are three main variants of participatory budgeting:
- the political stream (which aims to give citizens as much direct control and participation as possible)
- the good governance stream (which aims to foster trust between citizens and government)
- purely technocratic management (which is focused on cost-effectiveness)[38]

---

38 Yves Cabannes and Barbara Lipietz, 'Revisiting the Democratic Promise of Participatory Budg-

While on Arnstein's Ladder, the political stream of PB is an example that can range from 'partnership' to 'citizen control', its good governance stream is often 'placation', and technocratic management can descend into manipulation, coercing citizens into choosing options designed to force unnecessary austerity onto them.

On the 'wide and deep' axis, PB is very wide (in theory) regardless of the stream it belongs to, but its depth depends to a large degree on the importance of what is being decided upon. When decisions are superficial, citizens do not have to engage as deeply with societal and budgetary issues. When it comes to Fuller Democracy, while PB's saving grace is that it is issue-based, a great deal depends on how it is implemented.

These are rough estimates precisely because the potential of all of these instruments is high, but how they are used in practice all too often squanders that potential.

Democracy is an unnatural state, so in situations of neglect, all of these instruments tend to slide back down and to the left of these measuring scales, much like a ball that has been tossed upward will always fall back to earth. Keeping democracy going requires constant effort and vigilance. In everything you do, try to push the activity in question towards the top and the right of each of these graphs. For example, ask if you are merely placating participants, or if what you are doing is detached from the rest of your activities. As long as you are always working in these directions (upwards and forwards), you will make progress.

1.3 Conclusions

If one wishes to form or maintain a democracy, there are only a few things one really needs to do, but it is hard to do those things consistently. Thus, this book is about habit-forming. Whenever you start to feel lost, just return to these principles. Some of them may seem counter-intuitive since they contradict many of the buzzwords and unreflected promises so glibly made about digital democracy today. However, throughout this book it will hopefully become apparent as to why they are essential to a successful process.

Furthermore, we have to remember that technology changes, and a book that focused on technology and gadgets would quickly become outdated. But principles are true forever. In this book, we will use current cases to illustrate these princi-

---

eting in Light of Competing Political, Good Governance and Technocratic Logics' (2018) 30(1) Environment and Urbanization 67–84.

ples, but it is important to remember that these are just examples. The underlying principle is what is important.

Chapter 2
Benefits of Digital Democracy

The potential and wide-reaching benefits of digital technology were recognized early on by visionary thinkers like Buckminster Fuller, Erich Fromm and Alvin Toffler. A rudimentary digital democracy was even put into practice at an early date. During his 1992 US-presidential campaign, Independent candidate Ross Perot advocated for 'electronic townhalls', a call that coincided with several experiments in debating and mass voting on political issues via television. Shortly thereafter, in the early 2000s, Demoex (an internet voting party that started as a school project) fielded successful local politicians for over 10 years in Vallentuna, Sweden.[39] The Israeli thinker, Aki Orr writing simply on the basis of the invention of the ATM, and not the modern internet, already foresaw that direct democracy could include TV discussions on the topic at hand 'by panels of experts drawn by lottery, with the public phoning in to comment, criticize, or propose options'. In Orr's vision, people could then vote via ATM rather than visiting a polling station.[40]

While we've acknowledged some of the benefits of digital democracy in the previous chapter, here we will examine the most relevant claims in more detail. After all, in the intervening years, some of the areas that were previously speculated upon by visionaries have become filled with at least some data, and knowing what is possible and what isn't can prevent disappointed expectations as well as uncover overlooked opportunities.

2.1 Lowering Barriers to Participation

As we saw in Chapter 1, democracy requires mass participation. Thus, everyone should not simply have the theoretical opportunity to participate (although this is important), but also be in a reasonable position to actually do so. The impact digitalization could have on this – both positive and negative – has been the subject of a great deal of attention.

---

39 'Information about Demoex' (*Demoex*) <http://demoex.se/en/>.
40 Aki Orr, *Direct Democracy Manifesto: Politics for the 21st Century* <http://www.kulanu-nahlit.org/English.htm#mozTocId192120>.

https://doi.org/10.1515/9783110794465-006

2.1.1 Increasing Election Turnout

It was initially commonly believed that digital voting would increase election turnout, especially among younger voters, who were thought to be more technologically savvy. This hypothesis depends on the reason for non-participation being a lack of convenience: the idea is that people, particularly younger people, are not voting because it is too onerous for them to attend a polling station on a certain day. This line of thinking also gives rise to a specific fear about digital democracy: **click-button voting.** The idea behind click-button voting is that non-voters do not make the effort to understand candidates or their platforms, and also, due to this general apathy, do not make the effort to vote. If, however, they could vote online with a minimum of effort they would do so purely because it is convenient, while maintaining their apathy in every other respect. They would thus cast their votes 'at the click of a button' without thinking about their preferences and on the basis of completely superficial considerations. Those who fear click-button voting thus *agree* with those who think that internet voting will significantly increase badly flagging turnout – they just believe that it would do so for all the wrong reasons.

So far, neither hope nor fear has materialized.

Much of the concern about election turnout in Anglo-Saxon countries stems from the late 1990s and early 2000s when turnout significantly decreased in many Western nations. For example, turnout in British national elections remained consistently over 70% between 1922 and 1997, but dipped to 59% in 2001. It has since slowly recovered to 68.8% in 2017 and 67.3% in 2019. Voting among 18–24 year-olds (the 'youth' demographic of particular concern to many commentators) is estimated to have been 60–70% from the 1970s to early 1990s before crashing to under 40% in the late 1990s to early 2000s. It has since risen back to between 48–54%. 25–44 year-olds follow a similar pattern with a serious drop in voting setting in around 1997–2001 and never fully recovering.

If we look at the statistics over time, however, we can see changes in behaviour. In 2001, only 55.7% of 35–44 year-olds voted in the British national elections. Nine years later in 2010, this same group of people, now mainly in the 45–54 year-old category voted at a rate of 67.5%. By 2019, this group of now mainly 55–64 year-olds was voting at 72.8%. Similarly, 25–34 year-olds who voted at a rate of just 45% in 2001 were 18 years later (aged mainly 45–54) voting at a rate of over 70%.[41] This is in line with the vast majority of statistics on participation of all kinds: we see

---

41 Elise Uberoi, *Turnout at Elections* (House of Commons Library, 26 August 2021) 5 and 24 <https://assets-learning.parliament.uk/uploads/2021/12/Turnout-at-Elections.pdf>.

that as people age, more of them become politically active. The rate of political participation usually hits a peak around the ages of 40 – 75 and then slowly tapers off.

Table 2.1: British Voting by Age Group and Election Year

Age Group	1992	1997	2001	2005	2010	2015	2017	2019
18 – 24	67.30 %	54.10 %	40.40 %	38.20 %	51.80 %	51.60 %	48.60 %	54.50 %
25 – 34	77.30 %	62.20 %	45.00 %	47.70 %	57.30 %	51.80 %	50.60 %	54.40 %
35 – 44	78.30 %	70.20 %	55.70 %	61.60 %	64.40 %	60.60 %	59.60 %	60.90 %
45 – 54	81.80 %	76.40 %	63.20 %	65.50 %	67.50 %	70.10 %	70.70 %	71.00 %
55 – 64	78.10 %	79.90 %	64.00 %	72.60 %	69.80 %	74.40 %	82.50 %	72.80 %
65+	79.20 %	77.70 %	70.10 %	74.30 %	74.70 %	79.30 %	85.20 %	78.50 %
All	77.70 %	71.40 %	59.40 %	61.40 %	65.10 %	66.20 %	68.80 %	67.30 %
Cohort 1	Cohort 2							

Source: Elise Uberoi, *Turnout at Elections* (House of Commons Library, 26 August 2021) 5, 24.

In the USA, voting in Presidential elections also dipped among 18 – 24 year-olds and 25 – 44 year-olds, particularly in the years 1996 and 2000. By the 2010s, however, voting among 18 – 24 year-olds had recovered to the high 40s (about average for this age group). In the age groups 25 – 44 and 45 – 64 voting has declined by perhaps 10 % – 15 % since the 1970s.[42] That being said, overall, voter turnout in Presidential elections has remained fairly steady, and indeed, the 2020 Presidential election attained the highest voter turnout of any US Presidential election this century, including 51 % of 18 – 24 year-olds.[43] Voter turnout also declined rapidly in Canada between 1993 and 2008, hitting its all-time low at 58.8 % in 2008. It has, however, bounced back to 68 % in 2015 and 67 % in 2019, somewhat lower than the 70 – 80 % that was the norm from the 1950s to 1980s.[44] Considering this rebound in activity, the need for digital voting to counteract rapidly declining participation

---

[42] Aaron O'Neill, 'Voter Turnout in US Presidential Elections by Age 1964 – 2020' (*Statista*, 21 June 2022) <https://www.statista.com/statistics/1096299/voter-turnout-presidential-elections-by-age-historical/>.

[43] '2020 Presidential Election Voting and Registration Tables Now Available' (*United States Census Bureau*, 29 April 2021) <https://www.census.gov/newsroom/press-releases/2021/2020-presidential-election-voting-and-registration-tables-now-available.html>.

[44] 'Estimation of Voter Turnout by Age Group and Gender at the 2019 General Election' (*Elections Canada*) <https://www.elections.ca/content.aspx?section=res&dir=rec/eval/pes2019/vtsa2&document=p1&lang=e>.

is thus often overstated. This is quite fortunate, as it is highly questionable if offering digital voting alone could have any such impact.

The reasons for the slump in turnout around the turn of the millennium and its slow rebound in the following decades are unclear. However, the slump *precedes* widespread internet usage, so cannot have been caused by young people yearning for a more convenient internet vote. The factors are much more likely social: people aged 18–24 are far more likely to still be in education than they were in the 1970s and are far less likely to be integrated into the workforce or be homeowners – the spaces where one typically encounters political policy in the form of business regulation, tax, utilities provision and planning. In addition, further education is now far more likely to take place away from the family home so that students are not exposed to their parents' voting habits at election time and may not be registered to vote.

Moreover, until the 1970s the voting age was higher in many Western countries (21 as opposed to 18), and because the youngest voters vote the least, this naturally has an impact not just on the rate of youth voting, but also on the total voting statistics ('you're old enough to kill, but not for voting' as the 1965 hit song *Eve of Destruction* put it, referring to the fact that, at the time, Americans between the ages of 18–21 could be drafted to fight in the Vietnam War, but were not allowed to vote in elections). In other words, by lowering the voting age, we may have ensured that voting rates never fully return to their previous levels, and that a 69% turnout in 2017 may be equivalent to a 72% turnout in 1950, depending on demographics.

A similar point concerns immigration. As of the early 2010s, 40% of the population of Inner London was born outside of Britain,[45] while 3 million of New York City's 8.5 million residents are immigrants with ca. 1.3 million of these yet to acquire citizenship.[46] One-fifth of Paris residents are foreign born,[47] while in Vienna, the number of voting age residents not eligible to participate in elections has increased from 15% in 2000 to 31.5% in 2020, mainly as a result of immigration.[48] Even after they acquire citizenship, immigrants tend to vote at lower rates than

---

[45] Carolina Johnson, 'Engaging Democracy: An Institutional Theory of Participatory Budgeting' (DPhil Thesis, University of Washington 2017) 16 et seq.

[46] 'New York City' (*United States Census Bureau*) <https://www.census.gov/quickfacts/new yorkcitynewyork>; 'State of our Immigrant City: Annual Report for Calendar Year 2020' (*Mayor's Office of Immigrant Affairs*) <https://www1.nyc.gov/assets/immigrants/downloads/pdf/MOIA-Annual-Report-for-2020.pdf>.

[47] Alessio Surian, Foreword to Estela Brahimllari, *Multi-Layered Participatory Budgeting: The Case of Low-Income Neighbourhoods in Paris* (FrancoAngeli 2020) 9, citing INSEE.

[48] Monika Mokre and Tamara Ehs, 'If no Vote, at least Voice? The Potential and Limits of Deliberative Procedures for the Creation of a more Inclusive Democracy' (2021) 34(5) Innovation: The European Journal of Social Science Research 712, 716.

people who have been born in the country in question. Immigration rates to Western countries, and specifically to large metropolises, have been relatively high in recent decades, and this may also affect turnout rates, meaning that we are not necessarily comparing like with like over time.

It is also possible that during this time, electoral options have simply not appealed to many voters and that political activity has been channelled into protest and other movements. After all, turnout for referendums has at times exceeded electoral turnout: turnout in the Brexit referendum (2016) was 72%; turnout in the Scottish independence referendum (2014) was 84%; and turnout for the Quebec independence referendum (1995) was over 93%. Thus, we can see people turning out in very large numbers for votes on high-profile issues. At its deepest lows, the election slump period also coincided with a widespread anti-globalization and anti-war protest movement in many Western countries (an estimated 40,000 people participated at the 1999 anti-globalization Battle of Seattle, a number eclipsed by the millions who protested the Iraq War in 2003). Far from dissipating, political energy may simply have found other channels.

Because participation patterns can be explained by social factors and because the most serious voting slumps occurred pre-internet and have since largely recovered (despite the internet now being much easier to access than it was twenty years ago), it is unlikely that mere convenience is an overwhelming factor in people's decision to vote or not.

The only country where we have national level data on the impact that e-voting has on turnout is Estonia, and it bears out these suppositions. Estonia has allowed internet voting since 2005 and about one-third to one-half of Estonians today *do* cast their ballots from phones or computers at the click of a button, typically taking less than two minutes to do so.[49] Despite the ready availability of convenient, fast 'click-button voting', turnout has increased only slightly in national elections and somewhat more markedly in local and European elections (in the case of local voting by about 10%). However, numerous social factors likely also play a role: voting in European and local elections had been very low in the former Soviet-bloc country[50] and thus participation rates were much more likely to move up than down regardless of the methods of voting on offer.

Researchers who have analysed online voting in those Swiss cantons where it has been offered have come to similar conclusions – that online voting does not,

49 Taavi Unt, Mihkel Solvak and Kristjan Vassil, 'Does Internet Voting make Elections less Social? Group Voting Patterns in Estonian e-voting Log Files (2013–2015)' (2017) 12(5) PLoS ONE.
50 Kristjan Vassil, 'Introduction' in Mihkel Solvak and Kristjan Vassil (eds), *E-voting in Estonia: Technological Diffusion and other Developments over Ten Years, 2005–2015* (Johan Skytte Institute of Political Studies, University of Tartu 2016) 1, 11.

thus far, appear to increase turnout to any appreciable degree, and does not affect the outcome of elections.[51] It may have a very small mobilizing effect on occasional voters or previous non-voters, but is generally utilized by those who would have voted in any case even had e-voting not been available.[52] Researchers in Estonia also believe that the option of e-voting does have a small mobilizing effect on those least likely to vote – the young, less educated and those on a low-income, who are the most likely to switch from being non-voters to e-voters.[53] However, the vast majority of people who take up internet voting are people who would have voted, anyway.

Finally, in Markham, Ontario (a city of over 300,000 residents located near Toronto that has facilitated internet voting since 2003) just over 10 % of voters consistently say that they would likely not have voted in local elections had online voting not been available. Considering this together with the data from Estonia, it is therefore possible that the availability of online voting has a somewhat greater mobilizing effect for local elections (where participation rates generally start from a lower base rate) than for national ones.[54] Moreover, those who do cast an online ballot in Estonia rarely switch back to paper-based voting or lapse into non-voting and some researchers believe that this is evidence that e-voting, while not having led to large increases in voter turnout in the present, may still prevent further turnout decline in the future.[55]

This more modest supposition may be justified.

E-voting has long found a surprising degree of support among the general population: a 1994 American survey found that significantly more people favoured using interactive television for political purposes (85 %) than for other tasks, such as shopping or game shows.[56] This support has remained high around the world, despite significant challenges. Nearly 80 % of respondents in a 2013 Ghana-

51 Uwe Serdült and Micha Germann, 'Internet Voting for Expatriates: The Swiss Case' (2014) 6(2) eJournal of eDemocracy and Open Government 197–215.

52 Adrien Petitpas, Julien M. Jaquet and Pascal Sciarini, 'Does E-Voting Matter for Turnout, and to Whom?' (2020) 71(4) Electoral Studies 9.

53 Mihkel Solvak, 'Mobilization' in Mihkel Solvak and Kristjan Vassil (eds), *E-voting in Estonia: Technological Diffusion and other Developments over Ten Years, 2005–2015* (Johan Skytte Institute of Political Studies, University of Tartu 2016) 93, 100–104.

54 Nicole Goodman, 'Online Voting in the City of Markham: Patterns and Trends, 2003–2018' (November 2019) 20 <https://pub-markham.escribemeetings.com/filestream.ashx?DocumentId=19612>.

55 Mihkel Solvak, '"Stickiness" of eVoting' in Mihkel Solvak and Kristjan Vassil (eds), *E-voting in Estonia: Technological Diffusion and other Developments over Ten Years, 2005–2015* (Johan Skytte Institute of Political Studies, University of Tartu 2016) 117–126.

56 Evan I Schwartz, 'Direct Democracy: Are you ready for the Democracy Channel?' *Wired* (1 January 1994) <www.wired.com/1994/01/e-dem/>.

ian survey said they would be comfortable casting an e-ballot.[57] A survey of election officials in Botswana revealed that 93 % of them would be willing to use an e-voting system, while 92 % of students who took a similar survey gave the same answer.[58] In Markham, satisfaction with online voting has been extremely high, with 90 % of online voters reporting satisfaction in 2014 and 97–99 % reporting satisfaction in all other years. In every election between 2003 and 2018, over 90 % of respondents said they would be very likely to vote online again.[59]

In Kenya, a national survey conducted two months after elections that had to be re-run due to technical glitches with an e-transmission system found that just over half of all respondents felt that they 'mostly don't understand' or 'don't understand at all' what happened during the process of vote counting, and that only 49 % of people believed that the victorious candidate had 'really won'. Despite this, 58 % of respondents agreed that '[e]lections that use digital technology are always more free and fair.'[60] This is joined by favourable survey data from Australia, Catalonia, the Netherlands and Russia.[61]

Online voting, in other words, is more accepted by people than one would expect, and while offering online voting won't get people who dislike the options presented to them to magically vote, it still decreases the burden on voters who spend almost all of the time it takes to vote travelling to and from the polling station and very little of it actually casting their ballot. While there are no guarantees that they would do so, it would be a far better use of people's time to spend half an hour contemplating the candidates and their policy than driving to and from the polling station.

---

57 Samuel Agbesi, Fati Tehiru and Alexander Osei-owusu, 'Investigating the Feasibility of Implementing E-Voting System in Ghana' (2014) 10(1) International Journal of Innovation and Scientific Research 218, 225.
58 Lapologang Ntwayame, 'A Conceptual Model for Designing and Implementation of Secure and Trustable Remote Electronic Voting within the Developing World' (MSc, Botswana International University of Science and Technology 2018) 45 and 54.
59 Goodman, 'Online Voting in the City of Markham' 13–15.
60 Nic Cheeseman, Gabrielle Lynch and Justin Willis, 'Digital Dilemmas: The Unintended Consequences of Election Technology' (2018) 25(8) Democratization 1397, 1402.
61 Steve Baron, 'Internet Voting – What New Zealand can Learn from International Trials & Errors' (B.A. Paper, Victoria University of Wellington 2012), 22 et seq. <https://www.academia.edu/5426756/Internet_Voting_What_New_Zealand_Can_Learn_From_International_Trials_and_Errors> Valeria Babayan and A.V. Turobov, 'Not Unique, not Universal: Risk Perception and Acceptance of Online Voting Technology by Russian Citizens' (2021) Monitoring of Public Opinion: Economic and Social Changes 319, 330.

2.1.2 Enabling Voting from Abroad

Many countries offer certain categories of citizens the opportunity to vote in elections or referenda from outside the country. While some limit this right to military and diplomatic personnel, others extend it to all citizens living overseas. Moreover, today many people who do not reside abroad are still often temporarily out of the country, for example, on business trips or vacation, and they may miss out on chances to vote due to their absence.

Traditionally, voting from overseas has been conducted via postal vote or in-person at the embassy or consulate closest to the voter. Because in-person voting is so cumbersome under these circumstances, and internet voting is very similar but slightly more convenient than postal voting, where internet voting is available, ex-pat voters tend to adopt it quite quickly. About 5–6% of votes are submitted from outside Estonia in each election and approximately 90% of these votes are cast via the internet.[62] When the Netherlands allowed internet voting for people living abroad in 2006 about 20,000 voters used this option,[63] accounting for 63% of voters registered to vote abroad. Although voting by phone was also permitted, so few people took advantage of this option that it was discontinued.[64] Among Swiss citizens who genuinely live abroad (as opposed to merely residing over the border for economic reasons), few vote in elections or referendums. However, among those who do, about 40–60% have voted online where available with this rate growing by 2% per year.[65] Postal, proxy and e-voting all seem to increase turnout among ex-pat voters,[66] with one Swiss study concluding that internet voting could increase ex-pat turnout by about 4–6%.[67]

---

62 Taavi Unt, Mihkel Solvak and Kristjan Vassil, 'E-vote Log Files 2013–2015' in Mihkel Solvak and Kristjan Vassil (eds), *E-voting in Estonia: Technological Diffusion and other Developments over Ten Years, 2005–2015* (Johan Skytte Institute of Political Studies, University of Tartu 2016) 71, 73–74.
63 Guido Shryen and Eliot Rich, 'Security in Large-Scale Internet Elections: A Retrospective Analysis of Elections in Estonia, The Netherlands, and Switzerland' (2010) 4(4) IEEE Transactions on Information Forensics and Security 729, 734.
64 Baron, 'Internet Voting' 17.
65 Serdült and Germann, 'Internet Voting for Expatriates'. E-voting in Switzerland was suspended in 2019 although Swiss Post is developing a new system to be launched shortly ('E-Voting' *(Swiss Federal Chancellery)* <https://www.bk.admin.ch/bk/en/home/politische-rechte/e-vot ing.html>). Among the reasons given for developing this system is that the majority of citizens desire an e-voting option, and that it is particularly beneficial to Swiss citizens residing abroad (Simone Hubacher, 'Neuchâtel: the New E-Voting Hub' *(Swiss Post*, 25 August 2020) <https://www. post.ch/en/about-us/news/2020/neuchatel-the-new-e-voting-hub>).
66 Irina Ciornei and Eva Østergaard-Nielsen, 'Transnational Turnout: Determinants of Emigrant Voting in Home Country Elections' (2020) 78 Political Geography 16.

Some countries have also recently begun to offer alternative methods of representation, not just allowing but encouraging their diaspora to continue to participate in their home country's politics. For example, since 2012 France has divided non-French territory into 11 global constituencies, allowing eligible voters living in these areas to vote for their own representatives in its elections. Candidates campaign for election in these regions (e.g. 'Central America, the Caribbean and South America') much as they would if they were running on the territory of France. They often belong to one of the main parties contesting the election and successful candidates take a seat in the Assemblée Nationale. Unlike voters on French territory, ex-pat voters can use proxy, internet or postal voting to cast their ballot.[68]

In 2012 (the first year it was available), internet voting was used by 57% of ex-pat voters in the first round of elections and 54% in the second round (ca. 70% in North America and Europe where internet use is most widespread).[69] In the most recent June 2022 parliamentary elections (marred by bureaucratic error), nearly a quarter million French voters living abroad still cast their votes via the internet.[70]

The possibility of convenient internet voting from abroad does raise some questions, especially since many countries have a sizeable diaspora. For example, if one counts residents of Northern Ireland, who are entitled to Irish citizenship, there are close to as many Irish people living outside of the Republic of Ireland as in it. Even discounting those in Northern Ireland, over 20% of Irish citizens live outside of the State.[71] Similarly, more than 12% of Mexicans live abroad, main-

---

67 Micha Germann, 'Internet Voting Increases Expatriate Voter Turnout' (2021) 38(2) Government Information Quarterly.

68 Tracy McNicoll, 'Mapped: Expats Kick Off French Legislative Elections with Online Voting' *France 24* (27 May 2022) <https://www.france24.com/en/france/20220527-mapped-expats-kick-off-french-legislative-elections-with-online-voting>; Susan Collard and Elodie Fabre, 'Electronic Voting in the French Legislative Elections of 2012' in Dimitrios Zisiss and Dimitrios Lekkas (eds) *Design, Development and Use of Secure Electronic Voting Systems* (IGI Global 2014) 176, 178 and 191.

69 Collard and Fabre, 'Electronic Voting in the French Legislative Elections' 186 and 190.

70 Patrick Roger, 'Legislative Elections: First Round Kicks off for French Citizens Abroad, with Flawed Online Voting' *Le Monde* (4 June 2022) <https://www.lemonde.fr/en/politics/article/2022/06/04/legislative-elections-first-round-kicks-off-for-french-citizens-abroad-with-flawed-online-voting_5985648_5.html>.

71 This does not count people merely of Irish ancestry. Department of Foreign Affairs, Irish Abroad Unit, *Irish Emigration Patterns and Citizens Abroad* (20 June 2017) para. 3 <https://www.dfa.ie/media/dfa/alldfawebsitemedia/newspress/publications/ministersbrief-june2017/1-Global-Irish-in-Numbers.pdf>; Central Statistics Office, 'Population and Migration Estimates, April 2017' (28 September 2017) <https://www.cso.ie/en/csolatestnews/póessreleases/2017pressreleases/populationandmigrationestimatesapril2017/>.

ly in the United States.[72] It is estimated that over 15 million people of Lebanese descent live abroad, as compared to just 6 million in Lebanon itself.[73] Between 300,000 and 400,000 French citizens live in London, England alone,[74] five million US citizens live abroad (accounting for 2% of the population) and nearly 10% of British citizens do.[75]

It is theoretically possible that ex-pats, especially if encouraged to vote via the (for them easier) means of the internet, could end up deciding the outcome of an election or referendum, despite not having to live with its consequences if they remain abroad. In practice, however, many countries place strict time-limits on ex-pat voting rights. In France, by providing ex-pats with their own representatives, their influence also finds a ceiling – only 11 out of 577 seats in the Assemblée Nationale (or 1.9%) are devoted to ex-pats.[76]

Moreover, turnout among ex-pat voters starts from a very low baseline – in France there are 48.8 million registered voters, of which 1.4 million (3%) are registered abroad.[77] However, typically only about 40% of ex-pats vote in Presidential elections and 20% in legislative elections.[78] Similarly, fewer than one in five British citizens residing abroad voted in the 2019 British general election, while only 7% of American citizens resident abroad voted in the 2016 election.[79]

While internet voting from abroad has yet to make major waves in national elections, it is still an interesting point to watch, especially as out-of-country travel becomes ever more common and forms of internet voting make it easier to vote, increasing the chances that ex-pats – previously often subject to much more onerous procedures – will choose to do so.

---

72 *Latin American Economic Outlook 2010* (OECD 2009) 238.

73 Anna Pukas, 'Lebanese across the Globe: How the Country's International Community Came to Be' *Arab News* (4 May 2018) <https://www.arabnews.com/node/1296211/middle-east>.

74 Lucy Ash, 'London, France's Sixth Biggest City' *BBC News* (30 May 2012) <https://www.bbc.com/news/magazine-18234930>.

75 Germann, 'Expatriate Voter Turnout' 2.

76 Although ex-pats may also choose to vote as a member of the constituency in France that they last resided in before moving abroad.

77 Nathalie Stéphan, '48.7 million voters registered for the 2022 presidential election' INSEE Focus No. 264 (Institute National de le Statistique et des Etudes economiques, 24 March 2022) <https://www.insee.fr/en/statistiques/6327287>.

78 Collard and Fabre, 'Electronic Voting in the French Legislative Elections' 188.

79 Germann, 'Expatriate Voter Turnout' 2; Neil Johnston, *2016 Overseas Citizen Population* (Federal Voting Assistance Programme, September 2018) 8 <https://www.fvap.gov/uploads/FVAP/Reports/FVAP-2016-OCPA-FINAL-Report.pdf>.

2.1.3 Turnout in Participatory Budgeting

Another potential impact is voting in non-electoral activities like participatory budgeting (PB).

Considering how long it has been in place (over 10 years in some districts), PB in both Chicago and New York has low participation rates, generally between 1–3%.[80] Because non-citizens and residents over the age of 16 (or even 14) can vote,[81] but do not count as registered voters, the true participation rates in comparison to registered voters may be even lower in some cases. This low turnout could be inherent in the process, but could also be due to the fact that PB in the USA has mainly been conducted offline and involves comparatively little money (for the size of the municipalities involved) which is spent on a combination of 'nice-to haves' (e.g. underpass murals, pedestrian park paths) and rather boring necessities (e.g. repairing sidewalks, street lighting and resurfacing).[82] With PB in New York City (NYC) including an online component from 2022, it will be interesting to see if this affects participation rates.

Although the money at stake in PB in **Brazil** has been more significant, participation numbers haven't always necessarily been much higher. In the early 1990s, the city of Porto Alegre (population 1.4 million) was deciding over 20% of its local budget (and 100% of public capital investment) via PB, while Belo Horizonte (population 2.1 million) was deciding over as much as 50% of its capital investment (ca. 5% of the total budget) this way.[83] After six years of PB in Porto Alegre, ca. 1% of

---

80 PB started in Chicago in 2009 and in NYC in 2011 (Johnson, 'Engaging Democracy' 12). Comparing PB participation data to voter registration data revealed a PB participation rate of about 1–3%. In most NYC districts only a few thousand votes are cast, with most successful proposals receiving fewer than 1000 votes in favour.

81 Colin O'Connor, *Gotham Gazette* <https://www.gothamgazette.com/govermnent/5946-partic ipatory-budget>; Betsy Ribble, 'PBNYC: The Challenges and Opportunities of Scale' (*Harvard Ash Center, Medium,* 7 December 2016) <https://medium.com/challenges-to-democracy/pbnyc-the-chal lenges-and-opportunities-of-scale-951dabeae8d>; 'Chicago's Participatory Budgeting Project' (*Participedia*) <https://participedia.net/case/43>; Anna Clark, 'Is Participatory Budgeting Real Democracy?: Politics People's Choice Style in Chicago' *Next City* (28 April 2014) <https://nextcity.org/features/is-participatory-budgeting-real-democracy-chicago>.

82 Clark, 'Is Participatory Budgeting Real Democracy?'; 'Chicago's Participatory Budgeting Project' (*Participedia*).

83 Celina Souza, 'Participatory Budgeting in Brazilian Cities: Limits and Possibilities in Building Democratic Institutions' (2001) 13(1) Environment and Urbanization 159, 168; 'Building Trust & Breaking Down Complexity: The Past, Present & Future of Participatory Budgeting: Interview with Tarson Nuñez' (*Solonian Democracy Institute,* 24 November 2021) <www.solonian-institute. com/post/building-trust-breaking-down-complexity-the-past-present-future-of-participatory-budget ing>.

the population was taking part, despite steady increases since the process began. In Belo Horizonte, participation was between 1.8–2.5% of the population by 1995.[84]

In 2006, Belo Horizonte introduced **online participation.** That year ca. 174,000 participants (over 8% of the population) engaged and ca 124,000 in 2008 (ca. 6%), before declining again to 25,000 (1%) in 2011.[85] In the Brazilian state of Rio Grande do Sul, 63% of surveyed online participants said they would not have participated in PB if they were not able to vote online, and researchers concluded that ca. 8% of participants in the region (where PB was conducted online and offline) would not have taken part if online participation had not been allowed.[86]

In the idea generation phase of **Iceland's** 2022 online PB process, 17% of the total population of Iceland visited the page, with 0.4% submitting an idea (assuming one idea per person) and 2.3% actively participating (e.g. by submitting an idea, voting, etc.). These percentages more than double if we base them just on the population of Reykjavik, the area concerned (51% of the population visiting, 1.4% submitting an idea, and 7% participating actively as registered users). In 2020, 10,130 people actively participated, equivalent to 8% of the total Reykjavik population.[87]

Lisbon has offered PB both online and offline since 2008, with the exception of 2020 (due to the Covid pandemic). As of 2021, Lisbon PB is now fully 'digital' (no paper voting), with most votes being cast by SMS. The process started with only 2,802 votes in 2008, but increased dramatically every year before peaking at 51,591 votes in 2016. The number of votes has since reduced somewhat to 34,672 in 2018 (the last year for which figures are available). Because participants may cast two votes each (one for a public works project and one for an acquisition of public goods or services), the true participation rate may be anywhere between

---

84 William R. Nylen, 'The Making of a Loyal Opposition: The Workers' Party (PT) and the Consolidation of Democracy in Brazil' in Peter R. Kingstone and Timothy J. Power (eds), *Democratic Brazil: Actors, Institutions and Processes* (University of Pittsburgh Press 2000) 126, 135 et seq.; Souza, 'Participatory Budgeting in Brazilian Cities' 168 (accepting a calculation based on the city populations only and not the wider metro area).

85 Estela Brahimllari, *Multi-Layered Participatory Budgeting: The Case of Low-Income Neighbourhoods in Paris* (FrancoAngeli 2020) 63.

86 Tiago Peixoto, Paolo Spada, Jon Mellon and Fredrik M. Sjoberg, 'Effects of the Internet on Participation: Study of a Public Policy Referendum in Brazil' (2015) World Bank Policy Research Working Paper 7204, 3 and 20.

87 Percentages calculated by author based on a personal communication from Róbert Bjarnason, President Citizens Foundation, to author (11 January 2023).

the 'headline' number of votes (e. g. in 2016, 51,591) or half that number.[88] The population of Lisbon is ca. half a million residents, so this gives a participation rate of between 5 – 10 % for 2016 and between 3 – 7 % for 2018. The number of projects accepted to go forward to vote has decreased significantly since 2016 (182 projects, as opposed to 128 in 2017 and 122 in 2018). It may be that when fewer projects make it onto the final ballot this attracts fewer voters, as some groups lose their stake in the process when their proposal is rejected, and therefore do not encourage their members to vote.

Participatory Budgeting in **Paris** started in 2014, with 500 million EUR (5 % of the city's investment budget) allotted to the programme over five years (2014 – 2019).[89] These funds are divided between city-wide projects and projects particular to each of Paris's 20 districts. All residents of Paris above the age of seven, regardless of citizenship, may submit proposals and vote online or offline on the city-wide projects as well as projects in their own district.

As of 2018, ca. 2.5 – 4 % of residents took part in Paris PB with between 41 – 49 % of these voting online.[90] The number of paper voters increased slightly between 2015 and 2017, while the number of online voters remained fairly steady, likely due to organizers providing more voting booths around the city that encourage people to paper vote on the spot.[91] Each year more than 1,000 proposals are submitted to Paris PB out of a population of roughly two million residents (meaning at least 0.05 % of the population submits a proposal).[92] Paris PB has continued to grow since these figures were collected, now accounting for 25 % of the capital budget. 140,000 votes were submitted to the process in 2022, bringing the participation rate to ca. 7 % of the population.[93] If we compare these numbers to local voting in Paris, we can see that in the 2014 municipal elections, 33 % of the total popula-

---

88 'Edicões Anteriores' (*Lisboa Participa, Câmara Municipal de Lisboa*) <https://op.lisboaparticipa. pt/edicoes-anteriores> accessed 17 January 2023; 'Perguntas Frequentas' (*Lisboa Participa, Câmara Municipal de Lisboa*) <https://op.lisboaparticipa.pt/faqs> accessed 17 January 2023.
89 Brahimllari, *Multi-Layered Participatory Budgeting* 23.
90 Émilie Moreau and William Arhip-Paterson, 'Budget participatif de Paris: Qui sont les Parisiens qui y participants?' (2018) No. 123 Atelier Parisiene de Urbanisme 1 et seq <https://www.apur.org/ sites/default/files/documents/publication/etudes/note_123_budget_participatif.pdf?token= rsDSZWYi>; William Arhip-Paterson and Ari Brodach, 'Budget participatif de Paris: Analyse des votants papiers et de leurs pratiques' Rapport pour la Ville de Paris (December 2018) 2.
91 William Arhip-Paterson, 'Budget participatif de Paris: Tendances dans la participation' Rapport pour la Ville de Paris (February 2019) 12.
92 Arhip-Paterson, 'Tendances dans la participation' 2.
93 'Budget Participatif 2023: Deposez vos Idées' (*City of Paris*) <https://www.paris.fr/pages/budget-participatif-deposez-vos-idees-22902> accessed 21 February 2023.

tion and 58 % of registered voters cast a ballot,[94] so PB participation is now riding at close to one-quarter of local election participation.

While participation is definitely happening, it can be difficult to quantify what the precise increase is. For example, in some cases, we are comparing a general population which includes minors and non-citizens, and in others, voting is not always controlled to determine if voters are truly resident in the city. Furthermore, in some cases, PB may simply replace other forms of community consultation. However, that there has been some increase, especially in cases where tens or even hundreds of thousands of people vote, seems obvious.

The effect of offering PB online is also hard to determine, since different localities offer different participation modalities and different regions have different levels of internet access (especially across time). However, offering PB online does seem to have some effect – for one thing, participation is quite high in Iceland, where it is overwhelmingly online. The temporary boost in PB participation in Belo Horizonte as well as the steady high numbers of online participants in Paris and Lisbon also indicate that there are likely certain constituencies of residents who would not participate if this option were not available. Unlike the case for electoral voting, resources to raise awareness of and conduct PB are limited and they would likely not suffice to reach out to and facilitate these voters absent the efficiency of the internet.

2.1.4 Turnout on Online Consultation and Decision-Making Platforms

Where we can see a more substantial impact of internet voting on turnout (at least so far) is in voting within **professional and economic associations.** This is not insignificant as membership in such associations can number in the tens or even hundreds of thousands. One organization reported a jump in voting among members from 30 % to 80 % after it introduced online voting for elections to its board.[95] For professional associations, it appears that internet voting can boost turnout by 30–40 % on average,[96] although whether it can be sustained at this level is unclear.

---

94 Moreau and Arhip-Paterson, 'Qui sont les Parisiens qui y participants?' 4; participation was significantly lower in the French 2020 municipal elections, although this was likely partly due to coronavirus restrictions.

95 Interview with an official of the association (2022).

96 'Mr. SkyVote: "Our Voting Model is the Opposite of Rousseau"' *Breaking Latest News* (17 June 2021) <https://www.breakinglatest.news/health/mr-skyvote-our-voting-model-is-the-opposite-of-rousseau/>.

Some **municipalities** also offer ways to participate using other online platforms.

As of 2020, 62 municipalities, accounting for 53% of the population in Catalonia, were using the open-source software Decidim. Decidim has several functionalities, but is often used for planning consultations. For example, the Barcelona Action Plan for 2016–2019, which accounted for 40% of the municipal budget, was the subject of an online consultation which attracted 18,192 comments and 10,860 proposals from ca. 40,000 visitors. If we accept that each participant made only one comment, this would give an active online participation rate of 1% of the total population. Offline participation was also offered, but 70% of proposals were submitted via the online platform. Consultations in the smaller cities of Terrassa and Badalona typically generate hundreds of comments, which gives a similar participation rate, so we can see that this pattern is fairly consistent. The percentage of registered users (not necessarily participants) in municipalities using Decidim tends to vary from below 1% to over 15%.[97] Participation rates in other consultations have been more mixed. A consultation held by the New Zealand city of Hamilton (pop. ca 160,000) on its ten-year plan claims to have attracted 10 times as many responses as the last consultation on the same plan did, using Citizen Space developed by British company Delib.[98] In three cases where Ethelo, a Canadian online software, was used for local consultations, active participation averaged about 0.3–2% of the total population.[99] While these are not high participation rates, we can see that offering digital participation can result in increased uptake with many residents seeming to prefer this possibility.

Of course, platforms can also be used by **parties.** In this case, participants are drawn from a narrower pool of people who have at least some political interest.

Between 2012 and 2018, M5S (the Italian Five Star Movement) conducted 79 national votes using the platform Rousseau, which translates to an average of ca. 13 votes per year. Between 2014 and 2018, the Spanish party Podemos held 14 national votes, an average of 3–4 per year.

---

97 Rosa Borge, Joan Balcells and Albert Padró-Solanet, 'Democratic Disruption or Continuity? Analysis of the Decidim Platform in Catalan Municipalities' (2022) American Behavioural Scientist 7; Rosa Borge, Joaquim Brugué and David Duenas-Cid, 'Technology and Democracy: The Who and How in Decision-Making: The Cases of Estonia and Catalonia' (2022) 31(3) El Profesional de la Información 65, 72.
98 'Citizen Space for Hamilton City Council New Zealand' (*Delib*) <https://www.delib.net/citizen_space/resources/citizen-space-for-statutory-consultation>.
99 These cases were Lethbridge CIP, Okotoks 2080 and London Ontario, Carbon Budgeting.

Participation for Podemos online voting was:

- 54% of party membership in October 2014
- 43% for the election of Pablo Iglesias to Secretary General in November 2014
- 15.5% for online primaries in July 2015
- 4% for consultations on the party program in November 2015.

In 2016, Podemos started to distinguish between active and inactive members (anyone who had not used the platform for more than a year).

This gave the following figures for participation among active members going forward:

- 72% in April 2016 on whether there should be a PSOE-Ciudadanos government
- 60% in May 2016 on forming an electoral alliance with the Izquierda Unida
- 40% on the voting procedure for the second party congress in 2016
- 55% for the election of the Secretary General and the Citizen Council in February 2017
- 46% in March 2018 'on the use of the Podemos symbol in all electoral alliances'
- 31% on 'the proposal for a no-confidence vote to the conservative government of Mariano Rajoy' in May 2018
- Also in May 2018, the vote on whether Irene Montero and Pablo Iglesias should resign after having purchased an expensive home (against the party's socialist ethos) resulted in a turnout of 75% (190 000 votes).[100]

If we include passive members, the average turnout was about 26% across all of the votes held.[101]

The approximate turnout for Rousseau (including all members who joined but remained passive) was:

- 64% for primaries selecting MP candidates in 2012 for the 2013 elections
- 29% turnout for primaries in January 2018
- 13% on average for 20 consultations on the party programme
- 34% for the selection of presidential nominees (51 000 voters)

---

100 Marco Deseriis and Davide Vittori, 'The Impact of Online Participation Platforms on the Internal Democracy of Two Southern European Parties: Podemos and the Five Star Movement' (2019) 13 International Journal of Communication 5696, 5706.
101 Deseriis and Vittori, 'Impact of Online Participation Platforms' 5706.

- 76% for the reform of the party statute in 2016 (87 000 voters)[102]
- 70% for the 2019 national coalition agreement with the PD (80 000 voters)[103]

This is a fairly high participation rate when one considers that voting sometimes occurs over a single day.

It's interesting to compare voting within Podemos and the Five Star Movement to those countries where offline referendums are common, because, generally speaking, the more often referendums are held, the lower average turnout is per referendum.[104] Average turnout in Switzerland, which holds referendums at a somewhat lower rate than M5S held decisions (an average of 10 federal referendums per year were held in Switzerland over the same time period), is just over 40%, and in California it is 'as low as 35 per cent'.[105] This is despite the fact that in both jurisdictions citizen-initiated referendums must be able to prove a certain level of public support before being admitted to the ballot. At the same time, however, total participation *over time* in countries with frequent referendums is fairly high. For example, in Switzerland, although average turnout in referendums is usually in the 40s-60s in terms of percentage, the number of people voting at least once over two years is about 75%.[106] This turnover effect may also exist for the platforms we have been analysing here.

Unlike in national referendums, it is also possible for members to comment on these digital party platforms. While commenting has tended to decline over the years,[107] it is probable that in their formative years both Podemos and M5S were still heavily engaged in defining the party platform, and that after this stage, the focus increasingly turned to winning elections, and, in the case of M5S, governing on the basis of the agreed platform.

---

102 All numbers from Deseriis and Vittori, 'Impact of Online Participation Platforms' 5707. The last three percentage figures are my own calculation based on an average membership of 115,000 (this figure on membership from Marco Deseriis, 'Digital Movement Parties: A Comparative Analysis of the Technopolitical Cultures and the Participation Platforms of the Movimento 5 Stelle and the Piratenpartei' (2020) 23(12) Information, Communication and Society 1770–1786).

103 Number of online voters obtained from Interview with Davide Casaleggio, President and Founder, Rousseau Association (15 September 2020), calculation my own based on 115,000 members.

104 Matt Qvortrup, *A Comparative Study of Referendums: Government by the People* (2nd edn, Manchester University Press 2005) 30–31.

105 Graham Smith, *Democratic Innovations: Designing Institutions for Citizen Participation* (Cambridge University Press 2009) 118.

106 Uwe Serdült, 'Switzerland' in Matt Qvortrup (ed) *Referendums Around the World* (Palgrave Macmillan 2018) 87, 95.

107 Deseriis and Vittori, 'Impact of Online Participation Platforms', citing Mosca (2018), 13.

2.1.5 Conclusions on Turnout

When it comes to turnout, online voting may help to stem reduction in voting and possibly bolster it in those areas where participation is generally considered of lesser importance, e.g. in local elections and for ex-pats. This may become more significant in the future, as it has become more common for people to travel abroad and to live abroad for some time in their early careers. Enabling people to continue to be connected to their home country's political system may be beneficial if significant numbers eventually return at some point in their lives.

Technology can also enable new forms of participation and more participation in processes like participatory budgeting and consultation. Participation in these activities remains low-to-moderate compared to the total percentage of population, but still often represents a significant increase in total political involvement as tens or even hundreds of thousands of people take part in activities that were previously less accessible, and sometimes even closed off entirely from them.

2.2 Reducing Costs and Increasing Efficiency

Cost savings and improved efficiency are two of the most commonly cited advantages of digital technology, and there are some reasons to believe that these advantages transfer to digital democracy as well, especially at scale.

2.2.1 Streamlining Pre-Existing Activities

An Estonian study which attempted to quantify the costs of different methods of voting concluded that, if exercised by a large section of the population, e-voting was the most cost-effective, coming in around 60 cents cheaper per ballot than paper voting on election day and cheaper still than in-person forms of advance voting.[108] Professional associations have also reported substantial savings in postal costs when they offered online voting, while public servants reported that being able to export data from online public consultations saved them substantial time in preparing reports.[109]

---

[108] Robert Krimmer, David Duenas-Cid and Iuliia Krivonosova, 'New Methodology for Calculating Cost-Efficiency of Different Ways of Voting: Is Internet Voting Cheaper?' (2021) 41(1) Public Money and Management 17–26.
[109] Interviews (2022).

Voters also cast ballots more quickly online, **saving time.** An experiment in Ghana revealed that it took about half the time for voters to cast a vote electronically compared to paper voting, and that e-voting resulted in fewer errors than paper voting did.[110] In Estonia, it takes less than two minutes for a voter to cast their ballot online in elections, compared to an average 30-minute round-trip to a polling station.[111]

Even small-scale elections using Russian software Polys claimed to have saved time. For example, a student election at a Russian university with 14,000 voters taking part claimed to have saved ca. 30 work-hours in processing the results.[112] More complex elections, e. g. involving live debates between candidates or voting across different jurisdictions, can save even more time. The Russian political party Yabloko claims to have saved 145 work-hours by using Polys to facilitate voting in its primaries.[113] Voting for positions at the Russian Academy of Sciences involves voting at many different institutes, while the Asia Pacific Society of Spinal Surgery allows members to vote from many different countries. Both organizations have claimed to save time using Polys to facilitate these complex votes.[114]

Technology can also allow other activities to be completed more efficiently, particularly bureaucratic activities. For example, Prof. Beth Noveck of Northeastern University's Governance Lab suggests creating an online pool of experts to check patents quickly. This could help clear the backlog of pending patent applications that accrues partly through the difficulty of finding highly, and very specifically, qualified experts to examine claims.[115]

The largest savings by far, however, come from offering **public services** online. This isn't really democracy – after all, there is no collective decision-making or even public debate involved. Nonetheless, it is still important to think of this as part of the digital democracy ecosystem for two reasons: the first is that the substantial savings accrued by offering public services online and using tools to streamline the process can be repurposed to increase political participation; the

---

110 Agbesi, Tehiru and Osei-owusu, 'E-Voting System in Ghana' 226.
111 Unt, Solvak and Vassil, 'E-vote log files' 91.
112 'Large Scale Elections at RANEPA' (*Polys*) <https://ru.polys.me/success-stories/elections-at-rane pa> accessed 11 January 2023.
113 'Voting in the Primaries in the Yabloko Party' (*Polys*) <https://ru.polys.me/success-stories/ya bloko-party-primaries> accessed 11 January 2023.
114 'Online Election of the Director of the Federal Scientific Research Center of the Russian Academy of Sciences' (*Polys*) <https://ru.polys.me/success-stories/online-election-of-the-director-of-frsc ras> accessed 11 January 2023; 'APSS Council Member Election 2019' (*Polys*) <https://ru.polys.me/ success-stories/election-of-apss-board-members> accessed 11 January 2023.
115 Beth Simone Noveck, *Smart Citizens, Smarter State: The Technologies of Expertise and the Future of Governing* (Harvard University Press 2015).

second is that it is much easier to incorporate elements of digital democracy in a society where people possess a high degree of digital literacy and confidence in interacting with government online. Officials in some European countries, including Estonia, credit their online service provision for boosting participation in online democracy,[116] while election officials in Canada 'pointed out that the COVID-19 pandemic had naturally pushed people to use the internet to buy groceries and pay bills, which brought greater public trust and comfort in technology' and that they were therefore more 'relaxed' about online voting.[117]

Estonia, while it is best known for internet voting, also offers a highly integrated package of online services that residents can access using their digital ID. This is facilitated by a data sharing system called **X-Road** (now sometimes called X-tee) that supports the nation's 'once-only principle' – the idea that information should only have to be entered into the system once, and can then be accessed by any authority at need. For example, drivers do not need to carry their licence or vehicle registration with them, because police can access this information based on their ID-card and/or licence plate number.[118] Thanks to this system, Estonians can access over 75 different online services,[119] including tax reporting, child benefit payments, court services, and health information. Smart readers, necessary to use E-ID cards, can be purchased at supermarkets and convenience stores,[120] and the country has constantly updated its system to allow for novel forms of ID, such as Mobile ID and Smart ID (which, as the names imply, function on mobile and smart devices).

It has been estimated that if every citizen-facing transaction conducted over X-Road saves just 15 minutes of the citizen's time, this would mean that Estonia saved 2.8 million work hours in 2014 alone through digital queries. Realistically, likely double this time is saved.[121] Similarly, online information has made it possible

---

116 Interviews (2022).

117 Helen A. Hayes, Nicole Goodman, R. Michael McGregor, Zachary Spicer and Scott Pruysers, 'The Effect of Exogenous Shocks on the Administration of Online Voting: Evidence from Ontario, Canada' (International Joint Conference on Electronic Voting 2022) *Lecture Notes in Computer Science, Vol. 13553* (Springer 2022) 70, 83.

118 Kristjan Vassil, 'The Estonian e-government Ecosystem' in Mihkel Solvak and Kristjan Vassil (eds), *E-voting in Estonia: Technological Diffusion and other Developments over Ten Years, 2005 – 2015* (Johan Skytte Institute of Political Studies, University of Tartu 2016) 14, 28.

119 Vassil, 'Estonian e-government Ecosystem' 16.

120 Vassil, 'Introduction' 5.

121 Vassil, 'Estonian e-government Ecosystem' 34 – 36. In 2018, it was estimated that X-Road saved Estonia 1407 years of working time ('X-Road as Created by Cybernetica' (*Cybernetica*, 2 November 2021) <https://cyber.ee/resources/case-studies/x-road-as-created-by-cybernetica/> accessed 26 February 2023).

for Cabinet members to access data in real time, eliminating the need for reports (often quickly out-of-date) to be prepared for them. Cabinet meetings can also be organized using online tools to keep an overview of each subject under discussion. These measures have reduced weekly Cabinet meetings from 4 – 5 hours in length to as little as 30 minutes.[122]

Reaping these savings, however, requires significant initial investment and a commitment to continual renewal. It took more than five years for digitalized services to take off in Estonia in terms of citizen use. Researchers credit the **number of services available** as being more important than merely communicating the existence of such services to the public, as this is what makes adapting to a new system worth the time citizens must invest to change their habits.[123]

Estonia is not the only country to make significant progress in moving services online. Almost all Indian adults are now registered on **Aadhaar**, a digital identity system which records the resident's name, address, gender, date of birth, ten fingerprints and an iris scan (mobile and email are optional). Every person on Aadhaar has a twelve-digit identity code, which can also be used for commercial transactions, like banking. As in Estonia, it took time for the Aadhaar system to reap results – work was already underway in 2009. The government claims that Aadhaar has helped reduce identity theft and fraud, as well as making it easier for people to apply for government services and to access the financial system, something that has disproportionately benefitted the poor.[124] For example, India operates a system of food subsidies, which eligible residents can access via so-called 'ration shops'. Due to the previous paper-based nature of this system, it was easy for operators to skim food intended for the poor from the supplies, and it was difficult for those who moved to a new location to access their entitlements. In many areas, this has now been replaced with the Aadhaar system, where recipients' fingerprints are scanned before the rations are transferred.[125] These more comprehensive systems are joined by nations like Kenya and Ireland where passport applications, business registration and taxes can all be completed online.[126]

---

122 'Factsheet: E-Governance' (*E-Governance Academy*) <https://e-estonia.com/wp-content/uploads/e-governance-factsheet-sep2021.pdf> accessed 11 January 2023.

123 Vassil, 'Estonian e-government Ecosystem' 16 and 31.

124 'Aadhaar: A Unique Identity for the People' (*Unique Identification Authority of India, Government of India*) <https://uidai.gov.in/images/Aadhaar_Brochure_July_22.pdf> accessed 11 January 2023.

125 Vijayta Lalwani, 'Why has the Modi Government's Plan to make Food Grain more Accessible not Taken Off?' *Quartz* (7 July 2021) <https://qz.com/india/2030281/why-modis-one-nation-one-ration-for-india-hasnt-taken-off/>.

126 Nanjala Nyabola, *Digital Democracy: Analogue Politics: How the Internet Era is Transforming Politics in Kenya* (Zed Books 2018) 6.

Under the wrong circumstances, however, democracy-focused digitalization can also become a money-sink. In many African nations a large part of digitalization has been related to preventing voter fraud by using **biometric identification** (usually fingerprints taken digitally and compared to an existing database), as well as digital transmission of vote results from polling stations to a central counting centre. While it was initially hoped that this would save money, this hasn't always been the case. At times, developing nations are given or loaned large sums of money from donor countries and then expected to purchase biometric systems from that country's companies[127] – a practice not always in the best interests of the purchaser.

As this indicates, cost savings and efficiency gains heavily depend on the circumstances on the ground and the goals being pursued. It is very important to have a clear idea of where savings will come from and how long it will take to achieve them. It is also important to ensure that sufficient resources have been committed to the project to see it through.

This is even more true of the participatory aspects of democracy. Public services tend to be provided *anyway* – whether well or badly, efficiently or inefficiently. Thus, some level of cost already exists which can be cut using more efficient technology. However, when it comes to increasing political participation, the *opposite* is true. This *wasn't* something government was doing before, so it starts off *purely* as an expense.

2.2.2 Costs of Additional Participation

Many public bodies – even some of the most successful – have underestimated the resources required to make digital democracy (or indeed any kind of democracy) work. This is often because they ascribe to definitions of democracy that are synonymous with 'engagement' and 'participation' and are seen as 'nice-to-haves' and they therefore do not correctly assess the commitment that is necessary to make this participation sustainable.

Participatory budgeting, in particular, can be resource-intense. The participatory budget in Paris – one of the largest in the world in financial terms – was initially run by the city's Citizens' Participation Service. However, the project turned out to be more than the service could cope with and thus a specific PB department was created.[128] Paris PB had initially (in 2015) promised that each proposal submitted by residents would be reviewed by civil servants within 48 hours. This review would deter-

---

127 Cheeseman, Lynch and Willis, 'Digital Dilemmas' 1404.
128 Brahimllari, *Multi-Layered Participatory Budgeting* 104.

mine whether the proposal's cost estimate was accurate and whether it fell within the competency of the city council (both requirements for it to proceed to the voting stage). As it happened, Paris PB received 5,115 proposals and ended up having to create a task force (sometimes consisting of a dozen people pulled in from other projects) to sort through them in marathon sessions.[129] Even with the PB Department, which consists of 5–7 full-time staff,[130] Paris still struggles with the resources necessary to review and cost citizen proposals, as well as to perform outreach to inform citizens about the PB process.[131] In addition to the PB Department itself, Paris participatory budgeting has involved multiple stakeholders at a high level of bureaucratic responsibility,[132] as well as the agency responsible for organizing conventional elections to support voting.[133] As this indicates, PB often requires a high level of coordination, which is itself resource-intensive.

Lisbon, which has been running PB both offline and online since 2008 also requires a substantial level of resources. Lisbon City Council employs approximately 8,000 people, 70 of whom are involved in PB at some point of the process,[134] while a civil servant in Iceland (population ca. 370,000) described working 'all day and night' when PB is ongoing there.[135] Administrators who use Decidim in Catalonia, also confirmed that it was challenging to find the time to assess citizen proposals and provide responses, and difficult to coordinate action between different departments.[136]

Although New York City runs the largest instance of PB in North America,[137] several councilmembers have rejected opportunities to implement it in their districts precisely because it is expensive and time-consuming and they do not believe that it provides them with any additional input that would change budgetary decisions.[138]

---

129 William Arhip-Paterson, 'Wear and Tear: Civil Servants Grueling Implementation of Paris Participatory Budgeting (2014–2020)' (2022) COSTAction Working Paper No. 16/2022, 5.
130 Arhip-Paterson, 'Wear and Tear' 7.
131 Brahimllari, *Multi-Layered Participatory Budgeting* 105–106.
132 Brahimllari, *Multi-Layered Participatory Budgeting* 97.
133 Arhip-Paterson, 'Wear and Tear' 6 and 8.
134 Interviews (2022).
135 Interview with Eiríkur Búi Halldórsson, Project Manager – My Neighborhood, City of Reykjavik Human Rights and Democracy Office (22 March 2022).
136 Borge, Balcells and Padró-Solanet, 'Democratic Disruption or Continuity?' 6.
137 Ribble, 'PBNYC: The Challenges and Opportunities of Scale'.
138 David Brand, 'Queens' 14 Council Districts may Lose Participatory Budgeting for Second Year in a Row' *Queens Daily Eagle* (19 October 2020) <https://queenseagle.com/all/queens-may-lose-participatory-budgeting-for-second-year-in-a-row>; Abigail Savitch-Lew, 'Factcheck: Has Councilmember Perkins Ever Participated in Participatory Budgeting?' *City Limits* (25 September 2017); O'Connor, *Gotham Gazette*.

Councilmembers who do run participatory budgeting in New York usually have to devote one of their five full-time members of staff solely to overseeing it.[139] Some districts in Chicago have also stopped PB on the grounds that it was time-consuming and expensive with few residents voting,[140] and a number of small towns in Iceland that instituted participatory budgeting also eventually gave it up due to its resource-intensiveness.[141]

Digital tools, and sophisticated forms of participation generally, were invented for scale and if one doesn't need that scale, one also doesn't need digital tools. There are also many low-tech ways of enabling democracy. In Gambia, where illiteracy is high, voting is conducted using marbles as tokens and counting them with the aid of slotted boards.[142] The British grocery chain Tesco uses participatory budgeting to decide on the projects it funds as part of its corporate social responsibility efforts by giving shoppers tokens that they can throw into urns at the exit. Technology isn't the only way to accomplish democracy or facilitate participation, and is not necessarily always appropriate to the situation at hand.

That being said, in high-population, highly-literate societies, digital technology can be used to enable a level of coordination that would otherwise be impossible to achieve.

Up until this point, PB in both Chicago and New York has been subject to a cumbersome and lengthy offline process, which may explain some of its off-putting resource-intensiveness. Participating districts in each city start the process with neighbourhood assemblies to gather ideas before selecting delegates to work with experts and state agencies to turn those ideas (and others) into concrete proposals over several months. These proposals are then presented at neighbourhood assemblies where residents have a chance to request proposals to be added or removed from the list before it goes to voting.[143]

In both cities, councilmembers have used discretionary funds (called 'menu money' in Chicago) to facilitate PB. The amount of money so allocated is small, ca.

---

139 O'Connor, *Gotham Gazette.*

140 Clark, 'Is Participatory Budgeting Real Democracy?'

141 Interview Eiríkur Búi Halldórsson.

142 Nyabola, *Digital Democracy: Analogue Politics* 189; Ade Daramy, 'Why Gambians Won't Stop Voting with Marbles' *BBC* (1 December 2021) <https://www.bbc.com/news/world-africa-59476637>.

143 Daniel Williams and Don Waisanen, *Real Money, Real Power? The Challenges with Participatory Budgeting in New York City* (Palgrave MacMillan 2020) 44; O'Connor, *Gotham Gazette*; Ribble, 'PBNYC: The Challenges and Opportunities of Scale'; Chicago's Participatory Budgeting Project (*Participedia*).

$1 million per district.[144] In New York, the $32 million allocated via PB in 2014/2015 was 0.4% 'of the average $7.9 billion spent on city capital projects annually'.[145] More recent figures peg the proportion of the city's capital budget distributed via PB even lower – at 0.1%.[146] When the expense budget is taken into account, 'projects decided via PB account for about 0.03%' of New York City's total budget.[147] In Chicago, about one dozen aldermen use participatory budgeting, accounting for $12 million in funding. Chicago's city budget, which excludes payment for most major items like schools, parks, transit and housing, already comes to $8.6 billion, meaning that PB accounts for just 0.1% of this already reduced budget[148] (by comparison, from the beginning, PB in Paris was ca. 20 times higher in terms of monetary value than in New York, despite having only one-quarter of the population). PB done this way requires a high level of resources to allocate what is comparatively little money. Indeed, residents sometimes complain that PB projects are often limited to 'mundane things you can't possibly argue about'.[149]

Moreover, research indicates that those NYC councilmembers who claim PB would not change funding allocations may not be entirely wrong. A study comparing spending across NYC districts that did not engage in PB to districts that did, before they began PB and after doing PB for six years, came to the following results:

---

144 Clark, 'Is Participatory Budgeting Real Democracy?'; Williams and Waisanen, *Real Money, Real Power?* 23.

145 O'Connor, *Gotham Gazette*; 'Understanding New York City's Budget: A Guide to the Capital Budget' (*New York City, Independent Budget Office*) 1 <https://www.ibo.nyc.ny.us/iboreports/IBOCBG.pdf>.

146 Williams and Waisanen, *Real Money, Real Power?* 23.

147 Williams and Waisanen, *Real Money, Real Power?* 35.

148 Becky Vevea, 'What Would You Do With A Million Dollars? Whether Participatory Budgeting Is Worth The Effort' *WBEZ* (9 December 2017) <https://www.wbez.org/stories/what-would-you-do-with-a-million-dollars-whether-participatory-budgeting-is-worth-the-effort/ac8a69e6-8ad0-44bd-adb730de877601c6>.

149 Vevea 'What Would You Do With A Million Dollars?'

Table 2.2: Funding Allocations by Category in NYC.

District Type	Education	Housing	Highway & Traffic	Parks & Recreation	Housing Preservation
Non-PB district	43.68%	7.09%	2.56%	21.92%	3.81%
PB District (pre-PB)	35.97%	5.09%	2.58%	30.14%	6.83%
PB District (after PB)	42.03%	7.34%	4.58%	23.69%	2.78%

Source: Carolin Hagelskamp, Rebecca Silliman, Erin B. Godfrey and David Schleifer 'Shifting Priorities: Participatory Budgeting in New York City is Associated with Increased Investments in Schools, Street and Traffic Improvements, and Public Housing' New Political Science 190–192.

It would appear that those representatives who claimed not to need PB really did have a better idea of what their constituents wanted, as evidenced by the fact that other districts' spending was, in four out of five major spending categories, brought in line with them once they started PB. Thus, it would appear that PB *did* serve a purpose where it was utilized, but wasn't necessarily applicable to those districts where communication between representatives and citizens was already working well. So, in this case, they were both right: it is possible to come to the same conclusions using less resource-intense methods than small-scale, offline PB. However, this wasn't happening in many districts, so PB, despite being quite resource-intensive did fulfill a purpose here, and most likely *did* align spending priorities to better meet constituents' wishes. Whether this same purpose could be fulfilled in a less resource-intense manner by moving more of the process online, remains to be seen, but it is probable that with stringent management the overheads could be brought down and the outreach increased.

Nonetheless, because PB involves a kind of scalable mass participation that wasn't happening before, it will in some sense, always be an additional cost. The same may be said for other types of participation, such as consultation, planning and petitioning. If one were to create an online petition portal, this might increase the number of successful petitions and thus increase the workload to process them. The 'taking-in' and processing of more public input is itself always a cost (whether well or poorly managed).

However, that doesn't mean there aren't net savings. They are just harder to quantify, because they come predominantly in the form of avoiding long-term problems by ensuring greater accuracy and alignment between public wishes and government action. For example, savings may be generated by *not* building an expensive project no one wanted, or in avoiding the time and money wasted in political infighting.

2.2.3 Clientelism, Corruption and Fiscal Scrutiny

In Porto Alegre, where PB was first implemented, officials had believed that public transportation would be the most important concern for disadvantaged people, but instead they voted for better water supply and sewerage, which authorities then supplied.[150] While money spent on public transportation may not have precisely been wasted, had the government proceeded without consulting people, it would have inevitably spent a great deal of money addressing an issue of secondary rather than primary concern. As this indicates, online participation *isn't* necessarily about giving citizens more. It can also be about providing something different or even spending less.

In almost all instances of digital democracy that I have studied, participants chose to spend a large proportion of the discussion focused on money and ways to save it. Indeed, in both Okotoks 2080 and Lethbridge CIP (online consultations held in Alberta, Canada, detailed in Chapter 5) a very large percentage of comments concerned themselves with fiscal responsibility. Participants frequently viewed the projects presented by authorities as spectacularly overpriced and spent a great deal of time assessing whether or not the costs were reasonable or 'a good investment'. They often explicitly asked for the government to show them the pay-off in cost-benefit dollars over the lifetime of projects or just did the math themselves.

Participants also typically tended to frugality in their voting behaviour. For example, in the Lethbridge consultation participants voted down improving a path in the Japanese garden, a local recreational amenity and tourist attraction. While renewal would have been an aesthetic improvement, a frequently expressed sentiment in the comments was that because the path was still functional it simply wasn't a priority. A typical comment from Lethbridge CIP read: 'If this were my money (which it is as a tax payer) I would say that's too expensive'. Another, somewhat less diplomatically, accused the city of 'spending money like a drunken sailor'.

This should not be surprising: politicians are constantly pressured to spend money on prestige projects by various interests that promise to solve societal problems for a certain fee. Businesses do not approach governments with ideas about

---

150 Souza, 'Participatory Budgeting in Brazilian Cities' 167–168.

how to solve problems by spending no money whatsoever. That would be a completely pointless endeavour from their perspective. Politicians and public servants can feel pressured to take up these solutions – after all, they have to be seen to be doing something – and often the amount of money spent on an issue is viewed as a proxy for its importance to government. Indeed, politicians and government bodies often advertise how much money they spend on an issue, rather than whether or not they have resolved it.

By contrast the average person tends to ask what the goal is and how they can reach it, preferably without spending any money at all. This **scrutiny** is where savings come in. Far from happily spending money, people in Okotoks and Lethbridge rejected the majority of the proposals they were presented with, often with complaints about the 'ridiculous' costs and high payments to private contractors and consultants. Participants in NYC PB have also often complained that the costs of projects were 'astronomical' and 'shocking', with some researchers doubting if the cost estimates posted by civil servants are even accurate.[151]

This scrutinizing function of democracy is often overlooked, yet it is key to realizing one of the most important benefits of democracy. Organizers often frame democratic participation as a way for people to tell authorities what they want, but just as important is what they *don't* want.

This scrutiny helps to prevent clientelism – commissioning expensive (sometimes overpriced) public works, which may look impressive, but fail to fulfill the needs or wants of the populace. When these decisions are moved directly into the hands of the general public, it effectively ends the ability of politicians, civil servants and contractors to enter into procurement arrangements that may be corrupt or complacent, with too little regard for getting the best value for the taxpayer. In Brazil, the introduction of PB at least initially reduced the scope for this kind of backdoor decision-making.[152]

Another form of clientelism occurs when politicians spend public money on those areas of the locality that vote for them while excluding others. This has been an issue in both Brazil [153] and Chicago.[154] Former NYC mayor Bill de Blasio specifically connected using PB as a way to end abuse of funds, after a council-

151 Williams and Waisanen, *Real Money, Real Power?* 94–97.

152 Rebecca Abers, Igor Brandão, Robin King and Daniely Votto, 'Porto Alegre: Participatory Budgeting and the Challenge of Sustaining Transformative Change' World Resources Report Case Study (World Resources Institute 2018) 11 <https://files.wri.org/d8/s3fs-public/wrr-case-study-porto-alegre_1.pdf>.

153 Abers et al. 'Porto Alegre' 5.

154 Vevea, 'What Would You Do With A Million Dollars?'.

member allocated a significant portion of his funding to another district because he planned to run for Congress there in the future.[155]

Such behaviour doesn't even need to verge on the criminal. A major complaint in the Okotoks 2080 consultation was that civil servants were investing in prestige projects no one wanted. Participants did not believe that civil servants did this for material enrichment, but rather in order to win prizes allocated by outside bodies (e. g. federal agencies). This incentivized public bodies to spend taxpayer's money rather than save it.

Democracy can also 'save' money in other ways, by preventing economic freeloading and infringements on the rule of law. For example, if insurance costs are driving up prices for public projects, perhaps an examination of the industry or court-awarded damages is warranted in order to prevent the issue from ballooning. This has the potential to unravel cartels or other damaging practices throughout the wider society, and it is by doing these things that increased democratic participation saves costs and drives efficiency.

Thus, while there is a significant cost to implementing digital democracy, it can be expected that these costs are recovered in the long-run by avoiding forms of spending that do not enjoy popular support, and in uncovering costly malpractice.

2.3 Flexibility and Scalability

Digital democracy can be put into use very swiftly, as evidenced by the Taiwanese consultation at the beginning of the Covid-19 pandemic. Most digital tools are extremely flexible, and can thus easily be adapted to a wide range of scenarios as these arise – some tools with participatory budgeting capacity, like Ethelo and Delib, for example, have been repurposed to conduct carbon budgeting instead, in which citizens choose policy with the aim of reducing carbon emissions. As we have seen, while Citizens Foundation is best-known for PB, it is also used for general ideation and consultation in Iceland to generate feedback on various policies (such as the policy on multiculturalism) or on ongoing projects (such as the renovation of a large swimming complex).[156] In addition, public servants reported often finding multiple unexpected use cases for digital tools. One, for example had been using a consultation software externally, but also began using it internally to evaluate training sessions and the internal communication process.[157]

---

155 Sally Goldenberg, 'Mayoral Hopefuls Roast Council Pork' *New York Post* (9 July 2013) <https://nypost.com/2013/07/09/mayoral-hopefuls-roast-council-pork/>.
156 Interview Eiríkur Búi Halldórsson.
157 Interview (2022).

Voting tools also generally allow for the easy configuration of ballots, allowing different voting systems to be used and ensuring, for example, that gender quotas are fulfilled.[158] Digital voting cuts down on the guesswork involved in distributing ballots to each polling station, and thus the risk of overprinting by a wide margin or, worse, running out of ballots. This could ease the logistical difficulties in coordinating elections with very large numbers of voters. India with its 900 million voters uses direct recording electronic voting machines (stationary voting machines) in its elections.[159] Brazil, with about 150 million registered voters, also uses voting machines which transmit their results via satellite telephone to tabulating machines in Brasilia.[160]

Digital tools can also be easily scaled for use in small, large or specialist groups. For example, Discuto, an Austrian tool, was used by the Consumers' Association to develop certification criteria for its eco-label,[161] while SkyVote is often used at shareholder meetings. At the same time, tools like Rousseau or the Estonian i-voting system have handled tens of thousands or even millions of concurrent participants.

This flexibility also expresses itself in other ways, such as allowing people to access services or participate in decision-making more flexibly outside of normal working hours. An analysis of comments on 11 proposals discussed during the Lethbridge capital investment consultation showed that more than 70% of comments were made outside of normal working hours. The most common time for comments was the evening (6pm-12am) with 41% of all comments (many of them in the later hours), and the second most common time for commenting was during the night (12am-6am), accounting for 30% of all comments. The morning (6am-12pm) was the least popular time for participation, accounting for 7% of all comments, with the afternoon (12pm-6pm) still trailing out-of-hours commenting at 22%. Participants specifically mentioned this flexibility in their comments on the process, pointing out that it was often hard to attend real-life events at a certain pre-set time.

---

158 Interview with Vito Crimi, former Member of the Italian Senate and Deputy Minister of the Interior (3 March 2022).

159 Sanjo Faniran and Kayode Olaniyan, 'Strengthening Democratic Practice in Nigeria: A Case for E-Voting' (ICE Gov Conference 2011) 337, 337; Zuheir Desai and Alexander Lee, 'Technology and Protest: The Political Effects of Electronic Voting in India' (2021) 9(2) Political Science Research and Methods 398, 400.

160 Faniran and Olaniyan, 'Strengthening Democratic Practice in Nigeria' 338.

161 'Überarbeitung Umweltzeichen Tourismus – Überblick/Ausblick/Anhang' (*Discuto*) <www.dis cuto.io/en/informationsseite/ueberarbeitung-umweltzeichen-tourismus-ueberblick-ausblick-an hang>.

Others have also noted the advantages of online participation for those who cannot take time off work or afford childcare. Online, one can take part after children go to bed or while they watch a film or play. This can be particularly advantageous for single parents[162] or low-income people who do not own their own vehicles and find travelling to meetings more onerous.

All in all, the flexibility it affords is one the major benefits of taking democracy digital.

2.4 Access

Digital voting can enable people living with disability to exercise their democratic rights independently, more deeply, and in some cases, at all. In fact, facilitating voting for the disabled was a key reason for some American counties to authorize the use of online voting tool Voatz in elections.[163] Digital technology also makes it easier to provide ballots in more languages, as well as large-print ballots.[164] Many digital democracy applications comply with the Web Content Accessibility Guidelines which ensure that software is compatible with accessibility devices such as screen readers for the visually impaired.

Digital participation also allows for participation from inaccessible locations. For example, the company Berge Bulk used online voting to let employees vote for their Sailor of the Year. Offline voting would have been far more difficult to coordinate in this scenario since employees are generally at sea.[165] Similar arguments could be made for other remote locations.

A further (now obvious) use case concerns accessibility in emergencies, such as a pandemic. Municipalities that were already using online voting in Ontario, Canada were able to keep to their election schedule without major delays during the Covid-19 pandemic, while others struggled to implement safety measures to enable in-person voting.[166] This may have excluded some voters, particularly those most at risk from coronavirus.

---

162 Interview with Michael Neblo, Professor of Political Science and Director of the Institute for Democratic Engagement and Accountability, Ohio State University (1 April 2022).

163 Lucas Mearian 'Utah County moves to Expand Mobile Voting through Blockchain' *ComputerWorld* (21 October 2019) <https://www.computerworld.com/article/3446836/utah-county-moves-to-expand-mobile-voting-through-blockchain.html>.

164 Faniran and Olaniyan, 'Strengthening Democratic Practice' 337.

165 'Voting for "Sailor of the Year"' (*Polys*) <https://ru.polys.me/success-stories/voting-for-seafarer-of-the-year>.

166 Hayes et al. 'Exogenous Shocks' 73–74.

2.5 Non-Technocratic Advantages

While a great deal of scrutiny has focused on the technocratic advantages of digital democracy dealt with above, it is the non-technocratic ones that are the most interesting, especially as these often help to compensate for some of the downsides technology can bring, in particular, its cynical exploitation for surveillance and hyper-partisan politics.

2.5.1 Minimizing Distortions in the Political Process

There are two ways to minimize distortions in the political process: a) by including humans and excluding non-humans and b) by focusing on the concrete topic (issue-based voting). This is very important, because when political outcomes are distorted (that is, when the input of people's expressed wishes does not match the output of the results) it makes it easier to disguise cheating, which de facto encourages it.

2.5.1.1 Include Humans, Exclude Non-Humans

As we have seen above, democracy depends on each person using their own reason and knowledge to contribute to the formation of 'the general will'.[167] This truly means *their own* reason and knowledge, *not* someone's else's. When a participant fails to use *their own* reason and knowledge, they fail to contribute in any meaningful way to political decision-making and invalidate the reason for their participatory rights to exist in the first place. We saw this above with the Wisdom of the Crowd – it doesn't work if everyone agrees on their guess before submitting it – the guesses *have* to be made independently.

The unit of democracy is the individual – but this is always under attack.

Indeed, one of the most influential Founding Fathers of America, James Madison, repeatedly referred to the issue of 'faction' as one of the major weaknesses of America's constitutional design. Although it is taken for granted today, the modern party system did not fully evolve in America until well into the mid-19th century – decades after the founding of the State. This is also true in European countries; before the mid-19th century 'parties' were usually just loose groupings of like-minded politicians. Even long before this time, both the ancient Romans and Greeks had

---

167 Rousseau, *The Social Contract*, Chapter III.

tried to discourage factionalism – Roman election candidates were forbidden from pooling their resources to run for office together, while the Athenians went so far as to prohibit groups of friends from sitting together in some public forums.[168] As this illustrates, the issues created by blind adherence or unconditional support for faction have been known virtually forever, and it is a problem for all forms of government. Even emperors must balance competing factions in their territories.

Factional adherence isn't just a problem because it leads to strife (although it does). It also encourages intellectual laziness. To say, 'I think whatever my party or club of friends is thinking' is just another way of saying 'I'm *not* thinking'. Such empty repetition gives the impression that some ideas and opinions are much more widely shared than they in fact are. When organizations or cliques try to force viewpoints across or dominate the conversation, they are *interfering* with the democratic process, and just like interference with a television or radio signal, this creates distortion. If democratic participation is supposed to give us a picture of what society wants, they are blurring that picture. That is not good because what we *want*, in order to make sound decisions, is for our perception and reality to align to the greatest extent possible.

Individuals, fortunately, possess a limited capacity to distort democracy. No matter how vigorous the individual is, it is easy to trace their actions and statements back to them. They represent themselves and their strength is limited. Organizations, on the other hand, often claim to speak for large swathes of the population (frequently with little justification) and they have the resources (often obtained from wealthy individuals and corporations) to dominate conversations, for example, by sponsoring news coverage, producing expensive 'public information campaigns', paying for polls and 'research' to substantiate their claims, lobbying decision-makers, and hiring employees to maintain databases of 'followers' who are strongly encouraged to repost their content and to demand action on issues of concern to the organization. Many organizations even directly draft laws, and they often succeed in procuring a privileged position in conventional government, and even in international consultations.[169] This permits them a strong agenda-setting function that pushes other people out of the process. It tends to play in favour of the strong who are far more likely to have a stake in, or be employed by, such organizations. It is thus very much in the interests of marginalized sectors of society to constrain the direct involvement of non-human actors in democracy.

---

168 E.S. Staveley, *Greek and Roman Voting and Elections* (Thames and Hudson 1972) 191 et seq; Martin Ostwald, *From Popular Sovereignty to the Sovereignty of Law: Law, Society and Politics in Fifth-Century Athens* (University of California Press 1986) 418.
169 We will return to this point in more detail in later chapters, particularly Chapters 5 and 9.

Digital democracy can reduce the interference of these organizations, because in the digital space, it is possible to entirely exclude non-human actors, as well as making it impossible for participants to gain influence in the form of followers. Indeed, it is not only possible to do this, it is actually easier to do so than not to, because tightly controlling and verifying participants and starting each exercise afresh helps to maintain the security of the online system. Not only does this help to reduce distortion in the wider sense, it may also help to reduce polarization of the debate, as organizations, lacking a formalized presence on these forums, find it more difficult to whip up their followers to engage in harassment and distorting pressure tactics.

2.5.1.2 Issue-based Voting

Another key advantage of digital democracy is that it can facilitate direct voting on a greater number of issues than is normally practical in the offline world.

Voting on issues instead of all-encompassing platforms, can break the power of lobbies and voting blocs. This encourages more flexibility between the minority and majority which creates the **fluidity** that is necessary for a democracy to flourish.[170] For example, people may be in favour of conservation efforts and increased recycling, but against subsidies to energy providers. Under these circumstances, issue-based voting could give us a more accurate picture of the state of opinion than having to vote on a single broad environmental platform. It should also help to ensure that actions that *are* supported are implemented rather than being held up by disagreement on a related, but technically different, matter.

This is important, because most people's interests do *not* align neatly under interest groups or party platforms or a simple left-right ideology which has been inflated far beyond its usefulness. It may be useful to consider problems from a progressive angle or conservative angle, a Leninist angle or a libertarian angle, but we must always remember that these are attempts to understand reality. They aren't *themselves* reality. Excessive organization under these categories distorts our perception of political will and drives polarization by focusing on loyalties, doctrine and personalities rather than concrete facts. Demanding **alignment** to a party or creed as a pre-condition of participating in politics (as the representative electoral system de facto does) also makes it difficult to achieve action, sometimes leading to political gridlock.

This is where issue-based voting can really help. As Tarson Nuñez (an academic and former public official involved with PB in Porto Alegre) put it, in direct decision-making: 'You are not discussing if I'm more pro-State or against State or if

---

170 Fuller, *Beasts and Gods*; Orr, *Direct Democracy Manifesto*.

I'm a liberal or if I'm a socialist. You discuss which street you are going to pave, whether you are going to build a school, how much money you have to put in health facilities'.[171] Decisions may still be undergirded by theory, but this is different than being blindly steered by it, or worse yet, by group loyalty.

Of course, one can vote on issues offline as well, but this is a lot of work. In Switzerland, where referendums are common, postal voting is widely used to facilitate it with close to 90 % of people voting by post.[172] As this indicates, in those situations where frequent voting is possible, people begin to look for ways to optimize its efficiency, and digital technology can be very helpful here.

2.5.2 Counteracting Other Uses of Technology

Many uses of digital technology are highly coercive. This can include surveillance, censorship, neurolinguistic analysis of public sentiment, and attempts to manipulate public opinion (whether online or via more conventional means).

As we saw above, politicians sometimes reward those sectors of their constituencies that voted for them with extra spending, but this is only possible because they know who voted for them with a certain degree of accuracy, and this ability to determine how people vote is only increasing. To give just one glimpse into how far these capabilities have developed, during Barack Obama's re-election campaign in 2012, his team collected over 1800 pieces of data on almost every voter in America in order to predict how people would vote, and determine what messaging the campaign should target them with to procure their vote. This went so far as to assign each undecided voter a 'persuasion score' to denote how easy the campaign team thought it would be to persuade them to vote for their candidate.[173] This puts our current level of political privacy into perspective, and shows the extent to which surveillance capabilities already exist. This level of data would also make it easy to see who doesn't vote (and whose votes could thus potentially be falsified).

It is possible to think of myriad other ways to use technology to manipulate politics and restrict freedom. It would be possible, for example, for search engines like Google or Bing to manipulate search results and to curate information in non-transparent ways. New, more tailored, innovations like ChatGPT have increased

---

171 'Interview with Tarson Nuñez' (*Solonian Democracy Institute*).

172 Nobert Kersting, 'Online Participation: From 'Invited' to 'Invented' Spaces' 6(4) International Journal of Electronic Governance 270, 273.

173 Shoshana Zuboff, *The Age of Surveillance Capitalism: The Fight for a Human Future at the New Frontier of Power* (Public Affairs 2019) 122–123.

the potential scope and ease of such manipulation even further. In addition, many firms that claim to combat 'misinformation' on social media are actually corporate PR companies protecting their brands from criticism (thus stifling debate),[174] and social media companies and the intelligence services may co-operate to collect data and prevent the spread of what they see as misinformation.[175] Estonia plans to use its increasingly sophisticated algorithms to monitor traffic, match jobseekers with open positions and check up on whether farmers have completed the actions required to receive subsidies.[176] While such measures all have their benefits, they also give government more control over their people. Almost everything one does on the internet today is monitored, with website functionality simply denied to those who refuse to allow cookies (trackers), while home devices like FitBit and Alexa have become constant companions to millions of people. Some US cities have even used high-flying drones to continuously record the entire city on an ongoing basis so that footage can later be reviewed to find criminals.[177]

People are often concerned that digital democracy will 'change' politics in such a way as to increase surveillance, but the truth is that this surveillance is possible with or without democracy, and is, in many cases, already happening. One of the most important advantages of digital democracy is that it gives us the ability to 'level up' to the private sphere, using tools *as powerful* as those available to private interests to enable the formation of a public will that can make decisions on these points (rather than allow them to simply continue to be rolled out absent a collective decision-point). This, again, is in the interests of the most marginalized people who frequently have the least resources to allow them to defend against incursions on their privacy.

2.5.3 Increased Community Knowledge of Government Processes and Competencies

More widespread participation can also help to increase knowledge of government processes, competencies and budgets.

---

174 Heidi Boghossian, *"I Have Nothing to Hide": And 20 Other Myths about Surveillance and Privacy* (Beacon Press 2021) 41–44.

175 Ken Klippenstein and Lee Fang, 'Truth Cops: Leaked Documents Outline DHS's Plans to Police Disinformation' *The Intercept* (31 October 2022) <https://theintercept.com/2022/10/31/social-media-disinformation-dhs/>.

176 'AI "kratt" strategy' <https://e-estonia.com/wp-content/uploads/2020-april-facts-ai-strategy.pdf> accessed 11 January 2023.

177 Boghossian, *Nothing to Hide* 54–57.

FirstRoot, an American company, offers a child-friendly, digital PB product in schools that also comes with a pre-designed curriculum, while Aula, an off-shoot from the German Pirate Party, offers an online decision-making process geared towards schoolchildren. It is hoped that participating in such processes will increase students' level of knowledge and confidence when it comes to engaging with government processes later in life. Similarly, in PB processes in South Dublin, Paris and Lisbon, officials are supposed to provide reasons to citizens if their proposals are ineligible to go forward to the final voting stage. This helps participants to learn e. g. which department is responsible for a desired action. Other tools, such as Delib, seek to educate participants on the budgetary impact of their choices, e. g. the cuts to other services that undertaking a certain action would entail.

It is also an advantage of those tools that allow direct peer-to-peer conversation that information does not always come from government. In the Lethbridge consultation (referenced above), participants rarely made use of their ability to reply to others' comments inline, but when they did, it was often to provide information that another participant had requested. For example, there was some confusion on a proposal regarding the provision of emergency services, stemming from the fact that these services had recently been reorganized at provincial level. This was cleared up by participants who had knowledge of the recent restructuring sharing it with others in the comments section.

An early study of online crowdsourcing for legislative changes in Finland showed that although learning for learning's sake was not the primary motivation of participants for taking part, it was nonetheless a motivating factor and regarded as a positive attribute of the process.[178] In surveys on PB across the US, participants also noted that they learned about the formal operations of government through their participation in PB.[179]

Encouraging lifelong learning is a necessary part of democracy. When people are generally well-informed, they are able to react more quickly and flexibly to changing situations and to use knowledge acquired in one area to solve problems in another. A democracy *depends* on its people – so investing in them and ensuring they reach their full potential is critical. This learning does not necessarily have to happen online, but it does provide an efficient channel for doing so.

---

178 Tanja Aitamurto and Jorge Saldivar, 'Motivating Participation in Crowdsourced Policymaking: The Interplay of Epistemic and Interactive Aspects' (2017) 1 (CSCW) Proceedings of the ACM on Human-Computer Interaction, 1–22.
179 Johnson, 'Engaging Democracy' 81.

2.5.4 Fosters Accountability

As long as digital democracy *is* democracy and not merely 'engagement', 'involvement', etc., it also fosters accountability.

One of the negative attributes of purely representative systems is that policy failures generally simply result in those elected at the time being voted out of office rather than addressing the root causes of the failure. This often dooms the society to repeat the same mistakes.[180] By contrast, a digital democracy that enables everyone to take part in decision-making means that ultimately everyone is accountable for their own choices, as well as for taking action to achieve the policy they believe to be correct. One cannot simply blame others when things go wrong, one must undertake action to fix things. As we saw above, accountability is one of the most important and most neglected aspects of democracy. We cannot learn without accountability.

Digital decision-making helps ensure that chains of accountability are *crystal-clear.* This is important – muddying the waters of accountability with 'collaboration' and 'involvement' to the point where *no one* is definitively accountable for any decision is *not* innovative or anti-authoritarian or future-looking – it is a recipe for disaster.

It has been observed that where significant forms of participatory budgeting are offered, people pay their taxes more readily and also maintain public infrastructure better, since they feel more (rightly) like they ultimately have to pay for any damage.[181] This is certainly preferable to actions that *diminish* and discourage social accountability.

2.6 Conclusions on Digital Democracy Benefits

The benefits of digital democracy are not always what people think they are, and a great deal depends on how technology is used. However, these benefits, particularly the non-technocratic ones, are still substantial. While difficult to quantify, the savings engendered by transparently dealing with issues as they arise, preventing corruption and clientelism and creating a cycle of accountability, are potentially enormous. However, it is only possible to reap these benefits by adhering as far as possible to the democratic principles outlined in Chapter 1 and ensuring that

---

180 Orr, *Direct Democracy Manifesto.*
181 Yves Cabannes, 'Participatory Budgeting: Conceptual Framework and its Contribution to Urban Governance and the Millennium Development Goals' (August 2004) UN HABITAT, Urban Management Programme, Working Paper No. 140, 27.

the process is genuinely meaningful and results in significant outcomes for participants.

Chapter 3
Who Participates and Why?

The *idea* of increased citizen participation in politics is generally – if not universally – a popular one, even for people who don't take part themselves. In a New York survey, most people expressed satisfaction with the PB process, even if they had little knowledge of it.[182] In 2018, a local plebiscite in New York City approved the creation of the Civic Engagement Commission, which is charged with overseeing city-wide participatory budgeting, as well as boosting voter turnout. This would indicate that New Yorkers are generally favourably disposed towards increased civic engagement.

A survey in Belo Horizonte of PB delegates found that 85% approved of PB because 'it allowed the people to decide on how to invest the "government's money"'.[183] A 1994 opinion poll in Belo Horizonte found that over 67% of the population approved of PB, a greater percentage than approved of any other local government policy.[184] Likewise, four-fifths of those who answered a survey on the Lethbridge capital improvement consultation said they would 'be more likely to support decisions based on a process like this' despite concerns raised in the comments about technical security and inclusivity. When it comes to citizens, increased participation, including digital participation, tends to run through an open door in terms of theoretical acceptance.

This chapter will look at how this acceptance plays out in practice, examining both statistical data and qualitative interviews with participants in digital democracy processes to ask ourselves who participates in these processes and why they participate. Do some demographic sectors participate more than others? What do participants hope to achieve by participating? The answers to these questions are less mysterious than one might think.

3.1 The Digital Divide

It is important to remember that the vast majority of people involved with digital democracy do *not* propose to end offline participation, but merely to allow hybrid (online/offline participation) in which the advantages of the internet are used to

---

182 Williams and Waisanen, *Real Money, Real Power?* 93.
183 Souza, 'Participatory Budgeting in Brazilian Cities' 170, citing Somarriba and Dulci (1997).
184 Souza, 'Participatory Budgeting in Brazilian Cities' 170, citing Periera (1999).

https://doi.org/10.1515/9783110794465-007

supplement current face-to-face participation and provide a level of opportunity that was once infeasible due to offline limitations.

Nonetheless, a very large section of academic and 'grey literature' on this topic has been preoccupied by the so-called 'digital divide'. According to the OECD:

> the term "digital divide" refers to the gap between individuals, households, businesses and geographic areas at different socio-economic levels with regard to both their opportunities to access information and communication technologies (ICTs) and to their use of the Internet for a wide variety of activities.[185]

Although this is far less of an issue than generally perceived (since we are merely proposing *adding* to participation with digital democracy, not *abolishing* offline participation), it is still worth examining here, as the dynamics of this 'divide' have changed substantially since it was first identified as an issue in the mid-1990s.

3.1.1 Internet Access

3.1.1.1 Differences between Nations

Inflated worries about a digital divide fail to take two basic factors into account: the first is the natural diffusion of innovations,[186] and the second is the profitability of the IT sector. The internet only works through network effects, and thus there has never been an incentive for IT companies to hoard their technology.

Unsurprisingly, given the forces at work, internet access has increased very quickly worldwide (see Fig. 3.1). In the UK, 57% of households had internet access in 2006, a figure that had increased to 93% in 2019 and 96% in 2020.[187] Similarly, 94% of Canadian homes have fixed broadband internet.[188] Internet access in the US has followed a similar pattern covering 52% of adults in 2000 and 93% in 2021.[189] In 1997, about 5% of Germans were internet users. By 2021, this had increased to 94%, with 90% of households (and 100% of households consisting of

---

185 *Understanding the Digital Divide* (OECD 2001) 5 <https://www.oecd.org/digital/ieconomy/1888451.pdf>.

186 Everett M. Rogers, *Diffusion of Innovations* (5th edn, Free Press 2003).

187 'Internet Access – Households and Individuals: 2020' (*Office for National Statistics*, 7 August 2020) <https://www.gov.uk/government/statistics/internet-access-households-and-individuals-2020>.

188 'Access to the Internet in Canada, 2020' (*Statistics Canada*, 31 May 2021) <https://www150.statcan.gc.ca/n1/daily-quotidien/210531/dq210531d-eng.htm>.

189 'Internet/Broadband Fact Sheet' (*Pew Research Center*, 7 April 2021) <https://www.pewresearch.org/internet/fact-sheet/internet-broadband/>.

a couple with children) having Internet access by 2019.[190] In the same year, the number of people aged 16–74 who reported having never used the Internet was 8% over the entirety the EU – less than 5% in Ireland, Luxembourg, the Netherlands and the Scandinavian countries, but rising to 16% in Portugal, 17% in Bulgaria and 20% in Greece.[191]

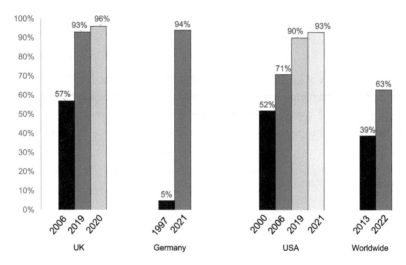

Fig. 3.1: Internet Access Rates over Time.

Broadband adoption, while slower, is still comparable, rising quickly in the United States from 1% in 2000 to 51% in 2007, 70% in 2013, and 77% by 2021.[192] In Canada, 72% of the population has high-speed broadband with government plans to expand this to 95% by 2026.[193]

---

190 'ARD/ZDF-Onlinestudie 2022: Mediale Inhalte verstärken Internetnutzung' (*ARD/ZDF*, 10 November 2022) <https://www.ard-zdf-onlinestudie.de/ardzdf-onlinestudie/pressemitteilung/>; Sylvia Behrends, Susanna Geisler, Kristina Kott and Michael Ziebach, 'Internetzugang, Datenreport 2021' (*Bundeszentrale für politische Bildung*, 10 March 2021) <https://www.bpb.de/kurz-knapp/zahlen-und-fakten/datenreport-2021/private-haushalte-einkommen-und-konsum/329906/internetnutzung/>.
191 'Offline in Deutschland: Mehrere Millionen Bürger leben ohne Internet' *Der Spiegel* (5 April 2022) <https://www.spiegel.de/netzwelt/web/internetnutzung-in-deutschland-mehrere-millionen-buerger-leben-offline-a-fc4b289d-a6bc-488c-837d-912bdd5263e3>; 'Households with internet access, 2010 and 2016 (as % of all households)' (*EUROStat*) <https://ec.europa.eu/eurostat/statistics-explained/index.php?title=File:Households_with_internet_access,_2010_and_2016_(as_%25_of_all_households)_F2.png>.
192 'Internet/Broadband Fact Sheet' (*Pew Research Center*).
193 'Access to the Internet' (*Statistics Canada*).

In 2013, over 2.7 billion people used the Internet, corresponding to 39 % of the world's population.[194] Ten years later, it is now estimated that only 37 % of all people on Earth have never used the internet – despite a population increase of almost a billion people (15 %) over the same time period.[195] By comparison, more than 80 % of people in the world have never flown in an airplane, despite the fact that commercial flight has existed for more than a century.[196]

A study of nine developing countries estimated internet access for basic and meaningful internet connectivity (see Fig. 3.2).

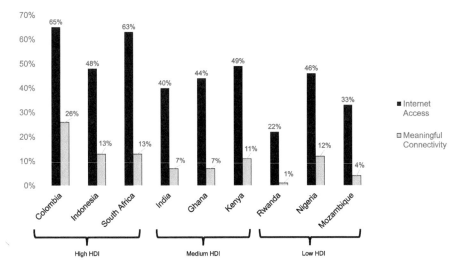

Fig. 3.2: Internet Access in Relation to the Human Development Index.
Source: Alliance for Affordable Internet; Human Development Index.

'Meaningful connectivity' was defined as having 4G connection speeds, owning a smartphone, having an unlimited access point to the internet, and using the internet daily. However, even those who did not meet this unusually stringent definition rated themselves almost as able to complete activities on the internet as those with

---

194 Sylvester Kimbi and Irina Zlotnikova, 'A Secure Model for Remote Electronic Voting: A Case of Tanzania' (2014) 3(4) Advances in Computer Science: An International Journal 95, 96.
195 'Offline in Deutschland' (*Der Spiegel*).
196 Lizzy Gurdus, 'Boeing CEO: Over 80 % of the world has never taken a flight. We're leveraging that for growth' *CNBC* (7 December 2017) <https://www.cnbc.com/2017/12/07/boeing-ceo-80-percent-of-people-never-flown-for-us-that-means-growth.html>.

'meaningful connectivity', indicating that even basic internet access was 'meaningful' to many people.

These statistics indicate that what we would expect to be true is, in fact, true: internet access loosely corresponds to each nation's level of development as measured by the UN's Human Development Index.[197] Canada, the US, UK and Germany are among the highest-scoring nations on the Index, coming in at places 16, 17, 13 and 6 (out of 189 countries), putting them all near the top of the Index's 'Very High' category. Colombia, Indonesia and South Africa are rated as 'High' (coming in at places 83, 107 and 114 respectively). India is ranked at place 131, Ghana at 138 and Kenya at 143 (all in the 'Medium' category), while Rwanda ranks at 160, Nigeria at 161 (average life expectancy just 54.7 years) and Mozambique at place 181 (all in the 'Low' category).[198] However, considering the vast gulf in development and living standards in these nations, the gap in internet adoption is less pronounced than one might expect.

To truly appreciate this, we need to remember the many things people in underdeveloped states *don't* have. For example, 86% of Nigerians lack access to a safely managed source of drinking water.[199] Only 59% of people in Kenya have access to safe drinking water and just 25% have access to facilities where they can wash their hands with soap at home.[200] 43% of Nigerians do not have access to grid electricity, and where power is supplied, outages are common.[201] Access to clean water is also an issue in Mozambique where 43% of children under 5 are also moderately or severely stunted due to malnutrition.[202] If we accept these numbers, it would appear that in some countries more people have access to the internet than to clean water, while in others access rates across these two goods are comparable. Yet we do not claim that the invention of water treatment caused

197 The Human Development Index measures quality of life across several factors, such as standard of living and life expectancy.

198 'Human Development Index' (*UNDP*) <https://hdr.undp.org/data-center/human-development-index> accessed 20 November 2022.

199 'Nearly one third of Nigerian children do not have enough water to meet their daily needs – UNICEF' (*UNICEF*, 22 March 2021) <https://www.unicef.org/nigeria/press-releases/nearly-one-third-nigerian-children-do-not-have-enough-water-meet-their-daily-needs>.

200 'Water, Sanitation and Hygiene – Kenya' (*UNICEF*) <https://www.unicef.org/kenya/water-sanitation-and-hygiene> accessed 12 January 2023.

201 'Nigeria to Improve Electricity Access and Services to Citizens', Press Release No. 2021/088/AFR (*World Bank*, 5 February 2021) <https://www.worldbank.org/en/news/press-release/2021/02/05/nigeria-to-improve-electricity-access-and-services-to-citizens>.

202 'WASH Situation in Mozambique' (*UNICEF*) <https://www.unicef.org/mozambique/en/water-sanitation-and-hygiene-wash> accessed 23 March 2023.

'a water divide' or that the invention of electricity caused an 'electrical divide', even though this is obviously the case. Similarly, many people in the world today are illiterate or functionally illiterate (as of 2015, 28% of Indians were illiterate, as were over 40% of Mozambiquans and 29% of Rwandans)[203] but we don't tell people who can read to check their privilege when they crack open a book or refer to illiteracy as 'book exclusion'. As this hopefully demonstrates the terminology around the digital divide is often a little overwrought.

This is all the more so as it runs somewhat counter to all of the other more distressing 'divides' in the world, and will likely continue to rapidly close, all other conditions remaining equal. This is partly because internet technology is still finding its saturation point and partly because many countries have significantly improved electricity access, which is necessary to power phones, computers and routers. In 1980, only 26% of Indian households had electricity access (15% in rural areas, a figure which had increased to just 55% by 2010).[204] In Tanzania in 2013, less than 20% of the population was connected to the national power grid with only 2% of users located in rural areas,[205] while in Kenya ca. 20–30% of the population was connected to the national power grid.[206] As of 2012, only 12.7% of homes in Kenya had access to the internet and to a computer, higher than both Ghana (2.7%) and Ethiopia (0.5%).[207]

This is changing rapidly. Today only 2.4% of households in India remain un-electrified,[208] while the power supply in Kenya has increased to cover 75% of the population.[209] Partly as a result of this, India alone is expected to see another 300 million internet users by 2025, increasing total usage in the country to ca. 900

203 Max Roser and Esteban Ortiz-Ospina, 'Literacy' (*Our World in Data*, 20 September 2018) <https://ourworldindata.org/literacy> accessed 19 March 2023.

204 Shalu Agrawal, Sunil Mani, Abhishek Jain and Karthik Ganesan, 'State of Electricity Access in India, Insights from the India Residential Energy Survey (IRES 2020)' (*Council on Energy, Environment and Water*, October 2020) <https://www.ceew.in/publications/state-electricity-access-india>.

205 Kimbi and Zlotnikova 'A Secure Model for Remote Electronic Voting' 96.

206 Mwangi Gakunga, 'Kenya Lauded for Achieving 75% Electricity Access Rate' (*COMESA*, 9 June 2021) <https://www.comesa.int/kenya-lauded-for-achieving-75-electricity-access-rate/>; Lily Kuo, 'Kenya's National Electrification Campaign is Taking Less than Half the Time it Took America' *Quartz* (16 January 2017) <https://qz.com/africa/882938/kenya-is-rolling-out-its-national-electricity-program-in-half-the-time-it-took-america/>.

207 Nanjala Nyabola, *Digital Democracy: Analogue Politics: How the Internet Era is Transforming Politics in Kenya* (Zed Books 2018) 36.

208 Agrawal et al. 'State of Electricity Access in India'.

209 Gakunga 'Kenya Lauded'.

million.[210] In some parts of the world, internet usage is increasing by as much as 40 % a year.[211] In Kenya, it has increased from 200,000 connections in 2000 to 30.8 million subscriptions in 2017, mainly using mobile phones as an access point.[212] As this indicates, internet technology has often leapfrogged traditional communications development. In 2013, there were fewer than 170,000 landline users in Tanzania – compared to 26.5 million mobile phone users.[213] Total mobile phone ownership in Nigeria is about 46 % (with access rates higher as people frequently share phones). This compares to the 0.2 % of households that have landlines.[214] This is significant, because while not all mobile phones are internet-enabled, they are still an important access point for internet in many developing countries.

The pace of development and its, from a Western perspective, somewhat whimsical order, was perhaps summed up best in a stand-up routine performed by South African comedian Trevor Noah, in which he recounted visiting Zambia to find its residents enthralled by the nation's first escalators, and taking videos of them on their iPhones and consulting voice assistants on how they worked.[215]

To put it in a nutshell: the trajectory for internet provision is still shooting upward in both developed and developing countries.[216] Connecting people remains the gateway to extremely profitable business. This is why not just internet adoption, but faster and better internet adoption is continually pushed by companies and government. In addition, satellite internet, such as StarLink will help to provide internet access to remote locations.

Nonetheless, clearly there is a divide that is directly related to the level of development. It is true that if we were to try to institute a global online-only digital democracy, citizens of the least developed countries would be at a disadvantage and could be excluded. While there are a few fringe groups that propose variations

210 'India to have 900 Million Active Internet Users by 2025, says Report' *Economic Times* (3 June 2021) <https://economictimes.indiatimes.com/tech/technology/india-to-have-900-million-active-internet-users-by-2025-says-report/articleshow/83200683.cms?from=mdr>.

211 Carmen Ang, 'These are the Countries where Internet Access is Lowest' (*World Economic Forum*, 17 August 2020) <https://www.weforum.org/agenda/2020/08/internet-users-usage-countries-change-demographics/>.

212 Nyabola, *Digital Democracy: Analogue Politics* 36.

213 Kimbi and Zlotnikova 'A Secure Model for Remote Electronic Voting' 96.

214 Ivan Forenbacher, Siniša Husnjak, Ivan Cvitić and Ivan Jovović, 'Determinants of Mobile Phone Ownership in Nigeria' (2019) 43(7) Telecommunications Policy, Article 101812, 2.

215 'Zambia Loves Escalators – Just Don't be Gay' (*Trevor Noah – It's My Culture*, 5 November 2018) <https://www.youtube.com/watch?v=L3SIdXPtB0M> accessed 21 January 2023.

216 Ofcom, *Communications Market Report 2021* (22 July 2021) <https://www.ofcom.org.uk/__data/assets/pdf_file/0011/222401/communications-market-report-2021.pdf>.

of such things (e.g. the Global Citizens Assembly),[217] we are very far from having a world government and few people view this as a desirable goal. So, for multiple reasons, while internet provision is an issue of access between developed and developing countries, it's less of an issue than many other areas of concern (lacking internet access for a day won't kill you – lack of clean water might), and not relevant to our project here, as we don't propose that the peoples of developed and developing nations should directly compete with one another in one world government, or even that residents of developed nations should be forced into online-only democracy. Local circumstances must always be considered, but in most cases digital access is increasing markedly. Rather than ending up with digital democracy mechanisms that cannot find a sufficient audience in online residents, we are more likely to arrive at a situation where there are hundreds of millions of additional online users who lack any channels for exercising digital democracy.

That being said, let us now turn our attention to other factors which may contribute to a digital divide.

3.1.1.2 Age

It is commonly believed that older people experience more difficulty in using the internet and that thus implementing any form of digital democracy (for example, planning consultations or online voting) or even internet service provision would negatively impact older people by disproportionately excluding them from public life. This hypothesis relies on taking statistics from a brief window in time, just as the internet was beginning to be rolled-out for household use, and then failing to revisit those statistics.

In 2000, 14% of people 65 and older in the USA used the internet. By 2021, that figure had risen to 75%, meaning that the rate of use among older users increased by 61 percentage points over 21 years. Over the same time period it increased by 50 percentage points for 50–64 year-olds (from 46% to 96%), by 37 points for 30–49 year-olds (from 61% to 98%) and by only 29 points for 19–29 year-olds (from 70% to 99%).[218] This is also true in the UK, where internet adoption has increased faster in older users than younger users.[219] Whereas 73% of UK households with a mem-

---

217 Funded by One Project, Climate Emergency Collaboration Group, the Calouste Gulbenkian Foundation, European Climate Foundation and the Scottish Government ('Funders' (*Global Assembly*) <https://globalassembly.org/about-2> accessed 12 January 2023)

218 'Internet/Broadband Fact Sheet' (*Pew Research Center*).

219 Susan Davidson, 'Digital Inclusion Evidence Review 2018' (*Age UK*, November 2018) <HTTPS:// WWW.AGEUK.ORG.UK/GLOBALASSETS/AGE-UK/DOCUMENTS/REPORTS-AND-PUBLICATIONS/AGE_ UK_DIGITAL_INCLUSION_EVIDENCE_REVIEW_2018.PDF>; 'Internet access – households and individuals: 2020' (*Office for National Statistics*).

ber aged 65 and older had an internet connection in 2019, this had already jumped to 80% by 2020. In Germany, the age gap continues to close as well: as of 2021, 100% of under-50s were online, 95% of 50 – 69 year-olds and 77% of over-70s (by comparison, in 2009 only one-third of Germans over 65 were online).[220] The use of broadband among older people may be lower in some nations, but is still generally comparable. In the USA, 70% of 18 – 29 year-olds have a broadband connection, which rises to 86% of 30 – 49 year-olds, before dipping again to 79% of 50 – 64 year-olds and 64% of people 65 years of age and older.[221]

According to a survey conducted by Civica, a British software provider: '79% of over 70s feel technology is helping public service organisations provide them and the wider community with better services. 74% now own a smartphone, 69% own a laptop (higher than those aged between 18 – 34) and 66% use smartphones daily.... Significantly, 59% see the benefit of voting online and the same percentage have registered to vote online'.[222]

Although Civica has a vested interest in believing these statistics to be true, it is still quite striking and in line with what other sources tell us about older people and the internet. For example, in Markham, the average age of online voters is 51 versus 44 for paper voters,[223] while another study showed that older voters who start voting online are more likely to continue to do so than younger voters are.[224]

The rapid closure of the gap in internet use among older people is likely partly due to the fact that internet services have become easier to use and provide greater utility, and partly because many people who are elderly today were middle-aged when internet use became widespread and they became used to it at that time (e.g. at work). For the most part, they haven't formed new habits as older people, but have merely retained habits from earlier in life.

Nonetheless, a small gap between younger and older cohorts will likely always remain. Statistics regarding internet use and age suffer from the fact that they generally place all people age '65 and up' into a single category. This is a legacy of

---

220 'ARD/ZDF-Onlinestudie 2022'; Behrends et al., 'Internetzugang, Datenreport 2021'.

221 'Internet/Broadband Fact Sheet' (*Pew Research Center*).

222 'Insights from our over 70s' (*Civica*) <https://www.civica.com/en-gb/campaign-library-uk/2020/a-word-from-the-wise/insights-from-our-over70s/>.

223 Nicole Goodman, 'Online Voting in the City of Markham: Patterns and Trends, 2003 – 2018' (November 2019) 22 <https://pub-markham.escribemeetings.com/filestream.ashx?DocumentId=19612>.

224 Fernando Mendez and Uwe Serdült, 'What drives Fidelity to Internet Voting? Evidence from the Roll–Out of Internet Voting in Switzerland' (2017) 34(3) Government Information Quarterly 511 – 523.

lower life expectancy in the past, as well as advertising categories that view retirees as a homogenous group (living on a fixed income). Unfortunately, this data fails to capture the fact that there are significant gaps in terms of physical and mental health for the 'young elderly' and the 'oldest olds'.

In particular, disability increases very sharply between 'young olds' and 'old olds'. According to Irish census statistics, 27.7% of females aged 70–74 have a disability compared to 73.3% over age 84.[225] This can often take the form of cognitive impairment. According to the American Academy of Neurology, about 8% of people aged 65–69 suffer from mild cognitive impairment, with this increasing to 15% in 75–79 year-olds, 25% in 80–84 year-olds and about 37% in those aged 85 and older.[226] While only 1.1.% of people aged 65–74 live in nursing homes, 15% of people aged 85 and above do, and roughly 50–70% of people living in nursing homes suffer from some form of dementia.[227] As long as cognitive decline continues to take its toll on the oldest olds (particularly those aged 85 and older), internet use (for any reason) is unlikely to reach parity with the younger cohorts. Where data is available, we can see that the pattern of internet usage is different for 'young olds' than it is for 'old olds'. According to UK statistics, 80% of 'young olds' (people between the ages of 65 and 74) used the internet recently, as opposed to only 44% of people 75 and older. In an online carbon budgeting exercise in London, Ontario (one of the few that statistically separated young and old olds in its survey data collection) we can see that while 66–79 year-olds were (typically) over-represented, accounting for 20% of participants but only 16% of the population, this was reversed for those over 80 who accounted for 2% of participants, but 6% of the population.[228]

In addition, there are sometimes surprising reasons as to why those elderly who are not on the internet choose not to be. Although there are often concerns that older people are excluded from internet use due to its unfamiliarity, this is true for only a minority of those who choose not to use the internet: 20% of UK households aged 65 and older without internet gave lack of skills as the reason, while 16% cited high costs. By contrast 7% cited privacy and security concerns

225 'Census of Population 2016 – Profile 9, Health, Disability and Carers' (*Central Statistics Office*) <https://www.cso.ie/en/releasesandpublications/ep/p-cp9hdc/p8hdc/p9d/>.
226 'Mild Cognitive Impairment' (*Cleveland Clinic*, 18 March 2019) <https://my.clevelandclinic.org/health/diseases/17990-mild-cognitive-impairment>.
227 'Nursing Homes' (*Health in Aging Foundation*, October 2020) <https://www.healthinaging.org/age-friendly-healthcare-you/care-settings/nursing-homes>.
228 'Census Profile, 2016 Census, London' (*Statistics Canada*) <https://www12.statcan.gc.ca/census-recensement/2016/dp-pd/prof/details/page.cfm?Lang=E&Geo1=CMACA&Code1=555&Geo2=PR&Code2=35&Data=Count&SearchText=london>.

as the reason they chose to remain offline, 12 % stated they had access to the internet elsewhere and almost two-thirds (64 %) claimed they simply did not need it.[229]

Similarly, while 6 % of Canadians (of all ages) reported not having home internet, 63 % of those 6 % simply didn't want it.[230] Thus, in developed countries, only about 2–3 % of the population does not have home internet despite desiring it. This is lower than the number of people living in accommodation that lacks a smoke alarm.[231]

Worries of older people struggling to use the internet have proven less urgent than they were once thought to be (at least in the developed world), and where they do persist, likely co-exist to some degree with age-related impairment and age-related poverty.

3.1.1.3 Poverty

Those who do not have home internet access (despite wanting it) likely disproportionately suffer deep poverty. This is true in both developed and developing countries – deep poverty is simply more widespread in the developing world. Almost one-quarter (22 %) of people in Britain (33 % of children) live in poverty.[232] However, only 6 % of people don't have the internet. This is comparable to the number of Britons who live in deep poverty (50 % below the poverty line) – about 7 % of the population.[233] Among British households earning between £6000–10,000 a year (and who often struggle to simply purchase food), only 51 % had home internet access,[234] as compared to 96 % of people nationally.

These figures are simply more stark in developing nations where low wages and precarious employment are more extreme. For example, the minimum wage in Nigeria is ca. $792 a year, while the cost of 1GB of data in Nigeria in

---

229 Davidson, 'Digital Inclusion' 20.

230 'Access to the Internet' (*Statistics Canada*).

231 Marty Ahrens, 'Smoke Alarms in US Home Fires' (*National Fire Protection Association*, February 2021) <https://www.nfpa.org/-/media/Files/News-and-Research/Fire-statistics-and-reports/Detection-and-signaling/ossmokealarms.pdf>; Department for Communities and Local Government, *English Housing Survey, Smoke Alarms in English Homes Report 2014–2015* (July 2016) <https://assets.publishing.service.gov.uk/government/uploads/system/uploads/attachment_data/file/539096/Smoke_Alarms_in_English_Homes_Full_Report.pdf>.

232 Social Metrics Commission, *Measuring Poverty 2020: A Report of the Social Metrics Commission* (Legatum Institute 2020) <https://socialmetricscommission.org.uk/wp-content/uploads/2020/06/Measuring-Poverty-2020-Web.pdf>.

233 Social Metrics Commission, *Measuring Poverty* 52.

234 Hannah Holmes and Gemma Burgess, 'Pay the wi-fi or Feed the Children: Coronavirus has Intensified the UK's Digital Divide' (*University of Cambridge*) <https://www.cam.ac.uk/stories/digitaldivide>.

2019 was $2.78.[235] The average broadband connection in the UK utilizes 429GB of data a month, while average mobile data use was 4.5GB per month.[236] A Nigerian worker on minimum wage would thus have to spend roughly 20 % of their income to access an equivalent amount of data as the average mobile user in the UK. Accessing a data package equivalent to that enjoyed by the average British household would cost (as of 2023) about $648 per year – close to the total income of a minimum wage earner.[237]

In addition, poverty is co-related with race and gender in some countries. The official poverty rate in the United States is 11.6 %: 12.6 % for women, 10.5 % for men, and 5.2 % for married couples. For male-householder families it is 12.7 %, for female-householder families it is 25.3 %. For people living with disability it is 24.9 %. The poverty rate for seniors is 10.3 %. By race, the poverty rate is as follows: Native American: 24.3 %; Black: 19.5 %; Hispanic: 17.1 %; White: 8.1 %; Asian: 9.3 %. 5.5 % of Americans live in deep poverty – less than 50 % of the poverty threshold.[238] In Britain, a head of household of Pakistani or Bangladeshi origin and having a disabled family member are among the most reliable predictors of poverty.[239]

However, if we look at these statistics, we can see that the number of Black Americans living in poverty is twice the rate of white Americans, but white Americans do not have twice the rate of internet access as Black Americans. In fact, there is barely a difference. In 2000, 38 % of Black American adults had internet access, compared to 53 % of whites. By 2021, 91 % of Black adults had internet access compared to 93 % of white adults. Hispanic adults, 71 % of whom had internet access in 2010 (when statistics for this demographic began to be collected), had surpassed whites by 2021 with a 95 % access rate.[240] The same can be said of gender: in the US in 2000, 54 % of men and 50 % of women used the Internet, compared to 94 % of men and 93 % of women in 2021. This is despite the fact that women and in particular single mothers are more likely to be impoverished.

---

235 Emmanuel Paul, 'The Cost of Internet Data in Nigeria is Increasing, but it is Not Really Obvious' *Techpoint Africa* (23 June 2020) <https://techpoint.africa/2020/06/23/internet-data-nigeria-in creased/>.

236 Ofcom, *Communications Market Report 2021* 2.

237 Samson Akintaro, 'Top 10 Internet Service Providers in Nigeria Offering Unlimited Data Plans as of January 2023' *Nairametrics* (January 2023).

238 John Creamer, Emily A. Shrider, Kalee Burns and Frances Chen, 'Poverty in the United States 2021: Current Population Reports' (*United States Census Bureau*, September 2022) <https://www.census.gov/content/dam/Census/library/publications/2022/demo/p60-277.pdf>.

239 Brigid Francis-Devine, 'Poverty in the UK: Statistics' (*House of Commons Library*, 29 September 2022) <https://commonslibrary.parliament.uk/research-briefings/sn07096/>.

240 'Internet/Broadband Fact Sheet' (*Pew Research Center*).

If we factor in broadband access, this changes, although not nearly as sharply as the differentiation in poverty rate: 71% of Black adults, 80% of white adults and 65% of Hispanic adults in the USA have broadband access. Again, real-life inequality decidedly outstrips internet inequality and the numbers of people who lack internet at all are comparable (and likely largely overlapping) to those people who live in deep poverty.

Internet adoption in developed nations is actually roughly on par with the adoption of smoke alarms. 92% of households in the US have at least one smoke alarm (not necessarily in working order), and the corresponding figure for the UK is 93%. This means that over 7 million households in the US and UK do not have a single smoke alarm, despite the fact that this inexpensive appliance cuts the rate of death by fire in half, and installing one is constantly encouraged in public campaigns.[241] In the UK, people who live in private rental accommodation, in a household where one or more members has a long-term illness, are single, on lower incomes, unemployed, or women were all less likely to have a smoke alarm, as were households headed by Indian, Pakistani or Bangladeshi persons.[242] Yet we rightly recognize that people having not installed a smoke alarm (also a piece of technology) is a social problem. You will never hear someone talk about a 'smoke alarm divide' because the issues people without smoke alarms face are rarely limited to smoke alarms and it would thus be inappropriately reductionist to refer to the issue this way – simply installing a smoke alarm will not make them less poor.

There is certainly a co-relation here – people living in deep poverty are less likely to have internet access – but if internet access is *less* unequal than other indications of inequality (like poverty itself) then it is an *ameliorating* factor, not an *exacerbating* factor. It may not have fixed our deepest social issues, but it also didn't cause *new* cleavages to open up.

Improving access probably depends on providing free internet (e.g. libraries, schools) and, most importantly, alleviating deep poverty generally. Still, it is important to keep this in mind and that while the internet is currently available to far more people than just upper middle-class residents (as was once feared), the poorest of the poor (generally single-digit figures in developed countries) are the least likely to be on the internet, as well as being the least likely to participate in politics generally.

---

241 Ahrens, 'Smoke Alarms in US Home Fires'; Department for Communities and Local Government, *Smoke Alarms in English Homes*.
242 *Smoke Alarms in English Homes*.

3.1.1.4 Income and Education

Gaps in internet access related to income generally and education still exist, but have decreased markedly in developed nations. In 2000, the highest and lowest income categories in the United States were separated by 47 percentage points (34% access rate for households earning under $30k and 81% for those over $75k). By 2021, this had reduced to 13 percentage points (86% for under $30k and 99% for over $75k). A similar reduction occurred vis-a-vis education. The gap between those who did not finish high school and college grads was 59 percentage points in 2000 (19% for those without a high school diploma and 78% for college grads), which had reduced to 27 percentage points by 2019 (71% for those without high school and 98% for college grads). [243]

Differences in broadband rates are more pronounced with this gap at 35 points on income (57% of those on less than $30k and 92% of those on over $75k) and 47 points on education (46% of those without a high school diploma versus 93% of college grads). [244] More highly educated, high-income people are thus more likely to have internet and more likely to have fast internet, despite those gaps closing considerably over time (and still closing). This is likely partly due to affordability and availability and partly due to different habits, e.g. needing internet for work, streaming rather than watching TV, etc. For example, an older person who does not have a high school diploma (more common among older people) and watches TV rather than streaming services, may use the internet regularly, but not feel the need for broadband. Still, it is important to bear in mind that there is a relationship here, especially in relation to the quality of the connection.

3.1.1.5 Location and Gender

Location and gender are factors that play out differently in different countries.

In the United States, the rural/urban gap for internet access was never extreme and has almost completely closed. In 2000, 42% of rural households had internet, compared to 53% of urban households and 56% of suburban households. By 2021, 90% of rural households had internet access, compared to 95% of urban households and 94% of suburban households. The difference in broadband adoption is also minor, with rural adoption of broadband coming in at 72%, urban at 77% and suburban at 79% in 2021.[245]

However, there is a significant rural/urban divide in high-speed internet access in Canada, with those living in or near metropolitan areas more likely (76%) to

243 'Internet/Broadband Fact Sheet' (*Pew Research Center*).
244 'Internet/Broadband Fact Sheet' (*Pew Research Center*).
245 'Internet/Broadband Fact Sheet' (*Pew Research Center*).

have high-speed internet than those living elsewhere (48%).[246] This is likely due to the fact that Canada is far more sparsely populated than the United States (there are 94 people per square mile in the US, versus 11 people per square mile in Canada).

The gap between rural and urban access to a meaningful connection (again with the caveat that this was a demanding definition) is sometimes also extreme in developing countries. For example, in Colombia 30.5% of urban users had high-quality internet, compared to 7.6% of rural users. In India, the figures were at 9% and 5.3% respectively and in Kenya 20.7% and 6.5%.[247]

In developing countries, as well as some developed countries with large rural areas, this would indicate greater difficulty in organizing nationwide digital efforts as opposed to those limited to a metropolitan area, although, we can expect that satellite-internet will likely have a beneficial impact on some of these figures.

While, there aren't meaningful differences in internet access by gender in most developed countries, many developing nations present a different picture with men often having greater access levels. For example, in Ghana 8.3% of men reported internet access that satisfied the criteria of 'meaningful connectivity' whereas only 4.8% of women reported the same. In India, the figures were 9.8% for men and 3.3.% for women. In South Africa this gap was less than in other countries with 16.4% of men and 12.1% of women reporting a meaningful connection. One study surmised that women were less likely to own mobile phones in Nigeria (a common access point for internet use), partly because women do not usually have purchasing power within the household. However, studies show that this gender gap tends to diminish over time as the technology in question becomes more common.[248] Thus, while it is a present reality, we can likely expect it to lessen over time.

3.1.2 Conclusions on Internet Access

Those who claim that the digital divide is 'reinforcing inequalities' choose their words poorly. To reinforce something means to make it stronger – reinforced concrete for example, is much stronger than regular concrete. By contrast, the inter-

246 'Access to the Internet' (*Statistics Canada*).
247 'Advancing Meaningful Connectivity: Towards Active and Participatory Digital Societies' (*Alliance for Affordable Internet*, 28 February 2022) <https://a4ai.org/research/advancing-meaningful-connectivity-towards-active-and-participatory-digital-societies/>.
248 Forenbacher et al. 'Mobile Phone Ownership' 8.

net is a relatively flattering mirror, smoothing away some of the inequalities that exist in society at large and making these less prevalent than elsewhere.

The digital divide (at least so far) is less severe than many commenters imagine and gaps are closing rapidly rather than expanding. There is nothing inherent about internet access that makes it prone to *generating* inequalities. This is all the more so, when we consider that many more people have the internet than the means to regularly personally travel to in-person meetings or complete other tasks, such as advertising, studying, connecting with loved ones, or applying for a job.

However, that being said, there are simple things we can do to render the inequality that does exist less (rather than more) of a problem.

3.1.2.1 Maintain Offline Options

Many commercial enterprises, such as banking, have tried to force customers online, since this enables them to shut down branch services and cut costs. In some cases, this has been mirrored by public services. One study showed that out of 100 randomly selected councils in England, 41 of them required benefits claims to be submitted online with 14 % not offering offline assistance for those unable to use the internet.[249] This is less than ideal – offline services and assistance should be maintained, even if it these options are rarely used. When they are used, it is likely to be by the most vulnerable citizens.

3.1.2.2 Use the Lowest Bandwidth Possible

As the statistics show, more people have basic internet access than broadband. While the broadband gap will doubtless close, there will always be new and better accessibility and affluent, better educated people will always be earlier adopters of these things, as they are with other appliances. Developers keep this in mind when designing digital tools, attempting to use the lowest bandwidth possible to achieve their goals (there are even competitions in which developers compete to write code as economically as possible). Still, it is important to ascertain the bandwidth a poorly connected user in your locality is likely to be able to avail of and to use applications that utilize the lowest bandwidth possible. People also become extremely frustrated when pages take too long to load, so it is important to use something that will load fast depending on capabilities on the ground, which may vary from region to region and country to country.

---

[249] Davidson, 'Digital Inclusion'.

3.1.2.3 Ensure Applications are Compatible with a Variety of Devices

Any application must work well both on computer screens and smartphones. Older adults have higher rates of vision impairment as well as compromises to mobility, such as arthritis, that can make them more likely to opt for a computer rather than the small screens and buttons of a smartphone.

At the same time, smartphones are heavily used by younger people, and a low-income person is more likely to possess only a smartphone (and no other internet capable devices) as it provides the best all-round functionality. As of 2021, 15% of adults in the US had smartphone-only access, especially 19–29 year-olds (28% of whom only have access via smartphone at home, a trait shared with 25% of Hispanics, 27% of people under $30k income (compared to 6% over $75k) and 17% of rural residents).[250] Ensuring that applications are mobile friendly in terms of display and usability will certainly (at least in the USA) benefit younger, Hispanic, rural and low-income people disproportionately.

Similarly, about 80% of all Canadians have a mobile data plan, including 470,000 people (1.5% of the population) without a home internet connection. While further research is pending, it is thought that these are disproportionately young people.[251] Mobile-only access is even more prevalent in developing nations. In Nigeria, over 93% of internet users accessed using a smartphone.[252] And people today *do* use their phones to participate democratically – 72% of site visits to Iceland's 2022 participatory budgeting site came from a smartphone.[253] A mobile-compatible strategy is thus essential, and the reason why many companies today develop 'mobile-first' applications.

3.1.2.4 State Provision or Regulation of Minimum Services

Due to the commercial incentives, private-company roll-out of internet access has worked relatively well. However, States can (and many do) fill gaps by offering free internet at public libraries, schools and community centres. Some municipalities, like the city of Paris, offer free internet on the Metro system.[254] Other countries,

---

250 'Internet/Broadband Fact Sheet' (*Pew Research Center*).

251 'Internet Access' (*Statistics Canada*).

252 Simon Kemp 'Digital 2021, Nigeria' (*DataReportal*, 11 February 2021) 23 <https://datareportal.com/reports/digital-2021-nigeria>.

253 Personal communication from Róbert Bjarnason, President Citizens Foundation, to author (11 January 2023).

254 'Paris Metro is Now 100% Covered with LTE' (*Connectivity Technology Blog*, 22 July 2020) <https://www.connectivity.technology/2020/07/paris-metro-is-now-100-covered-with-lte.html>; 'Pour une ville plein de vie' (*RATP Group*) <https://ratpgroup.com/fr/notre-contribution/pour-une-ville-pleine-de-vie/>.

like Germany and Taiwan have mandated minimum internet speeds that must be provided to every household with a fixed network internet connection. There are also several groups working in developing nations to provide internet connection. For example, in South Africa, Project Isizwe provides free wi-fi hotspots in low-income communities.[255] In addition, it is important for countries to break up cartels or monopolies that may form in private internet provision, as these can lead to substandard service.[256]

3.1.2.5 Education

It can be easy to assume that technologically advanced countries were *always* technologically advanced, but this isn't so. Estonia's digital divide was extreme when it first began to offer online services. In 2005, three years *after* Estonia launched its E-ID cards that serve as the access points to these services, only 58 % of Estonians aged 16 – 74 used the Internet, and only 37 % of households had an internet connection.[257] Today, the vast majority of Estonians use the internet, a development often credited to the availability of digital services and a comprehensive education programme that involved both public and private sectors.

Research from Taiwan shows a similar effect, finding that thorough digital education pursued by the Taiwanese government in schools since the 1990s has eliminated the differences in digital opportunity between individuals with high and low levels of general education. The government and private sector made particular efforts to reach out to rural areas, as well as ethnic minorities, women and the elderly with significant effect, although, as researchers note, these efforts were also helped by the simple fact that internet penetration and smartphones have become more widespread.[258]

Education and providing minimum public provision of services have worked well to dramatically improve literacy, nutrition and a host of other goals in the past, so it is not surprising that they should work well for internet provision, too.

---

255 'Our Work' (*Project Isizwe*) <https://www.projectisizwe.org/our-work/> accessed 21 February 2022.
256 This issue has surfaced in Canada, which has few internet providers and high costs, see e.g. Divya Rajagopal and Akriti Sharma, 'Canada's Anti-Trust Tribunal Clears C$20 billion Rogers-Shaw Deal' *Reuters* (30 December 2022) <https://www.reuters.com/markets/deals/canada-competition-tribunal-approves-c20-bln-rogers-shaw-merger-2022-12-30/>.
257 Piret Ehin, Mihkel Solvak, Jan Willemson and Priit Vinkel, 'Internet Voting in Estonia 2005 – 2019: Evidence from Eleven Elections' (2022) 39(4) Government Information Quarterly 1, 14.
258 Chia-Hui Chen, Chao-Lung Liu, Bryant Pui Hung Hui and Ming-Lun Chung, 'Does Education Background Affect Digital Equal Opportunity and the Political Participation of Sustainable Digital Citizens? A Taiwan Case' (2020) 12(4) Sustainability, Article 1359.

Now that we have established that theoretical access is less of a problem than one might think, and provided some ways to effectively deal with remaining inequalities, let us look at who actually does participate in political processes, and how digitalization can and does affect this participation.

3.2 Who Participates in Online Democracy?

Fears over unequal internet access have been used as a justification for refusing to pursue digital forms of participation on the grounds that such participation would structurally favour some sections of society believed to be the affluent and 'privileged' over others.

This argument, however, doesn't make a great deal of sense, because in traditional offline participation, affluent, educated people participate far more across all aspects of formal participation (including elections), as well as informally in 'civil society'. In addition, men are dramatically over-represented in almost all positions of power (even after many years of gender quotas), and middle-aged citizens tend to have the highest participation rates in traditional offline politics.

If we look at US voting patterns in elections, for example, we can see that voters are older (typically over 50), and much more likely to be white, highly educated and affluent (see Fig. 3.3)

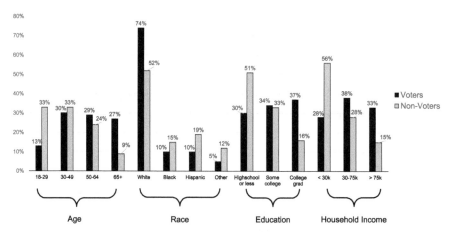

Fig. 3.3: Percentage of Overall Voters & Non-Voters by Age, Race, Education & Household Income in the USA.
Source: Pew Research Center.

As we can see, for example, college graduates account for 37 % of voters, but only 16 % of non-voters, whereas those with a high school diploma or less make up 30 % of voters, but 51 % of non-voters.[259] This represents a fairly typical pattern for participation in offline representative democracy to take, particularly in regards to age, income and educational attainment: the middle tends to be more accurately represented in participation – it is at the top and bottom margins where we see significant skewing. However, there is a flaw here: these statistics do not capture the truly rich, and they do not take into consideration the impact that inflation, particularly house price inflation, has had on real purchasing power. Incomes that would once have been considered upper middle-class or even affluent are now middling at best. Stopping income brackets at $75k or even $150k no longer adequately captures wealth disparity.

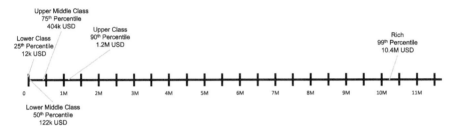

Fig. 3.4: Wealth Distribution in the United States.
Sources: Federal Reserve, 'Changes in U.S. Family Finances from 2016 to 2019: Evidence from the Survey of Consumer Finances' 37, https://www.federalreserve.gov/publications/files/scf20.pdf; 'Are You In The Top 1%?' *Forbes* (8 July 2022) https://www.forbes.com/advisor/investing/financial-advisor/are-you-in-the-top-1-percent/.

This diagram (see Fig. 3.4) shows the wealthy (not even the truly wealthy) and makes clear the gap that truly separates them from others, who by comparison are actually relatively close together in financial terms.

The truly wealthy take a disproportionate part in the *most* active forms of participation in traditional democracies – something not captured by general participatory statistics. For example, only 3 % of American families are millionaires, but millionaires compose the majority of the US House, Senate and Supreme Court. At the same time, more than half of Americans are working class, but working class peo-

---

259 'An Examination of the 2016 Electorate Based on Validated Voters' (*Pew Research Center*, 9 August 2018) <https://www.pewresearch.org/politics/2018/08/09/an-examination-of-the-2016-electorate-based-on-validated-voters/>.

ple have never held more than 2% of the seats in Congress.[260] Electoral campaigns are also frequently funded by the top 0.1% of wealthy citizens and corporations who also participate the most in 'civil society' organizations – groups that have insisted on becoming more and more heavily involved in political decision-making over the years.[261] Unlike many analyses, we will *not* lose sight of these most influential citizens, and we will do our best to avoid confusing them with people on household incomes of $100k/year (an income no longer sufficient to purchase a family home in many major Western cities).

Despite the fact that traditional participation has skewed towards the very wealthy since human records began (and, somewhat less concerningly and to a lesser extent, towards the older and more educated), and despite the fact that the very wealthy have significantly increased their stature and influence very recently, there is often:

a)   a fear that digital participation will skew demographic participation in an ambiguous way
b)   a demand that digital participation instantly eliminate *all* pre-existing societal skewing.

Here, we will examine the data we have to try to determine whether digital participation has an effect on demographic participation.[262] The good news is that digital democracy can – if done well – severely curtail the advantages of wealth – *the* major threat to democracy. The somewhat more ambivalent news is that it is less likely to *automatically* disrupt other long-standing general societal patterns of participation and we must, in fact, ask ourselves in more detail if and how this should be a goal.

---

260 Tiago Peixoto, 'Unequal Participation: Open Government's Unresolved Dilemma' (*Democracy-Spot*, February 2013) <https://democracyspot.net/2013/02/>.

261 See e.g. Linsey McGoey, *No Such Thing as a Free Gift: The Gates Foundation and the Price of Philanthropy* (Verso 2016); Gaëtan Cliquennois, *European Human Rights Justice and Privatisation: The Growing Influence of Foreign Private Funds* (Cambridge University Press 2020).

262 This is not always easy to do because some digital platforms intentionally do not capture demographic information about participants due to their commitment to privacy (Rosa Borge, Joan Balcells, and Albert Padró-Solanet, 'Democratic Disruption or Continuity? Analysis of the Decidim Platform in Catalan Municipalities' (2022) American Behavioural Scientist 7).

3.2.1 Participation in Internet Voting

Only 2 % of voters used internet voting in the first election in which it was allowed in Estonia and these voters were typically in early middle-age. This has changed markedly with the widespread adoption of the internet. Today, a 75 year-old is as likely to vote online in the next election as a 35 year-old.[263] Other factors that once strongly predicted the likelihood of being an internet voter – Estonian ethnicity (as opposed to Russian ethnicity), or having higher than average computer skills – have also lost their significance. Only those who report themselves as having poor computer skills are still less likely to vote online (and, of course, they can still vote offline).[264] In some respects, uptake is even the reverse of what would be predicted demographically. Although in 2005, 54 % of online votes were cast by men, by 2019 the situation had reversed with 54 % of internet votes cast by women. The most common online voter in Estonia today is female, middle-aged and mid-income – also the most common population demographic, making internet voters indistinguishable from the general population.[265] Furthermore, not only do older people in Estonia frequently vote online, they do so with more apparent ease than their younger counterparts, taking significantly less time to cast their ballots.[266] This finding confirms that claims of older voters struggling to complete digital tasks have indeed lost much of their saliency.

Internet voting has also proven beneficial to voters living in remote locations. People who live a 10-minute walk from a polling station are more likely to vote online than people who only live five minutes away. When voters are 15 – 60 minutes away from a polling station, 'only people with the poorest computer skills [are] somewhat less likely to e-vote in comparison to people with the highest skill level.' This is true regardless of age, education or income.[267]

Online voting arrangements in Markham, Ontario show a similar pattern. Markham has allowed internet voting in local elections for over 15 years and has conducted research into usage patterns at every election. While those using in-

---

263 Kristjan Vassil and Mihkel Solvak, 'Diffusion of E-Voting in Estonia' in Mihkel Solvak and Kristjan Vassil (eds), *E-voting in Estonia: Technological Diffusion and other Developments over Ten Years, 2005 – 2015* (Johan Skytte Institute of Political Studies, University of Tartu 2016) 57, 65.

264 Vassil and Solvak, 'Diffusion of E-Voting in Estonia' 66.

265 Ehin et al., 'Evidence from Eleven Elections' 8.

266 Mihkel Solvak, 'Mobilization' in Mihkel Solvak and Kristjan Vassil (eds), *E-voting in Estonia: Technological Diffusion and other Developments over Ten Years, 2005 – 2015* (Johan Skytte Institute of Political Studies, University of Tartu 2016) 93, 98.

267 Mihkel Solvak, 'Verification and Trust' in Mihkel Solvak and Kristjan Vassil (eds), *E-voting in Estonia: Technological Diffusion and other Developments over Ten Years, 2005 – 2015* (Johan Skytte Institute of Political Studies, University of Tartu 2016) 127, 135.

ternet voting *did* tend to be younger than the average voter in 2003, by 2018 this had shifted with the largest cohort of internet voters (around 30%) being 65 or over. At this point, the average online voter in Markham is slightly older than the average paper voter, slightly more affluent (household income being between $75–100k on average compared to $60–80k for paper voters (who however *are* younger and thus likely to be earning somewhat less)) and slightly more educated with 'some university' (the average paper voter had completed technical or community college). However, internet usage patterns were almost identical between paper and e-voters, indicating that lack of proficiency is not the reason for these minor differences in voting mode.[268]

Swiss researchers noted that while internet voters tended to be higher income and somewhat younger than average at the time statistics were collected (over 10 years ago), the most common predictor of whether someone used the internet to vote at the time, was how much they used the internet *in general*, and whether they lived far enough away from Switzerland that this was the most convenient voting option. They noted that high-income people who did not use the internet much, also did not use it to vote. Although younger, more educated, more high-income men were more likely to cast a ballot over the internet at the time, this was largely because they were the most likely demographic to be using the internet in the first place. The research did not reveal any significant demographic differences in terms of who online voters voted for. Researchers also noted that even if people of a certain political persuasion disproportionately vote online compared to other demographics this wouldn't mean they are voting more *because* it is online or that other people are failing to vote simply because online options are available.[269]

Estonian researchers came to similar conclusions, noting that parties with leaders who 'have actively campaigned against e-voting and publicly called on people not to vote online' tended to receive fewer online votes than other parties. However, this merely affected the *mode* of voting, not whether supporters voted at all or whom they chose to cast their vote for. There was no discernible pattern in terms of party choice in votes cast by former non-voters who took up e-voting,[270]

---

268 Goodman, 'Online Voting in the City of Markham' 21–22.

269 Uwe Serdült and Micha Germann, 'Internet Voting for Expatriates: The Swiss Case' (2014) 6(2) eJournal of eDemocracy and Open Government 197–215; Uwe Serdült, Micha Germann, Maja Harris, Fernando Mendez and Alicia Portenier 'Who are the Internet Voters' in E. Tambouris et al. (eds), *Electronic Government and Electronic Participation* (IOS Press 2015).

270 Kristjan Vassil, 'Political Neutrality of E-Voting' in Mihkel Solvak and Kristjan Vassil (eds), *E-voting in Estonia: Technological Diffusion and other Developments over Ten Years, 2005–2015* (Johan Skytte Institute of Political Studies, University of Tartu 2016) 142, 162; Kristjan Vassil, Mihkel

and as the researchers noted, even if people of certain political leanings (e. g. liberals or conservatives) had preferred to vote online as opposed to offline, this does not make their votes less worthy. Even if this had happened, forbidding internet voting for these reasons would amount to targeted voter suppression.

None of this should be surprising. As we saw above, online voting has a barely detectable impact on turnout. People *switch* to online voting because it is convenient, but few people who would not have voted offline do so online *just* because it is convenient. We also see that as internet access becomes more widespread, internet voting (where available) mirrors this access and is not confined to any particular demographic. While a few minor differences continue to exist, such as the skill levels among rural Estonian voters, the tendencies have been equalizing rapidly.

3.2.2 Participation in Participatory Budgeting

3.2.2.1 Participatory Budgeting in Brazil (Offline and Online)
Participatory budgeting is notable for the social conditions that first gave rise to it in Porto Alegre, Brazil, and that have influenced its implementation and analysis ever since.

Brazil experienced a military dictatorship between 1964 and 1985 and is one of the most economically unequal countries in the world with a Gini co-efficient higher than all but 16 States for which such data is available (its score is currently 48.9, on par with Congo).[271] Historically, the Gini co-efficient has been much higher (ca. 60 – 63 in the late 1980s), and in 1991 (around the time PB was first developed) over 20 % of Porto Alegre's population were living in favelas. By comparison, the USA's Gini co-efficient is 41.5 having risen from 38 in 1991. In the United Kingdom it is 35.1, in Canada it is 33.3 and in Germany 31.7.

Brazil's military rulers did allow opposition parties to exist, and one of these, the PT, was founded in 1980. PT stands for Partido dos Trabalhadores (Worker's Party) and, as the name would indicate, is a left-wing party that seeks to represent the interests of labourers or 'average workers'. This was the party that came to power in Porto Alegre in 1989 and which championed participatory budgeting.

It is not surprising that the PT would design and judge the success of PB (a mechanism it propagated) according to how well it delivered for its core support-

---

Solvak and Priit Vinkel, 'The Diffusion of Internet Voting: Usage Patterns of Internet Voting in Estonia between 2005 and 2015' (2016) 33(3) Government Information Quarterly.

271 'Gini Index' (*World Bank*) <https://data.worldbank.org/indicator/SI.POV.GINI> accessed 21 December 2022.

ers, given as it is a party formed to contest elections in explicit opposition to other parties, and thus to represent a certain segment (but not the entirety) of the Brazilian population. Studies of early PB in Brazil show that it did, to some extent, conform to its intended purpose as a vehicle for disadvantaged members of society to influence politics:

-   in 1998 11.4% of Porto Alegre residents earned **less than twice the minimum wage**, while 30.3% of people who participated in offline PB assemblies did
-   in 1995, it was found that while 15% of the Porto Alegre population identified as **non-white** 27% of those who participated in PB did
-   for thematic assemblies (city-wide meetings on district-spanning issues, such as transportation), this changed slightly. In 1995, 54% of these participants earned more than 5 times the minimum wage, almost identical to the population of Porto Alegre at large (53% in 1991)
-   women and men participated equally at the 'lower levels of the decision-making process', although **women** were less likely to be elected to be delegates to the Regional Delegate Forum or the Municipal Budget Council. As a result, a rule was introduced mandating that half of all electoral candidates must be women in 2003
-   PB also, as it was designed to do, increased funding for basic infrastructure in **poorer neighbourhoods**, although this also coincided with spending increases generally, some of which were generated by higher tax[272]

Few middle-class, upper-class or young people participated[273] and while tens of thousands of people participated in many years, participation numbers as a percentage of the population remained low.

As we can see, PB in its initial phases seems to have skewed *slightly* towards the poor, although by exactly how much is a matter of some dispute. Also, in at least some cases, despite being poorer and less educated than the average population, as many as 85% of participants were previously aligned to a civil society or-

272 Rebecca Abers, Igor Brandão, Robin King and Daniely Votto, 'Porto Alegre: Participatory Budgeting and the Challenge of Sustaining Transformative Change' (2018) World Resources Report Case Study, World Resources Institute 11 <https://files.wri.org/d8/s3fs-public/wrr-case-study-porto-alegre_1.pdf>.
273 William R. Nylen, 'The Making of a Loyal Opposition: The Workers' Party (PT) and the Consolidation of Democracy in Brazil' in Peter R. Kingstone and Timothy J Power (eds), *Democratic Brazil: Actors, Institutions and Processes* (University of Pittsburgh Press 2000) 126, 135.

ganization,[274] so PB was still, in many senses attracting those already highly engaged in politics.

At this time, PB was held offline in a similar fashion to that described in our earlier depiction of New York and Chicago (which were modelled after Brazil).

In later years, in some areas of Brazil, PB was also held online. This was done with the specific goal of broadening participation to attract greater numbers of young and middle-class participants,[275] and was, at least in some cases, a completely separate process than offline PB. This was initially extremely successful. Belo Horizonte held online PB in 2006, 2008, 2011 and 2013.[276] In 2006, almost 10% of the city's registered voters participated in the online process, compared with 1.4% who participated in the parallel face-to-face PB the same year.[277] However, the city did not collect information on the demographics of these participants, so we do not know if they were in fact younger and middle-class, and there is disagreement on research assessments in this regard.[278] What is certain is that the number of votes cast for projects in a given district was not related to average income in that district.[279] Participation in online PB then declined dramatically in 2011 and 2013 due to significant changes in the structure and poor project implementation (we will return to this in Chapters 4 and 8).

The state of Rio Grande do Sul also held PB online in 2011 and 2012. This PB also experienced high turnout rates (ca 15%), 15% of whom voted online.[280] Demographic information was collected by researchers in 2012, leading them to believe that online participation did succeed in attracting a significant number of additional participants who were more highly educated and higher income than average (bearing in mind that internet access was more limited in countries like Brazil in 2012 than it is today and that this was the organizers' intention).[281]

We can make two tentative conclusions based on this: adding internet voting probably does boost participation rates from where they otherwise would be, and

---

274 Stephen Coleman and Rafael Cardoso Sampaio, 'Sustaining a Democratic Innovation: A Study of Three E-Participatory Budgets in Belo Horizonte' (2016) Information, Communication and Society 4–5.
275 Coleman and Sampaio, 'Sustaining a Democratic Innovation' 5.
276 Coleman and Sampaio, 'Sustaining a Democratic Innovation' 3.
277 Tiago Peixoto 'E-Participatory Budgeting: E-Democracy from Theory to Success?' (2008) Zurich University, E-Democracy Center Working Paper 11 and 17.
278 Coleman and Sampaio, 'Sustaining a Democratic Innovation' 6.
279 Peixoto, 'E-Participatory Budgeting' 19.
280 Tiago Peixoto, Paolo Spada, Jon Mellon and Fredrik M. Sjoberg, 'Effects of the Internet on Participation: Study of a Public Policy Referendum in Brazil' (2015) World Bank Policy Research Working Paper 7204, 10.
281 Peixoto et al., 'Effects of the Internet on Participation'.

there are often differences in demographic participation in PB (compared to conventional participation), although this likely depends on pre-existing political affiliations, relatively low participation numbers compared to the total population, and the target audience of organizers.

3.2.2.2 Participatory Budgeting in New York City (Offline)

PB advocates in New York have – possibly even more than the PT in Brazil – pursued an explicit 'social justice' agenda. This is especially relevant, because during the voting phase of offline PB, volunteers typically set up stands on the street and thus can solicit votes from target demographics (e. g. younger or visible minority residents). Participatory budgeting in New York often also specifically encourages minority groups to participate in the process (with grants made available to non-profits to facilitate this).[282] At the same time, according to one writer/activist, councils in NYC should refrain from communicating about PB via social media or email as this would engage, 'a disproportionately white, highly-educated, and high income group, to the detriment of more diverse voices'. According to this writer, there are certain voices PB was 'meant to raise up' and that participants from other demographic backgrounds should not be allowed 'to drown out those voices'.[283] We thus have to see these statistics in light of this specific targeting, as well as the fact that these statistics are gathered and published by many of the advocates and organizers of the PB process itself. Some of the more salient points are as follows:

2011–2012

– Women participated more in local elections compared to their share of the population (by ca. 6 percentage points on average) and even more as PB voters (by ca. 10 percentage points on average) across the four districts using PB
– In those districts where Black voters took part in elections at higher rates compared to their percentage of the population, they took part as PB voters at even higher rates (by ca. 11 percentage points). However, in those districts where they participated less in local elections, they also participated less as PB voters.

---

282 Anna Clark, 'Is Participatory Budgeting Real Democracy?: Politics People's Choice Style in Chicago' *Next City* (28 April 2014) <https://nextcity.org/features/is-participatory-budgeting-real-democracy-chicago>.
283 Betsy Ribble, 'PBNYC: The Challenges and Opportunities of Scale' (*Harvard Ash Center, Medium*, 7 December 2016) <https://medium.com/challenges-to-democracy/pbnyc-the-challenges-and-opportunities-of-scale-951dabeae8d>.

– PB participation as it related to income was mixed over the various districts
– Those under age 35 participated at rates lower than their share of population, a trend reversed after this age (indeed those aged 65 and older represented 12 % of the population but 21 % of PB voters)[284]

2012–2013

– 62 % of PB voters were women compared to 51 % of the population in the districts covered by PB and 55 % of voters in the most recent local elections
– Asians, Blacks and Hispanics were all under-represented and whites were substantially over-represented (48 % of the population, but 64 % of PB voters (compared to 46 % of voters in local elections)). Black participants represented 17 % of the population in these districts and made up 17 % of voters in the most recent local elections, but only 12 % of PB voters (despite accounting for 27 % of budget delegates)
– Every income group under the $75k a year band was under-represented compared to their population share, with this reversed for those on higher-incomes (indeed, those earning more than $150k a year represented 12 % of the population, 14 % of budget delegates and 25 % of PB voters)
– The age trends remained the same as in the previous year, with those under 35 under-represented and those over 35 over-represented[285]

A longitudinal study between 2012–2016 showed:

– Voters aged 24 and under were under-represented initially, but over-represented by Year 4. The age group 25–34 were under-represented throughout. All other age groups were over-represented throughout (especially the age group 35–44, although this decreased over time)
– Those with only a high school degree were generally under-represented, although the extent to which this occurred varied by year. Those with graduate degrees were over-represented
– Those on incomes over $100k were over-represented in the beginning, but this over-representation had decreased significantly by 2016 to the point where participants were more or less average in terms of income

284 Alexa Kasdan and Lindsay Cattell, *A People's Budget: A Research and Evaluation Report on the Pilot Year of Participatory Budgeting in New York City* (The Urban Justice Center and PBNYC Research Team 2012) 77–80.
285 Alexa Kasdan, Lindsay Cattell and Pat Convey, *A People's Budget: A Research and Evaluation Report on Participatory Budgeting in New York City, Year 2* (Urban Justice Center 2013) 52.

- Whites were over-represented and Hispanics under-represented
- Women were consistently over-represented compared to men
- English-language speakers participated more, as did those born in the USA[286]

As we can see, in terms of participatory budgeting, demographic participation was a mixed bag. Sometimes, as in the case of women and Black voters in some districts, we can see that these groups were already participating at higher rates in local elections. Over-representation in PB voting simply mirrored, and in some cases intensified, this pre-existing pattern of engagement. The overall statistics also disguise demographic participation patterns that vary wildly district by district. For example, Black people represented 2% of residents in the 19th district and 0% of PB voters, 6% of residents in the 33rd district and 12% of PB voters, and 76% of residents in the 45th district and 89% of PB voters. Whites made up 53% of residents in the 19th district and 80% of PB voters, 74% of residents in the 33rd district and 69% of PB voters, and 11% of residents in the 45th district and 4% of PB voters.[287]

We can see some minority groups participating slightly more in PB than e.g. in electoral voting in some cases. However, because PB is open to non-citizens and minors (whereas electoral voting isn't), this may account for some, or even all, of the difference (in 2014–2015, 12% of PB voters were under the age of 18 and 10% of PB voters were not US citizens).[288] We also don't know the extent to which organizers are targeting these groups, and thus can't tell what participation may be inherently attributable to PB and what is purely a factor of e.g. targeting visible minority voters at offline voting booths.

Participatory budgeting in New York City does not just involve voters, but also the budget delegates who turn the ideas submitted by residents into concrete proposals and decide which of these proposals should go on the ballot. These roles are necessarily inhabited by those who have the time and inclination to take on the commitment of attending numerous face-to-face meetings. Unsurprisingly, those who could afford to act as budget delegates generally came from more affluent

---

286 Carolina Johnson, 'Engaging Democracy: An Institutional Theory of Participatory Budgeting' (DPhil Thesis, University of Washington 2017) 58 – 60.

287 Kasdan, Cattell and Convey, *Year 2* 53 et seq.

288 Ribble, 'PBNYC: The Challenges and Opportunities of Scale'; Colin O'Connor, *Gotham Gazette*, https://www.gothamgazette.com/govermnent/5946-participatory-budget; Carolin Hagelskamp, Rebecca Silliman, Erin B. Godfrey and David Schleifer, 'Shifting Priorities: Participatory Budgeting in New York City is Associated with Increased Investments in Schools, Street and Traffic Improvements, and Public Housing' (2020) 42(2) New Political Science 171, 194.

neighbourhoods, and up to 50 % of people who initially volunteer to be budget delegates quit the demanding role before the end of the process.[289]

Researchers who investigated PB in NYC reported that meetings (even initial meetings) were generally attended by those 'who had a direct stake in a particular outcome' and either arrived with or gravitated towards a particular proposal that they focused on championing throughout the process. Particularly those delegates with a high social standing, e.g. university lecturers, often succeeded in getting their pet projects onto the final ballot. Attendees would also at times make deals to vote for each other's projects, thereby effectively leaving others who could not afford to attend off the final ballot presented to the voting public.[290] Of all the people one pair of researchers were able to interview, all those who acted as budget delegates succeeded in getting their projects on the final ballot, whereas only 2 of 7 people who had made proposals, but did not become budget delegates did.[291] Although only 20 % of their respondents were delegates, they accounted for 80 % of the proposals included on the final ballot with 78 % of delegates and 19 % of non-delegates proposing a project that was ultimately funded via PB.[292]

Thus, as we can see, due to the way offline PB is structured,[293] being able to participate as a budget delegate is a significant advantage in terms of being able to steer the process and this may counteract participation by more marginalized people in other aspects of the process (idea submission, voting). This is because structuring PB this way creates a bottleneck (the budget delegate process) which prevents the natural fluidity and channelling of participation we spoke of in the principles above. This is a serious structural flaw that we will return to in later chapters.

3.2.2.3 Leith Decides Participatory Budgeting (Online and Offline)

Leith (a part of Edinburgh, Scotland whose inhabitants are overwhelming white and which includes some of the most disadvantaged parts of the city) has run a small PB project since 2010. Across six years of study, whites and Asians were

---

289 Daniel Williams and Don Waisanen, *Real Money, Real Power? The Challenges with Participatory Budgeting in New York City* (Palgrave MacMillan 2020) 66 and 79.

290 Madeleine Pape and Josh Lerner, 'Budgeting for Equity: How Can Participatory Budgeting Advance Equity in the United States' (2016) 12(2) Journal of Deliberative Democracy; Williams and Waisanen, *Real Money, Real Power?* 51–52 and 79 et seq.

291 Williams and Waisanen, *Real Money, Real Power?* 84.

292 Williams and Waisanen, *Real Money, Real Power?* 89.

293 There is some online collection of proposals, but this has not been emphasized by organizers until more recently, see e.g. http://ideas.pbnyc.org/place/654687 accessed 5 February 2023.

somewhat under-represented, with Afro-Caribbeans slightly over-represented. Those aged 46–65 and those aged 25 and under were over-represented, in the case of the 25-and-unders by a very wide margin. This may be because children as young as eight were allowed to participate and thus children were likely voting with their 46–65 year-old parents or grandparents. The age group 24–45 was slightly under-represented.[294]

3.2.2.4 Tower Hamlets Participatory Budgeting (Online and Offline)

Tower Hamlets is an urban area in central London, with a population of approximately 220,000. It is generally considered to be an underprivileged area and ca. 45% of its inhabitants were born outside the UK.

In 2009/2010, Tower Hamlets ran a PB project worth several million pounds in an effort to determine which projects and services would be maintained following the financial crash of 2007–2008. During this project, the 19-and-under age group was significantly under-represented, 20–25 year-olds were slightly under-represented, 26–43 year-olds were pretty much on target compared to the general population, and older people were over-represented. Men and women participated equally. White British people and Christians were significantly under-represented while Muslims and Bangladeshis were dramatically over-represented.[295]

In Tower Hamlets, Islam is the dominant religion with Bangladeshi being the most common ethnicity, and many non-white residents are successfully involved in electoral politics in the area, so we can interestingly see the local majority in terms of demographics mirrored in other forms of decision-making.

3.2.2.5 Civic Budgeting in Poland (Online and Offline)

Since 2018, all large Polish cities have been required to run a legally binding participatory budgeting exercise (called civic budgeting) with a value equal to at least 0.5% of the last municipal budget. These large cities have a combined population of 7,735,854 people, and in 2019, more than 1 million of them (ca. 1 in every 8 residents) voted in participatory budgeting.[296] The participation rates varied significantly from city to city, from a high of 40% in Rzeszow to a low of 6% each in Torun and Warszawa.

---

294 Johnson, 'Engaging Democracy' 111.
295 Johnson, 'Engaging Democracy' 118.
296 Agnieszka Szczepańska, Marek Zagroba and Katarzyna Pietrzyk, 'Participatory Budgeting as a Method for Improving Public Spaces in Major Polish Cities' (2022) 162 Social Indicators Research 231, 247.

All but four cities offered both online and offline voting, and in virtually all cities, a large majority of votes were cast online.[297] In some cities (Wroclaw, Warszawa, Torun, Szczecin, Rzeszow, and Lublin) almost all votes were. In those cities that *only* offered online voting, participation rates were slightly lower than in the other cities (13% as opposed to 17%). This may be reflective of 'missing' some voters who would only vote offline, but may also be reflective of the effort and resources put behind each project. A city willing to facilitate both offline and online voting may have been more assertive in advertising and running offline information sessions, which may have raised awareness and boosted total participation numbers. The cities that spent the most (more than 50 PLN per capita) had higher participation rates (21% on average) than those that spent the least (less than 35 PLN per capita with a 7% average turnout), but the sample size was small (two cities in each category) and there may have been other factors at play.[298] A relationship between cities with higher and lower-incomes and PB turnout could not be found.[299]

Researchers did, however, find that 30–50 year-old professionally-active people were the most likely to submit proposals to be voted on and the youngest and oldest cohorts were least likely to do so. Submitting a proposal was somewhat more demanding than in other jurisdictions in that each proposal had to include a cost estimate, 'be well-described and justified' and 'consistent with formal requirements, local plans, programs and strategies.' Researchers concluded that the factors leading to engagement with civic budgeting in Poland were too complex to be easily assessed and depended to a great extent on the specific locality in question.[300]

3.2.2.6 Participatory Budgeting in Lisbon (Online and Offline)

Portugal has official rules regulating PB which is also mandatory in public high schools.[301] PB in Lisbon presently distributes €2.5 million and is split between projects that cost less than €75k and projects that cost less than €150k. Following the Covid pandemic, where it had to be suspended, PB in Lisbon has chosen to go entirely digital with the goal of enabling more people to participate. As a result, meetings that deliberate proposals are now held over Zoom, and voting now occurs ex-

---

297 Szczepańska, Zagroba and Pietrzyk, 'Participatory Budgeting in Major Polish Cities' 239.

298 These statistics calculated by the author based on Szczepańska, Zagroba and Pietrzyk, 'Participatory Budgeting in Major Polish Cities'.

299 Szczepańska, Zagroba and Pietrzyk, 'Participatory Budgeting in Major Polish Cities' 246.

300 Szczepańska, Zagroba and Pietrzyk, 'Participatory Budgeting in Major Polish Cities' 248.

301 Giovanni Allegretti, 'Common Patterns in Coping with Under-Representation in Participatory Processes: Evidence from a Mutual Learning Space for Portuguese Local Authorities (LAs)' (2021) 34(5) Innovation: The European Journal of Social Science Research 729–765.

clusively digitally and via SMS. Turnout is facilitated by people sending text messages to contacts asking for their vote for a specific project. While little demographic information is available on voters, those in both the poorest and the richest neighbourhoods of Lisbon tend to participate the least in PB.[302]

3.2.2.7 Participatory Budgeting Paris (Online and Offline)

Online voting does not seem to have had a negative impact on marginalized residents in Paris. In 2016, the districts with the highest numbers of online voters in Paris PB were the 13th (which accounted for 13% of voters), followed by the 18th and 19th districts (all among the most disadvantaged areas of the city).[303]

The age, gender and location of participants has remained similar across the years. Those who submit proposals are most likely to be 30–50 year-old males, and those who vote are most likely to be 30–50 year-old females.[304] However, it is important to keep generalizations like these in perspective. 40% of all PB proposals are submitted by women,[305] so while men are 'most likely' to submit a proposal, a large number of women are also participating in this manner. The frequency and intensity of participation tended to be greatest in those aged approximately 40–74.[306]

Both proposers and voters were most likely to live in East Paris, which is generally more affordable in terms of living costs. Those who live in the West and Central areas, which account for a large proportion of the city's most expensive real estate, were the least likely to participate. Overall, about 18% of proposals and votes have come from people who live in low-income neighbourhoods.[307]

While each proposal must be submitted by an individual, associations are the ultimate source of ca. 20–25% of proposals, as well as often being the beneficiaries of funding allocated by PB. Organizations that described themselves as small were more likely to participate in public life via PB than other avenues. Of the organi-

---

302 Information obtained from interviews.

303 Émilie Moreau and William Arhip-Paterson, 'Budget participatif de Paris: Qui sont les Parisiens qui y participants?' (February 2018) No 123 Atelier Parisiene de Urbanisme 4 <https://www.apur.org/sites/default/files/documents/publication/etudes/note_123_budget_participatif.pdf?token=rsDSZWYi>.

304 William Arhip-Paterson, 'Budget participatif de Paris: Tendances dans la participation' Rapport pour la Ville de Paris (February 2019) 4.

305 Arhip-Paterson, 'Tendances dans la participation' 4.

306 William Arhip-Paterson, 'Budget participatif de Paris: Les comportements des participants numériques dans la durée', Rapport pour la Ville de Paris (April 2019); Arhip-Paterson, 'Tendances dans la participation' 17.

307 Arhip-Paterson, 'Tendances dans la participation' 9.

zations that participated in PB, 43 % described themselves as small, 27 % as medium and 30 % as large. This was the opposite of the other popular form of participating (local council). Among the organizations participating in this way, 38 % described themselves as small, 21 % as medium and 41 % as large.[308]

Online voting did not seem to have the negative impact on participation in Paris PB that some predicted the digitalization of democracy would have. Over half (54 %) of online voters are female.[309] About 14 % of those who voted online live in disadvantaged neighbourhoods, only slightly lower than the relative population of these neighbourhoods (16 % of the population of Paris). Disadvantaged neighbourhoods also accounted for about 16 % of all submitted projects, which is in line with their population, despite the fact that submitting proposals is a purely online process.[310] In fact, the districts that submitted the fewest proposals were the 7th, 8th and 16th – some of the most affluent areas of the city.[311]

Table 3.1: Participation in Paris PB by Arrondissement

Paris Arrondissement	Percentage Share of Population	Share of OnlineVote 2016	Deviation		Percentage of Proposers	Level of Disadvantage
1er	0.8 %	0.7 %	↓	0.1 %	1.2 %	12
2e	1.0 %	1.2 %	⇧	0.2 %	1.5 %	16
3e	1.6 %	1.6 %		0 %	2.3 %	15
4e	1.2 %	0.9 %	↓	0.3 %	2.1 %	11
5e	2.7 %	3.5 %	⇧	0.8 %	2.8 %	13
6e	1.9 %	2.5 %	⇧	0.6 %	1.4 %	18
7e	2.5 %	1.1 %	↓	1.4 %	1.5 %	20
8e	1.7 %	0.6 %	↓	1.1 %	1.7 %	19
9e	2.7 %	3.9 %	⇧	1.2 %	3.3 %	14

308 Mathilde Renault-Tinacci and William Arhip-Paterson, *Implications des Associations dans le democratie participative: le cas du budget participatif parisien* (Institut national de la jeunesse et de l'éducation populaire, September 2020) 13 <https://injep.fr/wp-content/uploads/2020/09/IAS38_democratie-participative.pdf>.
309 Arhip-Paterson, 'Tendances dans la participation' 13.
310 Moreau and Arhip-Paterson, 'Qui sont les Parisiens qui y participents?' 5.
311 Estela Brahimllari, *Multi-Layered Participatory Budgeting: The Case of Low-Income Neighbourhoods in Paris* (FrancoAngeli 2020) 155; Moreau and Arhip-Paterson, 'Qui sont les Parisiens qui y participants?'

Table 3.1: Participation in Paris PB by Arrondissement *(Continued)*

Paris Arrondissement	Percentage Share of Population	Share of OnlineVote 2016	Deviation		Percentage of Proposers	Level of Disadvantage
10e	4.2%	8.2%	⇧	4.1%	6.4%	8
11e	6.8%	8.1%	⇧	1.2%	8.4%	9
12e	6.5%	7.0%	⇧	0.5%	8.3%	7
13e	8.2%	12.8%	⇧	4.6%	8.0%	2
14e	6.4%	6.1%	⬇	0.3%	5.6%	5
15e	10.6%	7.3%	⬇	3.3%	7.7%	10
16e	7.5%	2.4%	⬇	5.1%	2.8%	17
17e	7.7%	5.6%	⬇	2.0%	5.7%	6
18e	9.0%	9.3%	⇧	0.3%	9.8%	3
19e	8.4%	9.1%	⇧	0.7%	10.2%	1
20e	8.8%	8.2%	⬇	0.6%	9.4%	4

The districts that contributed the greatest share of online voters (in terms of absolute numbers) were the 11th, 13th, 18th, 19th and 20th [312] – all but the 11th are among the most disadvantaged in Paris. In the 9th district, 65% of voters cast their votes online, compared to ca. 50% of voters in the 2nd, 6th and 10th districts. In all other districts, the majority of votes were cast on paper, whereby the 8th (an affluent district) had the lowest percentage of online voters at 22%.[313]

While it can be difficult to draw absolute conclusions from this data, since up to 30% of people who vote by paper cast their ballot in a different district than where they live (e. g. on their way to work or in a sporting club),[314] the information gathered from self-declared addresses indicates voters and proposers from disadvantaged districts participating at high rates. Fears that offering digital voting would exclude lower-income people are not evidenced here, although it is to be expected that the *most marginalized* people likely do not participate (those living in deep poverty, illegal immigrants, homeless people, the very 'oldest olds', etc.).

---

312 Arhip-Paterson, 'Tendances dans la participation' 13.
313 William Arhip-Paterson and Ari Brodach, 'Budget participatif de Paris: Analyse des votants papiers et de leurs pratiques', Rapport pour la Ville de Paris (December 2018) 4.
314 Arhip-Paterson and Brodach, 'Analyse des votants papiers' 14.

That offering online voting should not have this deleterious effect should not be terribly surprising. Paris, after all, has free public wi-fi, including 4G coverage throughout the Metro system,[315] and except during the pandemic (an exceptional situation) has also always allowed paper voting in PB. According to the World Bank, 86 % of all people in France use the internet,[316] while commercial research puts the figure higher at 91 %. 96 % of people aged 16 – 64 have a smartphone, 80 % have a laptop or desk computer, 50 % have a tablet, and 95 % of mobile connections are broadband.[317]

Fears of the process being dominated by a small group of people also seem misplaced. In Paris, thus far, 86 % of people who have submitted a project to PB have done so only once, and 70 % of people who have voted online have also only done so once (although some of them may have voted on paper in other years).[318] Only 3 % of participants have submitted a proposal every year[319] and these are more likely to ultimately be associations rather than individuals.[320] As this indicates, most people who do participate tend to do so intermittently. As we saw, this is the general pattern in those countries where referendums are more frequent. It was also the case in online PB in Belo Horizonte in 2006, where participants were allowed to vote for one project in each of nine districts. Despite having the ability to cast nine votes apiece, 172,938 participants cast only 503,266 votes between them with 74 % of participants casting a vote in three districts or less.[321] As this indicates, if anything, the issue faced is one of *retaining* participants through the years.

3.2.2.8 Participatory Budgeting Iceland (Online)

PB in Iceland has been running continuously every 1 – 2 years for over 10 years. Although they did not give exact figures, PB Iceland also reported that middle-aged people tended to participate the most and that young people and immigrants were hard to reach. Organizers were quick to point out that this is typical of polit-

---

315 'Paris Metro is Now 100 % Covered' (*Connectivity Technology Blog*); 'Pour une ville plein de vie' (*RATP Group*).
316 'Individuals using the Internet (% of population) France' (*World Bank*) <https://data.world bank.org/indicator/IT.NET.USER.ZS?locations=FR> accessed 28 December 2022.
317 Simon Kemp, 'Digital 2021: France' (*DataReportal*, 10 February 2022) 17 et seq <https://data reportal.com/reports/digital-2021-france>.
318 Arhip-Paterson, 'Comportements des participants numériques' 2.
319 Arhip-Paterson, 'Comportements des participants numériques' 10.
320 Arhip-Paterson, 'Comportements des participants numériques' 16.
321 Peixoto, 'E-Participatory Budgeting' 17–18.

ical participation generally, online, offline, traditional or new and that hiring a project manager might help to improve this situation.[322]

3.2.2.9 Conclusions on Participatory Budgeting

Because the total participation rates in participatory budgeting are respectable but generally not terribly high, it is likely that a large proportion of people take part having been triggered by an external event, e. g. passing an offline voting booth while out shopping. Spontaneity likely plays a greater role than in electoral voting, as marketing is less sweeping and participants do not feel as heavy a duty to participate, nor as if the consequences of doing so, or failing to do so, will be as great. This, the often low participation rates (in terms of total percentage of the population), and the efforts of some groups to particularly target certain demographics, are likely why we see demographics often tilting one way or another and not really mirroring the population. However, as we have seen, *how* they tilt varies considerably from place to place and time to time. The one relative constant is that older people tend to participate more, although this relationship was not quite as linear as it is with electoral voting, and sometimes the greatest participation came from the 'young' middle-aged (30 – 50 year age range). The age of participation has thus been pushed down slightly in some cases from where we typically see it in traditional offline participation.

3.2.3 Participation in Online Consultations with Voting

3.2.3.1 Lethbridge Capital Investment Programme, Alberta, Canada

As opposed to PB, whose adherents sometimes explicitly attempt to activate those not involved in politics, many online consultations are less prescriptive and may provide different insights on the issue of demographic participation.

In 2021, the city of Lethbridge, Alberta organized an online consultation on its 10-year Capital Investment Programme (CIP). This included a section for residents to comment and sometimes vote on various projects, ranging from sports facilities to trash disposal. Residents could choose to participate anonymously or to create a named account.

---

322 Interview with Eiríkur Búi Halldórsson Project Manager – My Neighborhood, City of Reykjavik Human Rights and Democracy Office (22 March 2022).

While the vast majority of people chose to comment anonymously,[323] 126 named contributors made a total of 366 comments. We can categorize these comments according to likely gender on the basis of names being typically strongly associated with male gender (e. g. John), female gender (e. g. Mary) or indeterminate/gender neutral (e. g. Terry).[324] If we accept this assumption as a rough reflection of reality, 59 of these commenters were (likely) men, 55 were (likely) women and 12 were unknown. 195 comments (or 53 %) came from male commenters, 124 (or 34 %) from female participants and 47 (or 13 %) from participants of unknown gender.

A total of 7,937 words were used in these comments. Of these, 55 % of words were from male contributors, 31 % from female contributors and 14 % from those of unknown gender. On one of the questions, a particular male contributor (an employee of an educational organization behind one of the projects) had become a defender of this project and thus an exceptionally frequent commenter. Eliminating his contributions gave a total of 339 comments from named contributors, 168 of which (50 %) came from males, 124 (37 %) from females, and 47 (14 %) from persons of unknown gender. The total words used in these comments were 7,213. Of these, 50 % of words were from male contributors, 35 % from female contributors and 15 % from persons of unknown gender. Thus, even after we remove the possible skewing effect of one particularly active male participant, we still see an apparent tendency of men to participate more than women, although this must be taken with the caveat that it is also possible that men felt more comfortable giving their names, and that we know nothing about unnamed contributors (the majority of all contributors). Although Lethbridge's male population slightly exceeds the female population,[325] the difference is too slight to make a significant difference in these figures.

Comparing these figures to traditional participation, we see that currently the Alberta Legislative Assembly has 62 male MLAs and 27 female MLAs, giving a ratio of 70 % male to 30 % female.[326] Lethbridge City Council has 7 male and 2 female members (78 % male to 22 % female).[327] The Canadian Parliament has 30.5 % female parliamentarians – the highest ever rate, obtained after the Liberal and NDP par-

---

323 Although some people complained that they had been unable to give themselves a handle and were thus forced to participate anonymously.

324 Hereinafter referred to as 'male', 'female', 'unknown' for simplification,

325 'Lethbridge Census Online, 2019 Census Results' (*City of Lethbridge*) <https://www.lethbridge ca/City-Government/Census/Documents/2019%20Final%20Census%20Report.pdf>.

326 'Members' (*Legislative Assembly of Alberta*) <https://www.assembly.ab.ca/members/members-of-the-legislative-assembly> accessed 22 December 2022.

327 'Mayors and Councillors' (*City of Lethbridge*) <https://www.lethbridge.ca/City-Government/City-Council/Pages/default.aspx> accessed 22 December 2022.

ties made running female candidates a priority in an explicit effort to boost their female MP numbers. Assuming that some commenters categorized under 'unknown' are not male, it does seem that allowing direct participation may have an immediate positive effect on male/female active participation rates (directly voicing an opinion on the matter at hand rather than merely voting for someone else), at least in regions where there is already a relatively high level of cultural equality between the genders. If all commenters categorized as unknown are, in fact, male this would give participation rates that more closely mirror those in elected representation, but still correspond slightly more accurately to the population in terms of gender.

The consultation in Lethbridge also asked participants for some demographic information.

According to the ca. 700 respondents, 20% of them lived in North Lethbridge, 44% in West Lethbridge and 36% in South Lethbridge. According to the census data, 28% of the population lives in North Lethbridge, 40% in West Lethbridge and 32% in South Lethbridge.[328] If we consider the margin of error due to the difficulty in getting an exact comparison (the census data includes some minors), we can see that respondents were fairly representative on this metric.

Age-related participation was also what we would expect (see Fig. 3.5).[329]

We can see that while the youngest cohort of voters remains the most underrepresented, the oldest voters are significantly less so and do not seem to have great difficulty in participating online. Participation follows the well-established pattern for most political activity (offline or online, traditional or new) with most people taking until their mid-twenties to become politically active, reaching their most active period between 35–65 and then declining again slightly with age (likely among the oldest olds).

Income presents a more difficult calculation (see Fig. 3.6). The survey conducted on the portal asked respondents for their pre-tax household income. This was among the least-answered survey questions with 20% of respondents preferring not to answer. In addition, there were some differences in how income was calculated for Lethbridge in the census data.

---

328 Calculated from '2019 Census Results' (*City of Lethbridge*) 4.

329 Due to different measurements among the youngest age groups and the fact that it stemmed from several years prior (2016), this data cannot give us a completely accurate comparison. This is complicated by the fact that Lethbridge is a university town, where the population of particularly the youngest voters tends to vary seasonally.

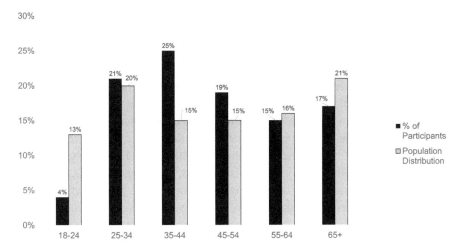

Fig. 3.5: Participation Rates by Age Group in Lethbridge.
Source: Lethbridge CIP survey and Census Profile, 2016 Census Lethbridge Alberta, Statistics Canada
(numbers are rounded).

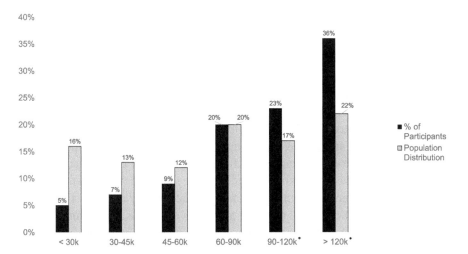

Fig. 3.6: Participation Rates by Income in Lethbridge.
Source: Lethbridge CIP survey and Census Profile, 2016 Census Lethbridge Alberta, Statistics Canada
(numbers are rounded). Population Distribution for 90–120k and >120k are approximate as source
data was grouped by 90–125k and >125k respectively.

We can see from this that higher-income households participated more than
lower-income households. However, we need to be wary of jumping to the conclu-
sion that this means 'the rich' are dominating participation. For one thing, those

on higher-incomes of ca. $125k are no longer necessarily 'rich' – an older four-bed family home in Lethbridge costs around $600k (a similar new home goes for over $800k) – completely out of range for a household earning a mere $125k – the current cost of an empty lot in Lethbridge.[330]

In addition, average household income (especially pre-tax) is not the most helpful way to calculate material well-being, since what household income means in concrete terms varies depending on the composition of that household. The average income for a 1-person household in the area is $47,375, whereas the average income for multi-person households is $107,266, and the average income for economic families with children is $132,348.[331] In other words, in many cases, where we are adding income, we are also adding people, without any clear way of determining material well-being per capita. It's possible for a young single person earning $30k a year to be as well-off materially as a couple with two small children earning $90k a year, yet the first would register in the second lowest income bucket and the latter in the second highest (in fact, if each partner participated, they would register at $90k *twice* despite actually splitting this income).

These figures also fail to take wealth into consideration, which is now an important component of material well-being. A person earning $40k who has inherited property, for example, may be as materially well-off as a person of the same age earning $80k-100k a year. This is even more true if the higher-earner has to provide for older relatives who are not part of their household.

It does stand to reason that people who have higher-incomes (rather than wealth from other sources) are the most likely to also throw themselves into participation, as they are more likely to be ambitious and driven people (this is, after all, likely how they are earning their income). However, we still don't know if they are a single 30 year-old driving a Porsche or an immigrant couple working long hours supporting their children and sending money home to their parents. Households today are diverse and until we capture the data to fully reflect this, it is hard to see privilege or lack thereof purely as a function of income. Participants *are* disproportionately higher-income, but they may or may not be disproportionately wealthy. Certainly, they do not necessarily belong to the category of *actually* wealthy people, who typically dispose over millions of dollars' worth of assets.

---

330 House prices obtained from real estate site <https://www.point2homes.com/CA/Real-Estate-Listings/AB/Lethbridge.html> on 17 December 2022.

331 'Census Profile, 2016 Census, Lethbridge' (*Statistics Canada*) <https://www12.statcan.gc.ca/census-recensement/2016/dp-pd/prof/details/page.cfm?Geo1=POPC&Code1=0467&SearchText=Lethbridge> accessed 18 February 2023.

3.2.3.2 Carbon Budgeting in Ontario, Canada

London, Ontario ran a carbon budgeting exercise on Ethelo in late 2021. In this exercise each participant had to achieve a certain carbon reduction, but had a choice of how to do it.

According to data collected by the organizers,[332] 51% of participants were born in North America, which compares to 81% of the population generally.[333] 2% of participants were Indigenous peoples, similar to the general population figure of 2.6%. According to census statistics, 51.5% of the total population is female and 48.5% is male. This was also reflected relatively accurately in participation with 46% giving their gender pronoun as 'she', 44% as 'he', 2% as 'they' and the rest preferring not to say or 'other'.

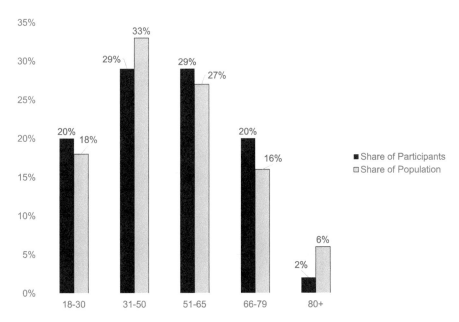

Fig. 3.7: Participation Rates relative to Population – London Carbon Budgeting 2020.

This was one of the few exercises that differentiated between 'young olds' and 'old olds' when it came to statistics collection (see Fig. 3.7), and we can see the predic-

332 'London Climate Action Plan Simulator' (*Ethelo*) <https://blog.ethelo.org/hubfs/Case%20Study%20Reports/London-report.pdf>.
333 'Census Profile 2016 Census, London' (*Statistics Canada*) <https://www12.statcan.gc.ca/census-recensement/2016/dp-pd/prof/details/page.cfm?Geo1=CMACA&Code1=555&Geo2=PR&Code2=35&Data=Count&SearchText=london>.

tions from earlier chapters bearing out; while those age 66–79 participated at a higher rate than their share of the population, those over 80 participated at much lower rates. It was also one of the few instances of participation where the youngest cohort (18–30) participated at more than its share of population (possibly as London is home to a large university).

3.2.3.3 Developing an Independent Political Platform, Ireland

Unlike the other uses of Ethelo mentioned here, this use-case took place in Ireland and had developing a platform for an independent political candidate as its object.[334] Participants were thus asked whether or not they supported a wide range of measures from funding options for healthcare provision to cannabis legalization to taxation policy. Participants were invited to participate via door-to-door canvassing, social media posts and leaflet drops.

Those between 31 and 65 were most likely to take part and these groups were over-represented at the expense of over 65 year-olds and under 30 year-olds (see Fig. 3.8). This was likely partly due to canvassing patterns that targeted estates rather than apartments and rural areas.

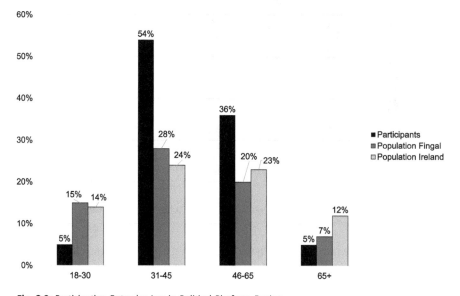

Fig. 3.8: Participation Rates by Age in Political Platform Design.

---

334 This candidate was the author who also collected and analysed all statistics.

All commenters chose to give their names. Assuming that names are real and reflect gender identity and ethnic heritage in stereotypical fashion, active male participants outnumbered active female participants by nearly 3 to 1. Nonetheless, the diversity of the exercise would appear to still compare favourably to electoral representation. Only 22 % of seats in the Irish Dáil (House of Commons) were held by women at the time[335] – and that only after gender quotas were introduced – whereas ca. 26 % of participants likely identified as female. Based on name, active participants of probable European heritage participated at a fairly robust rate (nearly 8 %), but those of non-European heritage were severely under-represented, and perhaps not represented at all. This is likely due to the small sample size, but is also in line with studies that show that immigrants from non-democratic countries or from countries where political freedom is low tend to participate less frequently than those who come from countries with a high degree of democracy and political freedom (recent immigrants account for the vast majority of non-ethnic-Irish residents in the area concerned). This may be even more the case for highly public forms of participation where fears of political intimidation, reprisals and violence are more likely to surface.

3.2.3.4 Your Priorities Legislative Consultation, Scotland

The Scottish Parliament used Your Priorities (from Citizens Foundation) to collect feedback from residents on a bill governing the use of fireworks in early 2022. 1,400 people took part, contributing a total of 1,600 comments and 11,000 ratings. 467 of these participants provided some demographic data about themselves. In this case, female participation exceeded male participation with ca. 55 % of participants describing themselves as a woman and 45 % as a man.[336] The age breakdown, again, tilted significantly towards the older demographics (see Fig. 3.9).

Of those who gave their ethnicity, 96 % said 'white', which is in line with the general population.[337]

---

335 Dan MacGuill, 'We now have more female TDs than ever before – but do we really have gender quotas to thank?' *The Journal* (1 March 2016) <http://www.thejournal.ie/women-in-32nd-dail-election-2016-2630150-Mar2016/>.

336 Three participants described their gender in another way, while an additional participant under the age of 16 is not accounted for in this data.

337 Participation and Communications Team, Scottish Parliament, *Fireworks and Pyrotechnics Articles (Scotland) Bill: Digital Engagement: Summary of Online Forum Submissions to Support the Criminal Justice Committee's Scrutiny of the Bill* (March 2022) <https://www.parliament.scot/-/media/files/committees/criminal-justice-committee/fireworks-bill-engagement-summary.pdf>.

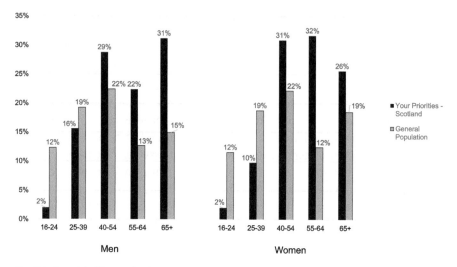

Fig. 3.9: Your Priorities Scotland vs. General Population.

3.2.3.5 Online Consultations, Finland

An early online consultation in Finland on the topic of Off-Road Traffic Reform (chiefly concerning snowmobiles and all-terrain vehicles)[338] attempted to crowd-source feedback by allowing participants to propose ideas for legislative reform on the platform, and to comment and like or dislike ideas. 743 people registered to take part, producing 500 ideas and 4,000 comments. 186 participants responded to a survey sent out by researchers, revealing the following demographics:

- 86% of respondents were male
- 45% were from rural areas
- 20% were 26–34 years old
- 46% were 35–54 years old
- 22% were 55–64 years old

Given as the topic itself was de facto targeted towards a specific group – mainly white, male outdoor workers, it is unsurprising that they participated.

---

338 Tanja Aitamurto, Hélène Landemore and Jorge Saldivar Galli, 'Unmasking the Crowd: Participants' Motivation Factors, Expectations, and Profile in a Crowdsourced Law Reform' (2017) 20(8) Information, Communication and Society 1239–1260.

A second online Finnish consultation concerned reform to legislation on condominiums. Researchers conducted a similar survey here with the following results:

- 61% of respondents were men, 67% of whom owned condominiums
- 24% had a masters degree
- 50% were retired
- 43% were over 65 years of age
- 33% were 55–64 years of age
- 49.7% were board members of their housing association
- 89% had voted in local or national elections in the past five years (compared to 70% of the general population)[339]

Again, the findings are unsurprising, as such apartments are typically owned by older men, so, again, we shouldn't be surprised that a consultation targeted to a certain demographic group results in participation from that group. In the reverse case, in an online consultation on poverty reduction in British Columbia in 2021, 63% of respondents identified with female pronouns and only 24% with male pronouns.[340] This should thus be taken as a reminder to be mindful of the subjects that are selected for wider participation and the impacts this could have on the demographics concerned. It certainly doesn't hurt to mix things up and cover a wide range of topics.

3.2.4 Participation in Online Deliberation

The statistics above have mainly come from instances of asynchronous participation (people can take part at a time of their own choosing and don't necessarily need to directly interact with each other). However, another model is presented by online tools specifically focused on deliberation, in which participants must take part synchronously (at the same time) and can directly interact with each other under the guidance of a facilitator.

Every Voice Engaged runs an online tool called Common Ground for Action which facilitates dialogue between small numbers of participants with the purpose

---

339 Tanja Altamurto and Jorge Saldivar, 'Motivating Participation in Crowdsourced Policymaking: The Interplay of Epistemic and Interactive Aspects' (2017) 1 (CSCW) Proceedings of the ACM on Human-Computer Interaction.

340 The remainder preferred not to say or used non-binary pronouns 'Poverty Reduction Prince George' (*Ethelo*) 35 <https://f.hubspotusercontent40.net/hubfs/6224498/Boilerplate/Prince%20George%20(1).pdf> accessed 12 March 2023.

of determining what participants agree on (what the 'common ground for action' is). The dialogue follows a series of 'issue guides' (pre-set manuals) that are intended to prompt participants to reflect on the pros and cons of various policy options. Participants engage in conversation about a topic (e. g. immigration) and plot their position on a visual graph. Facilitators are supposed to ensure that everyone has the chance to express themselves equally and that no participant dominates the conversation. Thus, these statistics derive from a more controlled atmosphere where an effort has been made to ensure equilibrium.

It is possible that this online environment (as opposed to face-to-face deliberation) could reduce the pernicious effects of arbitrary societal status, because in an online platform (particularly one where participants do not use video) it is much harder to tell someone's race, age or gender. Even when this is known, or possible to guess (participants generally use their first names), such considerations may retreat into the background when participants are not visible to each other.[341] This may help to prevent some member's contributions being given more weight than they deserve while others' are dismissed out of hand based on their origin. This is not simply about being fair to the participants (although this is important), but is tied to the hope that this will increase the objectivity of the discussion and lead to a focus on the issues rather than personality or other characteristics of the participants (much as direct democracy focuses on issues rather than the personality of electoral candidates).

Researchers studied data from 1,600 participants who took part in 275 different online sessions with Common Ground for Action over the course of three years.[342]Although it is possible to use the software in combination with Zoom[343] in these cases participants communicated with each other solely over text which (but for their names) hid their identities. In this facilitated atmosphere, women posted 8 % fewer comments than men, and non-whites posted an average of 16 % fewer comments. Participation tended to be highest for the 31–64 age group who posted on average 14–17 % more comments, while those over 65 posted 15 % fewer comments. Although women posted less often, they tended to use more words per post when they did, as did those aged 30 and younger. This evened up the participation of both groups to more average levels. However, non-white par-

---

341 Interview with Lori Britt, Professor, School of Communication, James Madison University (11 March 2022).
342 Ryan Kennedy, Anand E. Sokhey, Claire Abernathy, Kevin M. Esterling, David MJ Lazer, Amy Lee, William Minozzi and Michael Neblo, 'Demographics and (Equal?) Voice: Assessing Participation in Online Deliberative Sessions' (2020) 69(1) Political Studies.
343 Interview Lori Britt.

ticipants and those over 65 still participated less on this metric, with non-whites typically posting 17% fewer words per session on average and over-65s posting 24% fewer words.[344]

Perhaps unsurprisingly, non-white participants were significantly less satisfied with the outcomes of the deliberation 'relative to their white counterparts'.[345] Men also participated less when the moderator was identified as female (making participation in these cases de facto more equal) and men were less satisfied with the experience when women participated more. This shows an underlying societal issue – some men simply do not like women to participate and feel that equal treatment is, in fact, unequal to them. This doesn't seem to have *stopped* women from participating, but it does show that there are cultural biases that may cause some people to self-censor.

3.2.5 Conclusions on Participation Statistics

The truth is that these statistics don't really reveal any smoking guns in terms of participation. Small sample sizes (compared to the general population) and wide variations in how each participation is conducted (marketing, etc.) contribute to making comparisons difficult.

The youngest voters usually participate less, but this has been historically true across all forms of political participation (indeed, older people are thought to have participated more in democracy *in ancient Athens*). In some cases, there has been a higher rate of male participation, although several of the consultations were geared towards topics more typically associated with men, and gender participation is still more equal than, and in some cases the reverse of, most forms of traditional political participation. While there are fewer statistics available for race, where we have them, they seem relatively comparable in most cases, and in some cases, we even see minorities participating in very large percentages (e.g. in Tower Hamlets). In particular, we don't really see clear differences in terms of how people demographically participate based on the modality of participation according to the data collected so far.

Demographic differences are often reported in a profoundly exaggerated manner and haven't always been controlled for other factors. For example, older people do tend to participate a bit more (at least until they become very elderly), and they are often more affluent, but this is partly because they've had more time to

---

344 Kennedy et al., 'Demographics and (Equal?) Voice' 75 and 81.
345 Kennedy et al., 'Demographics and (Equal?) Voice' 79.

accumulate that wealth. The average 60 year-old is generally wealthier than the average 40 year-old, who is generally wealthier than the average 20 year-old. Similarly, immigrants, also tend to more often be people of colour. There are many reasons that immigrants participate less politically, but one key factor is that it simply takes some time to re-orient oneself to the politics of a new country. If we wanted to be more precise, we would have to start controlling for all of these factors.

In addition to this come many social factors. Why do older people use fewer words in online deliberation? Are they just more efficient? Likewise, women may impose a higher barrier in their own minds on when a thought is important enough to bother other people with it. Technology cannot change belief systems overnight and these beliefs are themselves constantly changing.

What technology *can* do is reduce *externally* imposed barriers, for example, if someone wants to take part more, but feels like they can't, because they don't have time or because they have to first be chosen by someone else to do so. I believe we can see these lowered barriers taking effect via the greater participation of women (in some cases slight, in some cases more extreme) on direct political matters, and by pushing the age range down in some cases (to 30–50) due to the lowered time constraints that digital participation enables. This is a fairly rough tendency, but with so many factors at play, this rough estimate is probably all we are going to get. It should, however, show that the value of democracy and digital democracy is not in achieving some kind of power-balancing between tribes, but in freeing people of unnecessary external constraints. Democracy is emancipatory – it brings freedoms, not outcomes.

3.3 Why People Participate (or Don't) According to Participants

In traditional elections, one of the most common reasons given for not voting is not being interested in politics or **not liking the options on offer** (meaning the person in question does not like the candidates or believes that elections will make no difference).[346] Reasons for not participating in other forms of digital or participatory democracy are similar, but also more varied.

---

346 Glenn Greenwald, 'Nonvoters are Not Privileged. They are Disproportionately Lower-Income, Nonwhite and Dissatisfied with the Two Parties' *The Intercept* (9 April 2020) <https://theintercept. com/2020/04/09/nonvoters-are-not-privileged-they-are-largely-lower-income-non-white-and-dissat isfied-with-the-two-parties/>.

Researchers investigating why people who had voted online in Paris's 2016 participatory budget did not repeat their participation in 2017, noted the single biggest reason given (at 50%) was having missed the voting deadline. Some respondents reported that they had been aware that PB was ongoing, but that they had **gotten busy** and it had slipped their mind.[347] Others (16%) were disappointed with PB, because their project had not been selected in the previous round, or they thought PB had been ineffective (13%), while 8% had been so overwhelmed by the number of proposals to choose from that they just hadn't voted.[348]

While many respondents expressed support for Paris PB, common complaints included:

– that people were being asked to vote again without knowing what had become of the first round of projects they had voted on in 2016 (**no follow-through**)
– that the projects were **too bland** and superficial and gave a cosmetic appearance of participation
– that basic services such as street cleaning were inappropriately placed on proposals
– a perception of **double standards** regarding which projects cleared the pre-checks and went through to the voting stage[349]

Similar complaints surfaced in the United States, with PB participants irritated at being asked to vote for basic necessities like school bathrooms, which they felt should not be in question.[350] Under these circumstances, people can feel like they are being manipulated into making false trade-offs under the guise of participation. Marketing was also an issue. A survey of PB voters in NYC revealed that of 78 respondents, only 15 had been able to attend neighbourhood assemblies to propose ideas. 84% of non-attendees said that they had been **unaware of the process**, while the remaining 16% cited time constraints.[351]

Another study that asked participants why they did not want to participate in a deliberative exercise (i.e. why they did not answer 'yes' to the question of whether they would, in theory, be willing to deliberate) revealed the top reasons to be not

---

347 William Arhip-Paterson, Ari Brodach and Titouan Tence, 'Budget Participatif de Paris: Etude de le repetition de vote numérique à deux éditions consécutives', Rapport pour la Ville de Paris (May 2018) 15.
348 Arhip-Paterson, Brodach and Tence 4, 13 and 14.
349 Arhip-Paterson, Brodach and Tence 24.
350 Williams and Waisanen, *Real Money, Real Power?* 96.
351 Williams and Waisanen, *Real Money, Real Power?* 86.

knowing enough to participate (42 %), being too busy (31 %), disliking conflict (29 %) and the fact that the process would not lead to a binding decision (26 %).[352]

Another team researched participation in The Great Debate (Le Grand Débat), a nationwide consultation in France in which people could attend local meetings but also submit comments online. According to official sources, 1.9 million online contributions and 27,000 letters and emails were received,[353] not, however, notably, from Paris's most disadvantaged areas (the residents of the so-called 'banlieue').

The study showed that the residents of these disadvantaged neighbourhoods had a 'thorough knowledge' of the event, but consciously chose not to participate.[354] The Debate was variously referred to by residents who took part in a focus group as 'a charade', an exercise simulating care, and as intended to legitimize pre-decided 'solutions' with a veneer of citizen participation. It was also described as a trick to reinforce elite domination and 'gross manipulation…by those who are in power'. Respondents complained about topics being pre-selected with one stating: 'The system is more and more capable in luring the people to take part in elections, consultations, polls and referendums, and to pretend it implements the will of the people, while in practice such Great, Average or Small Debates are useless'.[355]

The researchers noted that the people they spoke to were perfectly comfortable with public discussion, had plenty of ideas for how things could change, and reported that they would have had time to attend or participate in the Great Debate had it been worth their while to do so.

Subjects thus portrayed an attitude fairly common in studies into the economically disadvantaged: a conviction that participation would not benefit them and was thus generally not worth their time. Somewhat less well-publicized, however, is the fact that this conviction is often shared by higher-income people, including those who *do* participate.

Participants in lengthy consultations in Okotoks, Lethbridge and Finland all frequently expressed the view that likely no one was listening to what they were saying and that what they were doing was useless. These participants were often highly motivated, articulate and had, at least in some cases, above average incomes and education levels.

---

352 Neblo et al., 'Who Wants to Deliberate' 32.

353 Le grand débat nationale <https://granddebat.fr/> accessed 1 March 2023.

354 Sergiu Miscoiu and Sergiu Gherghina, 'Poorly Designed Deliberation: Explaining the Banlieues' Non-Involvement in the Great Debate' (2021) 34(5) Innovation: The European Journal of Social Science Research 694, 695.

355 Miscoiu and Gherghina, 'Poorly Designed Deliberation' 703–704.

This is interesting, because organizers often attempt to convince disadvantaged people to see the utility of participation for them. But if even higher-income people who are participating are not convinced of this utility, it is hard to see how this would work. It still leaves us, however, with the task of understanding how similar perceptions can result in such divergent behaviour. Why do higher-income people participate in things they think are useless?

There are two streams of thought concerning why people choose not to take part in political activity. The first (sometimes associated with 'stealth democracy') asserts that people want politics to function with the minimum amount of work from their side. They only participate in order to prevent problems (corruption, decisions counter to their interests, etc). Thus, the less people trust politicians, and the unhappier they are, the more likely they are to become politically active. The second stream, generally associated with participatory and deliberative democracy, believes that people want to participate more in politics, but refrain from doing so because they feel frustrated and disempowered by the current mechanisms for participating available to them.[356] What both streams have in common is that they acknowledge that participants are seeking some kind of utility in return for their participation. The first stream posits that as long as the utility occurs without the participant contributing, they will remain happy to ride on the coattails of others and not necessarily take part themselves; whereas the second stream postulates that if people believe that the participation process is fair and effective they will enjoy, rather than dread, participating in it.

The truth is that there are probably both kinds of people in the world and that if politics 'worked better' possibly some people would drop out of participation and others would start. However, as politics is unlikely to reach a state of perfection, it is probable that both of these motivating factors will continue to co-exist in some measure. I think of these streams in a slightly different way as 'optimists' (those who attempt to fight back against a corrupt system (who I believe to typically be the societal 'high achievers')) and 'pessimists' (those who feel the system is too corrupt for this to function (who I believe to more typically be marginalized people)).

That these two groups share convictions about utility, but differ in how they engage with them, is likely a reflection of Maslow's Hierarchy of Needs. Those in a more advantageous position can sometimes afford to participate without assurances of utility because they have enough security to indulge less pressing needs (assuaging their conscience that they tried, getting things off their chest, etc),

356 Michael Neblo, Kevin M. Esterling, Ryan Kennedy, David Lazer and Anand E. Sokhey 'Who Wants to Deliberate and Why?' (15 September 2019) HKS Working Paper No. RWP09–027, 4–8.

and because their life circumstances have led them to believe that sometimes things work out anyway even absent any real evidence that they are going to ('I didn't think I'd get that job, but I threw my hat in the ring and it worked out!'). By contrast, those in a disadvantageous socioeconomic position have little energy to fulfill those secondary needs and are less inclined to believe things will 'work out' absent very convincing evidence that they will ('I fulfilled all of the criteria, but they still didn't take me'). This is not a good state of affairs either way, and the only way to rectify it is to make whatever you are doing obviously and incontrovertibly useful as this will have a positive impact on both groups, both of which experience cynicism and flagging motivation, but deal with it differently. This is important to recognize, because much of the grey literature on this topic focuses on making participation 'fun' and/or about pursuing a nebulous 'good of humanity' under the erroneous understanding that these factors are the decisively motivating ones. Few, if any people want these things – not even the people who already participate.

Finnish participants in the Offroad Traffic Reform consultation gave, as their reasons for participating:

- civic duty (they would have felt guilty for not taking the chance to air their views)
- affecting the law
- to deliberate with and learn from peers.
- to set the record straight about what they thought was false information or wrong (stupid) conclusions, etc.[357]

Although participants may have had fun or learned as part of the process: 'Having fun, passing time, enjoying problem-solving, feeling creative, and advancing one's career were not the driving factors of participation in crowdsourced policy-making.'[358]

The most common motivations people gave for participating in the similar participation on housing law were:

- Solving problems in the housing companies
- Improving the law

---

357 Aitamurto, Landemore and Saldivar Galli, 'Unmasking the Crowd' 10–11 and 18.
358 Aitamurto, Landemore and Saldivar Galli, 'Unmasking the Crowd' 18.

– Learning about the law

Participants tended to have clear ideas about what should be done and how it should be achieved. They were not particularly interested in 'the common good' in the sense many writers mean, but rather in having the law changed to the way they thought was best. Discussion and learning was undertaken in the interests of achieving that goal ('a better law') rather than for its own sake. This does not mean that participants did not enjoy discussion with others and learning, but how much they enjoyed it purely for its own sake was limited.[359] Utility, as always, remained to the fore, with, I believe, the relatively prosperous and the socially disadvantaged differing in how they cope with a lack of utility. Increasing the utility of such participation and making it obvious is thus of paramount importance, in addition to other such steps as improving marketing (more detail below on this). How exactly this should be done, however, depends on the fundamental beliefs one has about democracy, and above all, what democracy is. To understand this fully, we have to take a brief detour into a concept that has recently become entangled with the idea of democracy (and which always resurfaces in some form or other over the years).

3.4 Democracy as Social Justice?

As we saw above, there are two main configurations for society to take: the first is when the poor and middle work together to reduce the power of the rich – democracy. The second is where the rich utilize the poor to reduce the power of the middle – mob rule followed by oligarchy. This is extremely relevant to our considerations here, as it influences how we should conceptualize democratic participation and the question of who participates in relation to social goals. We will use the example of participatory budgeting here, since a great deal has been written on the relationship between PB and social justice. However, the general considerations can be applied to any form of participation.

3.4.1 Accountability, the Scrutinizing Middle and Class Interests

As we saw earlier, participatory budgeting was initially adopted in Brazil by the PT, a left-wing party that advocated 'inverting priorities', that is realigning public pol-

---

359 Aitamurto and Saldivar, 'Motivating Participation in Crowdsourced Policymaking' 15.

icy in areas like healthcare and education to favour the poor.[360] This kind of 'priority inversion' has been standard policy in most Western nations since WWII, where robust social services and tax-funded healthcare and education (although now waning) have disproportionately benefitted the poor and have worked to prevent the levels of poverty common in Brazil. By Western standards, such a goal is thus not necessarily that radical. Furthermore, despite its commitment to the least affluent members of society, the PT sought to utilize PB to engage the broader public in policy-making and avoid a situation where participatory events were composed solely of their own party supporters. The PT also neither fully embraced 'the orthodox Marxist-Leninist strategies of taking advantage of democratic procedures to undermine "bourgeois democracy" from within',[361] nor came to view democracy as having mere 'tactical utility', i.e. being a means to achieving a predetermined end.[362]

Many Western activists, however, have taken a significantly more radical and partisan approach to PB in specific and political participation in general. This approach is often self-contradictory and poorly expressed, but there is a certain strand of rather anti-democratic thought that continuously, if in somewhat scrambled fashion, continues to resurface throughout it, and which we will seek to come to grips with here, because it leads a lot of people astray in implementation and turns what is supposed to be democracy into something else entirely. It's a perfect example of mangling different goals together and confusing democracy with these separate issues (which, as we saw in Chapter 1, should always be avoided).

In this activist view, the middle class dominates conventional political participation, in the sense that 'white, middle and upper class voters' are 'far more likely to vote' in elections and thus enjoy 'an outsized influence in their neighbourhood'.[363] Those who are not members of 'the popular classes' are sometimes referred to as 'the dominant classes' in the literature,[364] and regarded by some as inherently conservative and repressive. As we saw above, some have even gone so far as to discourage public officials from communicating about opportunities for democratic participation in ways that would engage, 'a disproportionately white, highly-educated, and high income group', because these are not the voices innovations like PB were 'meant to raise up'.[365] Because they view the middle class as the prime

360 Nylen, 'The Making of a Loyal Opposition' 131–132.
361 Nylen, 'The Making of a Loyal Opposition' 127.
362 Nylen, 'The Making of a Loyal Opposition' 130.
363 Clark, 'Is Participatory Budgeting Real Democracy?'
364 Heloise Nez, 'Les budgets participatifs européens peinent à lutter contre la ségrégation' (2013) 74 Mouvements 123, 123 and 128.
365 Ribble, 'PBNYC: The Challenges and Opportunities of Scale'.

driver and beneficiary of traditional politics, some of these 'democracy' activists believe that efforts should be made to reserve or protect *alternative* modes of participation for the class *they* claim to represent (marginalized people, which can also include people who do not have the right to vote because they are too young or are non-citizens). Thus, the primary point of PB (and other instruments of participatory democracy) is not to provide an *additional* means to participate for *all* citizens (since they believe that in this scenario of free participation some demographic groups would inevitably participate more than others), but rather an *alternative* means for *some* citizens to pursue pre-determined goals not met under the conventional system, such as 'more equitable spending'[366] helpfully defined as spending that is 'fair and unbiased'.[367] Other, not necessarily widely-shared, 'social justice' goals are often espoused in loose connection with democratic participation, such as 'the critical transformative deconstruction of patriarchy'[368] 'prison abolition',[369] including undocumented immigrants in political participation, incorporating critical race theory into its design,[370] preventing commercialized urban renewal, and advancing LGBTQ+ interests. In the United States, these values and goals tend to match up with the current policy of the urban progressive wing of the Democratic Party, but not necessarily with society as a whole.

This points up the basic fact that, as we saw earlier, *what* is equitable and *what* is 'socially just' are exactly the things that are up for debate in a democracy. When organizers pre-decide the outcome and thus admit that participation has only been enabled as a means of reaching a certain goal, one robs *all* participants of their agency and makes participation itself pointless (again, see Chapter 1 on this point).

---

366 Hagelskamp et al., 'Shifting Priorities' 192–193; one of the researchers defined 'more equitable spending' as 'the ultimate goal of PB' ('New Research on Participatory Budgeting Highlights Community Priorities in Public Spending' (*NYU*, 22 July 2020) <https://www.nyu.edu/about/news-publications/news/2020/july/new-research-on-participatory-budgeting-highlights-community-pri.html> accessed 17 January 2023); Pape and Lerner, 'Budgeting for Equity' 2–3.

367 *PB NYC Rulebook* (New York City Council) 4 and 18 <https://www.participatorybudgeting.org/wp-content/uploads/2016/10/PBNYC2016_2017-Rulebook_PBP.pdf>.

368 Alessio Surian, 'Foreword: Power and Soft Policies' in Brahimllari, *Multi-Layered Participatory Budgeting* 13.

369 Carolin Hagelskamp, Celina Su, Karla Valverde Viesca and Tarson Nuñez, 'Organizing a Transnational Solidarity for Social Change through Participatory Practices: The Case of People Powered – Global Hub for Participatory Democracy' (2021) American Journal of Community Psychology 294, 295.

370 Celina Su, 'Beyond Inclusion: Critical Race Theory and Participatory Budgeting' (2017) CUNY Graduate Center.

If the prime goal at hand is to reverse inequities and increase socioeconomic equality (if that political decision for a particular interpretation of 'social justice' has *already* been made, in other words), then the PT in Brazil did the right thing upon ascending to national power in 2002 – it neglected its previous star policy of PB (which, as we will see, decayed somewhat as a result) in favour of simply mandating the outcomes the party had already decided it wanted and which it gained the right to impose by virtue of winning the election. While an imperfect method of measuring popular will, this at least confers some legitimacy and, crucially, accountability for decisions made.

We have to ask ourselves: if activists are determined to achieve social justice goals, why do they choose to do so via highly controlled forms of participatory democracy (both online and offline)? In particular, why are they so insistent on determining who should and should not participate? The answers to these questions are far from innocent and highly detrimental to democracy, which is, as we saw above, largely a form of middle-class government.

The need to achieve pre-determined goals via an ostensible 'democracy' rather than simply impose the policy one has already decided upon only makes sense in one particular case – where one lacks the legal right to make such an imposition, but is determined to do it anyway. There is a group of people that strongly supports 'social justice' goals (on some level), and yet lacks the legal standing to impose them on society, because they have failed to win the right to do so (e.g. via election). This group is the very wealthy – vanishingly small in numbers, yet rich in...well, riches. And they have used these riches to insert themselves into social justice movements and 'democracy', conflating in the process these two very different things.

For example, People Powered (which co-directs PB in NYC) receives funding from the William and Flora Hewlett Foundation and One Project,[371] as well as from the Ford Foundation, the National Endowment for Democracy, Porticus (founded by the Brenninkmeijer family (banking and investment managers)) and the American Council of Learned Societies[372] (which in turn receives millions from wealthy individuals and foundations including over $5 million each from the Carnegie Corporation of New York, the Robert H.N. Ho Foundation, the Henry Luce Foundation, and the Andrew W. Mellon Foundation). The Brenninkmeijer's current

---

371 'Funding' (*People Powered*) <https://www.peoplepowered.org/funding> accessed 17 January 2023.

372 'Partners: Funders' (*People Powered*) <https://www.peoplepowered.org/about/partners> accessed 17 January 2023.

holdings (COFRA) are located in Switzerland.[373] One Project has received funding from Justin Rosenstein, who founded tech company Asana together with Dustin Moskovitz,[374] as well as by an organization called Monster Growth Ventures. A filing for a Monster Growth Ventures LLC in Delaware, indicates its directors as another company called 'Paracorp', but an SEC document from 2013 lists its co-manager as Dustin Moskovitz together with holdings of millions of Facebook shares (Moskovitz's former workplace).[375]

Such foundations also fund 'research' into democracy.

Out of the four authors of one article analysing American PB, for example, three of them were affiliated with Public Agenda: Carolin Hagelskamp (Senior Fellow); Rebecca Silliman (Senior Research Associate); and David Schleifer (Vice President and Director of Research). According to Public Agenda (which is itself a 'member' of People Powered), its recent supporters include most of the wealthiest donors in the USA, some of whom also directly fund People Powered (meaning both 'researchers' and the project they are 'researching' are partly funded by the same entities). These include Democracy Fund (funded by Pierre Omidyar) the Bill and Melinda Gates Foundation, the William and Flora Hewlett Foundation (also directly funding NYCPB/People Powered), the National Endowment for Democracy (which also funds People Powered), the Kresge Foundation and the Toronto Dominion Charitable Foundation.[376] Together, these foundations hold assets of well over $11 billion and represent some of the richest entities and people in the entire world. While they may want to improve the lives of the poorest, they have no reason to be interested in a society that gives decision-making power to the majority – a very different thing. The fourth author of the aforementioned article, Erin B. Godfrey, was previously at the Urban Institute, which in 2021 received over a million dollars each from Wells Fargo, the Bill and Melinda Gates Founda-

---

373 'Working, Investing and Giving Together' (*COFRA Holding*) <https://www.cofraholding.com/en/family/> accessed 17 January 2023.

374 Rosenstein also lists himself as a co-founder of One Project on his LinkedIn Profile, <https://www.linkedin.com/in/justinrosenstein/> accessed 25 February 2023.

375 OneProject.org, Form 990-PF (2015) available at 'Non-Profit Explorer' (*ProPublica*) <https://projects.propublica.org/nonprofits/display_990/463259572/12_2017_prefixes_45-46%2F463259572_201512_990PF_2017120715013752> accessed 25 March 2023; OneProject.org, Form 990-PF (2019) available at 'Non-Profit Explorer' (*ProPublica*) <https://projects.propublica.org/nonprofits/organizations/463259572/202043219349102909/full> accessed 25 March 2023; Open Corporates <https://opencorporates.com/companies/us_de/4603076>; Document SG 13/A, United States Securities and Exchange Commission <https://www.sec.gov/Archives/edgar/data/1326801/000119312514040883/d672846dsc13ga.htm> accessed 25 February 2023.

376 'Our Institutional Supporters' (*Public Agenda*) <https://www.publicagenda.org/about/our-funders/> accessed 17 January 2023.

tion, JP Morgan Chase and the Mastercard Impact Fund.[377] Other research has also been funded by Democracy Fund.[378]

The immense gap in resources between these funders and even the 'average' millionaire, let alone middle-class person, is extreme (see Fig. 3.10).

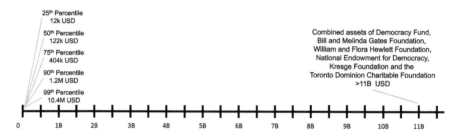

Fig. 3.10: Wealth Comparison – General Population vs. Selected Funds & Foundations

Such funding patterns have begun to influence a very large slice of the non-profit space, and this influence is likely the reason that so much writing on democracy has recently taken a peculiarly antagonistic view towards the middle class, painting Finnish kindergarten teachers as a 'civic elite' being amplified in consultations,[379] building a monument to slaves in Portugal as merely helping those

---

377 'Annual Report 2021' (*Urban Institute*) <https://www.urban.org/sites/default/files/2022-10/2021%20Financial%20Report.pdf>.

378 e.g. Hagelskamp, 'Shifting Priorities' was funded by Democracy Fund, while PB researchers Wampler, McNulty and Touchton thanked numerous supporters in a recent book (*Participatory Budgeting in Global Perspective*), including the Hewlett Packard Foundation and Reboot, which is in turn sponsored by Harmony Labs, whose 'collaborative' advisors include representatives from Democracy Fund, YouTube, The Solutions Journalism Network, VoteRunLead, Mozilla and Future Majority, an organization strongly affiliated with Democratic Party donors ((Reboot Democracy) <https://www.rebootdem.com/> accessed 22 February 2023; 'People' (*Harmony Labs*) <https://www.harmonylabs.org/people> accessed 22 February 2023; Maggie Severns, 'Top Dem Strategists Launch Secret Money Group to Rebrand Party' *Politico* (29 April 2019) <https://www.politico.com/story/2019/04/29/democrats-money-future-majority-1291388>. Harmony Labs is funded by the Bill and Melinda Gates Foundation, Open Society Foundations and Google (among others) and has the mission of optimizing the media to benefit people ('Mission' (*Harmony Labs*) <https://www.harmonylabs.org/mission> accessed 22 February 2023) and 'increasing the efficacy of narrative change work' ('Projects' (*Harmony Labs*) <https://www.harmonylabs.org/projects> accessed 22 February 2023)).

379 Monika Mokre and Tamara Ehs, 'If no Vote, at Least Voice? The Potential and Limits of Deliberative Procedures for the Creation of a More Inclusive Democracy' (2021) 34(5) Innovation: The European Journal of Social Science Research.

'who already have a seat at the table',[380] creating parks in Paris slums as 'gentrification',[381] and any one white, middle-class or who is a 'homeowner' as a 'usual suspect' and part of the group of people 'with the most power' in society who will inevitably 'dominant' other more 'marginalized' people.[382] After all, someone must be to blame for inequality, and it cannot be high-minded funders with their billions in assets and, in some cases, artfully avoided taxes (which have, of course, been sucked out of the very social programmes that have a proven track record of reducing inequality).

While not everyone is funded by these entities,[383] their influence is such that it has become necessary to pay lip-service to these trendy views or risk accusations of bigotry. On the flip-side making remarks about the alleged iron-fisted power of quite ordinary people under the current electoral-representative system is not questioned, although it deserves to be.

It is likely due to its close association with large funders that the social justice theory of class warfare which pits the middle class against the poor so often edits out the very demographic that socialist political thought traditionally considered to be of great concern: the very wealthy. This omission is all the more noteworthy when one considers that the very wealthy are currently enjoying an enormous resurgence of both wealth and power in the Western world, and that their existence thus represents a greater social injustice than at any time since the Great Depression. Indeed, New York City (home of much of the PB rhetoric in the USA) may be as unequal today as Brazil was in the 1980s.[384] To top things off, a considerable proportion of mainstream opinion is united behind the idea that the extremely wealthy exert undue influence over representative democracy today,[385] thanks to

---

380 Giovanna Coi and Aitor Hernandez-Morales, 'Living Cities: European Cities' Big Cash Handover' *Politico* (21 April 2022) <https://www.politico.eu/article/europe-big-city-cash-handover/>.

381 Brahimllari, *Multi-layered Participatory Budgeting.*

382 Josh Lerner and Donata Secondo, 'By the People, For the People: Participatory Budgeting from the Bottom Up in North America' (2012) 8(2) Journal of Public Deliberation, Article 2, 6.

383 I have carefully noted the chains I have investigated.

384 Edward L. Glaeser, Matt Resseger and Kristina Tobio, 'Urban Inequality' WP 2008 10 (Harvard Kennedy School, Taubman Center for State and Local Government) <https://www.hks.harvard.edu/sites/default/files/centers/taubman/files/glaeser_08_inequality.pdf>.

385 Martin Gilens and Benjamin I. Page, 'Testing Theories of American Politics: Elites, Interest Groups and Average Citizens' (2014) 12(3) Perspectives on Politics 564–581; Paul Krugman, 'Why Do the Rich have so much Power?' *New York Times* (1 July 2020).

the clever exploitation of minor distortions in the electoral process,[386] leaving almost no room for the average person to influence political decisions.

Instead of focusing on these obvious issues, the social justice view of democracy has identified the problem, but not the cause, editing the world to consist solely of the poor and their middle-class oppressors who need to be contained under controlled forms of participation (that determine both who should participate and what conclusions they come to). The prime movers behind these deterministic 'social justice' views of democracy (and against emancipatory versions of democracy) are, as we have seen, extremely wealthy foundations (non-humans). *They* are the entities who should have no place in democracy – not the middle class.

The view of 'democracy' as highly circumscribed participation directed at achieving pre-determined goals and with a targeted mobilization of non-voters, young people (sometimes too young to vote) and the impoverished cuts out a very important element of democracy: the scrutinizing middle. As we saw in Chapter 1, democracy is not about feeling good, engagement or generating ideas, it is about *scrutiny*. And effective scrutiny requires high information, reasonably secure participants: the middle class.

That the middle class is essential to democracy is a basic truth that has been recognized since Aristotle's time. Indeed, there can be no democracy that does not have the middle class as its backbone. Middle class participants often attempt to find flaws in new policy before they adopt it, and precisely because they have some resources to fall back on, they are harder to influence and their objections cannot be easily brushed aside. In particular, they are rarely grateful for what they regard as basic, taxpayer-funded services (this lack of gratitude has been recast as 'privilege'). By contrast, the very poor are the most susceptible to vote-buying and clientelism[387] – this is, after all, what being 'vulnerable' means. The vulnerable, per definition, rarely have the resources to stand up for themselves and question authority,[388] and having nothing, even small gifts can provoke their gratitude. In developing countries this can reach the extremes of vote-buying in ex-

386 Roslyn Fuller, *Beasts and Gods: How Democracy Changed Its Meaning and Lost Its Purpose* (Zed/Bloomsbury 2015).

387 Nylen, 'The Making of a Loyal Opposition' 133.

388 Nick Pearce, 'Juncture Interview: Bonnie Honig' *IPPR* (6 March 2013) <https://www.ippr.org/juncture/juncture-interview-bonnie-honig>.

change for small amounts of food,[389] but in richer nations, the relationship is simply less flagrant – as we saw in regards to clientelist behaviour in Chicago and New York.

This, of course, doesn't mean that one should ignore poor people or fail to support them. They do need to be included – it's just not in our interests to *exclude* others or view their participation as a negative (as some advocate) to do so. We will only succeed in keeping our democracy if the poor and middle classes work together and the poor increasingly become middle class, rather than the other way around. As we saw on the diagram above (Fig. 3.4), the vast majority of people from the poor to the upper-middle-class are fairly close together on the wealth distribution scale – at least compared to the wealthy. Their interests are thus more aligned – they must all pay tax, they must work to sustain their standard of living, and they all depend at some point in their lives on social services provided by the State or mass insurance schemes. It is between the upper-middle-class and very wealthy that a dis-alignment occurs on these basic life conditions. By seeking to exclude the middle from participation or denigrating them as 'the usual suspects' the very wealthy evade scrutiny of their actions and thus accountability. Poor people will never be helped by disenfranchising middle-class people. This can only help the rich, as it removes their strongest class enemy.

Any form of stable and free government, and we know this from Montesquieu, depends on checks and balances to function.[390] This does not mean that in a democracy every citizen must be continuously involved in every single decision – instead it means having the institutions that enable citizens to check up on the responsible person or entity's work, to hold them accountable for that work, and (in a democracy) ensure that it aligns with the democratically decided upon action. This was the thought behind the separation of powers: the idea that the executive, legislative and judicative should act as a check on each other. Checks and balances also existed in ancient democracy – people who served as officials in Athens were subjected to intense scrutiny in all of their actions and punished harshly for wrongdoing and mistakes. Unfortunately, the importance of checks and balances and **appropriate boundaries** has gone under today in a craze for 'collaboration', which erases accountability for choices. This is why the scrutinizing functions of the relatively well-resourced and educated have come to be so under-appreciated.

---

389 Interview Patricia Namakula, 'Democracy and Digitalization: A Ugandan Perspective' (*Solonian Democracy Institute*, 16 September 2022) <https://www.solonian-institute.com/post/digital-democracy-a-ugandan-perspective>.
390 Charles Montesquieu, *The Spirit of Laws, Volume 1* (Thomas Nugent tr, first published 1748/1752, Batoche Books 2001) Book XI, Ch. VI.

That such people often disproportionately participate (as we saw in the statistics above) is not necessarily a bad thing, since they are often demanding and full of energy with interests that are still largely aligned to those less affluent. When 'inclusivity' efforts start to focus on excluding such people on the grounds that they are already 'privileged' it is really just the government trying to pick its own boss, hopefully a less-informed, less-confident, more time-pressed boss, rather than the one who is demanding, informed, full of energy and likely to determine the true causes of inequality. Social justice activists' dismay with middle-class participation in democracy, including those methods of democracy made possible by digital technology, only serves to increase that injustice by inaccurately attributing its cause to the middle class and thus allowing the true perpetrators to continue their behaviour.

For example, PB that is deemed insufficiently social justice-oriented has sometimes been blamed for 'gentrification'. The idea is that high house prices are caused by middle-class people moving into low-income neighbourhoods and voting for projects such as parks. This, it is conjectured, drives up property prices, in turn leading to landlords raising rents and evicting lower-income people. Those so evicted are replaced by more higher-income people who vote for yet more frills, making the neighbourhood nicer yet, and touching off an apparently vicious cycle of neighbourhood improvement. In this manner, even if money is ringfenced for low-income neighbourhoods, it may be 'sucked up' by these pockets of higher-income gentrifiers who vote in larger numbers. Thus, the money does not go to the benefit of its intended recipients and something should be done to prevent the middle class from dominating such participation.[391]

The evidence for such a scenario is at this point inconclusive,[392] but anecdotally we don't necessarily see higher income (but still middle class) participants selfishly voting for ornamental things. In 2016, the project that garnered the most votes in Paris PB was 'Solidarity with the Homeless',[393] while the disproportionately higher-income participants in the Lethbridge CIP voted to expand a public library, but against an expensive performing arts venue. The affluent middle in other words, chose to put free books above 'the theatre' – something that will disproportionately benefit the disadvantaged.

However, quite beyond the fact that there isn't grave interest disalignment between the poor and middle, the sums of money involved in PB (and other forms of democracy) cannot possibly be having an impact on big-ticket economic issues like

---

391 Brahimllari, *Multi-layered Participatory Budgeting*; Nez, 'Les budgets participatifs'; Coi and Hernandez-Morales, 'Living Cities'.
392 Brahimllari, *Multi-layered Participatory Budgeting*.
393 Surian, 'Foreword' to *Multi-Layered Participatory Budgeting* 10.

the international housing market. The housing bubble is caused by a lack of financial and building regulation (for example, allowing practices like blind-bidding on
houses, interest-only mortgages, and corporate ownership of entire housing estates
at preferential tax rates), extremely low interest rates and the excessive concentra-
tion of jobs, as well as extremely high internal and external migration into a few
large metropolises. None of these things were *caused* by PB and thus they can't be
fixed by doing PB better. Putting a park somewhere is neither here nor there when
people are manipulating the LIBOR rate and getting away with it. The focus on
mortgage-holders and urban parks obscures the cause of much of the impoverish-
ment and inequality in society today – the super-wealthy and their extremely
short-sighted economic policies.

One can, of course, pursue social justice, or any other aims, *within* a democracy, but it is important not to confuse this *with* democracy. This is even more
of an issue when 'social justice' views itself in opposition to the middle class
and erases those issues caused by immense wealth discrepancies (such as the
housing crisis). When this happens, almost any method used for participation
slides down the measurement scales we outlined in Chapter 1 and becomes a
kind of manipulation or therapy in which participants are 'guided' into giving
their assent to the actions organizers have already determined they should take.

In summary, PB as a way to counteract middle-class participation in elections
would make sense if middle-class participation in elections was the source of poor
people's problems. Unfortunately, no one five hundred years from now is going to
write a history of our time as one where the middle class really peeled away from
the poor in terms of material well-being. This is the age of the rise of the oligarchs,
in which the power of the middle class has greatly diminished. 'Social justice warriors' who view the middle and poor in opposition to each other are doing nothing
more than helping the oligarchs finish off the middle class, and when they finally
achieve that democracy will cease to exist and instead groups will be handed their
'equitable' due as determined by those running the system.

I have devoted such a large segment of this book to dealing with this somewhat
faddish, esoteric view, because these theories of democratic participation from
the marginalized are often foisted onto organizers by generously-funded NGOs.
These theories are often presented as scientific expertise, when they are in reality
deeply flawed, anti-democratic foibles that will inevitably produce the *opposite* results of what they claim to want. If anything, these attitudes are preventing digital
technology from unfolding its true emancipatory potential for democracy and society in general.

The obsession with the particular, not at this point widely shared, values of 'social justice' is also misguided precisely because it fails to comprehend the long-term impacts digitalization will have on politics. According to Amara's Law, formulated by American futurist Roy Amara, we overestimate the impact that technology will have in the short term and underestimate the changes it will bring in the long term. Three examples from the past illustrate this concept: the automobile, voting in elections and the printing press.

Early adopters of automobiles were often wealthy individuals who employed chauffeurs to drive and maintain their vehicles. It took time for one entrepreneur, Henry Ford, to figure out how to mass produce his prime product – the Model T – to the point where it became affordable for one of his own assembly line workers.

Cars thus started as the preserve of very wealthy people and even with the advent of Ford, the main market for drivers was still men. Pre-1920 fewer than 20% of drivers in the United States were women, and this became a lifelong difference: in 1969 only 20% of women who had reached driving age before 1916 held a drivers' licence, as opposed to 62% of men of the same age.[394] Nonetheless, cars allowed women who did take up driving to travel independently, and some Black Americans credit owning a car with allowing them to avoid the worst instances of racism they would otherwise be subjected to when using public transit.[395] Civil rights organizers used a car pool system to sustain the bus boycott in Montgomery Alabama, and Black Americans were *disproportionately* employed in the high-paying auto industry.[396] However, then as today, Black American households are more likely to not have a car than white households (18% vs 6%).[397]

Things progressed similarly with voting in elections. In the United States, women did not vote in the same numbers as men did for decades after they were given the right to do so. It is estimated that one-third of eligible women voted in American elections in 1920 compared to two-thirds of men. By 1960,

394 Stephen J. Dubner, 'Mothers and the Model T' (*Freakonomics*, 4 December 2009) <https://freakonomics.com/2009/12/mothers-and-the-model-t/>.

395 Jay Driskell, 'An Atlas of Self-Reliance: The Negro Motorists' Green Book [1937–1964]' (*National Museum of American History, Behring Center*, 30 July 2015) <https://americanhistory.si.edu/blog/negro-motorists-green-book>.

396 Larry Copeland, 'Blacks Feel Auto Industry's Pain: It was Road to Middle Class' *USA Today/ABC News* (21 January 2009) <https://abcnews.go.com/Business/story?id=6694808&page=1>.

397 'Car Access' (*National Equity Atlas*) <https://nationalequityatlas.org/indicators/Car_access#/>, although it should be noted that Black Americans are less likely to live in very rural areas where cars are more necessary ('Racial and Ethnic Minorities, Economic Research Service' (*US Department of Agriculture*, 13 October 2020) <https://www.ers.usda.gov/data-products/chart-gallery/gallery/chart-detail/?chartId=99538)>.

still only about 70 % of women were voting compared to 80 % of men.[398] Only starting in 1980, did women vote in elections in equal numbers to men in the United States.[399] Women have also been found to participate less often in Swiss referendums, likely because some of them obtained the right to vote in the 1970s and had thus already developed non-voting habits. As researchers noted, ironically, enfranchising people can sometimes lead to lower turnout rates in the short-term, as it can take several decades for behaviour to fully adjust to the new circumstances.[400]

We have seen women becoming more emancipated over time, as their political participation is normalized and advances are made in e.g. changing related laws. But we have not seen it happen overnight, and it is hard to see how success would have occurred if we had, for example, prevented men from voting during the time it took for women's voting patterns to equalize with theirs.

Finally, and most relevantly here, the printing press is often credited as one of the most important inventions in human history. The printing press (moveable type print) was invented around 1440 by Johannes von Gutenberg who died 28 years later in 1468.

By 1480, Gutenberg's invention had spread rapidly around Europe, but its most famous and impactful user, Martin Luther, would only be *born* in 1483. During his lifetime, approximately one-third of *all* books printed in Europe were authored by Martin Luther.[401] Thanks to Luther's industriousness, by the time he *died* in 1546 the Reformation was just getting under way. This would (eventually) break the absolute power of the Catholic Church, paving the way for more scientific, rational inquiry, the French Encyclopédistes and political thinkers who disseminated knowledge, often via printed pamphlets, the advent of mass literacy (which did not occur until the 19th century in Europe and still hasn't occurred in parts of the world today), new social theories, such as socialism, representative government, and rights for women (all fought out and propagated via print), mass education (enabled by print), and eventually new inventions like television and radio

---

398 Jennifer M Piscopo, 'How Women Vote: Separating Myth from Reality' (*Smithsonian Magazine*, 6 October 2020) <https://www.smithsonianmag.com/history/how-have-women-voted-suffrage-180975979/>.

399 Amelia Thomson-DeVeaux and Meredith Conroy, 'Women won the Right to Vote 100 Years Ago. They Didn't Start Voting Differently from Men until 1980' (*FiveThirtyEight*, 19 August 2020) <https://fivethirtyeight.com/features/women-won-the-right-to-vote-100-years-ago-they-didnt-start-voting-differently-from-men-until-1980/>.

400 Uwe Serdült, 'Switzerland' in Matt Qvortrup (ed), *Referendums Around the World* (Palgrave Macmillan 2018) 87, 95.

401 Nicholas Davis, 'This is What Martin Luther Tells Us About Today's Technological Disruption' (*World Economic Forum*, 31 October 2017), citing Andrew Pettegree <https://www.weforum.org/agenda/2017/10/what-we-can-learn-from-martin-luther-about-todays-technological-disruption/>.

(based on the work of Michael Faraday, a man born into relative poverty, and unlikely to have been recognized before the Enlightenment). The abolition of slavery was primarily championed by Protestant sects, such as the Quakers, as well as African-American Protestant churches. In this context, teaching slaves and freed slaves to read was often viewed as an important component of full emancipation. The free-flow of science, rationalism, and independent learning made possible by the printing press, led to antibiotics, central heating and, one day, the invention of digital technology.

However, the march of history was not all one way. Before the printing press, communication was often verbal, so we could argue that a switch to writing placed blind people and, of course, illiterate people at a disadvantage. Oral historians and entertainers as well as the monks who created beautiful illuminated manuscripts were put out of work. Braille was not invented until close to 400 years after the invention of the printing press. Female literacy rates were also historically much lower than male literacy rates – in England about 5–30% for much of the pre-modern period, whereas for men they were about 40–70% (depending on location).[402] The printing press also enabled the rise of Protestantism which, together with the backlash, provoked hundreds of years of war in Europe and the deaths of millions of people.

In the long run, of course, the effects of the printing press have been more equalizing than un-equalizing. Thanks to modern science enabled by this exchange of knowledge, fewer people go blind (e. g. from cataracts or early childhood illness), and those who do benefit from a far higher of standard of living than in the past, just as women have benefitted from reliable birth control, also enabled by science, enabled by literacy.

The emancipatory power of digital technology will unfold, just as the potential of the printing press unfolded. To name just a few minor examples, in a recent survey large majorities across all African nations and India said the Covid pandemic would have been much worse without the internet (when we include 'somewhat worse' it was about three-quarters of people); in Colombia and Indonesia 47% and 30% respectively said living through lockdown would have been 'much worse' without the internet.[403] Automatic translation can also now help people participate despite language barriers. This gives people independence, saves money and may help to preserve lesser-spoken languages. Automatic translation

---

402 Max Roser 'Literacy Rate in England and the UK since 1580' (*Our World in Data*) <https://ourworldindata.org/literacy#historical-change-in-literacy> accessed 25 February 2023.
403 Teddy Woodhouse, 'Advancing Meaningful Connectivity: Towards Active and Participatory Digital Societies' (*Alliance for Affordable Internet*, 2022) <https://a4ai.org/wp-content/uploads/2022/02/FullreportFINAL.pdf>.

also helps gather input from these languages, broadening the impact of work published in them. Quite apart from this, of course, technology has enabled us to do so much more, so much cheaper. We can send a book, or a thousand books, around the world in an instant, we can diagnose and research health issues with greater accuracy, we can likely go to Mars and mine asteroids, and get an instant alarm if our elderly relatives experience a fall. Although all changes will not be beneficial, there is no way to short-cut this process and to instantly reduce inequalities between groups to zero. Even those people who have been willing to kill millions to achieve this goal (for example, Pol Pot or the Russian Bolsheviks) have never yet succeeded.

3.4.2 How to Help

As the above indicates it is very important to distinguish between

a) reaching out to under-represented demographics and encouraging them to get involved, as well as creating a conducive atmosphere for that involvement (e.g. preventing bullying, accommodating attendance, providing support such as sign-language translation, etc.) and
b) viewing some groups of participants as 'less worthy', and refusing to engage in ways that may be beneficial to them or attract them to participate. This attempts to close off democracy from 'inside enemies', in this case other people, which is also a form, in addition to all of the other problems it generates, of sabotage and over-alignment as discussed in our original principles.

Fortunately, there are many things we can do to encourage participation. Some of these are simultaneously pursued by activists and academics who also seemingly ascribe to more divisive and exclusionary tactics; others are more radical, but also more likely to have salutary results, including for the most vulnerable.

3.4.2.1 Communicating about the Opportunity to Participate

As we saw, one of the biggest single reasons people give for failing to take part in political participation outside of elections is that they were unaware of the opportunity in question. This is often due to poor communication on the part of organizers. Even researchers have reported great difficulty in getting clear time schedules for democratic opportunities from authorities.[404] This is particularly

---

404 Williams and Waisanen, *Real Money, Real Power?* 44–47

important, because the most vulnerable people are the most likely to give up if it is a struggle to pin down the time, place or other details of participation, whereas the more demanding members of society find it easier to deal with such set-backs. Thus, when communication is poor it stands to reason that this will disproportionately exclude the disadvantaged.

The level of communication required to achieve adequate awareness is *much* higher than many believe, and is one of the main expenses of 'democracy'. Most civil servants who have successfully implemented elements of digital democracy state that they went to a great effort to publicize it both online and offline. Some have a communications plan for every consultation with a specific person dedicated to promoting it, and able to use various channels to achieve this, e.g. press releases, corporate communication, advertising on the local transport network, etc. Organizers have also at times used QR codes that people can scan to participate.[405] An Icelandic organizer described the four-to-six weeks he spends promoting PB to the public as very challenging as he tours schools, rest homes and other institutes to make people aware of it. This marathon of informative events is necessary, despite the fact that most citizens are already aware of participatory budgeting in general, and his work consists primarily of reminding everyone when it starts and encouraging them to participate.[406]

The level of effort required to attain awareness is not surprising when one considers the level of media coverage surrounding electoral politics. Even outside of elections, major politicians feature on the news, political programmes and in newspapers every single day. When an election is called, this coverage increases, with formal government information, official debates (both national and on constituency level), posters, the publication of policy programmes, issuing pamphlets, and canvassing potential voters both in public places and on doorsteps. In some countries, like the United States, this is supplemented by rallies, direct phone calls and substantial media advertisement. Depending on the country and election, millions to billions of dollars are spent, and while much of it is spent by campaigns for certain parties or candidates, all of it gets the message out that an election is happening, along with details about where, when and why each person should vote. In some nations, people even go door-to-door registering voters. In others, like Australia, voting is compulsory. Despite all of this, people tend to participate at levels between 60–80% – far from universal.

As long as resources are insufficient to achieve an adequate level of marketing, organizers will always be fighting a losing battle on this point. However,

---

405 Interviews (2022).
406 Interview Eiríkur Búi Halldórsson.

there are things one can do to try to keep the process as fair and efficient as possible, even in the face of insufficient resources:

- hold **information** events **targeted** to various communities[407]
- ensure that **subject matter** of interest to a variety of groups is put forward for democratic decision-making.[408] Some commenters believe that more marginalized people would participate in PB if it included funding for ongoing expense items (e.g. staff, ongoing programmes), rather than capital investment projects.[409] Some districts in NYC do now allow this,[410] as did Tower Hamlets.[411]
- use public stands to raise awareness and encourage people to vote, e.g. at subway stations[412] or, as in Paris, using **mobile ballot boxes** which can be moved around the city with bicycles[413]
- include information in **official communications** (for example, online voters in Markham overwhelmingly reported hearing about online voting from the voter information package[414] while Lisbon PB displays the projects up for vote in their Citizen Shops (public facing stores that people visit to complete public business))
- send **reminders** (the Danish Society of Engineers has held elections for its Board of Representatives using Assembly Voting since 2007. Despite this long use, organizers send an email letting its 100,000 voting members know that voting has opened, followed by three reminders plus an SMS text with a direct link)[415]
- distribute **leaflets and fliers** with information on the process
- raise awareness through **door-to-door** visits
- include **various languages** in informational activities wherever possible (including door-to-door visits)
- **subsidize** the financial **costs of participation** (in NYC, transportation, food and childcare is sometimes provided for people attending PB meetings)

---

407 Ribble, 'PBNYC: The Challenges and Opportunities of Scale'.
408 Allegretti, 'Common Patterns'.
409 Hagelskamp et al., 'Shifting Priorities' 195.
410 *PBNYC Rulebook* 18.
411 Johnson, 'Engaging Democracy' 106.
412 Vevea, 'What Would You Do With A Million Dollars?'.
413 Brahimllari, *Multi-layered Participatory Budgeting* 109 and 130.
414 Goodman, 'Online Voting in the City of Markham' 11.
415 'How the Danish Society of Engineers Navigates Complex Elections with Assembly Voting' (*Assembly Voting*, 20 May 2022) <https://assemblyvoting.com/customer-stories/how-the-danish-society-of-engineers-navigates-complex-elections-with-assembly-voting/>.

– **use social media** (in 2022, Iceland reported that half of its PB page views were directed from Facebook, facilitated by the fact that many people share their ideas and proposals on the social media site. A Canadian climate budgeting exercise reported that its advertisements on Instagram were the most successful at attracting visitors to the site, followed by Facebook.)

It should, however, be noted that many organizers do many of these things, yet still have fairly low participation numbers in terms of the percentage of the population. This is sometimes simply because it takes time to grow new habits. It took until 2016 (5 years) for PB in Iceland to reach more than 20,000 unique visitors, which doubled to 40,000 in 2019, before increasing to well over 60,000 in 2020.[416] However, we can also do things that are much more radical in terms of equalizing participation *without compromising democratic principles.*

3.4.2.2 Pay for Participation

Something truly advantageous for the economically disadvantaged is to compensate everyone for the time they spend participating in politics. In fact, this compensation could even take the form of high-speed internet access. This would have the salutary effect of erasing any residual digital divide issues (as well as preventing such a divide from arising in the future). Paying participants in internet access is not lucrative enough to attract many people of a middle-class background and up to participate, and possibly not enough to motivate less affluent people to participate *just* for this payment. But it does decrease this barrier to participation, contribute to economic equalization and provide the least affluent with a tool with which they can do many other things to improve their lives. It should be noted that compensation for time spent participating is different than paying people for the *level* of their engagement, e.g. the number of comments they make, etc. and that it is important to bear this differentiation in mind. It may sound like an odd idea, but the ancient Athenians actually did something similar, paying people a small amount of money for every (in their case generally day-long) session they attended. This allowed the population, which had a high rate of self-employment, to take time away from work to participate, as it reduced their losses for that day.

3.4.2.3 Ringfence

While foundations might fund non-profits that execute 'democracy' projects, like PB, the money for the projects themselves comes from tax. Taxes are normally re-

---

416 Personal communication Róbert Bjarnason (11 January 2023).

distributive (they are disproportionately collected from the rich and disproportionately given to the poor), so if PB (or other forms of democratic decision-making) is not at all redistributive or significantly less redistributive, this could cause a problem.

How likely such a thing is to actually occur is unknown. After all, we already live in majority-rule democracies, yet have established redistribution mechanisms that disproportionately benefit the poor. Why people would suddenly make wildly differing choices in more direct voting processes is unclear. Indeed, forcing funding decisions to go through a transparent process should theoretically *lessen* the pressure wealthier residents can bring to bear on decision-makers.

That being said, issues may arise in some circumstances. In PB in large cities, residents are often only allowed to vote for city-wide projects and projects in their own districts. If people are asked to vote under these circumstances, it is understandable that they may not realize that others have not been provided for. This is further complicated by the fact that participants are often told that the money they are using is disposable.

However, if all else fails, one can simply ringfence a certain level of funding for target groups. Paris officials were initially concerned that there was a low rate of voting from low-income neighbourhoods resulting in fewer projects being approved there (although this seems to have been transitory with voting rates improving markedly). As a result, starting in 2016, authorities ringfenced 30 % of the PB budget (€30 million) for these neighbourhoods.[417] One can do this for any group one wishes to specifically target – young people, ethnic minorities, etc.

There are downsides to this practice, as it can lead to fractures in society if done too often. However, in some cases it is the obvious choice. If one has a budget to address the needs of migrants, for example, there really is no reason why migrants shouldn't be the ones voting on it. For example, the Taiwanese city of Taoyuan held a PB process in 2017 with a budget of 40k EUR for 'leisure activities for migrant workers' (110,000 of Taoyuan's 2.1 million inhabitants are migrant workers). Although everyone in Taoyuan was entitled to vote, of the 3,052 people who did so, only 285 were Taiwanese citizens.[418] As one can see, it may have been defensible to ringfence voting in such a project, but it proved to be unnecessary – and this is often the case.

A related issue could surface if large organizations (e. g. large sporting associations) mobilized their members to participate in the interests of the organization,

---

417 Brahimllari, *Multi-Layered Participatory Budgeting* 109.
418 Brahimllari, *Multi-Layered Participatory Budgeting* 63 et seq.

which could lead to this group always 'winning' public voting processes. This isn't necessarily always a negative (after all, such organizations do have to have those members in order to mobilize them), but if such practices go beyond an acceptable limit, one can simply ringfence funding according to certain categories, allocating a minimum budget to sports, arts, etc. It is also possible to limit how much funding any one organization can receive over a certain time period (e.g. five years) in order to prevent the process from being dominated by a few groups.

Some forms of public participation seek to counteract this kind of organizational domination by requiring participants to vote for multiple projects. This prevents them from just ticking a box on behalf of an organization without even considering the other options.[419]

3.4.2.4 Maintain Transparency Through the Process

The origins of proposals, as well as how votes are tabulated should be clear throughout any process. When small, labour-intensive groups are inserted into the process, especially where they are not publicly accountable (as in e.g. budget delegates in American PB), this tends to go to the detriment of more marginalized people. The least well-off are also the least likely to be able to take the time to participate as budget delegates, and as we saw above, delegates are often successful at getting their preferred projects on the ballot. An open and transparent process that is obligated to give equal treatment to all proposals is preferable to this.

3.4.2.5 Avoid Anything that is Not One Person-One-Vote

Each affluent person is one person and each vulnerable person is one person. This is the most basic egalitarian dimension of our existence, which is why the principle of one-person, one-vote must be maintained.

This means barring NGOs from directly taking part in the process. More affluent people are far more likely to be members of NGOs, which effectively allow them to 'vote twice'. Cutting out NGO participation and forcing their members to participate as mere individuals would be something that would be far more fair to low-income and marginalized people. It also means jettisoning practices that entitle people to act as representatives for abstract entities like 'nature' or 'future generations'.[420] If participants want to advocate for nature or future generations they are certainly free to do so, but elevating some people to this position creates inequality. It not only opens the door to abusing this position, but also raises the

---

419 Johnson, 'Engaging Democracy' 87.
420 As Allegretti suggests in 'Common Patterns in Coping with Under-Representation'.

question as to why others should not be entitled to represent 'industry' or 'finance' or any other component of our society.

That many people feel entitled to claim to be the representative of an external good that is beyond debate is one of the key contributors to polarization in representative democracy today. This fiction allows people to avoid responsibility and thus accountability for the policies that *they* are advocating. They may do so because they believe their policy is e.g. good for nature, but at the end of the day, *they* are advocating it, nature isn't.

3.4.2.6 Set Maximum Contributions

Another way to make participation more fair is to set maximum contribution lengths. Lethbridge CIP, for example, limited comments to a certain number of characters. While participants could simply make further comments if they were so inclined, few of them did so. Similarly, most PB projects allow people to submit as many proposals as they like. While, as we have seen, few people submit multiple proposals, if this ever became an issue, this could always be limited to e.g. one proposal per year.

3.5 Conclusions on Participation

One of the principal objects and advantages of digital democracy lies in enabling all people to participate equally in decision-making, rather than leaving this task in the hands of a group of representatives who are, due to their small numbers, vulnerable to elite capture. However, despite its very point being to enable unlimited, universal participation, this area has become convulsed in a debate about who exactly does participate in practice, and this debate is often conducted on the basis of obsolete or incomplete statistics.

This debate on demographic participation has been accompanied by an odd acceptance that 'democracy' *is* an elite-captured process that consists of very wealthy funders creating opportunities for the permanently impoverished to 'feel heard' on some issues while downgrading 'the usual suspects' who participate most often. These suddenly-imposed and self-contradictory goals make technology responsible for 'solving' problems that are social.

As we see technology diffuse across society, as in Estonia, we unsurprisingly see those who participate digitally mirroring the societal demographics. The strength of digital democracy is not to impose a societal recalibration, but rather to remove barriers to participation. When people do not need to pass through a filter (e.g. election) to participate, a certain source of distortion is removed, and people are more emancipated than they were before, when they were unable to take part in politics directly and thus depended on others, who may or may not have had their best interests at heart.

Democracy depends on as few people as possible being either extremely rich or extremely poor, and for this reason it is important to continually fold people back into the democratic process with appropriate supports. I have outlined above some ways to do this that are effective and that do not compromise democratic principles of free participation. However, much also depends on the decisions made *within* a democracy to make decisions that maintain this *social* calibration, rather than seeking to impose strictly equal (or even unequal) formal participation goals on a society that one accepts is deeply materially unequal. Such a situation is far more likely to lead to civil strife than to democracy.

Chapter 4
The User Experience

When it comes to digital democracy, there are two kinds of users that must be kept in mind: the end user (the citizen) and the public administrator utilizing digital tools as part of their job. We have talked about the user experience above in a more material sense (why do people take part, why don't they); this chapter will now turn to exploring this experience in a more formal sense, focusing on the structure and fluidity of the process.

4.1 The End User

4.1.1 Avoiding Frustration Time

It is often said that on the internet **attention spans** are short. However, it may be more accurate to say that it is easier to leave a virtual space than a real one, where such behaviour is considered rude and requires the person leaving to make a plausible excuse. We have all sat through long meetings for no better reason than that we couldn't think of a way to leave. But just because we endured doesn't meant we found the experience helpful or even enjoyable. The social barriers to leaving such a situation aren't as formidable on the internet, so it is more accurate to think of it not as a space where attention spans are low, but where standards are high.

In addition, the internet allows tasks to be completed very quickly (indeed, efficiency is one of the key benefits of digital technology). The average Estonian takes less than 2 minutes to vote in elections, while in the 2022 idea generation phase for PB in Iceland, the average page visit length was just under 3 minutes.[421] The average visit length to Lethbridge CIP 2021 (a more involved process) was 12.5 minutes, for the London Ethelo on carbon budgeting it was 14 minutes, and for a poverty reduction engagement in Prince George, British Columbia it was 15 minutes.[422] Although we can see people spending more time on a site when the task demands it, generally speaking, time is of the essence and choosing or building a software that is intuitive for the end-user to navigate is imperative. This is another reason why it is so important to strip organizers' partisan demands from the design process and

---

[421] Personal communication from Róbert Bjarnason, President Citizens Foundation, to author (11 January 2023).

[422] 'Prince George Poverty Reduction' (*Ethelo*) 3 <https://f.hubspotusercontent40.net/hubfs/6224498/Boilerplate/Prince%20George%20(1).pdf> accessed 12 March 2023.

https://doi.org/10.1515/9783110794465-008

focus on the user, *what* they are trying to do and *why* they are trying to do it. In particular, it is important to minimize the time the user spends in what I call Frustration Time.

Frustration Time is composed of two closely related concepts: **Frustration Time** proper and **Boredom Time.** Frustration Time proper is the time spent doing something that does *not* lead to a result. For example, a citizen is told about a consultation, but when they log in to the site, it hasn't been posted yet. Boredom Time occurs whenever the user experiences boredom, e.g. waiting for a page to load, or experiencing participation at a start-stop pace with a comment here or there, but generally flagging momentum. When people are not in Frustration Time, time runs quickly. But the moment Frustration Time enters the picture, time runs very slowly indeed. People remember all of the other tasks they need to get done, and once they leave the participation site to perform those tasks they are unlikely to return.

There are a few key things one can do to reduce Frustration Time:

– The more **intuitive** something is to use, the less Frustration Time it generates. Therefore, always make it obvious what the next step is and prompt people to actions. This can be as simple as prominently displaying the 'next' button and ensuring that the most common features ('next', 'login', etc. are in the same places they usually occupy in commercial applications (known as 'the familiarity principle')). Intuitive design is often among the qualities people say they like best about the digital tools they prefer.[423] In addition, the more people can navigate a system independently, the fewer resources need to be devoted to aiding them.
– Ensure that participation can occur at **scale.** More comprehensive and far-reaching participation that happens at less frequent intervals is preferable to a constant trickle of flagging participation. This is an advantage of synchronous participation – it is less flexible, but for that it funnels all activity through a narrow timeframe and this helps to maintain a certain momentum.
– Avoid **unnecessary lags**, e.g. forcing people to wait for approval before their comment is posted. If you are concerned about comments (e.g. for legal reasons) consider something like Citizens Foundation's comment flagger. This monitors the conversation for toxic language (e.g. profanity) and flags these comments to moderators.

---

[423] Interview with Vito Crimi, former Member of the Italian Senate and Deputy Minister of the Interior (3 March 2022).

- Similarly, try to ensure that tasks can be completed with the **fewest clicks possible** (endless clicking was a complaint about digital tools that users sometimes brought up in interviews). In cases where there is the potential for participants to generate a great deal of information (e. g. by commenting), creating a hierarchy by up/downvoting comments or arranging them by most liked/useful can reduce frustration and fatigue.
- Always aim for **maximum clarity** in stating the purpose of participation, as well as the subject matter to be decided over. Although the Lethbridge CIP was an exceptionally clearly formulated consultation, when it transitioned from voting on cultural and sports projects to commenting on critical infrastructure without explanation, this immediately generated confusion among participants and thus frustration and misunderstandings with the process.
- Ensure **disability access** is functioning, and that compatibility with different operating systems and browsers has been assured. Bear in mind that some people experience colour vision deficiency, which means it can be difficult to distinguish between shades of colour or in more rare cases, they may see no colour at all. Thus, using a system that is dependent on being able to distinguish colours could cause an issue for some users.
- Include a mechanism that allows participants to **go back** or undo an action, as well as, where appropriate, mechanisms for logging on and off.
- Ensure that someone is reachable to **provide help** whenever the system is live.

Digital tools require constant maintenance and improvement, and aging digital applications become hard to navigate very quickly. Commercial providers generally provide updates, but if you are creating your own software, you will need to update it at fairly frequent intervals, and this should be planned in as a cost from the beginning.

4.1.2 Verification vs Ease of Access

One of the key trade-offs that must be balanced in any system is between security and ease of access. The more convoluted the sign-in process to any digital application, the more people fail to register at all. Neuchâtel in Switzerland, for example, for many years had the lowest rates of online voting in the country, a circumstance that has been attributed to the fact that it also had the most extensive sign-in procedure.[424] The introduction of a much more cumbersome verification process has also been blamed for reduced participation in online PB in Belo Horizonte.[425]

In practice, many instances of digital democracy do not utilize secure registration checks. Instead, they allow people to simply participate on a public webpage or with an easily faked email address (that generally receives a one-time use token), under the understanding that there is little to be gained from rigging a vote on small, local projects, and that the key challenge for organizers is to attract participants at all rather than to screen for fake ones or double voters. Others seek to piggy-back on pre-existing structures and allow participants to use their Facebook or Google sign-in to participate.[426]

The consequences of open access can be mitigated on the back-end by filtering out accounts that are obvious duplicates, but this is a rough rather than exact science. Although fewer people participate (at least initially) when doing so requires a high level of verification, there are downsides to not verifying users. Not only does it mean that organizers are unsure about the validity of results, participants also sometimes express concern that others may vote more than once, skewing the outcomes. Lack of verification also tends to send a signal that the exercise is not entirely serious, a nice-to-have, as opposed to a binding decision. To be truly secure, all participants would need to be compared to the official voter register at some point in the process.

4.1.3 Information Organization

One of the most common requests from digital democracy participants is for more information. Some of these requests are quite specific, for example, to specify the intended beneficiaries of proposals (e.g. cyclists, older people), information on how money is being spent, or for statistics related to the problem at hand.

---

424 Uwe Serdült and Micha Germann, 'Internet Voting for Expatriates: The Swiss Case' (2014) 6(2) eJournal of eDemocracy and Open Government 197, 202.

425 Stephen Coleman and Rafael Cardoso Sampaio, 'Sustaining a Democratic Innovation: A Study of Three E-Participatory Budgets in Belo Horizonte' (2016) Information, Communication and Society 1, 7–8.

426 Participation and Communications Team, Scottish Parliament, *Fireworks and Pyrotechnics Articles (Scotland) Bill: Digital Engagement: Summary of Online Forum Submissions to Support the Criminal Justice Committee's Scrutiny of the Bill* (March 2022) <https://www.parliament.scot/-/media/files/committees/criminal-justice-committee/fireworks-bill-engagement-summary.pdf.>

It is important to provide information in a manner that doesn't clutter and confuse the experience, and that also does not steer the conversation. Unfortunately, the more information one provides, the harder it is to avoid this. In some ways, this is an advantage of sourcing ideas from the public (e. g. for PB) because one can then let members of the public make the argument for their own project without having to worry about whether it is biased or not.

Participants themselves have offered some ideas for presenting additional information online (all of which are technically possible):

–   Provide a separate page with information for each proposal under discussion
–   Provide links or text that can expand for those who want it
–   Include figures and displays of proposed projects
–   Create a mechanism for participants to ask questions to the council, staff or citizens behind proposals
–   Offer more information on costs

Visualization can be an aid to providing this information, and there are several forms for this to take:

1.   Illustrating Projects or Ideas
2.   Data Visualization
3.   Dialogue Visualization

4.1.3.1 Illustrating Projects or Ideas
People are generally attracted to pictures, and news stories and ads that include pictures or video receive much more attention than those that do not. It thus often helps to provide visualizations of intended projects or works for people to consider. For example, a recurring demand from participants in Okotoks 2080, which included a large component on housing, was for visual representation of what some forms of housing would look like. Of course, the extent to which visualization is possible always needs to be weighed against the locally available bandwidth. Nonetheless, this is a long-standing component of most offline consultations, which usually include models or illustrations of the intended works, precisely because it makes it much easier for people to imagine the finished project. Provided the bandwidth is available, it is possible to enhance this digitally with rudimentary VR experiences that allow the user to 'walk-through' the finished product.

It is also possible for participants to interact visually, by e. g. dragging and dropping a pin on a map to designate where they think a facility should be located, rather than attempting to describe the location verbally, which can lead to misunderstandings. Participants can use the same basic features to draw their preferred route for a one-way-traffic system or to define the area they think a park should cover. Delib's CitizenSpace Geospatial is a good example of this in practice.[427]

4.1.3.2 Data Visualization

Data visualization requires significantly more care than illustration. For one thing, it requires that the relevant data be available at all. This is part of the reason why a section on service provision was included in Chapter 2: getting clean data and making it presentable is imperative to facilitating participation, and this in return requires a reasonable level of internal organization. The data required to support public decision-making usually *exists* in every public system, it's just not easily accessible. From a data privacy point of view, this is the worst of both worlds. Because the data exists, a determined person can potentially find out quite a lot of information about any other person (vast data leaks are but one aspect of this). However, at the same time this information is not organized and used constructively. As long as this continues to occur, we are subjected to the downsides of the information age (erosion of privacy) without the upsides (data is available to underpin new discoveries and make better decisions).

When information *is* available to the public, it is all too often out-of-date. Real-time data, that is data that is instantly accessible and available to process, is becoming the norm commercially, and, as we saw, is now also used in cabinet meetings in Estonia. This saves the need to make rough extrapolations from old data, which can often lead to error. Improving data management within government is a task long overdue in many nations and failure to properly complete this task will have serious consequences both for democracy and service provision generally.

Once it exists in organized form, however, a key issue with *any* data is that it is rather easy to manipulate. For example, one can simply fix the x or y axis of a chart to make differences appear more sensational than they are, or start a graph at a certain historical point in order to cut off data that could interfere with a pre-determined interpretation of events.

This is a thornier issue than is often acknowledged, because a certain amount of pressure to open up government data comes from foundations and other special interests who often pursue governments to release data so that they can use it to pressure government to do what *they* want to do. Such organizations have the clout

---

427 'Place-Based Engagement with CitizenSpace Geospatial' (*Delib*) <https://www.delib.net/citizen_space/geospatial> accessed 25 February 2023.

to produce unending data visualizations (often misleading) as to why their preferred solution is the right one, and the resources to push government to adopt it. Attempts to procure and use data just to drive a certain agenda can chill government willingness to share it with anyone.

Because it is so easy to deceive with data visualization, it is better to focus on illustration (architectural plans, etc.) instead. However, there are also four simple principles for data visualization one can follow to mitigate its potential for deception:

1. Make the entire data set available instead of just picking out key highlights
2. If you release data on the same issue repeatedly over time, try to avoid changing the format it is released in, as this makes comparisons over time very difficult
3. Make data highly customisable, so that the user can select what they want to drill into
4. Analyse before you summarise (show your work).

The key is to present data in ways that are understandable without compromising its integrity. Let's consider two cases where data visualization could be helpful. The first is in budgeting.

As previously mentioned, Lethbridge CIP (an online consultation on capital investment) put forward a proposal to build a new performing arts centre in the city, projected to cost $100 million. Many residents found this price exorbitant and the project was rejected by voters in the online consultation. The only figure citizens had to work with in making this decision was the final price tag with no way of easily assessing whether the project delivered value for money. Governments could, of course, share line-item level data to show e. g. how much of the total budget is for the land purchase, construction, insurance, furnishings, etc. but often worry that this would overwhelm citizens as it would necessitate hundreds of line-items for every proposal.

However, there is no need to ask citizens to comb through thousands of lines of an Excel sheet. As long as data is captured at the line-item level, it can be grouped by cost category and then by project. Cost category could be shown as a pie chart, with citizens having the ability to click into each slice of the pie to get further breakdowns by cost category. Drill down far enough and one ends up at a line-item analysis, but one doesn't have to begin this way and data is easier to digest when it is peeled down. Modern data visualisation tools like Tableau, Microsoft Power BI or QlikView can be used to present this data in an intuitive, user-friendly format which does not require citizens to have any particular computer skills. Showing data in this way allows citizens to make more informed decisions.

In the above example, the civic centre might be rejected if citizens can't see the value at top line level, but if e.g. the land is the main cost driver, a modified proposal to build the centre on a more affordable site might very well be approved.

The fact that few people will have the time and skill to analyse raw data is immaterial – it only takes one person to look into it and explain it to everyone else. Everyone should have the opportunity to examine the primary source and to scrutinize, or listen to the scrutiny of others. Simply making it available so that it *can* be verified often goes a long way towards allaying suspicions.

Another use case for data visualization is in scenario analytics – 'what if' scenarios.

To take another real-life example from Lethbridge CIP, the city proposed building a new operations depot to store equipment in a different part of the city where it could be accessed more easily. This was one of the proposals on which participants felt they had the least information, reflected in both the comments and a high number of neutral votes. Without understanding how this would facilitate access to equipment, the normal traffic flows and time expected to be saved, residents were simply at a loss as to whether the new investment presented value for money.

This is a common issue when it comes to traffic and transportation measures. These often require an iterative calculation to determine the true changes they would bring, as traffic alterations often divert traffic to or from another destination (e.g. making one road a pedestrian zone diverts traffic to a parallel street). It would have been possible to include predictions (categorized according to probability) of the various outcomes to be expected from building the new depot (as these surely existed in the city's calculations). This would have helped citizens to understand why the proposal was being made in the first place and assess whether or not the expected gains were worth the expense.

4.1.3.3 Dialogue Visualization

A third form of visualization concerns the dialogue between participants and/or the decision-making process itself.

For example, pol.is, sometimes used in Taiwan (see Fig. 4.1), invites users to 'approve', 'reject' or 'pass' on initial statements provided by organizers. They can also submit their own statements, which are passed on to other users to approve, reject or pass on.

Based on their answers, users are visually clustered into different opinion groups on-screen so that people can see where participants stand on different points of the discussion. The object is to identify statements that the members of these different groups agree or disagree on and use them to develop new statements which may further convergence. For example, if most people disagree with the statement 'liquor stores should be allowed to open 24/7' there is an incentive to create a new, more restrictive statement about when they should be allowed to be open.

Conceptualisation of Grouping on pol.is

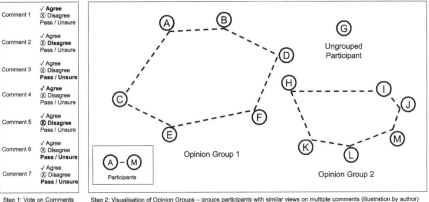

Fig 4.1: Conceptualisation of Grouping on pol.is.

Common Ground for Action (see Fig. 4.2) uses a similar system for participants to place themselves on a map in relation to the issue being deliberated. They may change this position as the discussion unfolds. Their own placement then flows into a visualization of the group's stance on a particular action, e.g. 'promote English as our common language' in regards to the integration of immigrants to the United States.[428] In this way, all participants are aware of the current state of group opinion on a range of different options – something that isn't always necessarily clear purely from commenting.

Other tools, like Loomio, also include visual aids like a pie chart, which is displayed next to the conversation and updated in real-time according to how participants are voting.[429]

This type of visualization, particularly that employed by pol.is and Common Ground for Action, makes sense in those instances where the focus is on attempt-

---

428 Scott London and Mary Engel, *Immigration: Who Should We Welcome, What Should We Do?* (National Issues Forums Institute 2020) 17.
429 Richard Bartlett and Marco Deseriis, 'Loomio and the Problem of Deliberation' *Open Democracy* (2 December 2016) <https://www.opendemocracy.net/en/digitaliberties/loomio-and-problem-of-deliberation/>.

ing to hammer out a resolution that achieves the highest consensus possible. However, such tactics can also leave issues unresolved if the process is poorly managed and consensus comes at the price of any clear, actionable outcomes.

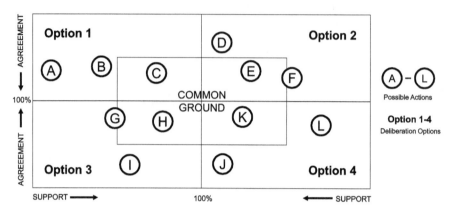

Fig. 4.2: Visualisation of Common Ground for Action.

4.1.4 Thresholds

Ideally, citizens should do as much of the 'work' of participation as possible, because this decreases the opportunity for distortions (intentional or unintentional) to enter the process. Outcomes are the most accurate when everyone represents themselves and speaks for themselves, rather than someone else helping them or making guesses and assumptions on their behalf. In order to support this direct participation, it is necessary to introduce some structure into the process from the very beginning.

This is important because it is fairly common to equate making virtually no demands on the participant as 'user-friendliness'. For example, a common point of view would be that if anyone can submit a proposal or idea with few requirements on precision or detail, that this is more inclusive and user-friendly than forms that require more input from the initiator. Unfortunately, in these cases the structure, sorting and filtration is then just carried out by someone else at a later stage, often with little public oversight. This is where the transparency and scrutiny of the process is so frequently lost.

Commenters sometimes complain that any structure necessarily privileges some forms of acting or makes certain decisions more likely. While this is true, it is still far preferable to what is sometimes called 'the tyranny of structureless-ness'.[430] When the structure of participation is inefficient or altogether missing, nothing gets done, the momentum deflates, and you enter **Frustration Time.** In creating thresholds to channel initiatives through the decision-making process, it is important to rely on the democratic principles outlined above in order to maximize emancipation and minimize opportunities for elite capture and the distortion that facilitates it.

4.1.4.1 Support Test

One type of threshold is to demand that proposals or ideas demonstrate a certain level of support before moving on to the next step in the decision-making process. This is familiar from offline petitions and citizen-initiated referendums in Switzerland and California where supporters are required to gather a certain number of signatures for their proposal in order to get it placed on the ballot.

Podemos used this type of threshold online, requiring proposals to receive a certain number of endorsements from other users to move on to the next stage and become the subject of a general vote. Few initiatives have ever moved beyond this stage (none in Podemos where the threshold is 10%) and only a few in Madrid (which used a similar product, Consul) where the threshold was set even lower at 1%.[431] Some earlier tools like Appgree and Postwaves also used this method, with Postwaves testing support for an initiative among a small number of randomly selected participants and only moving to larger groups if a majority of them voted in favour.

The advantage of these types of thresholds is that they preserve the organic nature of open idea generation without wasting everyone's time on fringe, unpopular initiatives. In addition, when initiatives are pushed out to participants to test support (as they were in Postwaves), there is no need for groups to have the financial reserves necessary to publicize them and attract support. This circumvents issues like those arising in California where well-funded special interests have the ability to disproportionately collect the offline signatures necessary to put an issue up for vote.

It is important to remember that the goal of democratic participation isn't necessarily to get the maximum number of issues on the ballot, regardless of the level

---

430 Jo Freeman, 'The Tyranny of Structurelessness' (1972) 17 Berkeley Journal of Sociology 151–164.
431 Marco Deseriis, 'Reducing the Burden of Decision in Digital Democracy Applications: A Comparative Analysis of Six Decision-Making Software' (2021) Science, Technology and Human Values 1, 21–22.

of support they enjoy. When too many issues are up for debate at the same time, this floods the public space and makes meaningful, focused conversation difficult. Even in Switzerland, 62% of referendums between 2012 and 2018 failed, despite the fact that they all start with a substantial base of support, either from the government or a citizens' initiative.

4.1.4.2 Formal Criteria

Another form of threshold is to develop formal criteria that allow infeasible proposals to be rejected at an early stage in proceedings. Using Rousseau, the M5S parliamentary group rejected proposals that were unconstitutional, financially infeasible or that contradicted pre-existing policy.[432] This helps to prevent time being wasted on debating proposals that cannot be implemented anyway, and to focus scarce resources on those that have a realistic chance of success. Spending an inordinate amount of time discussing proposals that will never be implemented (e.g. because the authority in question does not possess the legal capacity to do what is being asked of them) is one of the more common pitfalls of public participation, particularly offline where conversation is often easily side-tracked.

If you are collecting ideas from the public, it is important to make the criteria that a proposal must fulfill in order to continue through the process as clear as possible. For example, if a project must fall within the legal competencies of the municipality to be eligible, then it makes sense to include information on what the competencies of that municipality are in plain language.[433] This can initially be resource-intense, but it also minimizes the submission of ineligible ideas (and inevitable disappointment) as well as creating a resource for citizens to learn from. Such criteria can, of course, be revisited, especially if they are too restrictive, but this structure must exist in the first place if it is to be revised and optimized.

4.1.4.3 Requiring some Structure and Thought from the Participant

Digital democracy can easily turn into 'metrics democracy', that is measuring 'the strength' of democracy almost exclusively on 'how many ideas are submitted' and 'how many comments are made'. Organizers and activists who view democracy this way often encourage people to submit whatever ideas or comments they

---

432 Marco Deseriis, 'Direct Parliamentarism: An Analysis of the Political Values Embedded in Rousseau, the 'Operating System' of the Five Star Movement' (2017) 9(2) eJournal of eDemocracy and Open Government 60.

433 The City of Paris does this well for Participatory Budgeting: <https://www.paris.fr/pages/budget-participatif-deposez-vos-idees-22902> accessed 18 February 2023.

have, however flippant or inconsequential they may be, because they are intent on 'driving the numbers'.

The truth, however, is that there are few truly original ideas, most ideas are deeply flawed, most people aren't particularly creative, and creativity itself does not make an idea viable. Incorporating idea generation into the democratic process *is* important, but it has value mainly as a way to ensure that ideas aren't kept *off* the agenda by others (as we saw above, a sovereign who can only say 'yes' or 'no' to the ideas presented to them has less power than one who also comes up with their own ideas).

Ideation is *part* of the process, but it is by no means the *whole* process. It is important to recognize this, because it tells us everything about how decision-making should be structured. If the problem is that we 'just don't have enough ideas' (which would require us to believe that the government as well as the millions of experts employed worldwide in any given field *literally* do not have even *an idea* of what to do) then focusing a great deal of attention on unstructured idea generation would make sense. But if the problem is something else, for example, poor implementation of policy, then focusing excessively on idea generation doesn't make sense.

In truth, there is a surfeit of ideas in the world with governments being lobbied to implement them from every side, every single day. We are not, as a civilization, out of ideas. What democracy is really about is *scrutinizing* and *voting* on the oversupply of ideas that are out there. We must *choose* which ideas we would like to pursue and implement them well. Starting this scrutiny at an early phase in the funnel actually helps us to ensure that the things people want *do* have a reasonable chance of progressing through the decision-making funnel – that their ideation, in other words, was not in vain. It's better (also from the citizen's perspective) to have one idea that goes somewhere than ten ideas that don't, and that is why it is actually in their interests to make some minor demands on them at this early point in the process in order to prevent ideas from being intentionally or unintentionally ignored or manipulated.

Crowdsourcing, for example, (simply asking people to submit ideas) is one of the easiest ways to give the impression that an idea originated 'from the people' and that authorities are merely obeying that wish, when in reality they are picking through the surfeit of ideas and selecting the ones they were going to do anyway. If one crowdsources for long enough, every possible idea will be mentioned at some point, so it is simply a matter of patience. Similarly, if ideas are vague enough, authorities can pour their own content into them – indeed, they are practically compelled to do so.

If we look at this in practice, we can see that in the New York PB, which now uses Decidim to gather ideas online,[434] the ideation phase is not particularly well-structured and this can lead to vague proposals being submitted.

For example:

Public Safety
African International Collaborative Center_AICC

10/06/2022 Report
What problem would you like to solve?
crime
Why is it important to solve? Why is it relevant for the community?
for safety in the community
What idea do you have to address the problem?
Increase the presence of cops
Who would that help?
General public
What neighborhood would benefit from your idea?
Bronx[435]

Another reads:

The People's Mic
Canvas Institute

10/13/2022 Report
What problem would you like to solve?
The need for more veteran aid programs
Why is it important to solve? Why is it relevant for the community?
it is important to compensate those who protected and served this Nation
What idea do you have to address the problem?
Install more veterans appreciation service/centers
Who would that help?
Military veterans and their families

---

434 Ethan Geringer-Sameth, 'Civic Engagement Commission to Launch Citywide Participatory Budgeting after Pandemic Delay' *Gotham Gazette* (1 May 2022) <https://www.gothamgazette.com/city/11269-nyc-civic-engagement-commission-participatory-budgeting>.
435 'The People's Money: 2022–2023' (*NYC Civic Engagement Commission*) <https://www.participate.nyc.gov/processes/Citywidepb/f/304/proposals/2353> accessed 11 February 2023.

What neighborhood would benefit from your idea?
Staten Island and other boroughs of New York[436]

Such proposals don't include even an approximate idea of costs or the agencies involved, and fail to quantify what e.g. 'more' (cops or veterans' centres) would look like. Checking back on the proposal page after the submission window had closed,[437] revealed that more ideas had been submitted, but very few were any more specific.

However, more importantly for our point here, neither of these issues was unknown prior to these submissions. Crime and the poor treatment of veterans have been staples of political discussion and television plotlines for decades. Participants may experience some relief in expressing these sentiments (therapy), but they are already well-known to people living on the other side of the world, much less to politicians in the United States itself. The reason for inaction is *not* a lack of knowledge, so merely reiterating ideas is *not* going to improve things. By over-estimating the importance of ideation and failing to structure and refine this point, the true power is actually moved somewhere else in the process.

Because vague ideas (to the extent that they meet the eligibility criteria in the first place) need to be turned into proposals, NYC PB utilizes the budget delegate system described above. Because budget delegate meetings involve a small number of people, generally working behind closed doors (or at least with little scrutiny), it is easy for government agencies to withhold information from delegates, as well as for them to discourage proposals they dislike by costing them too high or low in order to ensure they fall out of the scope of the budget. Government agencies may also directly pressure delegates to choose the agency's preferred proposals.[438]

In NYC, very few proposals make it onto the final ballot. For example, in District 45 in 2011–2012, of 281 proposals only 13 made it onto the ballot, while in District 39 there were 866 proposals, but only 20 went onto the ballot.[439] While some of this is likely due to consolidating similar projects, it is still a very high rejection rate (95% and 98% respectively – by comparison the rejection rate in Lisbon is ca. 66%). This astronomical rejection rate amounts to de facto pre-deciding the out-

---

436 'The People's Money' <https://www.participate.nyc.gov/processes/Citywidepb/f/304/proposals/2507?page=2> accessed 18 January 2023.
437 'The People's Money' <https://www.participate.nyc.gov/processes/Citywidepb/f/303/> accessed 18 January 2023.
438 Williams and Waisanen, *Real Money, Real Power?* 52–57 and 73–74.
439 Alexa Kasdan and Lindsay Cattell, *A People's Budget: A Research and Evaluation Report on the Pilot Year of Participatory Budgeting in New York City* (The Urban Justice Center and PBNYC Research Team 2012) 65 and 56.

come, since once a project is included in these short ballots it has a fairly high chance of success. Clearly, in cases like these, proposals do need to be refined or filtered, but the budget delegate process obscures this step which can leave it open to manipulation or, just as bad from a public participation perspective, perceptions of manipulation.

It may be more transparent and accountable to take an approach more common in Europe where governments either put forward their own proposals (as Tower Hamlets did in 2010),[440] or for officials to vet proposals put forward by citizens according to clearly established criteria, while demanding slightly more from participants in terms of their submissions in order to reduce the level of adjustment needed at this stage.

For example, Paris PB requires people to submit proposals online, including a short description, location of the project and budget estimate. PB in Lisbon also establishes a theme that proposals must relate to (in 2021 it was sustainability and sport).[441] Submitted proposals are often more thorough and specific than in NYC. For example, in Lisbon a proposal to create a pathway along an area that was de facto used as a shortcut by many pedestrians included a photo of the location, a thorough justification for the proposal, as well as a map with a pin of the location in it.[442] When a proposal is rejected, officials must give the reason for the rejection as well as the rule it is based on – the proposal described above was rejected because the land the proposed path would traverse was privately owned. Many other proposals, however, were rejected with more vague reasons, such as 'contradicts or makes other projects infeasible'. This still, however, seems preferable to a process that alters proposals possibly beyond the intentions of the original proposers.

Thresholds, although they are much maligned, can be a useful tool for keeping participation focused on a manageable number of options at any given time, as well as for allowing participants to focus on completing the cycle from ideation to vote to implementation, rather than getting stuck in an endless cycle of ideating.

---

440 Carolina Johnson, 'Engaging Democracy: An Institutional Theory of Participatory Budgeting' (DPhil Thesis, University of Washington 2017) 106.

441 Lisboa Participa (*Câmara Municipal de Lisboa*) <op.lisboaparticipa.pt/> accessed 18 January 2023.

442 '#2 Cricao de Caminho Pedonal com a Apoio para Bicecletas' (*Lisboa Participa, Câmara Municipal de Lisboa*) <https://op.lisboaparticipa.pt/propostas/604f388a6a7c8600a9eba5bb> accessed 18 January 2023.

4.1.5 Avoid Digital Sprawl

Measuring public participation in terms of the length of time a participant spends on it or the number of comments made is something that has been taken over directly from marketing and social media companies that seek to maximize engagement so that they can sell more advertising. Such yardsticks are not completely appropriate for democracy. After all, no one is seeking to maximize their *input* in a democracy. People are seeking to maximize their *utility.* If we look at studies into participation, we notice that there is a certain point at which this utility begins to taper off and the participation enters into a state of diminishing returns.

A study into a particularly lengthy digital consultation on housing legislation in Finland (which consisted of two periods of consultation separated by one year) noted that participation on the platform occurred in waves, peaking in week 2 and again in week 5 of the initial consultation period. It then hit a saturation point, following which the number of new ideas decreased, eventually to zero. When the second round of participation opened up a year later, fewer than half the number of ideas were received, compared to the first phase, with fewer new users signing up. While the number of comments remained fairly consistent with the first phase, in the second phase, activity peaked early and then decreased. Participants who were interviewed also felt that at a certain point, the process hit its saturation point, stating that most of the possible perspectives had been covered, ideas were getting repetitive, the process started to degenerate into negative complaints, and it was time to quit.[443]

Similarly in the Lethbridge CIP, which generated thousands of comments, there were generally 1–5 core feedbacks on each issue, e.g. regarding waste disposal, a common feedback was to weight the trash bins as they tended to fly around in Lethbridge's windy weather. While there are always a few one-off original comments, the core themes generally come out quite quickly, and don't merit endless discussion (no one disputed that trash bins were flying around or that it would be nice if they didn't).

Most people quickly tire of repetition, which generates Frustration Time, because the participation is demanding one's attention, yet progress is not being made. This is where structure is so needed to keep the process moving along. It's important to take the time one needs to make a consultation, participatory budget or anything else meaningful, but one should always strive to take the mini-

---

443 Tanja Aitamurto and Jorge Saldivar, 'Motivating Participation in Crowdsourced Policymaking: The Interplay of Epistemic and Interactive Aspects' (2017) 1 (CSCW) Proceedings of the ACM on Human-Computer Interaction 1–22.

mum time necessary to achieve this and not regard democracy purely in terms of the length of time and effort it required.

One can work against repetition by grouping proposals that have a common location or goal together (e.g. five proposals to repaint fences in five different areas, may become one proposal called 'repainting fences in these five areas'). In Iceland, PB tools group similar proposals together so that voters can browse topics of interest to them rather than becoming overwhelmed with the total offerings.

Similarly, service provision should also be consolidated. The Estonian one-stop shop is ideal from a user perspective, as residents must only memorize one set of codes to access services. At the opposite end of the spectrum, the web portal *Smart Dublin*[444] is supposed to offer a digital future for Ireland's capital, but merely serves as a holding place where citizens are required to download an app for virtually every separate process (for example there is an app devoted to consultations in part of Dublin and another to allowing the user to alert emergency services as to the whereabouts of 'rough sleepers'). This fragmentation of services is a time sink for both users and administrators and therefore discourages any use at all. Precisely because the internet allows us to escape so many constraints of space and time, it is necessary to impose a few sensible ones to regain structure and avoid digital sprawl.

4.1.6 Fun and Gamification

An idea that frequently circulates in discussions of digital democracy, and indeed democracy more generally, is that if it were more fun and, in fact, like a game, more people would participate.[445] Attempts at 'fun' and gamification can range from making the participatory atmosphere more festive, to turning the issue into a competitive challenge to 'solve', to rewarding people who participate more with status (badges) or material rewards (prizes). This is different than pay-for-participation. Pay-for-participation is not a game. Like jury duty pay, it simply aims to offset lost income while the participant fulfills their public duty and to even up the playing field for the less affluent.

I believe that focusing on gamification is a mistake for multiple reasons. The first is that democratic participation is, at the best of times, only a limited amount

---

444 *Smart Dublin* <www.smartdublin.ie> accessed 18 January 2023.
445 See e.g. Josh Lerner, *Making Democracy Fun: How Game Design can Empower Citizens and Transform Politics* (MIT Press 2014).

of fun – there are many things that are much, much more fun. When we compete on the axis of fun, we are setting ourselves up for failure.

The second is that the moment something serious is at stake, any activity no matter *how* previously pleasant, immediately ceases to be fun. While professional athletes, musicians and comedians may love what they do, they also have to do their job when it isn't fun – and a lot of the time, it isn't. The only way democracy could be fun is if nothing truly important rested on the outcome – and in that case, it wouldn't be democracy.

The third is that construing choices as a game or puzzle (e.g. 'balance the budget', 'solve world hunger') obfuscates that the choices one makes are going to have very real, potentially very serious, consequences. Democracy is anything *but* a game. Encouraging people to think otherwise could lead them to act irresponsibly and in ways that aren't appropriate to the reality of the situation.

Finally, as adults, we have limited time for fun in our lives and we don't need to have fun in order to do things. We do not clothe our children or vacuum our floor because we experience unbearable joy in so doing. On the contrary, we are mainly motivated by duty and problem avoidance in almost everything we do, and it is an interesting fact, in this context, that older voters (who vote the most) tend to give 'civic duty' as their reason for doing so. In other words, the people who vote *the most* do *not*, in fact, necessarily feel particularly happy or special for doing so. Quite the opposite – they feel that it is a minor obligation they need to fulfill in order for democracy to continue to function and that they would be remiss for failing to complete it.

This is significant unto itself, because it reveals a lot about what truly motivates people. This is all the more important as the harder our life circumstances, the more we only have time for duty. Portraying democracy as 'fun' also portrays it as frivolous, and if we insist on doing this, it is likely that those who consider themselves to have more time and leisure will show up and those who feel they must focus on work will not.

Despite knowing all of this, the hype around gamification led me to doubt myself enough to try a gamification experiment when I used Ethelo to develop my own electoral platform (outlined in Chapter 3), offering prizes to the people who commented the most, etc. I could not discern any impact this had on participants' behaviour (indeed the winners expressed practically no interest in collecting their prizes) – and it's probably best that it didn't. After all, is it really in the best interests of clear decision-making if people comment in order to win a prize or acquire status, or only when they feel they have something to say that they have put thought into?

It's not that participants can't have fun or that democracy necessitates deadly seriousness at all times, but democracy is a lot more important than just 'fun' and when we make it a social activity or competition we are actually devaluing it into just another pleasant activity. Democracy is worth doing regardless of whether or not it is fun.

4.1.7 Choice over Modes of Interaction

The level of interaction people prefer in digital participation varies according to the personality of the participant and how they feel about the issue at hand. However, generally speaking, on any given issue, more people will choose to participate in a passive fashion, with proportionally fewer people choosing more active forms of participation.

For example, on the Lethbridge CIP, few people uploaded a profile photo despite having the opportunity to do so, and some of those that did used a logo or other generic photo rather than a photo of themselves

In the Scottish Consultation on fireworks safety legislation, there were 8,679 votes cast (somewhat more than 1,000 per proposal) and 1,187 comments, giving a ratio of one comment for ca. 7.3 votes. In the Finnish housing consultation, 232 ideas, 2,901 comments, and 8,526 votes were submitted,[446] meaning there were about three times as many votes as comments and more than ten times as many comments as ideas. In the Okotoks 2080 consultation, one comment was posted for every 7.5 votes, while in the Lethbridge consultation, one comment was posted for every 10.5 votes.[447] An analysis of four random questions for which voting was possible revealed one comment posted for every 9.5 votes cast and one reply for every 11 original comments (direct comments on the proposal). Favourites outstripped comments slightly with one favourite for every 8.6 votes cast or every 0.9 comments. An analysis of 11 proposals, some of which did not include a voting element, revealed one reply for every 9.75 direct comments, and one favourite for every 1.2 comments. Pol.is also noted this same ratio of approximately ten votes to every comment on its platform.[448] Considering the stability of this ratio across platforms over different time periods, it is thus safe to say that people tend to vote far more often than they comment (approximately ten times as often, in most cases) and to favourite about as often as they comment.

In those cases where replying to other participants was possible, this mode was rarely used. In Okotoks 2080 participants exclusively addressed themselves

---

446 Aitamurto and Saldivar, 'Motivating Participation' 15.
447 Analysing 17 proposals for which full data was available.
448 Colin Megill, 'Pol.is in Taiwan' (*Medium*, 25 May 2016) <https://blog.pol.is/pol-is-in-taiwan-da7570d372b5>.

to public officials, rather than replying to one another. When participants did use the reply function, it was often to answer a request for information from another participant, e.g. in Lethbridge CIP:

> Comment: Where are the potential locations?
>
> Reply: The proposed location is currently 28 St N and 12 Ave N on the southeast corner.

In the various instances where Ethelo was used, participants did sometimes indirectly comment on other comments *in* their comment, e.g. 'I agree with the other commenters here' or make a comment that picked up a theme from a previous comment, but without directly replying to it, e.g. 'I agree with the concerns around drought and water usage'. There was thus a slightly higher level of interactivity than the statistics alone would suggest.

However, as we can see, there tends to be more passive than active participation and people do not typically 'max-out' their participatory opportunities. In Lethbridge CIP the average length of comment was 22 words, although the character limit allowed for ca. 50 – 55 words. Those who commented more often tended to keep each comment brief, while others made one all-encompassing comment. The 8 users with the lengthiest comments (all above 44 words) only commented once.

Participants in the Ethelo consultations stated that they liked the ability to vote. While many people said that they enjoyed reading others' comments, this did not (at least at this point) translate into any apparent wish to have a long conversation with those people.

This commenting pattern was similar when Barcelona used Decidim to formulate its Action Plan (described in Chapter 2). 88 % of the more than 18,000 comments received were direct reactions to the initial proposal and did not lead to further conversation with other participants. However, when someone did reply to a comment from another user, it often triggered a long conversation (the original commenter received a notification that their comment had been replied to). Negative comments (comments speaking against a proposal) were also more likely to trigger discussion.[449]

This would indicate that conversing with others is not necessarily a particularly important part of the process for many people, possibly because participants

---

449 Rosa Borge, Joaquim Brugué and David Duenas-Cid, 'Technology and Democracy. The Who and How in Decision-Making: The Cases of Estonia and Catalonia' (2022) 31(3) El Profesional de la Información; Pablo Aragón, Andreas Kaltenbrunner, Antonio Calleja-López, Andrés Pereira, Arnau Monterde, Xabier E. Barandiaran and Vicenç Gómez, 'Deliberative Platform Design: The Case Study of the Online Discussions in Decidim Barcelona' (2017) International Conference on Social Informatics 277–287.

correctly assume that officials are the decision-makers, and thus focus on convincing them rather than their fellow citizens. However, it is also unsurprising that opposition to proposals tends to trigger the direct discussion that does occur, as when all are in agreement, there is simply very little to say. The lower levels of organic dialogue between participants may also speak against deliberation as a widely preferred form of participation. That being said, the advantage of digital technology is that one size does not have to fit all.

Some people like to be more active (e.g. commenting); others to be less active (e.g. liking others' comments); others prefer just to vote and not to interact with others. This is likely simply a matter of personal preference: some people, for example, are more extroverted and enjoy sharing their thoughts, others are introverted and are just as happy not doing so, although they may enjoy reading other people's comments. It is therefore advisable to offer a spectrum of participation that offers the opportunity to be very active, but doesn't demand it in order to have one's preferences count.

4.2 The Administrator

Unlike many other applications, digital democracy tools do not just need to satisfy the end user, but also public officials who are responsible for administering them. The two main issues of concern here are how efficient the tool is in terms of use for the administrator and how easy it is to retain and grow participation.

4.2.1 Ease of Use and Integration

One of the key concerns for administrators is how easy a new platform is to use and how efficient it is to integrate into the existing system. A major point of concern here is fragmentation, with multiple tools being used to perform different processes with little integration between them. Sometimes, the citizen experience proceeds smoothly, but the administrator experience is time-consuming and scattered.[450] It is thus always important to also inquire about the administrative side of any tool and to prefer those with single integrated portals. Some providers also provide coordination, input and consulting services to make integration easier.

Integration is especially necessary when administrators need to continue to process the data that has been gathered (and when it comes to democracy one gen-

---

450 Interviews (2022).

erally does). Many providers have made efforts to streamline their process, for example, information that was once provided in a pdf can be provided in a Word document to enable further processing, or proposal submissions that were once spit out in an Excel sheet (disorienting when there are 1000 or more proposals) can be further processed in the system itself or in a CRM system.

When choosing or developing a tool, it makes sense to think a little about what the organization in question would realistically like to be doing in three or five years' time and to pick (or develop) a software that will consolidate as many of those tasks as possible.

4.2.2 Stickiness of Participation

Democracy is mass decision-making. It is not clear that generating 800 throwaway ideas is better than 100 actionable ones or that taking three hours to complete a process is superior than taking 30 minutes to do so, but it *is* clear that a vote with 50 % of the population participating is likely more representative and will be viewed as more legitimate than one in which only 1 % participates.

However, it is important to temper the expectation of large-scale participation with patience. As we have seen, most digital systems take many years to fully catch on, and reaching meaningful levels of participation depends on people coming back to participate again. This can be difficult, because many instances of digital democracy start afresh on each occasion, meaning that every time there is, for example, a consultation or participatory budget, organizers have to go out and attract people to take part. This is very time-consuming and in the previous chapter we saw the lengths organizers have to go to to try to ensure everyone truly has a chance to participate.

An alternative method is to develop a community of participants who are signed into the application and who receive notifications when a decision is put forward. This is how associations and political parties work – they send messages to their registered members when it is time to vote (and even then, as we saw in Chapter 2, participation rates often fluctuate with some members lapsing into passivity). The problem with applying this tactic to democracy in general is that it can become self-limiting, especially if efforts to reach out to additional participants lose steam. In this case, one ends up creating a community composed of a subsection of the population.

A more decentralized manner of creating online communities has been pioneered by PlaceSpeak in Canada. People register on PlaceSpeak and then receive notifications when an opportunity to participate in their area occurs (e. g. when a consultation in the area they live in is posted). People can also express interest in an issue. When a certain level of interest is reached among registered residents, local authorities are notified and encouraged to organize a consultation on this point. Civocracy, a European software, also allows citizens and residents to sign up to projects they are interested in (e.g. schools), while Delib, a consultation software widely used in the UK, geo-tags consultations, which can be particularly useful when dealing with more complex jurisdictions.[451]

Thinking about the stickiness of participation is very important – if we had to register to vote at every election, we would probably all vote less often. Having to attract each participant from scratch for every process is probably over-idealistic, and organizers often mention this as a major challenge, simply because it is hard to raise awareness.

Fortunately, once people *are* registered on a platform, they generally participate at fairly high rates within the immediate exercise. When I organized my campaign platform on Ethelo, 92% of registered users participated with two-thirds of those active participants voting on 90% or more of the issues put to them. In the Finnish online consultation on housing legislation, 1,300 people visited the site resulting in 566 registrations (a conversion rate of almost 45%). 60% of registered users participated actively.[452] In Lethbridge CIP 2021, 4,097 people visited the site, of which 2,007 participated, a conversion rate of again roughly 50%. In the carbon budgeting exercise run in London, Ontario, out of 12,190 site visitors, 1,263 took part (just over 10%). In an engagement on poverty reduction in Prince George, British Columbia, 1852 site visits resulted in 814 participants (a 43% conversion rate).[453] The Scottish consultation on Fireworks Safety attracted 12,000 site visitors and 1,400 participants (a conversion rate of just under 12%).[454] These high conversion rates may be partly due to insufficient marketing ensuring that only those with a particular interest in the topic at hand hear about it in the first place. However, as we can see, once people visit the site, the conversion rate to participation is often surprisingly high, especially considering that additional registration steps are sometimes required. The same could be said of participating once people sign up. The upside of this, is that one generally ends up with engaged and energizing participation. The downside is that it is difficult to achieve afresh every time an opportunity to participate is offered.

---

451 Interviews (2022).

452 Aitamurto and Saldivar, 'Motivating Participation' 8.

453 'Prince George Poverty Reduction' (*Ethelo*) 3.

454 Scottish Parliament, *Fireworks and Pyrotechnics* 2–3.

4.3 Conclusions on the User Experience

The importance of organization has often been neglected in the discussion of digital democracy. Although most of the things mentioned in this chapter are quite simple from an intellectual point of view, implementing them well is still challenging and requires constant focus and attention to detail.

Chapter 5
Communication

As we saw above, there is an unfortunate misconception that social media *is* digital democracy, and that any digital democracy would and should run along the lines laid down by the most ubiquitous social media companies. This understanding is deeply flawed. Not only does social media lack organized decision-making capabilities, its underlying logic is very different than that of democracy. Social media's purpose, as the name implies, is to be social, that is, to socialize and to maximize the time spent socializing. This is, however, not the purpose of democracy, which is to facilitate collective decision-making among free and equal citizens. One does not communicate in a democracy purely for its own sake. The communication is directed towards a goal – coming to a resolution on a certain point. Thus, we have to ask ourselves: since it is not to socialize, what is the purpose of *peer-to-peer* communication in a democracy? After all, this is precisely what the internet has changed – our ability to speak to each other, not just in small groups but at scale, without necessarily involving intermediaries, such as professional politicians or media personalities. We often hear that peer-to-peer communication is good for democracy, but *why* is it good?

5.1 Theories of Communication: A Brief Overview

There are three main ways to look at the purpose of peer-to-peer communication:
1) Deliberative Theory
2) Agonistic Theory and
3) Media Distortion Theory

5.1.1 Deliberative Theory

Deliberative theory, currently very popular in activist circles, postulates that communication serves the following points: encouraging consensus; participants accepting decisions as fair; learning about the experience of others; and examining evidence rationally and objectively in order to come to the best outcome for 'the common good'. While there are many variations of this theory, proponents gener-

https://doi.org/10.1515/9783110794465-009

ally believe that everyone should engage in deliberation, that is a public participation where they share and attempt to rationally justify their views to others.[455]

There are several drawbacks to this theory, especially when it is taken to extremes.

The first is that it can be conducive to groupthink which actually interferes with rational decision-making and the Wisdom of the Crowd. This is mainly due to the fact that although participants are explicitly exhorted to rationally justify their positions, they are also exhorted to empathize with other participants and see things from their point of view. Thus, participants are asked to simultaneously do two diametrically opposed things. Even the mere act of encouraging people to share their personal experiences with each other before coming to a decision incurs social pressure which inevitably causes people to confuse individual circumstances with general statistics and to attempt to keep the good opinion of the group by anticipating what others will approve of. These are not necessarily the best circumstances under which to make a binding decision.

The second drawback is that some adherents of this theory (often activists) have preconceived ideas of what 'the common good' is and host deliberation purely as a means of trying to coerce others into accepting those views. As a result, in practice a large portion of deliberation is based around deliberating how to achieve a pre-decided goal.[456] This is due to some activists having committed a gross oversimplification in their understanding of deliberation. Because it is believed that deliberation makes it more likely for people to accept that an outcome is fair – because they understand the reasons for it, as opposed to having it simply imposed upon them for no given reason – activists have understood this to mean that all they have to do is explain 'the right solution' *at* an audience and that audience will accept *that* solution. After all, they have now been told 'the reasons'. This requires those in charge to be extremely overconfident in their own solutions. However, this kind of highly directed deliberation can give the appearance of 'working' because forcing people to justify their views to near strangers (sometimes in the presence of selected experts who have explained the 'correct' outcomes) provides a powerful lever to pressure them to (at least outwardly) accept those foregone conclusions.

This can lead to a lack of respect for our inherent equality, as well as a tendency to intentionally encourage over-alignment. Some researchers and activists focus on achieving consensus as the ultimate goal of deliberation. The more consensus

---

455 Some examples of those writing on deliberation include Jürgen Habermas, Joshua Cohen, Lynn Carson, Iris Young, Ian O'Flynn and John Dryzek.
456 We will return to this in detail in Chapter 9.

there is, the better the process and the more 'right' the answer must be. However, it is impossible for a democracy to run this way.

Thirdly, although it ostensibly favours 'ordinary people', explaining one's political views generally requires a very high degree of articulation, especially since most views do not, in the final analysis have a *completely* rational explanation. Generally speaking, we *rationalize* our beliefs, that is, we find a cover that makes what we believe anyway sound plausibly rational. Highly educated, literate and higher-income people tend to have the most practice at exactly this activity. It doesn't mean their views *are* more rational – just that they are better at making them *sound* rational. People who do not spend their days verbally explaining themselves often find this more challenging. With deliberation, we thus run the risk of highly articulate people running rings around those who are less articulate, not because they are smarter or more likely to be right, but simply because they have spent a lot of time honing this particular skill-set. This can intimidate those less able to express themselves into going along with those who can.

This isn't always how deliberation is used, and some deliberative democrats explicitly reject extreme uses, but it is still important to consider these weaknesses which can be exploited.

5.1.2 Agonistic Theory

Agonists (also known as agonistic pluralists) believe that there are conflicting interests in any society and these interests cannot be reconciled purely through deliberation, because they are based on actually existing circumstances.[457] If I am using a river to power the waterwheel of my mill and someone else wants to build a dam upstream to provide a drinking water reservoir, we have a problem, especially if I don't want to give up my mill no matter the compensation being offered. Thus, although communication serves to clarify positions and examine the facts, it doesn't necessarily bring people closer together. Sharp divisions may continue to exist.

Agonists believe that there are few, if any, politically 'right' decisions based on a universal common good. Instead, politics is ultimately about making choices. It is

---

457 On agonism and the general de-politicization of politics see: Chantal Mouffe, 'Deliberative Democracy or Agonistic Pluralism' (2000) Institute for Advanced Studies, Vienna; Bonnie Honig, *Political Theory and the Displacement of Politics* (Cornell University Press 1993); Peter Mair, *Ruling the Void: The Hollowing of Western Democracy* (Verso 2013); John Matsusaka, *Let the People Rule: How Direct Democracy can Meet the Populist Challenge* (Princeton University Press 2020).

emancipatory – we have *agency*. Without this, there would be no diversity. As Aki Orr put it: 'Choices cannot be taught. To choose is to prefer. People prefer what they consider best. What is 'best' is determined by values, not by skill. No amount of skill – or information – will convince a religious person to vote for abolition of religious education'.[458]

Agonists may also favour debate, or other forms of communication, as opposed to deliberation, and be comfortable with formats where people can lay out their position and criticize the other side freely. Communication isn't generally aimed at convincing one's opponent, but rather at undecided or weakly committed voters. It serves to elucidate the points of contention and clarify facts around an issue that has arisen, but, above all, to *contest* the political space. Agonists accept that there are winners and losers of every decision, and are somewhat less enthusiastic about the idea that loss is acceptable in the service of 'the common good'.

It is not necessary for every single voter to directly participate in agonistic communication. Instead, many voters may rely on others putting their thoughts into words and then scrutinizing these others and deciding who they agree with most. Indeed, this is likely to be the case, because public debate is not always for the faint-hearted, and succeeding often requires a certain degree of articulation. That being said, the logic of agonistic pluralism is to determine which position or side will win in a reasonably respectful manner, whereas the logic of deliberation is to try to come to the one right (or at least 'best' or 'most just') answer. We can say generally that deliberative democrats (at least the extreme ones) want to depoliticize politics and agonistic pluralists generally want to re-politicize politics. Peer-to-peer communication can increase pluralism by reducing barriers to participation and allowing a greater variety of views to be expressed.

However, people can sometimes take agonism to extremes (in which case, it tends to go over into pure antagonism), making spurious claims and performing theatrics that serve no purpose. Some aspects of the American legal system, in which court cases can be performative in an effort to play to the press, are an example of this. The trick for democracy is to try to channel the energy of contested politics into avenues where political adversaries focus on the issues rather than on utterly destroying one another, and to try to create a situation where losers are not permanently trapped in their position.

---

458 Aki Orr, *Direct Democracy Manifesto: Politics for the 21ˢᵗ Century* <http://www.kulanu-nahlit. org/English.htm#mozTocId192120>.

5.1.3 Media Distortion Theory

A third theory is that peer-to-peer communication in democracy primarily serves the purpose of cutting down on the impacts of propaganda and misinformation.[459] This is especially the case in a society that lacks a media that works on behalf of 'the people'. In Western countries today, a large proportion of the media is sponsored by corporate advertising and wealthy donors who pay for content. This has become a norm rather than an exception. For example, two organizations ultimately funded by eBay billionaire Pierre Omidyar (Democracy Fund and Luminate) donate ca. $30 million annually to journalistic enterprises, such as the Center for Investigative Reporting, ProPublica and the Institute for Nonprofit News.[460] Other major donors to news organizations (local and national) include the Chan Zuckerberg Initiative, the MacArthur Foundation, Ford Foundation and Knight Foundation to name but a few. These organizations explicitly pursue a strategy of sponsoring what they view as desirable content and encouraging this content to be widely published, as it is available for free.[461] This undermines independent journalism, skews the national conversation in a manner that no longer accurately reflects public opinion, and doesn't necessarily satisfy public demand for answers or facts. Such 'journalism' is generally also explicitly partisan, with facts that contradict the 'narrative' or 'story-telling' of the publication intentionally omitted.

The point of peer-to-peer communication is thus to circumvent what is essentially commissioned propaganda as well as the high costs associated with mass media production, and allow people to directly contribute their own information and experience in the interests of producing a more accurate picture of reality. The well-known weakness here is that due to the lack of quality controls, in addition to well-researched and elucidating information, a great deal of vulgar and logically flawed information is also produced and it can be difficult to even find well-produced information amidst all the dross.

---

459 Roslyn Fuller, *Beasts and Gods: How Democracy Changed Its Meaning and Lost Its Purpose* (Zed/Bloomsbury 2015).

460 Roslyn Fuller, 'Power before People: The Global Crisis of the Faux Democracy Industry and Its Consequences' (Eastern Economics Association Annual Conference, 26 February 2021); 'Grant Search: Public Integrity' (*MacArthur Foundation*) <https://www.macfound.org/grants/?q=center+for+public+integrity> accessed 12 February 2023; Ford Foundation, Database search for the Center for Investigative Reporting <https://www.fordfoundation.org/work/our-grants/awarded-grants/grants-database/?q=Center%20for%20Investigative%20Reporting&p=1> accessed 12 February 2023. 461 'Steal Our Stories' (*ProPublica*) <https://www.propublica.org/steal-our-stories/> accessed 12 Feb 2023.

While each of these theories has something to be said for it, I believe that the deliberative theory is the weakest, especially when it comes to large-scale participation, and in particular, because at bottom, it seeks to depoliticize politics and deny the reality of different interests. This effectively – and rather against the intentions of many deliberative democrats – erases marginalized people under the pretence that they have been 'included' in the process. It may be the most harmonious and idealistic, but it is ultimately the most damaging for the reality of democracy.

However, before moving on, we should also ask ourselves one additional question when it comes to communication and that is: is sharing political views – particularly online – always good?

5.1.4 Is Sharing Always Good?

We use the secret ballot precisely so that people do not have to publicly state their politics and thereby risk being bribed or intimidated into voting a certain way.

Socializing is no different. We interact with others precisely in order to influence them and that can be positive (e.g. convincing), but also negative (browbeating, social pressure). The more we interact and share, the more handholds we give people to exercise this influence over us. According to legal scholar Spiros Simitis 'Personal information is increasingly used to enforce standards of behavior', a state of affairs incompatible with democracy, 'which depends upon a reservoir of individual capabilities associated with autonomous moral judgment and self-determination.'[462] According to Paul Schwartz, another legal scholar, 'The more that is known about a person, the easier it is to control him. Insuring the liberty that nourishes democracy requires a structuring of societal use of information and even permitting some concealment of information.'[463]

I have also argued that constitutional law acknowledges that:

> a private sphere is necessary to enable the development of personality…[T]o be under constant observation, exposed to constant judgment, impairs our abilities to think and develop as humans…it is necessary, for ourselves and for the health of our democracy, that we

---

462 Spiros Simitis, 'Reviewing Privacy in an Information Society' (1987) 135(3) University of Pennsylvania Law Review 710, cited in Zuboff, *The Age of Surveillance Capitalism* 191.

463 Paul M. Schwartz, 'The Computer in German and American Constitutional Law: Towards an American Right of Informational Self-Determination' (1989) 37 American Journal of Comparative Law 676, cited in Zuboff, *The Age of Surveillance Capitalism* 191.

each have somewhere to retreat, where we are safe from the judgement of others and alone with our own thoughts.[464]

Indeed, a lack of privacy is characteristic of totalitarian governments that maintain their absolute control by forcing actions into a public sphere where they may be judged, punished or 'corrected'.

These considerations are especially relevant when it comes to online commenting on digital democracy platforms, where records may remain long after the issue in question has been decided upon. Some M5S members, for example, claim they were purged from the party after it split from its digital provider Rousseau, and that this was easy to achieve, as administrators could see their commenting history and determine their sympathies.[465]

It is also important to recognize that in addition to the downside of public oversharing, the upsides of continuous political communication are also limited. It is often awkward and even fruitless to spend an inordinate amount of time discussing issues with those who have deeply different points of view, and insisting upon doing so can even lead to people hardening their positions (almost every extended family simply doesn't discuss politics for this very reason) or being talked into decisions they later regret. Obviously, one needs to have some communication in a democracy, but how much of it and how obligatory it should be are open to question. It *isn't* simply a case of 'the more the better'.

Based on the considerations above, there are four main options we could choose from when it comes to facilitating peer-to-peer communication in a digital democracy:

1. It is either obligatory or highly encouraged for each participant to share their views and justify their opinions (for example, Common Ground for Action)
2. Commenting is optional and interaction between participants is possible, but not particularly encouraged (e.g. Ethelo)
3. Commenting is possible but interaction between participants is not – participants can leave a comment, but cannot reply directly to others (e.g. Citizens Foundation, PolCo)
4. No commenting is possible (e.g. SkyVote Cloud)

---

464 Roslyn Fuller, 'A Call to Re-Embrace our Privacy' *Los Angeles Review of Books* (31 August 2021).
465 Personal communications with the author. The veracity of these claims is disputed, but it shows the issues at play here.

As we have seen, the first option is too open to manipulation, and interferes with independent reasoning and thus with the Wisdom of the Crowd, while option 4 precludes getting the benefit of circumventing the media and preventing distortions.

Options 2 and 3 would seem to carry the most benefits for democratic decision-making in terms of peer-to-peer commenting with the fewest downsides, as they facilitate an exchange of communication while still permitting people to retain their privacy according to their own judgement. If some people wish to act more publicly and attempt to influence others, they can, but it is not a requirement to have one's vote counted.

Of course, beyond these basic structural considerations, there are still many difficulties with peer-to-peer interaction in digital forums. Thus, we will discuss how to facilitate this interaction in a more constructive manner, and discourage abuse while preserving the freedom and individuality necessary for democracy.

5.2 Understanding Abusive Behaviour: The Dark Triad

The Dark Triad refers to three related personality traits: Narcissism, Machiavellianism and Psychopathy. While no one is completely devoid of these attributes, some people exhibit them to a much higher degree than others.[466] Narcissists tend to *truly* believe that they are the centre of the universe, that they are more skilled and popular than they are, and to demand unending attention. Psychopaths tend to be 'dead inside', lack empathy, and are often impulsive. At their most extreme, psychopaths have been known to kill others simply out of curiosity or boredom. Machiavellians tend to be highly ambitious and focused on callously manipulating others to get what they want (the character Littlefinger in the popular book and television series *Game of Thrones* was a classic Machiavellian). Ca. 4% of the population are thought to be clinical narcissists, while 1% are clinical psychopaths (Machiavellianism is not an officially diagnosable personality disorder). However, people can also possess these attributes at a high but subclinical level. This means that a non-negligible minority of people possess these characteristics to a degree that regularly affects their social behaviour.

Some of the behaviours associated with the Dark Triad include:

– frequent lying (including fraudulent behaviour)

---

466 Delroy L. Paulhus and Kevin M. Williams, 'The Dark Triad of Personality: Narcissism, Machiavellianism and Psychopathy' (2002) 36(6) Journal of Research and Personality 556–563.

- sabotaging others (in particular with frivolous claims, intentional misunderstandings, or by spreading gossip about them)
- scapegoating (picking someone to blame for all ills and mistakes)
- attention-seeking (often leading to ever more outrageous behaviour)
- projection (claiming others are doing what the Dark Triader is, in fact, doing)
- disingenuously playing the victim (a devastatingly effective tactic, often used when they are finally caught engaging in any of the other behaviours)

Some of the ways this manifests on social media are:

- claiming that anyone who does not agree with the Dark Triader is inherently evil and thus an acceptable scapegoat for their ire
- spreading false information, either as a form of attention-seeking (narcissism) or as click-bait for profit (Machiavellianism)
- misportraying others or intentionally reading negative intentions into their statements or actions (however far-fetched)
- encouraging others to bully, ostracize or cancel another user
- acting impulsively ('hot takes')
- refusing to take responsibility for proven past mistakes, false claims, etc.
- consistently seeking to portray oneself in an unrealistically positive light
- blatantly flattering or pandering to others in order to ultimately use them (Machiavellianism)
- engaging in wars of attrition or feuds well past the time anything useful has been said
- publicly celebrating the deaths of their opponents

As if this weren't bad enough, preliminary research indicates that people who score highly in Dark Triad traits (as well as the related traits of sadism and spitefulness) may disproportionately become addicted to social media.[467] In fact, those who score highly in Dark Triad traits may be predisposed to addiction in general,[468] and Dark Triaders, particularly narcissists and psychopaths, struggle with poor impulse control. It therefore seems plausible that they would quickly suc-

---

467 Kagan Kircaburun and Mark D. Griffiths, 'The Dark Side of Internet: Preliminary Evidence for the Associations of Dark Personality Traits with Specific Online Activities and Problematic Internet Use' (2018) 7(4) Journal of Behavioural Addictions 993–1003; Lennart Fryth, Bernad Batinic and Peter K. Jonason, 'Social Media Use and Personality: Beyond Self-Reports and Trait-Level Assessments' (2023) 202 Personality and Individual Differences, Article 111960.
468 Guyonne Rogier and Patrizia Velotti, 'Narcissistic Implications in Gambling Disorder: The Mediating Role of Emotion Dysregulation' (2018) 34 Journal of Gambling Studies 1241–1260.

cumb to the temptation to use social media to try to fulfill their (destructive) psychological needs. Dark Triad behaviour on social media is thus often both compulsive and abusive (just as it is in real life), and to some extent commercialized social media caters to this disturbed behaviour precisely because the people perpetrating most of it are their best customers.

It's this behaviour, perpetrated primarily by a minority of individuals, that accounts for most of the disturbance in our communication today. It's not just 'people' in general, it truly is *some* people with particular characteristics, and it is important to remember that they also perpetrate these behaviours in real life. The internet did not change their personality or cause this behaviour (although it would be classic Dark Triad projection to claim that it did); it just gave them yet another avenue to channel it into.

Our goal is not to diagnose and root out individual behaviour, but rather to minimize the scope for abuse in online peer-to-peer communication by stopping those aspects of communication that are almost uniquely attractive to Dark Triaders and most easily exploited by them. The following provide some guidelines on how to do this.

5.2.1 Avoid Stable Hierarchies

It is typical of social media that most users 'follow' the accounts they like. Unfortunately, some Dark Triaders are very adept at attracting a large number of followers often using strategies that other people may baulk at, such as:

- doing what they believe their followers want to see, creating an endless hall of mirrors (inimical to democracy where everyone is supposed to contribute independently)
- competing to say the most outrageous and extreme thing possible in the interests of attracting more followers and proving their 'commitment' to a cause or 'side'[469]
- projecting a lifestyle far above the one they are actually enjoying in an insatiable cry for attention
- endlessly updating their status and constantly patrolling their online image

---

[469] For a description of this general phenomenon see, Hugo Mercier, *Not Born Yesterday: The Science of Who We Trust and What We Believe* (Princeton University Press 2020).

They then seek to use their accumulated followers as a weapon against others, demanding that they harass or cut contact with those who have had the temerity to displease or oppose the Dark Triader.

In contrast to commercial social media, none of the working systems of online democracy that I have examined over the past 15 years use 'follower' systems, and this is likely one of the reasons they report few (sometimes zero) incidences of harassment and bullying. If a person with half a million followers starts to pick on someone else or make unfounded accusations, it's very hard for their victim to defend themselves, especially if the bully encourages their followers to engage in a coordinated attack with the goal of permanently damaging their victim's reputation or driving them from the platform. If a person without followers attempts the same thing, it is still an unpleasant experience, but decidedly easier to deal with.

As this indicates, there are many reasons why the follower system is not just unpleasant, but actually counterproductive to democracy. In order to be equal, every participant must start from the same position. We want (as we saw above in the principles) to avoid dependency, because when two million people allow themselves to become dependent on one person's decision, we suddenly don't have two million brains scrutinizing the issue – we only have one, who has, for all intents and purposes, mentally enslaved the others. This spurns *all* of the advantages of democracy and democratic equality and substitutes a pro forma, mob-like participation in its place. This is why claims that social media is *an excess of democracy* are completely incorrect. Social media is profoundly anti-democratic in the way it is structured and it facilitates anti-democratic behaviour and outcomes by instituting hierarchies that lend themselves to perpetrating abuse.

5.2.2 Thwart Cliques

While mutually friending people (as people frequently do on Facebook or when they connect on LinkedIn) is preferable to following in that it at least creates a more egalitarian relationship between the people so bonded, it is still far from ideal, as it can lead to the formation of online cliques. Cliques impair judgement and, in the worst case, can gang up on other participants. At other times, they work together to amplify their own content (favouriting, linking to each other) to the extent that it pushes others out of the conversation.[470]

Clique formation has become prevalent on some forms of social media with users proving quite inventive in how they go about constructing these kinds of 'clubs'. For example, over the past few years, Twitter users have figured out a way to identify who is on their 'team' by using certain acronyms or symbols in their profile description (e. g. the British or European flag to indicate their stance on the Brexit referendum), thus *pre*-organizing into squads that adhere to a certain position. This is a prime example of the Iron Law of Oligarchy at work – power is constantly coalescing and seeking to perpetuate itself under all circumstances. People don't *need* to identify their positions in their profiles; they *choose* to form teams against opponents and to make this group loyalty central to their identity.

The ease with which cliques proliferate in even the most petty and inconsequential environments will be known to anyone familiar with local politics. Indeed, clique-formation is a problem that has been known since the dawn of time. In the Council of 500 in Athens (a largely administrative body), members were prohibited from sitting with their friends for exactly this reason. In a democracy, every citizen *owes* the State (the collective) their judgment. When one unthinkingly gives someone else's judgement one is essentially committing fraud. While focusing on emotional ties may be appropriate for socializing, in a digital democracy environment, participants should not have 'friends', as they are there to act professionally, not socially.

5.2.3 Status should not Supplant Achievement

Modern representative democracy and social media suffer from a similar flaw – they both make it easy for people to project an artificial construct of themselves. Politicians and parties are famous for doing this and for encouraging people to vote based on how much they like a candidate's *image.* This turns politics into a popularity contest and the people best able to win it are often the most manipulative.

Social media revolves even *more* around image – who has the most followers, who has the best photos, who has the most likes and compliments. This means an emphasis on a kind of empty status rather than achievement, and this status can become semi-formalized.

---

470 See e. g. Nanjala Nyabola, *Digital Democracy: Analogue Politics: How the Internet Era is Transforming Politics in Kenya* (Zed Books 2018) 92.

Twitter's former blue check programme was a prime example of the issues with status on social media. The programme started as a way to distinguish parody accounts from genuine ones. For example, if Barbra Streisand were on Twitter, her account would have a blue checkmark next to it to distinguish her from an account devoted to imitating the famous singer. However, the blue check programme eventually morphed into the equivalent of a 'VIP' status. Blue checks were given out according to opaque criteria and came to be viewed purely as a status symbol which made their bearers (in some indefinable way) more important than other users. Blue check holders then proceeded to spend most of their time boasting in truly grandiose fashion, giving innumerable 'hot takes' on every possible issue, and attacking each other continuously.

That the behaviour of so many of those given exalted status took this negative turn should come as no surprise. Dark Triaders are far more likely to participate in settings where they can acquire status. Particularly narcissists often insist that they be recognized as 'more important' than others and that they be able to conduct arguments, and preferably all interactions, from this vantage point. Giving some people a status marker, especially one that did not bear any known relationship to easily ascertainable achievements, provided a perfect attraction for Dark Triaders, some of whom may have even paid to acquire this status. Stripping this status away and forcing Dark Triaders to communicate from a position of equality within digital democracy forums is not something that appeals to them, and thus doing this should encourage them to minimize their interactions with others, rather than maximizing them.

For the same reasons, digital democracy tools should also discourage users from sharing social photos of themselves on the platform unless doing so serves a purpose. Not only does allowing people to project an image compromise privacy, it can lead to status (based on appearance), vanity, and people de facto using the forum as a dating site.[471]

5.2.4 Dealing with Bots and Bot-Like People

Because the commercial value of social media companies depends on having the maximum number of users and engagement, they are somewhat disincentivized to prevent and eliminate bots (automatic programmes that seek to pass for real users while pursuing some other aim). Fortunately, the nature of public democracy

---

471 Some very early iterations of digital democracy platforms fell victim to this issue, before quickly course-correcting.

tools makes it very hard for bots to gain access to the system in the first place and very easy to detect. Even many tools that allow open-access participation (e.g. on local consultations) include features that filter out bots, and the more security there is around setting up an account, the easier it is to prevent a bot from gaining access to the system. Nonetheless, it is important to always dedicate some time and energy to controlling this problem, particularly in open-access systems. As programming becomes more advanced, and bots are better able to imitate human beings, this could become more of an issue for open-access participation (where anyone can participate on a public website without having to sign in).

Bot-like people are another problem entirely and they come in two main forms: the serial repeater and the copy-paste commenter.

5.2.4.1 Carthago Delenda Est (The Serial Repeater)

In ancient times, Cato the Elder, a prominent Roman statesman, was in the habit of closing each and every one of his speeches with the phrase 'Carthago delenda est', which means 'Carthage must be destroyed' (Carthage being an enemy city, which the Romans did, in fact, eventually destroy). In other words, in Cato's opinion, the threat posed by Carthage was being dangerously ignored by his fellow citizens, and to remedy this he adopted the somewhat irritating habit of unrelentingly making this point, even if the rest of his speech concerned an entirely different topic.

There are people who use similar tactics to bring their points across today, although they often lack Cato's finesse. For example, in Okotoks 2080, one participant commented 'eliminate the sustainability department' on almost every proposal. Another participant in the Lethbridge CIP responded to a large number of proposals with strident accusations of white supremacy (often only tangentially related to the matter at hand). While in some cases, these types of comments may originate from a genuine obsession with the point at hand that the person feels must be reiterated as a matter of importance, they are also sometimes narcissistic attempts to hijack the conversation and force it into a path more congenial to the relentless poster.

Interestingly enough, such comments are much easier to ignore online than they are offline (e.g. at an offline consultation or townhall meeting) where they tend to instantly derail the conversation. However, despite persistent and intentionally provocative commenting, these participants (and others like them) were almost completely ignored by other participants online. Unless intense repeat commenting becomes disruptive and begins to interfere with other people's contributions, it is probably best to do likewise. Allowing other participants to flag comments can also allow such situations to be dealt with in the event that they get out of hand.

5.2.4.2 Copy-Paste Comments

Another form of bot-like participation is the copy-paste re-post. This occurs when the commenter does not post their own original content, but instead re-posts content copied entirely from another source.

This is a particular issue, because many activist organizations intentionally create pre-formulated posts for their adherents to use. These tactics are frequently used during election campaigns to flood candidates with a wave of identical messages and influence or intimidate them into taking the desired action. When I ran for election as an Independent candidate in my constituency in 2016, the majority of the thousands of emails I received from potential voters were copy-paste messages of this type. One of the most frequent originated from an environmental NGO. It was quite belligerent in tone and ended with a promise from the sender to confront me about my environmental record when I canvassed them at their door. The message also included the sender's full name and address (given to prove that they lived in my constituency).

It was therefore quite easy for me to determine that some of these messages came from people I *had* recently canvassed, and who had *not* raised any such issues to me while I was standing right in front of them, specifically inviting them to do so. Others came from people I proceeded to canvass (none of whom raised these issues). On one occasion, upon receiving the email yet again, I promptly replied to the constituent who sent it, outlining my environmental policy, and asking why he hadn't raised this issue to me as promised a mere 48 hours previously when I had, in fact, been standing on his doorstep actively attempting to engage him in political conversation. He did not respond.

Given these circumstances, it is very hard to know how seriously one should take such copy-paste messages. Some people may simply be too shy to bring things up themselves, but in many cases it seems that the person posting the message is merely the intermediary of the ultimate sender (usually an NGO), and that they often do *not* entirely stand behind the content being posted – they merely succumb to posting it due to its convenience.

This type of submission is not particular to the internet. In offline consultations organizations and companies sometimes encourage people to sign pre-formulated submissions that the organization then sends to authorities in bulk. Offline, this is generally tolerated, but I believe a much harder line is necessary in digital democracy forums, precisely because the ease of reposting is so negligible as to empty such copy-paste participation of any meaning whatsoever while simultaneously clogging the discussion for everyone else. In a digital forum, one should either search and delete for such identical posts, or use a tool that offers automatic collection of them for administrators to review and delete. Retaining them would allow a level of distortion into the arena that serves no purpose, as it is unclear how much support such messages actually enjoy. Participants, after all, still have their vote which they may exercise without any need for justification and may also comment 'no' or 'disagree' or simply like another comment without the need to rely on pre-formulated justifications.

5.2.4.3 Coordinated Disruption

A third threat could stem from entities paying or otherwise rewarding others to participate in the online discussion. After all, companies already pay social media 'influencers' to essentially do the same thing today, crowding out other brands.[472] This is another reason why it is important not to allow followers. If a participant has a large number of followers, it attracts others to pay them, legally or illegally, for their endorsement.[473]

Coordinated disruption is, unfortunately, a real threat for digital democracy. Political partisans already encourage their followers to visit retail sites like Amazon and systematically down-rank products the group disapproves of, while others (such as Tea Party and Indivisible activists) attend physical townhall meetings with the explicit goal of disrupting them (indeed some organizations even produce handbooks instructing their members on how to achieve this). It is therefore not unreasonable to assume that such organizations could encourage their members to join online discussions with the explicit goal of disrupting them or swamping them with their own views in a coordinated takeover. This is yet another reason why (as we saw above) it is important to advertise widely and reach out to all groups, as well as to focus on concrete issues which lend themselves less to hyper-partisan behaviour.

We can also imagine the same thing happening the other way around – someone seeing a comment they dislike on a digital democracy forum and then attempting to cancel the poster on social media. The possibility for such retaliation remains a thorny issue of public participation which we will cover in more detail in Chapter 7.

---

472 Nyabola, *Digital Democracy: Analogue Politics* 6.
473 Nyabola, *Digital Democracy: Analogue Politics* 91.

5.2.5 Don't Judge Success on Engagement Alone

It's now fairly well established that users often engage more with content that outrages or offends them, possibly because this activates our threat reflexes. Unfortunately, these reflexes play straight into the hands of Dark Triaders who are often masters at generating outrage.

There are two ways we use the word 'controversial' today: one is to mean that something generates controversy, because many people feel strongly for and against the issue at hand. But another usage is to indicate that an idea or view is simply extremely unpopular, without there being deep societal divisions about it. Competing purely on engagement numbers can often lead people to compete on being outrageous and controversial, as this is a cheap, fast way to increase involvement. While it is important to encourage as wide a participation as possible, it is also important not to give in to this temptation.

When a proposal meets with a high level of approval or seems 'like a no-brainer' to participants, there simply isn't much to say about it. Thus, although lack of participation *can* signal apathy and dissatisfaction with the choices on offer, it can also signal complacency and a high level of satisfaction. People are less likely to vote in referendums, for example, when they believe the outcome is already assured.

5.2.6 Say No to Infinite Interaction

Some Dark Triaders particularly love to feel important and thus view it as necessary to continuously state their position on all matters. They will thus often engage in obsessive (if contentless) posting to each other while others tune out of the process.

This can easily be resolved by limiting the number of posts anyone can make, as well as the manner in which they can make them. For example, on Ethelo, there is generally a character limit on the comments one can make under each post. One can, of course, simply continue what one was saying in a further comment, but it does discourage this behaviour by making it inconvenient. It also encourages people to try to make their point with a certain degree of brevity. Common Ground for Action achieves the same outcome via facilitation which is aimed at preventing a few people from dominating the conversation, regardless of whether this originates in mere gregariousness or selfishness.

Others discourage direct confrontation by separating comments into 'for' and 'against' or 'pro' and 'con' columns. This means that each side cannot interact with the other directly, making it impossible for them to enter a flame war with each other. However, each participant's input is still preserved in comment form which may influence others. Both Citizens Foundation and PolCo use this method.[474]

Asynchronous digital participation itself may also discourage endless fights. Because participants are online at different times, they rarely reply directly to others' comments and when they do it tends to be in slow-motion. The quick back and forth of a social media war of attrition is extremely difficult to establish under these conditions.

5.2.7 Establish Clear Guidelines

Because Dark Triaders are experts at manipulation, it is important to make all rules very clear and to lay them out in advance. Otherwise, those who feel entitled to manipulate the process will simply bend them until they have lost all meaning. In particular, if one allows comments to be deleted without very clear guidelines governing this process, one is highly likely to end up with a time-consuming 'war of deletion' in which the argument centres on what is and what is not deleted.

5.2.8 Utilizing Expertise in a Dark Triad World

Expertise and achievement *are* important for democracy, and while everyone has a right to their own opinion, this is a far cry from accepting that all opinions are based on plausible evidence or at least well-intentioned educated guesses.

It is, unfortunately, not uncommon today to come across people who believe themselves to be experts on subjects they know virtually nothing about. This is particularly an issue for narcissists, who often genuinely believe in their own false perception of their abilities, but is also an issue across the Dark Triad, as most people who score highly in these characteristics possess a flair for projecting an unrealistically positive version of themselves. Worse, these self-anointed experts often act in bad faith with little regard for the consequences of their carelessness. This behaviour isn't confined to isolated commenters who have little chance of influencing others, but extends into seemingly professional NGOs and think tanks whose proclamations (often outrageous, exaggerated or just superficial) are blindly repeated by media. This has created enormous confusion in society and there are now widespread doubts as to the value of expertise.

---

474 Information obtained via interviews.

This extremely serious problem is often met with a knee-jerk demand that people should simply trust experts more, glaring mistakes and clear failures of those who have been proclaimed to be experts, notwithstanding. This, it is said, would be good for democracy. But in fact, the opposite is true. Democracy is *the opposite* of trust. Democracy is about *scrutiny*. Far from blindly accepting ideas that seem to make little sense on the surface, democracy is about taking ideas that seem like perfectly good ideas and subjecting them to rigorous tests in case they harbour a hidden flaw. When the consequences are serious – as they are in a court of law or in a democracy – even the most seemingly water-tight case deserves to be scrutinized. Real experts are also usually happy to explain themselves (rather than attempting to shut the conversation down) and to acknowledge the limits of their knowledge as well as human knowledge in general (expert advice is a best guess, not a prophecy).

There are two things we can do here. Firstly, instead of complaining about a lack of trust, experts (real experts) need to make a commitment to try to live up to democratic scrutiny and to firmly but politely stand up to people who claim to be experts, but fail to live up to the standards we would normally expect an expert to adhere to.

Secondly, even in the absence of a good education system, there is one fairly quick way to sort reliable from unreliable experts – and that is to look at their track record. This is not a perfect system (someone could give good advice a few times, all the while plotting ultimate betrayal), but it's fairly good. Politicians utilize exactly this tactic whenever they run 'on their record'.

Judging experts on their record, however, presents some difficulties because it requires democracy to go on for long enough for people to be able to judge experts' contributions against reality. This requires that such experts be identifiable – that there is a record of what they have said that we can measure against outcomes. While creating permanent records for ordinary citizens is fraught with issues pertaining to surveillance (as outlined above), it would seem not too much to expect that those who want to call themselves experts are willing to stand on and be judged by their record. This is, after all, analogous to how we have been running offline democracy up to this point, where 'ordinary citizens' can cast their votes anonymously, but those who wish to exercise influence, e.g. by publishing a newspaper article, are expected to sign their name to it and bear the consequences if they are mistaken.

5.2.9 Conclusions on the Dark Triad

It is important to recognize that social media doesn't *cause* Dark Triad behaviour –
it just gives it an outlet. People who behave badly online would not *be* better people
without social media and they would still be interfering with democracy in face-to-
face settings. They are an eternal problem for *any* political system.

The digital democracy systems that exist have thus far experienced the issues
caused by Dark Triaders to a remarkably low degree, with many operators reporting that they have rarely if *ever* had to remove a participant from their sites.[475]
One researcher reported that they had used Common Ground for Action to run
a deliberation that had attracted over 1000 comments. The rules of the deliberation
were such that if two people judged a comment or question to be inflammatory,
vulgar or abusive, that comment would be filtered out. No comments had to be filtered.[476]

One of the reasons for this is that the vast majority of people do not score
highly on Dark Triad traits. In fact, most people tilt towards the so-called Light
Triad rather than Dark Triad. This means that the bulk of humanity is not merely
neutral, but actually leans slightly towards the following qualities:

1. a strong belief in humanity
2. empathy
3. a dislike of self-promotion.[477]

Such people may strongly disagree or even have a spat and say things they regret,
but they do not engage in the continuous destructive behaviour that is characteristic of those who score highly on the negative personality traits.

Although this is encouraging to know, it likely does not fully explain the mainly
quite good behaviour so far observed in digital democracy forums. Thus far, most
of these forums tend to revolve around fairly small-scale decisions rather than 'the

---

475 Interviews with operators (2017–2022).

476 Michael A. Neblo, Kevin M. Esterling and David M.J. Lazer, *Politics with the People: Building a
Directly Representative Democracy* (Cambridge University Press 2018) 89 (the authors see this primarily as a factor of facilitation and deliberation not replicable to other online forums, although
others without such facilitation report equally low numbers of incidents).

477 Scott Barry Kaufman, 'The Light Triad vs Dark Triad of Personality' *Scientific American* (19
March 2019) <https://blogs.scientificamerican.com/beautiful-minds/the-light-triad-vs-dark-triad-of-
personality/>; Kylie Andrews, 'The Dark Triad Sums up Psychopaths, but the Light Triad Defines
Saints' *ABC News* (15 May 2019) <https://www.abc.net.au/news/science/2019-05-16/psychopaths-nar
cissm-the-dark-triad-fascinate-us-the-light-triad/11093104>.

big issues'. It is likely that those who score highly in Dark Triad traits are less attracted to such forums and their limited audience than they are to commercial and social media. As digital democracy grows, it is likely that it will have to contend with such behaviour and adapt accordingly, although hopefully some of the tactics outlined above will help to control the issue. The more a process can focus on issues and avoid back-stabbing, politicking, and wheeling-dealing, the less people become fatigued by the process. The endless drama fuelled in part by negative personality traits is exactly what most people hate most about 'politics'.

5.3 Observations from the Field: Okotoks 2080 and Lethbridge CIP

Much of what one reads about commenting in digital democracy forums is actually based on commenting on social media, which, as we have seen, is very different and does not readily transfer. This section will detail what I learned from two use cases of Canadian software Ethelo in Alberta, Canada. Both cases produced extensive data on how people engaged in digital democracy in an atmosphere where they self-selected to participate and there were few controls.

The first use case occurred in Okotoks, a rapidly growing town ca 15 minutes by car from Calgary (a large city of a million inhabitants). In 2021, the population of Okotoks was 30,405. The subject of the Okotoks consultation was the new Municipal Development Plan (MDP) 'Okotoks 2080', intended to 'guide future growth and development as the town's population grows to an anticipated 70,000 – 90,000 people by 2080'.[478] The town administration put 42 different elements of this plan up on Ethelo and invited residents to comment and vote[479] on a 5-point scale on each element which ranged from 'totally oppose' to 'moderately oppose', 'neutral', 'moderately support' and 'totally support'. Only five of the proposals put forward received over 50% of the combined 'totally support' and 'moderately support' vote. Some proposals received as little as 16% approval, while others went as high as

---

478 'Okotoks 2080' (*Ethelo*) <https://okotoks-2080.ethelo.net/page/welcome> accessed 16 February 2023.

479 In this context, we will use the term 'vote' to describe those situations where participants can indicate a measurable preference on a particular proposal or recommendation, whether through indicating 'yes/no', selecting a position on a scale or up/downvoting. Whether or not organizers intend this to count as a 'vote' or merely a 'feeling', etc. is not relevant as this very inclarity is part of the problem.

66%.[480] There were a total of 749 comments, giving an average of close to 18 comments per proposal.

In Lethbridge, a city of 100,000 people, a 2-hour drive south of Okotoks, Ethelo was used for a digital consultation on the 10-year Capital Investment Programme (CIP) in 2021.[481] There were three phases to this consultation, although this was not immediately apparent – projects put forward by community groups for voting; feedback on general infrastructure (e.g. electricity, water, internet, waste); and feedback on the Ethelo process itself. The capital cost and annual operating cost were given for each proposed project, which was often illustrated with a photo (sometimes a generic stock photo) or diagram. These projects were typically very large, generally costing a minimum of several hundred thousand dollars, with many coming in in the millions or even tens of millions of dollars. Each proposal also featured a description (ca. 100 words) of what the money would be used for with specific outcomes to be achieved. If something were to be built, for example, the exact square meters, seating capacity, etc. was stated in the description. Often a reason was also given as to *why* the proposal was being made.

One example of a descriptive paragraph reads:

> This project is the expansion of the Crossings Branch Library into the undeveloped space of 2,588 square feet. The project will include extending the children's area, improved teen area, creation of a new public meeting room, additional public washrooms and staff workspace, a strategic redesign of the library to provide better access to washrooms and staff support. Includes additional furniture and collections.[482]

While 105 projects (most of them bundled into packages) were listed, only 29 could be voted upon, and 11 of them cleared the 50% hurdle on approval (totally support and moderately support votes). Over 2,000 people took part, generating over 10,000 comments.

What is interesting about both Okotoks 2080 and Lethbridge CIP is that they did not occur in a lab, where scientists often introduce artificial constraints in an attempt to isolate variables. Unlike in PolCo or Your Priorities, these fairly large groups also involved people being able to actively reply to and debate each

---

480 'Okotoks 2080' (*Ethelo*) <https://okotoks-2080.ethelo.net/page/collective-results> accessed 16 February 2023.

481 'City of Lethbridge Capital Budget' (*City of Lethbridge*) <https://lethbridgecipbudget.ethelo.net/page/welcome> accessed 16 February 2023.

482 'City of Lethbridge Capital Budget' (*City of Lethbridge*) <https://lethbridgecipbudget.ethelo.net/page/Community%20Group%20Projects> accessed 16 February 2023.

other without facilitation, so it is a good opportunity to observe these dynamics potentially playing out. It also should be noted that many Canadians (including Albertans) consider Alberta to be 'the Texas of Canada', by which they mean they stereotype its inhabitants as not only failing to conform to the national standard of politeness, but actually being proud of their refusal to do so.[483] So, for many Canadians, if an online consultation was going to go wrong and get really polarized, it would be in Alberta – exactly why these made such interesting test cases.

Some observations on this participation process are detailed below.

5.3.1 Little to No Groupthink

In both Okotoks and Lethbridge, no matter how many comments were expressed in a certain direction, there was always at least one participant who took a contrary stance. Participants did not seem to experience any discomfort at this (they did not apologize for or relativize their position), nor did they do anything to indicate that they were being contrarian for the sake of it.

In addition to this, in the case of Okotoks 2080, despite the fact that most participants were very strongly opposed to the majority of proposals, they still accepted and voted for the few they liked. Participants clearly did not reject proposals out of hand, despite the fact that they had rejected many previous proposals and were in some cases clearly annoyed and offended at the general direction the proposals presented by government were taking. Similarly, in Lethbridge it was possible to track named commenters who voiced clear and strong opposition to many proposals, but then came across one they liked which they endorsed in the comments.

It would appear that people are significantly less carried away by their emotions and significantly less prone to knee-jerk reactions than is commonly thought. This is in line with research that shows politically unaligned individuals and those who do not constantly follow politics take in more information and are more likely to change their minds based on new information than those who consider themselves 'political junkies'.[484]

---

483 This entire reddit thread is devoted to discussing whether or not these stereotypes are true: <https://www.reddit.com/r/Calgary/comments/lp1m2a/is_alberta_the_texas_of_canada/>.
484 Charles S. Taber and Milton R. Lodge, 'Motivated Skepticism in the Evaluation of Political Beliefs' (2006) 50 American Journal of Political Science 755–769; Richard F. West, Russell J. Meserve and Keith Stanovich, 'Cognitive Sophistication does not Attenuate the Bias Blind Spot' (2012) 103(3) Journal of Personality and Social Psychology 506–519.

Commenters *did* certainly influence each other to some extent, for example, comments sometimes followed a similar track for a little while, e.g. clusters of comments about shale pathways, clusters of comments about maintenance, clusters of comments about signs, but this was fairly mild. It is possible that group-think (at least in settings where there is no hierarchy or concerted effort to attain consensus among face-to-face participants) is overestimated in the literature.

5.3.2 Address Underlying Issues

Deep, unresolved issues surfaced in both the Okotoks and Lethbridge consultations.

In Okotoks, this issue was an ongoing water shortage, prompted in part by the rapid growth of the town. The fact that Okotoks 2080 focused on growing the population even more rapidly inflamed residents, particularly as they had previously capped population growth in an effort to mitigate the water supply issues. While the water supply was explicitly addressed in some of the Okotoks 2080 questions, it also had implications for many others (e.g. more housing), and it was frequently mentioned in comments as an underlying issue that needed to be resolved *before* the proposal at hand could be addressed. References to water were possibly the single most common comment in Okotoks – in fact, the word 'water' was mentioned 122 times by participants.

In Lethbridge, the unresolved issue was a bridge that had long been promised but never constructed. This bridge was of major importance, as most of Lethbridge's growth is concentrated in the oxbow of a river with little possibility for the residents to flee should a fire (a major hazard in the region) break out. The missing bridge and its relation to various proposals accounted for a large number of comments, and it was clear that this issue was preventing the community from moving forward on some proposals. As these examples show, if there is an important unresolved issue in your area that everyone is already aware of and that has a bearing on the process at hand, this issue should be dealt with first.

5.3.3 Avoid Perceptions of Manipulation

There is a reason we focused on manipulation in the introduction and why it features so prominently in Arnstein's Ladder of Participation.

No one appreciates being asked their opinion on the *details* of a plan they believe is *fundamentally* wrong or counter to their interests. This came through very clearly in the Okotoks consultation where many of the proposals were directed at facilitating compact living and pedestrianizing the town. As many participants pointed out, they explicitly rejected high-density living every day, simply by not moving to nearby Calgary. Furthermore, proposals for pedestrianizing, abandoning cars or using bikes were met with objections regarding the inclement weather of Okotoks, which has been known to experience snowfall in August and where the daily mean temperature is below zero degrees Celsius half of the year.

Because so many proposals ran so counter to what was considered to be the basic, most intrinsic goods of the participants' lifestyle, several accusations were made that the engagement amounted to 'social engineering'. A recurrent accusation throughout the process was that it was manipulative and that the government was trying to get them to approve of the high-density, pedestrianized living that they rejected and believed was inappropriate for their location.

In this case, it would likely have been better for the organizers to consult with citizens at an earlier point in the process to come up with ideas better suited to the location and population, as presenting them with multiple ideas that seemed out of sync with public opinion raised suspicion among participants.

5.3.4 Avoid Euphemisms and Any Other Inclarity

Perhaps the most violent reaction to be observed in both consultations was to euphemisms. For example, in Okotoks 2080, participants were quick to realize that 'non-traditional' and 'non-market' housing meant smaller, more cheaply produced housing, and they became extremely irate that this was not addressed directly. Participants proceeded to relentlessly object to what they termed 'lame buzz words' and 'management speak' throughout the course of the consultation.

NGOs and political advisors constantly push for better 'messaging' and using shiny new terms to put a spin on things, but this underestimates the level of intelligence of the population and is thus insulting – with predictable results.

Perhaps one of the most aggressive comments in Okotoks (in relation to building non-market housing) was:

> WTF is non-market housing? English, mother-commie! Do you speak it?! Quit hiding behind weasel-words. State exactly what you are proposing and we will decide.

Another commented, on a proposal to introduce a 'Sustainability Scorecard' for development plans:

> If I see this word "sustainable" one more time I am seriously going to scream. Oh, I see the person below has already said the same thing. Good grief, stop this b.s. I am opposing it because I have no clue what you mean or how you would be able to produce it.

Others were somewhat more polite in expressing their annoyance. In response to the proposal: 'Facilitate development of an Innovation Precinct centered on innovation and sustainability. This would include shared resource use and programming, and by-product synergies'

a participant commented:

> Best use of buzzwords and vague platitudes in this survey so far. With folks like this at the helm, we can't help but innovate our way to progressive excellence.

Another comment explained the issue to the organizers in a less hostile fashion:

> Words like 'innovation' and 'sustainable' are weasel words. They make us feel good but can be so broad in definition that they can be meaningless and confusing. Why not try to define what specific characteristic you think will make a real difference and set targets or performance measures around that. Eg. Net zero energy use, or more employee density, etc

Anyone planning a consultation should heed this advice. Like their counterparts in Okotoks, participants in Lethbridge also became instantly hostile to euphemisms. As one Lethbridge participant put it in the feedback section: 'While some descriptions were clear, others were too vague, and therefore, "suspicious"'.

Participants also frequently complained that when objectives were vaguely formulated, they would mean different things to different people, meaning there would, in the end, be no clarity on what people had actually voted for, giving organizers an unacceptably wide margin to interpret the results.

This proved to be a justified concern. While some participants shrewdly narrowed in on euphemisms, others were genuinely confused by them. For example, in relation to a proposal about emergency shelters in Okotoks, some people understood this to refer to homeless shelters, others to detox centres or shelters for victims of domestic violence, while a few took it to refer to emergency weather shelters (e. g. from tornadoes). Participants were thus answering completely different questions, depending on how they understood the original wording of the proposal.

Democracy requires *clarity* – it does not work well on the basis of euphemisms and platitudes. Democracy is about *scrutinizing*. We can't scrutinize something when we don't even know what it is.

Interestingly, participants in Belo Horizonte's 2013 online PB also expressed extreme annoyance with vague proposals, e. g. to build a 'space for sport, culture and leisure' at an unspecified location, complaining that they could not vote for something they didn't even understand,[485] so this appears to be a widely-held concern.

5.3.5 Assertiveness is not Aggression

Even during the most hostile interactions and discussion of unpopular measures on Okotoks 2080, there was still a high-level of constructive feedback from some commenters and this constructive criticism was generally well thought-out and specific. For example, on a proposal concerning infill building (building between existing buildings), a commenter expressed concern about fire safety, suggesting purpose-built row housing would be safer. A proposal about active transportation and public transit was met with detailed comments made with reference to the population, bus size, previous bus provision experiments the participants had lived through, queries for more information, and references to regional integration plans (rail, etc.).

Annoyance generally took the form of biting sarcasm rather than thuggish rudeness. For example, in answer to a proposal in Okotoks 2080 to 'Encourage development to prioritize protection of conservation areas by clustering density' a participant responded:

> Clustering density? Just curious: is there any other type of density? Is there any non-clustered density? Semi-clustered density? Uniformly distributed density?

I followed up this line of inquiry with Stéphan De Loof, probably the participant who had taken the most flak on the Lethbridge CIP as the defender of an improvement to a Francophone school. This was one of the few discussions on either Ethelo consultation that had resulted in comments being flagged to organizers. De Loof reported himself as not remotely fazed by the (relatively minor) hostility, which he accepted as it was a part of his job to inform the public whenever questions arose on projects his employer FrancoSud was involved in.

Participants occasionally engaged in slightly snippy interactions during the Lethbridge consultation. For example, on one question concerning the local art gallery, a participant commented:

---

485 Stephen Coleman and Rafael Cardoso Sampaio, 'Sustaining a Democratic Innovation: A Study of Three E-Participatory Budgets in Belo Horizonte' (2016) Information, Communication and Society 12.

> I have never been to the art gallery I think it's a waste of money

To which they received the reply from another participant:

> How do you know it's a waste of money if you've never been? Or is anything you don't personally use a waste in your opinion?

However, such interactions were uncommon and rarely went beyond one back-and-forth exchange.

Due to the nature of the exercise, it is unclear if people would come back to check comments later on and potentially change their vote. It seems unlikely that very many did, and this is both a blessing and a curse of asynchronous participation. Because people often do not return after they are finished voting and commenting, interaction between participants was fairly limited (more like a message board than a discussion) and neither degenerated into endless fights, nor ended up getting off-topic via a long comment thread.

Mass participation means accepting people's general communication patterns. While most people are not mean-spirited, they do not always express themselves in the genteel manner some researchers and activists would like to see. As long as this doesn't cross into slurs, outright bullying or similar behaviour, it should not be taken as a pretext to interfere with the process.

5.3.6 Fiscal Responsibility a Major Concern

One of the most common issues raised both in Okotoks and Lethbridge was fiscal responsibility. A discussion of the costs as well as the economic advantages and disadvantages of various policies occurred on almost every proposal, even in the absence of financial information (i.e. without a prompt to do so). Participants were rarely ideologically committed to one policy or another, preferring to focus on any given proposal's economic efficiency and the return for the community. Many participants indicated in the comments that they intended to vote negatively on proposals that did not deliver clear value.

A major reason given for voting negatively was the view that projects were over-priced (as we saw this also occurred in NYC PB). While participants were not always against spending or even a direct increase in their own expenses (feedback on a proposal to introduce organic waste collection for a small monthly fee in Lethbridge was generally positive), they insisted on value for money, frequently assessing whether or not the costs of certain projects were reasonable or 'a good investment'. Indeed, participants often explicitly asked for the government to show them the pay-off in cost-benefit dollars over the lifetime of projects. When such information was not available, participants simply did the math themselves. It was also common for people to suggest cheaper alternative actions to the ones proposed or to state that while they weren't against a project, they simply didn't think it was worth the money.

A typical comment from Lethbridge CIP read:

> If this were my money (which it is as a tax payer) I would say that's too expensive.

Another read:

> I moderately support [rather than totally support] this because the estimated cost is RIDICULOUS! If there was a reasonable cost estimate I would support 100 %.

As this indicates, participants displayed a high degree of financial acumen, frequently commenting on the macroeconomic implications of decisions (e.g. on property tax and house prices), as well as debating the level of government that was responsible for various categories of spending (province, municipality, etc.). Far from greenlighting every project or engaging in frivolous spending, participants tended to view the government as frivolous spenders who needed to be contained.

As we saw above, businesses are not in the habit of approaching governments with ideas about how to solve problems by spending no money whatsoever (that would be pointless). Worse, the amount of money a government is willing to spend on an issue has come to be seen as an indication of how much they care about it. This incentivizes fiscal recklessness, and the fiscal conservatism of voters could help to correct this.

It is also notable that rather than voting for 'frills', participants were far more concerned with using resources to fulfill basic needs – which goes to the benefit of the least affluent. Saving money can also help those most in need, for example, by enabling a reduction in sales tax or increasing pensions. Thus, although self-selected participants tended to be higher-income than average, they acted in a way that would benefit disadvantaged people (and, over time, prevent them from being disadvantaged).

This bolsters the evidence for what is thought to be one of the major benefits of digital democracy and wider participation generally: that involving more people in decision-making can cut down on clientelism and save costs by avoiding spending money on things citizens don't particularly want (as discussed in Chapter 2).

5.3.7 Future-Focus

Participants in both Okotoks and Lethbridge were very forward-looking in their comments – at times more so than government planners, debating (without any prompts to do so) the future of offline retail, the impact of remote work on transportation and internet infrastructure, and the potential for moral hazard on a proposal to incentivize landowners to retain mature trees on their properties. This indicates that there is a lot of untapped potential for making policy that takes our future trajectory into account. This could help to more quickly negotiate some bureaucratic processes which can take an unhelpfully long time to travel up and down the government hierarchy. Too often, this results in governments solving yesterday's rather than tomorrow's problems (much like the Soviet GOSPLAN system once did with disastrous results).

5.3.8 Specificity – Local vs National Information

Both Lethbridge CIP and Okotoks 2080 concerned local topics and there was a high level of consensus regarding the local facts. When participants referred to a certain street or sports centre, they expected the other participants to have seen these things with their own eyes and that the truth of what they were saying was easily ascertainable.

This is very different on a national level, where people rely on reporting by others. When that reporting is slanted, it can confuse the situation, as participants aren't in a position to ascertain facts themselves. This illustrates the difference between peer-to-peer communication where participants serve as eyewitnesses (e.g. 'that bus goes by my house, it's empty most of the time'), and social media which is driven almost entirely by media intent on 'story-telling', creating 'a narrative' and, above all, generating clicks. This shows the value of using peer-to-peer communication to circumvent media distortion, but it is also important to keep in mind that the incentive to be less than truthful will always be greater on a national than a local level. That being said, there are always some people who live locally and who can attest to local circumstances with evidence if need be.

One of my favourite examples was a case on social media concerning German-American commenter Yascha Mounk. Mounk previously worked with former British Prime Minister Tony Blair (who contributed substantially to the Second Iraq War) and is generally committed to a hawkish American foreign policy. Shortly after a poison attack on a former Russian agent in Salisbury, England, Mounk tweeted that over 500 people had been poisoned in Salisbury, using this to justify his hawkish attitude towards Russia. However, this version of events was instantly contradicted by residents of Salisbury, who were certain that in their city of 40,000 people they would have noticed 500 dropping dead by poisoning.[486] If Mounk had stated that there were fears that up to 500 people may have been exposed to poison, he would have been more accurate, but he chose to overstate his case. National journalists and commenters frequently engage in this kind of behaviour (it keeps them in the headlines), but it isn't helpful, and it is to be hoped that local people with their specific knowledge can help to counteract convenient, and unfortunately often inaccurate, narrative-building.

5.3.9 Consistency

Comments and voting were consistent in the sense that similar questions got similar results. Participants were, in other words, coherent in their preferences (a point that is often contested in the literature). Some even engaged in a kind of consistency patrol of the organizers, pointing out proposals that were potentially at odds with each other or with the goals that were allegedly being pursued. Participants also made connections between proposals, seeking to consolidate them into fewer (cost-saving) items or to point out things like, 'if we did A, do we really need B?' etc.

This shows that people often keep all of the options in mind and compare and re-evaluate as they move through the decision-making process, and that at least some people seek consistency and efficiency while doing so. Participants also referred to related projects in the area that were not part of the proposal, tying in general knowledge and seeking to create consistency across the region. Again, this shows the positive scrutinizing function that digital democracy can have, which particularly makes such comparisons and inconsistencies easier to discern than they would be in a face-to-face setting.

5.3.10 Little Reference to Personal Circumstances

In contrast to the fad to focus on 'lived experience' participants rarely relied on or sanctified their individual experience. Some did occasionally bring it in, e. g. on disability access, a participant commented, 'Get someone in a wheelchair to give guidance. Often I go to newly renovated facilities and can't use them.' This was rare and usually tightly focused on the issue at hand. There were no instances of any-

---

486 Roslyn Fuller, *In Defence of Democracy* (Polity 2019) 179 et seq.

one trying to claim that their circumstances outranked others or made them more worthy of consideration. At least in some societies the demand for focusing on the personal sharing of experiences seems fairly limited, although it may also be that forms of participation that are somewhat more technical simply attract people who prefer to communicate with each other on a more technical, less personal, basis.

5.3.11 Misinformation

Participants were direct about confronting anyone they thought was spreading misinformation, often accompanied by offers to provide the other party with evidence as to why their assertions were incorrect. For example, several anti-fluoride comments in regards to water provision were met with others reassuring the commenter that fluoride is not toxic in the amounts used in drinking water. Although people corrected the original commenter, they seemed unflustered by these comments being made. The paranoia that false information would have an outsized effect on everyone's thinking and irrevocably contaminate the process simply didn't exist in real life (as it does in media narratives).

5.3.12 Fluidity

There was a turnover of named commenters throughout the Lethbridge consultation, showing this was not just a case of the same named commenters commenting on every question. Some people did not comment the entire way through, but gave feedback in the end. Others started commenting three-quarters of the way through. Some people only commented on issues of particular concern to them. Thus, there was a certain fluidity to the process. This matches up to the information we have on PB in Paris, where there is also a high turnover in people submitting proposals and in voting. While this raises some issues for retention, it does show that at least at this point, these processes are not necessarily *dominated* by a small group of superusers.

5.3.13 Minority Participation

There were several proposals in the Lethbridge CIP which could have been seen to have a bearing on minority participation.

The first concerned a proposal to expand the gymnasium at a French language school (Ecole La Verendrye Gymnasium Expansion). This proposal was unsuccessful in the sense that it did not receive a majority vote in favour (although it was still funded by the city). French is a minority language in Lethbridge and the school is also open to children who speak English as a first language, but whose parents prefer them to be educated wholly or partly in French in order to give them proficiency in both official languages.

This was the only proposal in either Ethelo consultation that had a clear champion, that is someone who openly and consistently advocated for the proposal. This was Stéphan De Loof who works for FrancoSud, the organization that runs French-language education in southern Alberta. Due to the existence of a champion, this was by far one of the most interactive proposals in Lethbridge CIP – out of 54 replies to comments, 27 of them were made by De Loof, who, unlike many people, commented during office hours, as it was part of his job to do so.

Because schools in Canada are generally public and funded by the province, the proposal generated confusion as to whether this was a public or a private school (with strong opposition to funding a private school). However, in addition to the hostility generated by participants believing they were being asked to upgrade schools on their own dime, this was one of the very few proposals that resulted in a small number of comments (three) being flagged. One comment claimed that Francophones were 'resistant to the English-speaking community' and that they had kicked the commenter's child out of day care. This was flagged four times and De Loof confronted the commenter about 'false information' and invited them to contact him personally with complaints. Another comment, also flagged four times, claimed the school was 'biased toward the French'. A third comment, flagged once, claimed the school was 'only open to Francophones'.

The proposal also attracted what could be considered 'anti-racist' comments. One commenter defended people's right to be educated in French, while another said that they were happy that the city was working with the Francophone community. As mentioned above, when I spoke to De Loof about his experience and the flagged comments, he reported himself completely unbothered by it.

A second example concerned a proposal for formulating an 'Indigenous Place-making Strategy'. This was one of the vaguest proposals in the Lethbridge CIP, and involved contracting a specialist to perform a feasibility study and 'implementation strategy' to 'meaningfully engage Indigenous Peoples'. It was also unclear to online participants whether the proposal had the support of the local Indigenous community, which forms a small percentage (ca. 5%) of the local population.[487]

On this proposal, favourites outstripped comments by a significant margin (an unusual situation), indicating that people did not wish to comment on the matter themselves, or perhaps felt they were not *entitled* to comment on the matter themselves. There was also a large number of neutral votes, presumably by people who did not consider themselves directly affected by the issue. Those who did comment, however, fell quite clearly into three different camps, with little direct engagement between them. The first side could be termed pro-reconciliation and strongly supported funding for Indigenous peoples whom they viewed as the victims of colonization. The second side felt that 'enough had been done' and that some minorities should not get special treatment. Some of these comments were rather 'othering' and vaguely, if not pointedly, hostile. The third group simply exhorted authorities to work with Indigenous communities more closely, and expressed the view that if they were going to hire someone to do a study that person should be an Indigenous person (comments to this effect were the most favourited).

The conversation did, however, seem to occur largely without the involvement of Indigenous people themselves. On closer examination, this turned out to be because the proposal, like all proposals included in the online consultation, had actually been formulated over a long time period, in this specific case, with the involvement of the Indigenous communities in the area. It was, like the other proposals put forward, not seriously up for a vote in the online discussion (despite the fact that participants could vote on the aforementioned scale). In addition, while some members of the Indigenous community live in Lethbridge, many others live on a nearby reserve (land legally reserved for use by Indigenous communities). Many reserves are sparsely populated and internet access is not as developed as it is within cities like Lethbridge. The Blood 148 Reserve, located just outside of Lethbridge is territorially the largest reserve in Canada (over 500 square miles) with a population of ca. 12,000, which equates to ca. 4–5 people per square mile. Reserves are also partly self-governing, because unlike the case with other minorities, relations between Indigenous peoples and the Canadian government are regulated by treaty. Many Indigenous peoples thus have parallel systems of governance and consultation, sometimes conducted according to traditional practices. In this case, however, the proposal did affect the residents of Lethbridge, as it proposed alterations to the appearance of the city (rather than being a matter car-

---

487 More information on the process is included in *City of Lethbridge: Indigenous Placemaking Strategy and Public Realm Audit* (City of Lethbridge, 13 April 2022).

ried out on the reserve) and involved spending municipal funds (hence its inclusion in the process).

The Indigenous Place-making Strategy also failed (very narrowly) to obtain a majority of totally and moderately support votes, but (as with other projects) seems to have continued to move forward through the process.[488] This is an interesting point as it raises an issue about participation on points that concern small minorities (single digits of the population), in circumstances where there are differing legal regimes in place.

Another 'minority-interest' example concerned upgrades to an arena which would provide more changing rooms and bathrooms for women and people with disability. This was estimated to cost $6 million, with an operating cost of over $100k a year, and the arena in question was old and dilapidated. While participants were supportive of providing 'changing rooms for women and 'female identifying people", as one commenter put it, they were against sinking such a massive amount of money into a facility many believed would not be in use much longer. A similar but broader proposal also made provision to include gender neutral bathrooms across facilities. While some participants were uncomfortable with this proposal, others were supportive, there were few comments, little argument, and the proposal enjoyed one of the highest levels of consensus in favour in the entire consultation.

We can see that obsessive culture wars are something that occur more in news media where people are rewarded with high 'engagement' for being contentious, but that it doesn't necessarily flow into the dynamic of direct democracy to the same extreme extent (at least so far).

We can also see the limits of studies that just measure how often 'minority' goals are approved without considering all of the other factors, such as being connected to what is perceived as a ludicrous cost (as in the case of the changing rooms). However, it also raises questions as to who should vote on issues that may be of greater importance to numerically very small minorities, and where the majority of voters seem to view that matter as not particularly being their business (e.g. Indigenous Place-Making).

---

488 See e.g. David Opinko, "'Oki" Signs with Indigenous Art to be Displayed across Lethbridge' *Lethbridge News Now* (28 September 2022) <https://lethbridgenewsnow.com/2022/09/28/oki-signs-with-indigenous-art-to-be-displayed-across-lethbridge/>.

5.4 Observations on Scottish Consultation on Fireworks Regulation

Unlike in Lethbridge and Okotoks, every aspect of the Scottish consultation on fireworks regulation attained a vote in favour, however, the ratio of votes varied considerably. While having to pay a licence fee was one of the least popular measures (with 319 votes against), making it illegal to give some kinds of fireworks to under-18s was one of the most popular (receiving only 39 votes against). Thus, we can see here as well, that participants are differentiated in their opinions and even those opposing some forms of regulation support others. As in the Lethbridge and Okotoks consultations, in Scotland Fireworks, people also gave comments to improve the bill, and also sometimes disagreed with a proposal, not because they disagreed with its object or purpose, but because they thought it would be ineffective to achieve that purpose (similar to Albertans disagreeing with a proposal not because they disagreed with its object, but because they thought it was too expensive).

5.5 Conclusions on Communication

So far, we see far less vitriol in digital democracy than we see in conventional politics and on social media. Part of this may be due to the fact that participants are often required to agree to be reasonably polite. It is also possible that this partially stems from the lack of organization among participants. Political organization, of necessity, involves drawing boundaries and sharpening divisions, often in ways that are intended to endure over years. For a party, the best, and most secure voter is one who truly hates the other parties. Professional campaigns of division, however, often require a great degree of organization and a certain amount of money. One has to *mobilize* one's core supporters.

   If one excludes non-human actors, however, and strips off the ability of any individual to retain a network of followers, this kind of mobilization becomes very difficult to achieve. When people cannot be mobilized to adhere to a political side, they have to be convinced on each policy. This circumstance alone serves to somewhat deflate the kind of hysterics and enmity often employed by conventional political campaigning. It's simply less useful in this atmosphere. Similarly, with no obvious influencers on the opposing 'side', participants are left without a clear target to 'take down'. This again disincentivizes needlessly antagonistic commenting. Debate may still be acrimonious (and there is no reason it should be conflict-free) but at least this acrimony will not be fuelled to fever pitch by organized forces capable of sustaining long-running conflict. Left to their own devices, people tend to behave, if not like saints, at least within the bounds of the reasonable.

However, even if we facilitate peer-to-peer communication on an equal basis within digital forums, this would still occur against a backdrop of radio, TV, traditional and social media, where much of the content is funded by special interests. Unlike in Rousseau's time, we are all subjected to a flood of information every day, which is ubiquitous and, frequently, outrageous. These forces will likely be able to insert themselves into digital democracy in some form or other. Even if they are locked out of directly participating themselves, they will strive to find ways to influence the process.

Without breaking up media cartels and sufficiently taxing the wealthy so that they are unable to fund vast information empires that monopolize conversation, this will continue to have a detrimental impact that we can only hope to contain by introducing rules that make it unpleasant for those with high levels of negative personality traits to take part and difficult for them to seize control of the process. Organizers also have a role to play in getting things off to a good start by being forthright and honest in their interactions with the public and avoiding perceptions of manipulation.

Chapter 6
Voting

The purpose of voting is to measure support for a decision. It is supposed to give us clarity on what our political will is – a much more complicated task than it at first appears.

6.1 Some Issues Relating to Interpreting the Meaning of Votes and Comments

One of the major issues with voting in elections is the problem of wasted votes.[489] Wasted votes are votes that do not have an impact on the outcome of a decision. For example, if a candidate requires 100 votes to be elected and they receive 200 votes, 100 of those votes were technically unnecessary. The outcome would have been the same even if all of those voters stayed at home. The same can be said of all those people who cast their votes for losing candidates. If we take a first-past-the-post election with four candidates, one of whom receives 58 votes, another who receives 57 votes, another with 34 votes and another with 20 votes, we can see that out of 169 votes cast, 111 of them are 'unsuccessful' votes. They don't go on to influence the decision-making process on specific issues.

Parties attempt to minimize their wasted votes, and often don't pursue voters whose votes won't result in a seat for their party. The need to win election as a prerequisite to doing anything else and the issue of trying to minimize wasted votes at best lends itself to a manipulative process and a sort of paint-by-numbers, managerial style of government. At worst it leads to gerrymandering and parties working to skew the process to win the most seats with the least votes. This can at times lead to situations where the party that wins the most votes (known as the popular vote) fails to win the election because another party manages to take more seats.[490] As this indicates, we don't, after elections, always end up with a very clear idea of what the population wants. Indeed, an entire class of political pundits makes a living trying to guess. It is not a very good state of affairs for nations that are supposed to be governed by the will of the people, that no one can even identify what that will is.

---

489 Roslyn Fuller, *Beasts and Gods: How Democracy Changed Its Meaning and Lost Its Purpose* (Zed/Bloomsbury 2015) 43–121.
490 Fuller, *Beasts and Gods* 43–121.

https://doi.org/10.1515/9783110794465-010

To complicate matters, an election is also merely a decision-point on who will make future decisions. It is actually quite unclear what people are even voting for in elections: is it for a candidate who they believe will make the best decisions on their behalf as issues arise in the future? Or is it for someone who will implement a specific policy that they have promised during their campaign? Commentators today often complain that voters do not pay attention to 'the issues', but the issues are not necessarily the object of an election. Voters do not cast their votes for issues, they cast them for a person who *then* deals with the issues. *All* of them. This raises more questions. How many issues does a voter have to agree with a candidate on in order to give them their vote? One important issue? Half the issues? Perhaps they just *disagree* with a competing candidate very strongly on one issue? It is not unusual in our present system for someone to be elected to run a country simply because the population intensely dislikes the personality or a single policy of their main competitor. Elections give us very little information about what people actually want, and this is why there is so much guesswork involved in trying to determine what any given election means.

This is why voting directly on issues helps so much to bring *clarity* to the situation, and it is why this major advantage of digital democracy, which enables cheaper and faster voting, and thus more votes on more issues, should not be neglected.

Similarly, assessing the comments people make on social media or other forums and trying to guess what they mean is also generally far more inconclusive than many political analysts would have one believe. Comments are not always equivalent to statements of intent and it is often impossible to interpret a comment as a definitive yes or no on the proposal at hand. A salesperson might show me a piece of furniture in a store, and I might say something like, 'It's a bit tall.' Is that a yes or a no on this cabinet? Chances are that even I don't fully know my own mind yet. I may well come around to liking it and even being glad that it is tall. Equally, it is possible to occasionally want to express annoyance at something that can't be rectified or regarding which one has no better ideas.

Due to the lack of definition inherent in a great deal of self-expression, it is much harder to make assumptions about what people are thinking than is commonly believed, and it is also quite difficult to extrapolate where any given person will come down on a topic. For example, on the Lethbridge CIP, at times, previously irate and difficult people came out to condemn colonization and the 'ignorance' of their fellow citizens, while others of a sunny disposition seemed to out themselves as borderline racists. A similar incident occurred much later in the feedback section, where a named commenter who had been vigorously anti-spending throughout the process, stated that homeless housing should have been included as a proposal (this was, in fact, later incorporated into the budget by the City Council). While participants are consistent in the sense that they do not make decisions that materially contradict each other (e.g. 'we will not plant more trees in the park if we just decided to stop planting them in the cemeteries due to drought'), they are not predictable in that they do not adhere to pre-defined ideological camps.

This is part of the reason that being specific and focusing on issues helps digital democracy decisions to be more accurate than general surveys (the preferred form of 'engagement'). If one asks for e.g. agreement on the statement: 'The government should spend less money', a person might say 'yes' to that because they agree the government should, generally, spend less money. However, we still can't interpret that as a de facto vote against any specific form of spending (e.g. homeless housing), although this blanket interpretation is generally exactly what happens with surveys – researchers ask for 'sentiment' on general statements and then extrapolate a level of agreement or disagreement with specific policy that this information does not suffice to support.

People also often seem to comment more when they disagree with a proposal. In the Scotland Fireworks consultation, a government bill was broken down into its various components and participants could 'vote' (using thumbs up/thumbs down) on each component of the bill and leave a comment (in this case separated into for and against categories).[491] Those who voted 'no' commented at a higher ratio than those who voted 'yes' on 7 out of the 8 sections put up for vote. As this illustrates, commenting may diverge from voting behaviour in the sense that many people choose not to comment and are sometimes indeed 'a silent majority' (or a greater majority than they appear to be). On one question on the Scottish Fireworks consultation, for example, there were 83 comments in favour and 77 against. Had the software only allowed commenting rather than voting as well, one might conclude that sentiment was quite evenly split on this issue. However, the vote on this point was actually 66.5% for to 33.5% against.

Similarly, voting helps when the conversation takes an unexpected turn. On a proposal concerning a sports facility on Lethbridge CIP, the location of the facility came to be a major issue, making it difficult to interpret comments as supportive or not supportive of the proposal as opposed to just the location.

This lack of definition is why social listening (scraping information about what people are saying about a given topic from social media) and sentiment analysis

---

491 Participation and Communications Team, Scottish Parliament, *Fireworks and Pyrotechnics Articles (Scotland) Bill: Digital Engagement: Summary of Online Forum Submissions to Support the Criminal Justice Committee's Scrutiny of the Bill* (March 2022) <https://www.parliament.scot/-/media/files/committees/criminal-justice-committee/fireworks-bill-engagement-summary.pdf>.

aren't always great ideas – the signal it gives is not very clear, and those who engage in such activities often believe they have received much more accurate information about what people are thinking than they have.

When it comes to digital democracy tools, sentiment analysis, thus far, only exists at a rudimentary level. For example, CitizenLab, a Belgian software, allows administrators to sort comments thematically, e.g. for those comments relating to 'work' or 'health and welfare'. It's also possible to generate a keyword map from comments (sometimes called a word cloud), which can help to show major areas of concern that organizers might otherwise overlook.[492] ZenCity also performs basic sentiment analysis, generating insights such as that 26% of online interactions about housing are negative and 7% are positive, or that housing accounts for 51% of the conversations on Planning and Development. It can also report on trending topics and popular words.[493] CiviQ, an Irish provider, generates a graphic output illustrating how participants' views align or don't align in a conversation (i.e. what the main sources of agreement and conflict are). It's important to keep things at this level where the gleanings remain closely connected to the facts (e.g. housing isn't going very well) without reading too much into it. Attempting to overly-anticipate people's wishes, even if done with benevolent intentions, can become manipulative and rob participants of their agency.

In summary, neither commenting nor voting on broad platforms, as e.g. in elections, gives us much clarity about what voters want, but with digital democracy platforms that allow both comments and voting on specific issues we can start to achieve some clarity, as the input given by participants starts to generate a clearer output. However, even here, we can see that this clarity is not absolute. For example, in both the Lethbridge and Okotoks consultations, participants sometimes expressed a 'conditional acceptance' of proposals, meaning a participant agreed to a proposal as long as it was 'not funded by my tax' or if the proposal was implemented 'within reason'. Other forms of conditional acceptance were more specific, such as comments to the effect that increased building of accessory dwelling units would be acceptable if off-street parking was provided and safety and building standards were assured. This also points up the need for clarity, and more reliable

---

492 'Automated Text Analysis Tool' (*CitizenLab*) <https://www.citizenlab.co/platform-features/in sights> accessed 22 January 2023; James Aung, 'How to Leverage AI in Community Engagement' (*CitizenLab*, 15 June 2022) <https://www.citizenlab.co/blog/civic-engagement/how-to-leverage-ai-in-com munity-engagement%ef%bf%bc/> accessed 22 January 2023.

493 'Data Snapshot, The Housing Crisis in the UK: An Analysis of Resident Discourse' (*Zencity*) <https://zencity.wpenginepowered.com/wp-content/uploads/2022/10/Data-Report-The-Housing-Crisis-in-the-UK.pdf> accessed 22 January 2023; 'Community-Based Insights for Better City Management' (*Zencity*) <https://zencity.io/zencity-for-cities/> accessed 22 January 2023.

feedback could have been provided if citizens had had information on whether these conditions were fulfilled.

The act of voting is so important, because it is the decision point in any system. It eliminates (or at least reduces) guesswork and thereby creates accountability. Whatever a voter may think, say or feel, ultimately they cast their chips down in a certain place. We don't need to really speculate anymore about *why* they did so. Only they really know why, and that's fine, because *they* become accountable for making that decision. Clarity and accountability are thus the two things we are trying to achieve with voting, and, as we can see, this is often much more difficult than is commonly believed. Still, creating systems that maximize that clarity and accountability is much more helpful than relying on systems that don't.

6.2 Modes of Voting

All voting systems have advantages and drawbacks. An advantage with digital democracy, however, is that rather than having to permanently commit to one voting system, one can more flexibly choose different methods depending on the needs of the situation.

6.2.1 Binary Yes/No Voting

Binary voting is familiar to most of us as the way we vote in referendums – yes or no on a single question. Binary voting has the virtue of providing absolute clarity on what voters would ultimately choose on a given issue. This is important, because conditionality and 'nuance' can sometimes be overrated when one wants to embark on a clear strategy or deal with a time-sensitive issue.

The disadvantage of such votes is chiefly that what can be expressed by them in terms of preferences is quite limited. Even in a 'yes or no' referendum, the voter may prefer a third mediating option. For example, a question could be, 'Should cannabis be legalized?' and the voter might be of the opinion that it should be legalized for medical use, but not for recreational use. However, due to the way the ballot is constructed they are unable to express this and can only vote yes or no to the question posed. For this reason, referendums are sometimes called 'blunt instruments' – they count a vote for or against as a vote 'completely for' or 'completely against', with no 'conditional' for or against. Voters are forced to choose between the limited options presented, sometimes without having had the opportunity to shape those options.

Another disadvantage to straight binary voting is that it can be hard to relate a decision-point to *other* decision-points. In California, for example, each referendum must only concern a single subject area. This makes sense if one considers that referendums are often an attempt to achieve clarity on a single point and that including multiple subject areas would negate this advantage. Unfortunately, however, these restrictions can also mean that voters become 'trapped' by outcomes that create other problems in different areas. For example, one might vote that tax should not be raised in a certain area, but without the power to cut costs or raise tax in a different area, this can cause problems down the line. Thus, voters may have simply shifted the problem into another area without having conclusively resolved it. This is even more the case in situations where initiating a referendum is difficult or impossible (as when only governments may propose referendums), meaning voters could end up with an unexpected situation that they now lack the means to address.

Of course, many of these issues can be overcome by involving people in the ideation phase as well, e.g. facilitating petitions or debate/deliberation that would potentially serve to formulate the final ballot question. Digital decision-making also gives us the opportunity (given the lower online costs) to hold a series of referendums in quick succession. Thus, people could initially vote on a broad strategy and then narrow that down through a series of votes (e.g. 'should euthanasia be legal?' – 'yes'; 'should it be allowed in non-terminal cases?' – 'no'; 'should a medical professional be allowed to initiate a conversation on euthanasia' – 'no', etc.). One could either do this instantaneously, e.g. every voter answers 5 or 6 questions that are then instantly tabulated into a final result, or one could intersperse renewed debate at every step. For example, if the majority of people answer that euthanasia should not be legal, one does not necessarily need to proceed with questions relating to the conditions of legality. With digital technology, we don't need to give up the clarity of straight binary voting in order to handle complex multi-faceted questions quickly. Clarity and complexity are far easier to combine online using the kind of decision-tree described here. This represents a real breakthrough in the form mass decision-making can take.

6.2.2 Voting on a Scale

The single transferable vote (STV) used in some countries is, in some sense, a form of voting on a scale. In this system, voters place a '1' next to their preferred candidate, a '2' next to their second most preferred candidate and so on. STV is sometimes used in multi-member districts, where more than one candidate is elected. It has the virtue of allowing more diversity than the first-past-the-post systems used in many Anglo-Saxon countries, but it takes a long time to tabulate results from paper ballots and rarely makes major changes from what results would have been based on 'the first round' (where people put the '1' on their ballot).

Of course, online, calculating such preferences is no work at all, and as a result one can easily use scales like this to vote on all manner of things. In the Albertan consultations we analysed above, voters were able to choose between 'totally oppose', 'moderately oppose', 'neutral', 'moderately support' and 'totally support'. The key advantage to such voting is that it gives a clearer idea of the range of support behind any given vote. For example, one can easily see if a proposal enjoys a high amount of strong support *and* strong opposition, or if it enjoys only bland weak support. This allows us to identify those points on which there is a high degree of consensus and those on which there is a high degree of conflict. As we have pointed out, this is likely much more accurate than making such assessments based on comments alone.

This kind of voting also works well for those systems where multiple options are selected by voters, and they thus need to prioritize those options rather than ranking them all equally (just as in STV one differentiates one's most preferred candidate from one's second choice). This can be done through weighting. For example, a 'totally support' vote could be weighted at twice the value of a moderately support vote, or one could simply assign each part of the scale a number 1–5 (or -2 to +2) and take the proposals that score the highest in absolute terms, whether that is through having many 3s and 4s or 1s and 5s. Alternatively (or additionally) one can require that a proposal receive a majority of 'support' votes (setting a floor on the level of support a proposal must receive to be successful). When it becomes easier to count votes, it opens up many options for configuring that counting.

We can also make this type of voting more complex, asking people to vote across different scales at the same time, with each scale representing a different criterium. While in Lethbridge and Okotoks, participants used a single 5-point scale (totally oppose to totally support) on each item, a different exercise in Prince George used two scales for participants to rank each of a series of recommendations on poverty reduction: how impactful a given recommendation was likely to be and how urgent it was.[494] Voting across multiple spectrums simultaneously was always *possible*, but, of course, digital technology makes it easier to maintain oversight over this process, both for the voter and during the counting process.

That being said, there are disadvantages with complexifying the voting process – the main one being that it can reduce the clarity of the outcome. Voting on too

---

many options at once carries the risk (if the design is poor) of coming up with a 'design by committee' outcome that doesn't satisfy anyone.

Including a neutral voting option in voting scales also raises questions around how to interpret it. Is it a vote for, against, or not a vote at all? In Lethbridge CIP, out of the 29 proposals that were voted on, only 11 received 50% or more supportive votes (totally or moderately support). If one simply discounts neutral votes, this increases to 18 proposals, moving a further 24% of proposals across the line from a non-majority to apparent majority vote. If we go one step further and count neutral votes as votes in favour of a proposal (as some organizers do), only two proposals still fail to hit the bar of an apparent majority vote 'in favour'. Indeed, under this method of measuring, a proposal with just 17% of the moderately and totally support vote share (the lowest of any proposal in the exercise) was able to cross the line to be considered a vote in favour.

Out of 42 proposals in Okotoks 2080, only five received more than 50% of moderately and totally support votes. If we discount neutral votes, the number of 'approved' proposals more than triples to 17, meaning 12 proposals move from a position of not having attained the majority of totally or moderately support votes to counting as votes in favour. If we count neutral votes as votes in favour, this number increases again with 28 proposals achieving a level of apparent 'support' of 50% or above.

As this demonstrates, overly generous interpretations empty voting of its purpose by erasing distinctions between levels of support, and transforming nearly every proposal into a positive vote in favour. Therefore, if one does take advantage of a voting scale to weight votes this way, it is important to make the cut-off for the level of support high enough to make the exercise meaningful. Voting on a scale only makes sense if you are using that scale to create differentiations and distinctions. If one uses STV to vote for five candidates in a district with five available seats and only five candidates run, it becomes meaningless.

Considering the rhetoric of 'scarce resources' and 'too many competing priorities', it makes sense to either de facto count neutral votes as votes against or at the very least exclude them from the final count (as would be the case, for example, in a referendum in countries that do not demand a minimum participation rate). We should also ask ourselves if it is worth the time and effort to commit resources to projects that citizens are not decisively in favour of. When few projects receive enthusiastic support, it is an opportunity to go back to the drawing board and come up with proposals citizens are more enthusiastic about, or to save the resources from these projects and reinvest them into other larger projects, possibly of more interest and utility to citizens. One can do almost anything with different types of voting, but it is important to have an idea in your mind of what voting expresses and how much support is enough to justify the time and expense of carrying out any given policy, bearing in mind the opportunity costs of doing so.

6.2.3 Adjusting Vote Weight, Individually and Collectively

Digital voting also allows for vote weighting to be easily implemented. Ethelo allows participants to increase or decrease the weight they give to their votes on certain subjects. For example, a participant might weight 'sports' as more important than 'arts and culture' to them. Participants made use of this possibility in both Lethbridge and Okotoks adjusting the relative importance of certain categories of expenditure.

Another way to weight votes is to retroactively alter results to conform to population demographics. For example, if 15% of the population is under the age of 30, but only 5% of participants are, one can increase the weight of votes cast by participants under 30 until it is equivalent to 15% of the input. Whether this is a good idea is another question.

There is no particular reason to believe that all those under 30 share the opinions of those in that age group who took part. If anything, we might well conclude the opposite – if they did share those views and attitudes, if they were, in other words, truly similar to those who participated, they likely would have taken part as well. More importantly, however, retroactive vote weighting contravenes the fundamental logic of democracy as an emancipatory process in which all people have agency and thus accountability for their actions. This is what differentiates it from so many processes geared at *figuring out* what people want.

The vast majority of political research is aimed not at producing democracy or emancipating people, but primarily at trying to *second-guess* what the population thinks and *anticipate* how they will react to any given policy. For this reason, researchers often worry about selection bias when they conduct surveys or focus groups, because they are trying to find *the truth* about people's behaviour. If only people over 60 are willing to talk about whether they like apples, we may get a very skewed picture of the apple-eating habits of the population. We also need to get some 30 year-olds and 15 year-olds to tell us what they think of apples. Often, such research is conducted on behalf of a third party, like a supermarket, that is going to take action based on it. If the information is incorrect, obviously we are setting that client up for failure. They may believe they are going to sell a lot more apples than they are, if the habits of 60 year-olds cannot be applied to the entire population.

However, in democracy, we are not attempting to solicit information to give to another power to make decisions for us. We are instead directly making the decision, which is unto itself, a completely different *kind* of decision. Democracy is not used to answer technical questions such as 'how many apples does the average person eat?' For that we use the process outlined above. Instead, it is used to ask questions like: 'How much pesticide are you willing to tolerate in order to get affordable apples?' or 'Should farmers be allowed to grow genetically-modified apples?'

Only the voter in question can know what they think about these things and since everyone has the opportunity to contribute to these decisions, the onus is on the voter to express themselves. If one cannot be bothered to participate, then that apathy *is* actually reflected accurately in the outcome. When we start altering votes based on who 'should' have participated while making assumptions about how those participants would have voted based on their demographic characteristics, not only do we run the risk of making a mistake while doing so, we are applying the logic of enlightened despotism that passively discourages accountability by telling the voter that if they do not take the trouble to express themselves, someone else will step in and try to fix the issue for them. In other words, we reduce both clarity and accountability – the two things voting is supposed to achieve.

6.2.4 Scenario-Building

It is also possible to use digital technology to build dependency paths into the decision-making process. For example, preventing participants from voting on items that stand in contradiction to each other, or from choosing options that when aggregated go beyond certain constraints. For example, if one were designing a community centre, one could say that it should include one sports element. The outcome would thus select the sports element that received the highest level of approval or consensus, rather than recommending that the centre consist solely of twenty different sports facilities, with no arts or meeting facilities. This works (to some extent) to prevent the 'design by committee' pitfalls mentioned earlier, and ensure a more balanced outcome between different interests. Similarly, one might want to offer different options for building a bike path, e.g. with different materials as part of a wider consultation on a park design. The outcome should not include three bike paths, even if they were all quite popular, but rather the path that received the most votes *and* is compatible with the other popular options. Software can either perform these calculations automatically in the background and/or explicitly ask participants to 'pick one of each category', etc.

6.2.5 Cumulative Voting

Rather than allowing each participant to vote once on each agenda item, cumulative voting allocates each voter an equal number of votes that they can distribute across options as they like. For example, each voter might be given ten votes for an agenda with ten items on it. Rather than cast one vote on each item, they could choose to refrain from voting on two items and distribute their ten votes over the remaining eight items, or they could place all ten votes on one item, or cast them in any other possible combination. A version of this occurs in some forms of participatory budgeting, when rather than simply voting on the options they like the best, participants distribute the available budget across their favourite projects. If they want to put the entire budget onto one very expensive project they can.

Cumulative voting has been advocated by some people, such as American legal scholar Lani Guinier,[495] as a way to combine voting equality with minority protection, as it allows minorities to focus their votes on the items most important to them. If something is very important to a minority, but less so to a majority, this can be captured with cumulative voting, and it prevents situations where a passionate minority is outvoted by a disinterested majority. Because everyone receives an equal number of votes, cumulative voting does not contravene the principle of one-person, one-vote in the sense of being inegalitarian. It also does not necessarily create solid, unchanging minority groups.

However, it could lead to confusion in the sense that in this scenario it is hard for voters to know how other voters are allocating their votes. One does not, after all, want to put more votes on an issue than one has to to prevail on that issue. This could lead to tactical voting, as well as tactical voting that goes wrong if voters become confused about general sentiment and put more or fewer votes on an issue than they would have had they been able to correctly assess that sentiment. This could lead to outcomes few, if anyone, wants, and demands for re-votes. Cumulative voting could thus be appropriate to some circumstances and inappropriate to others.

---

495 Lani Guinier, *The Tyranny of the Majority: Fundamental Fairness in Representative Democracy* (Free Press 1994).

6.2.6 Liquid Democracy

Liquid democracy is a voting method that was championed by the German Pirate Party. Under this system, participants can vote directly on issues or delegate their votes to another person whom they trust or believe to be more knowledgeable on the issue to hand. Unlike a representative democracy in which voters delegate their vote on all issues to their chosen representative for a set time period, under liquid democracy voters can delegate their votes to various people and withdraw all or any of those delegations at any time. For example, a voter might choose to vote directly on matters related to taxation, but to delegate their votes on education to Person A, their votes on healthcare to Person B and their votes on foreign policy to Person C. These delegates then cast votes on behalf of all those who have delegated their voting power to them. For example, if 1000 people delegate their vote to Tina, when Tina casts her vote, it counts as 1000 votes for the option she has chosen. Similarly, if 1000 people delegate their vote to Tina and Tina in turn delegates her votes to Robert, then Robert casts all those votes and possibly votes from other delegates as well.[496] The idea is that delegates would be held on a shorter accountability leash than politicians currently are in the electoral system, because their 'constituents' could retract their delegated votes at any time if the representative displeases them. Some people argue that in a liquid democracy, votes could also be delegated to 'trusted institutions' like NGOs.

The main issue with liquid democracy is that, despite being rather complicated, it doesn't effectively counteract the Iron Law of Oligarchy. On the contrary, it explicitly allows people and entities to accumulate power in the form of delegated votes, and once this happens, such entities always seek to expand or retain that power.

This is a particular danger when we consider giving NGOs the ability to collect votes. As we have seen, NGOs are now often highly centralized, extremely well-funded entities that receive a large portion of funding from economic elites. While it is not always easy to hold politicians to account for their actions, non-governmental organizations enjoy *no* accountability or oversight. However, because they dispose over vast resources, it is to be expected that such NGOs would act exactly like parties, soliciting the votes of individuals, producing a stream of propaganda about their own success and policy, and competing with other NGOs for votes. Nothing would change, except that in the absence of focal points like elec-

---

496 See e.g. Bryan Ford, 'Delegative Democracy' (2002) Unpublished paper. Available at <http://www.brynosaurus.com/deleg/deleg.pdf> and 'Delegative Democracy Revisited' Blog post available at <https://bford.github.io/2014/11/16/deleg.html>.

tions, as well as formalized public debate, there would likely be even *less* scrutiny of their actions. This is more or less the same when it comes to delegating voting power to individuals. In the absence of elections, these individuals would likely be subjected to less oversight and scrutiny of their actions, because there are no collective focal points for people to hold them accountable. Instead, individuals would likely canvass others to solicit their votes, those able to raise the most funding or support (e. g. from corporations or philanthropists) would likely be the most successful at this, some would likely find ways to combine resources, and we would be right back where we started. After all, elections are also just a form of delegation. They are merely more regularized and regulated.

In addition to this, liquid democracy squanders the opportunity for independent thinking presented by digital technology. Participants are instead explicitly invited to turn *off* their thinking and delegate it to someone else. Liquid democracy thus throws away *all* of the accountability advantages that can come with digital democracy. Indeed, it is even less accountable in some ways than representative democracy is, because at least in representative democracy voters are often invited to contemplate the issues and 'think it through' for themselves. The idea is often that a voter *agrees* with a candidate or party about priorities or the best course of action, not that they simply trust them to 'know more'. Liquid democracy, however, emphasizes trusting delegates who 'know more' about a subject, absolving the average voter from the expectation to acquire and use this knowledge themselves.

Finally, because different people make decisions on different topics, liquid democracy also has the potential to result in self-contradictory policy, which (according to the theory) must be resolved by appealing to a super-committee or the populace as a whole. This means we are, in the final instance, brought back to either representative or direct democracy as the ultimate method of decision-making (after all, nationally elected governments are exactly the super-committee charged with resolving all conflicting interests in society and pursuing a coherent policy that includes health, security, tax, transportation and the rest of it).

For all these reasons, liquid democracy is essentially a huge amount of work to get back to a system that is almost guaranteed to become a less accountable version of representative democracy.

6.2.7 Quadratic Voting

Like cumulative voting, quadratic voting allows participants to place more than one vote on each proposal, with the twist that these votes become progressively more 'expensive'. For example, if everyone starts out with 10 voting 'tokens', casting a single vote on a proposal would cost one token, but casting two votes on a single proposal would cost four tokens and three votes would cost nine tokens, etc. (hence why this kind of voting is 'quadratic'). This is supposed to discourage people from placing too many votes on a single proposal. One could, of course, achieve the same thing by just giving every voter in a cumulative voting system five votes for ten proposals or declaring that each voter can only allocate a certain maximum (say two or three out of 10 votes) to any particular proposal. However, this begs the question as to why one would first introduce a system like cumulative voting (the prime advantage of which is the ability to weight one's vote) and then seek to constrain it in this manner.

The answer is that quadratic voting stems from the same kind of effort to depoliticize the public sphere as so many other 'democratic innovations' we have seen throughout this book. It is worth reflecting on this here as the same sentiments are continuously repeated in the discourse of so many 'think tanks' and newspapers without examining whether they make sense. The advantages of quadratic voting have been described as 'limit[ing] the influence of politics and self-interest' in legislatures, as well as preventing strong or 'fringe' opinion from being expressed in the voting system.[497] Quadratic voting has sometimes been billed as a way to make hard choices, 'like whether addressing the opioid crisis is more important than reducing the cost of health care, or choosing between making college or housing more affordable'.[498]

It is unclear as to why limiting the influence of politics *in politics* is a good idea or why anyone should not vote in their 'self-interest'. One is granted a vote *precisely* as a means via which to represent one's interests. That's the *point* of it. The general will or common good is formulated via a combination of those interests and the voter's own views on what is best for society – it is not some other thing decided on by some other force.

It is also hard to see how quadratic voting would force Americans to make 'hard choices' between e.g. resolving the opioid crisis or lowering the costs of healthcare. After all, one could still just put one vote on each proposal, exactly as one could do under regular cumulative voting. In fact, there is more incentive to prioritize more strongly with the regular form of cumulative voting, because the cost to putting additional votes on a proposal is lower. One loses the ability to place

497 Matt Prewitt and Paul Healy, *The Handbook for Radical Local Democracy v2.0* (RadicalXChange Foundation) <https://www.radicalxchange.org/media/papers/The_Handbook_for_Radical_Local_De mocracy.pdf> accessed 22 January 2023.
498 Brian Eason, '$120 Million in Requests and $40 million in the Bank. How an Obscure Theory Helped Prioritize the Colorado Budget' *The Colorado Sun* (28 May 2019) <https://coloradosun.com/ 2019/05/28/quadratic-voting-colorado-house-budget/>.

that vote somewhere else, but not at double or triple the rate as one does under quadratic voting. Thus, theoretically, cumulative voting should allow for better prioritization.

However, more noteworthy is the emphasis on forcing people to 'make hard choices' and accept that their options are limited, even when there is no good reason for believing that they are. Why *would* Americans have to choose between addressing the opioid crisis or reducing the cost of healthcare, after all? Shouldn't they save on something less existential or close some tax loopholes to fund both? In fact, surely addressing the opioid crisis *would* reduce the cost of healthcare as there would be fewer people in medical treatment related to opioid addiction? Similarly, if one thinks about it, how *would* paying more for a house make college cheaper? Is tuition funded directly by mortgage interest payments? Why were both house prices and college tuition more affordable in the past? Indeed, why would any of these issues need to be addressed by spending taxpayer money when they can all be addressed via market regulation (and indeed *are* addressed by market regulation in many other countries)?

This effort to bake manipulation into the process and force participants to make unnecessary false (and therefore 'hard') choices is extremely common in most forms of democratic 'innovation' today, which focuses almost exclusively on *controlling* voters rather than emancipating them. In the *Colorado Sun*, Radical-XChange President Mark Prewitt referred to quadratic voting as imposing 'a cost on fanaticism...If you feel so strongly about one issue that you're willing to allocate all of your voice credits to one issue, your overall say in the system is quieter.'

On the surface this seems to be an obsession with fixing a problem that doesn't currently exist. The great contribution of one person, one vote, *is* that it is one person, one vote, regardless of the level of enthusiasm anyone feels when they submit their ballot. Indeed, the principle of one person, one vote could in some sense be considered to be the most socialist invention of all time. But it is worth thinking about quadratic voting in a little more detail, precisely because these muddled sentiments on 'mitigating extremism' and promoting 'hard choices' are so often both voiced and praised, despite making a very limited amount of sense.

'Reducing fanaticism' as the goal of a political system only works if one believes that the definition of fanaticism is widely known, agreed upon, and impervious to change. But again, *the point* of politics is to determine what we regard as right and wrong, useful and spurious, sensible and fanatic. The Quakers were widely regarded as abolitionist fanatics in their day, as were suffragettes. Many 'fanatical' freedom fighters fought wars of liberation against colonization. How else to describe someone like Símon Bolívar, who spent his entire fortune in the efforts to liberate South America from Spanish rule, or Gandhi, who went to jail repeatedly and adopted an extremely ascetic, religiously motivated lifestyle, or Patrick Henry's 'Give me liberty, or give me death' speech? Strong feelings are as liable to be grounded in rationality as not, or to enjoy our ultimate endorsement as not. It is the very *strength* of democracy that minority views have a chance to interact meaningfully in the political system and (if they can persuade others) to grow. Voting systems that seek to manipulate or constrain outcomes to subjective preferences are *not* democracy.

Like liquid democracy claims to be direct democracy, but systematically gets rid of all its advantages, quadratic voting claims to be cumulative voting while getting rid of all *its* advantages.

6.3 Conclusions on Voting

It requires few words to describe and analyse voting systems, yet it is one of the most important decisions to make. Particularly when it comes to digital democracy, the choices one can make here are endless and thus the task more daunting. Generally speaking, it is best to focus on whether the system one uses achieves that clarity and accountability that is the purpose of voting, and to use the simplest system possible to complete the task adequately.

Chapter 7
Security

Security is probably the single most discussed aspect of digital democracy.

The most difficult option to manage from a security perspective, and the one people tend to think of first when they hear the words 'digital democracy', is to leave the current system of representative democracy in place unchanged and use digital voting *just* to replace paper voting in elections (as is the case in Estonia). For this reason, this section is going to start with an explanation of election security.

7.1 Paper-Based vs Online Voting Security

It is important to understand digital security and electoral security in context. Although many people in Western countries tend to equate the internet and particularly internet voting with increased security risks, this is not uniformly the case around the world. Indeed, comparing elections worldwide shows that the issue of security is not necessarily purely one of developing a perfectly secure system (although technical security is important), but also of enforcement and incentives.

7.1.1 Understanding the Essence of Election Security

7.1.1.1 The Hot Gates

In 480 B.C., a brief but famous battle was fought near the Gulf of Malia in ancient Greece. This became known as the Battle of Thermopylae and it was part of a wider war fought between Persian and Greek forces. At the time, Persia was a large and well-developed empire and the Greek states were small and fractured. Thus, the Persians were in an advantageous position in terms of both numbers and resources, and they invaded the Greek states with the object of incorporating them into the empire (and also to punish them, because the Greeks were rather provoking in a whole number of ways).

In order to try to prevent the invasion, the Greeks deployed small groups of fighters to block the Persian advance at strategic sites and thus give their fellow citizens a chance to evacuate, prepare, or fight at sea. They chose to make one such stand at Thermopylae, which at the time was a narrow pass along the Mediterranean coastline close to hot springs (hence the name of 'hot gates'). Here, a group of Greeks led by the Spartan King Leonidas did indeed hold off the massive

https://doi.org/10.1515/9783110794465-011

Persian army for several days, before ultimately, and somewhat anti-climactically, being betrayed, encircled via a lesser-known route around the battle site, and killed.

While it is much celebrated as an act of patriotic heroism, whether or not the Battle of Thermopylae had much of an effect on the course of the greater war is disputed. However, it does illustrate two things that are relevant here: 1) a narrow pass is easy to defend; 2) any route around said narrow pass ruins the whole strategy.

Modern elections are like the Battle of Thermopylae, a vicious struggle to **control a narrow bottleneck** that grants access to other things (for example, making laws as one likes). If one fails to win this battle, one fails to win access to all of the things on the other side of the gate (see Fig. 7.1).

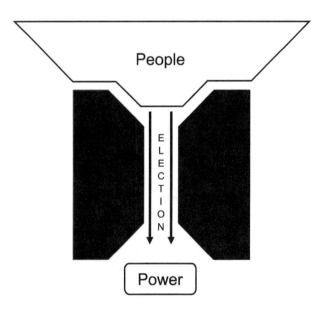

Fig. 7.1: The Hot Gates of Election.

As a result, everyone is highly motivated to win elections, and a small, seemingly insignificant location (election day) becomes a site of intense focus, a place into which huge resources are poured in an attempt to own that space. Because victory is everything in elections, the incentive to use whatever means are at one's disposal to win is enormous. And when people are sufficiently incentivized, it is very difficult to prevent them from cheating, breaking laws, and generally doing whatever they need to do to prevail.

If you win an election, you can lock in your powerbase for several years. During this time, you can pursue the policy you like, or leverage your experience to move to a higher-paying job. In addition, successful politicians are able to reward those who have helped them with the resources of the State.[499] This need not even involve corruption. For example, a candidate sponsored by oil and gas companies may continue to rely on oil and gas, while those sponsored by renewable energy may give out large solar and wind power subsidies. It is possible that both sides believe that their choice is also the right one for the country, but there is a lot more riding on these decisions than just ideology. This makes people desperate, giving them **an incentive** to cheat (e.g. gerrymandering, vote-rigging, false claims, etc.).

The gate or bottleneck of elections is what creates **the opportunity** to cheat in democracy, because you can control it with a smaller force than you would need to prevail in society generally. Any system that allows these bottlenecks to be created will always turn into a system of minority rule for the simple reason that it is possible for a minority to 'hold the pass' against the majority. This is the first thing that needs to exist for security problems to arise in any voting system: incentive and opportunity. This opportunity is even greater in societies that experience extreme inequality, because it ensures that the minority 'holding the pass' has an even stronger starting position.

7.1.1.2 Inequality as a Driving Force of Vote Rigging

Democracy as a form of government is usually preceded by a levelling event that reduces pre-existing economic inequality. For example, in ancient Athens, democratic procedures were only (gradually) put in place following an event known as the Seisachtheia (shaking off of burdens), which was a kind of debt cancellation. The Seisachtheia did not make all Athenians equally wealthy (far from it), but it did end the most extreme forms of inequality that had created **dependency** between Athenian citizens and as a result it 'reset' societal relations. Other times when democracy has moved forward (if in different ways) include after the War of Independence in America, following the French Revolution and, in a large portion of the world (including America and Europe), following World War II. These levelling events (particularly war) tend to destroy wealth or outright target inherited privilege (such as the French Revolution) while simultaneously creating a situation of solidarity among 'ordinary' people (e.g. through having to

---

499 See Roslyn Fuller, *Beasts and Gods: How Democracy Changed Its Meaning and Lost Its Purpose* (Zed/Bloomsbury 2015) for a full description of this process.

defend the country together). As a result, some scholars view war, or at least existential crisis, as a crucible of democracy.

Likewise, it is an axiom of classic democratic philosophy that it depends on a large middle class with few (if any) very rich or poor people. This is because very rich people inevitably manage to create dependencies with very poor people. Regardless of how benevolent their intentions may be, this makes the poor easy to manipulate, they become the mere tools of their rich benefactors and we enter a period of mob rule rather than democracy.

This is important to recognize because there are an almost infinite number of ways to cheat at elections that have nothing to do with the actual voting. For example, one can engage in gerrymandering, essentially rigging each district to the point where no meaningful political contest takes place. Voter intimidation can also become an issue, as can vote-buying. Vote-buying is rife in many developing countries,[500] and it only works when inequality is so severe as to allow many votes to be bought cheaply. It should be noted that this does not need to be explicit, but if a candidate gives a voter something (a kilogram of sugar, for example), it becomes exponentially more likely that they will vote for that person, rather than for someone who has given them nothing. While it is often most flagrant in developing countries, tacit vote-buying is not unknown in developed countries, either – representatives often reward their voters and supporters with lucrative contracts or a publicly-funded project in their area. When I ran for election, it was not uncommon for constituents to contact me and offer me their vote in exchange for pulling strings in their favour, and I have spoken to many people who support other politicians precisely because they believe the politician has successfully engaged in such behaviour on their behalf.

In recent decades, flagrant bribery has been less widespread in developed nations, because people have been more economically equal and, as a result, it is a) simply too expensive to directly buy them off and b) most of them are not desperate enough to ask for such favours. However, this is changing, as inequality in developed nations increases and we see a resurgence of private patronage and philanthropy, as well as the decline of post-war social services. These social services had previously broken the patronage link, by creating a system where people paid into collective 'charity' institutions like welfare or unemployment insurance that they were later entitled to collect from according to democratically agreed rules (rather than at the discretion of a specific person). This made people depend-

---

500 'Interview with Patricia Namakula: Democracy and Digitalization: A Ugandan Perspective' (*Solonian Democracy Institute*, 16 September 2022) <https://www.solonian-institute.com/post/digital-democracy-a-ugandan-perspective>.

ent on the State, not specific other people within that State. One cannot, in a modern Western State, receive a greater pension than one is due according to the rules. But one can receive a greater pension from a billionaire by pleasing them. This is how buying people starts. When people are in deep dependency relationships, democracy is just a pretence. The 'pass' to power becomes narrower and narrower and it becomes easier and easier for a tiny minority to hold it with minimal effort.

7.1.1.3 Political Polarization (caused by Economic Inequality) as a Driving Force of Vote Rigging

When societies become more unequal *despite* continuing to grow economically (as many Western countries are) it is because some segment of society has figured out how to capture a greater piece of the economic pie for themselves. This can only happen in a democracy by *excluding* others from decision-making – reducing the impact of their votes from where they would be under a system of equality. This is already occurring, and as more and more people fall out of the middle-class democratic system, many of them become 'clients' of more powerful members of society – both economically and socially. Today, far fewer people own small businesses or belong to member-funded social organizations.[501] Instead, they work at large corporations or 'civic' organizations that are funded with the proceeds of these large organizations. In this situation the biggest 'players' become more and more powerful, sucking up more and more wealth. Inevitably, they all run into resistance – some from those who have been left out of the process, but others from the other 'big fish' out there.

And that is when the real battle begins.

Because these titans no longer need to expend much effort in keeping the majority at bay, they fight each other. In their efforts to attain supremacy and achieve their goals (which could be to make more money or to achieve a societal goal), such entities enlist the help of all of those beneath them (their clients) often through a mixture of reward and threats (see Fig. 7.2). As this continues over years, it gradually becomes impossible for anyone to claim to be neutral, as this is seen as synonymous with being on the other side. All newspaper articles, all research, all casual comments on social media are judged according to what side is believed to be served by them (regardless of their intentions). This is the death of independence and thus the death of thought. The USA is the prime example of this precise phenomenon at the moment, but the Weimar Republic went through a similar event in the 1920s, as did the Roman Republic shortly before its end. This hyper-partisan-

---

501 Robert D. Putnam, *Bowling Alone: The Collapse and Revival of American Community* (Simon and Schuster 2000).

ship is exactly the kind of super-factionalism that the American Founding Fathers warned against. However, it is important to remember that it is not caused merely by intense feeling on either side of the divide, but that it also *depends* on having the resources to enlist a significant segment of society to fighting one's cause and perpetuating this struggle. Strong feelings are a given of the human condition – having the resources to indulge them society-wide (as e.g. some Roman Emperors did) is really the crucial factor that *can* be affected by our choice of societal rules.

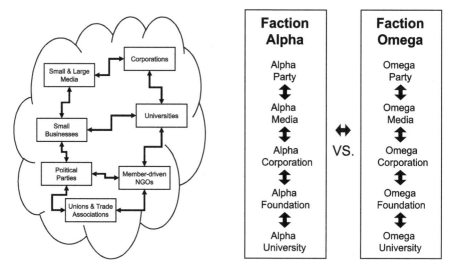

Fig. 7.2: Dispersed Independent Democracy (left, in cloud) vs. Over-Alignment (right, in columns).

The duration of this all-encompassing political struggle then really takes its toll. As time goes on, each side becomes more and more obsessed with the other side's obliteration. If this goes on for long enough, eventually it comes to be believed that *nothing* is neutral or unbiased, also not the system for counting votes or determining democratic outcomes. These political partisans (not necessarily the majority of all people) lose respect for this system the moment it fails to deliver the outcome they 'know' to be right. They then begin to agitate for the system to be changed to deliver those outcomes (they begin, in other words, to undermine the basis of their civilization in pursuit of their own preferred outcomes).

It is not unusual today to come across people who suggest that following facts is 'playing to a side' or 'being a traitor' and that one must adjust facts to fit the outcomes that 'are needed'. In this atmosphere, vote rigging is not a possibility, but a moral duty.

This fatal flaw in the basic power dynamic of electoral democracy is why I do not advocate simply voting digitally in elections and instead adhere to a more encompassing view of democracy (outlined in Chapter 1) which includes mass participation in all phases of the process from ideation to decision-making to implementation. This is what is necessary to break up these factions – dispersing power, not consolidating it. Elections create the 'hot gate', the single point of vulnerability to attack, they are not robust or resilient and they frequently cause the kinds of distortions (over a long timeframe) that lead to all of the problems I have outlined above. This is a *social* problem, and thus cannot be *technically* fixed, but rather socially mitigated at best.

7.1.2 Security in Paper-Based Elections: Comparisons and Considerations

7.1.2.1 Paper-Based Voting Around the World

When we look at paper-based voting systems worldwide, we see that there is nothing particular about paper that instantly and reliably places paper-reliant elections beyond dispute. Instead, the dynamics of incentive plus opportunity to rig are plain to see.

Indeed, in nations where more is at stake in elections, where the possible paths the country could take are more divergent, or where the rewards of victory (or consequences of defeat) are greater, there is often more vote-rigging. In the West, we also recently see disputes about election security as pivotal, high-stakes battles between elites and populists come to depend on the outcome of a few all-important voting events. Indeed, two-thirds of all US Presidential elections this century have been highly disputed. When less existential questions were at stake, as in previous decades, contention was also minimal.

Paper-based voting has also been the subject of enormous controversy in many other nations and has not, of itself, brought security and stability to the practice of voting and electing leaders.

Some of the issues experienced with paper-based voting include:

- ballot box snatching and stuffing
- difficulty in timely delivery and distribution of electoral materials (e.g. ballots, voter rolls)
- biased electoral officials
- altering results after votes have been counted
- disenfranchisement of eligible voters (by e.g. striking them from the register)

- registering underage voters
- 'ghost' voters (voting under the name of a deceased person who has not been stricken from the register)
- long queues for voting (which can amount to voter suppression)
- multiple registrations of people who are entitled to vote but have been entered into the system more than once (possibly due to a change in location) with the duplicate records never having been cleaned from the register[502]

Due to all these problems, in developing countries electronic voting is sometimes seen as a potential method for *preventing* vote fraud, inaccurate counting and corruption.[503] After all, it eliminates much of the risk that comes with transporting filled ballot boxes through remote areas, where they may be stolen or tampered with, and allows the register of voters to be better tracked and revised for accuracy. This is worth thinking about, because developing nations sometimes have *far* tighter official election security measures than most Western states, and comparing the two really gives us an insight into the entire issue of social versus technical security.

In Canada, people can vote just by having someone accompany them to the polling station and vouch that they are who they say they are.[504] In the Netherlands, voters receive a polling card before the election, although they are rarely required to present this or any other form of ID before voting. Because Dutch law has recently expanded to allow voters to cast their ballot at any polling station, electoral officials have begun to demand polling cards – creating issues since voters do not always receive them. In other words, people neither followed nor cared very much about following the official security guidelines. What would likely be portrayed as a scandal and obvious opportunity for election malfeasance in a devel-

---

502 Nwogu Emeka Reginald, 'Mobile, Secure E-Voting Architecture for the Nigerian Electoral System' (2015) 17(2) IOSR Journal of Computer Engineering 27–36; Sanjo Faniran and Kayode Olaniyan, 'Strengthening Democratic Practice in Nigeria: A Case for E-Voting' (ICE Gov Conference 2011) 337–340; Samuel Agbesi, Fati Tehiru and Alexander Osei-owusu, 'Investigating the Feasibility of Implementing E-Voting System in Ghana' (2014) 10(1) International Journal of Innovation and Scientific Research 218–231; Nic Cheeseman, Gabrielle Lynch and Justin Willis, 'Digital Dilemmas: The Unintended Consequences of Election Technology' (2018) Democratization 1397–1404.
503 Reginald, 'Mobile Secure E-Voting'; Cheeseman, Lynch and Willis, 'Digital Dilemmas'; Lapologang Ntwayame, 'A Conceptual Model for Designing and Implementation of Secure and Trustable Remote Electronic Voting within the Developing World' (MSc, Botswana International University of Science and Technology 2018).
504 'Vouching' (*Elections Saskatchewan*) <https://www.elections.sk.ca/what-we-do/glossary/vouching/> accessed 23 January 2023; 'FAQs on Voting' (*Elections Canada*) <https://www.elections.ca/content.aspx?section=vot&dir=faq&document=faqvoting&lang=e#a4> accessed 23 January 2023.

oping country is treated as merely a minor annoyance in a 'stable democracy', where we are so confident in our social security that our lackadaisical approach to technical security has gone unnoticed.

It is even possible for a voter to allow someone else to cast their vote for them (voting by proxy) in the Netherlands, simply by signing their polling card and handing it over to the other party. Intended to be used in cases of illness and travel, this practice did lead (because it provided the opportunity) to some people soliciting the votes of many others and casting them en masse (vote harvesting). As a result, the rule was tightened so that any person can only cast votes on behalf of two other people.[505] In addition, advance voting, postal voting and drop-off-ballot voting are increasingly used in many countries, without necessarily including a great deal of security around these procedures.

Contrast this to the level of official formal security in some developing countries. Voters in many nations such as Nigeria, Brazil, Kenya, and Tanzania must register to vote in person (not the case in most Western countries), submitting biometric data which can range from thumbprints, to all ten fingerprints, to photos to signatures. All of this data is stored in a database and voters often receive a voter card at the time of registration.[506] In the case of Tanzania, such national ID cards include microchips containing an image of the cardholder, their fingerprints and all of the 'cryptographic keys, random number generators and algorithms needed to carry out all the computations on behalf of the voter'.[507] On polling day, voters are generally recognized via scanning their fingerprints on a touchscreen. About half of all African nations now use systems which include biometric voter registration and identification and/or electronic results transmission to the central tabulation centre.[508] In Brazil, officials also issue ID to act as a backup in case of system failure. For example, if the scanner does not recognize a voter's fingerprints (as sometimes happens), the voter can show his or her photo ID and still vote.[509]

---

505 Bart Jacobs and Wolter Pieters, 'Electronic Voting in the Netherlands: From Early Adoption to Early Abolishment' (2009) Foundations of Security Analysis and Design 121–144.

506 Reginald, 'Mobile Secure E-Voting' 28 and 31; 'Biometrics' (*Tribunal Superior Eleitoral*) <https://www.tse.jus.br/eleitor/justificativa-eleitoral/consequencias-para-quem-nao-justificar> accessed 23 January 2023; 'Biometria' (*Justiça Eleitoral*) <https://www.justicaeleitoral.jus.br/biometria/> accessed 23 January 2023.

507 Sylvester Kimbi and Irina Zlotnikova 'A Secure Model for Remote Electronic Voting. A Case of Tanzania' (2014) 3(4) Advances in Computer Science: An International Journal 95, 96.

508 Cheeseman, Lynch and Willis, 'Digital Dilemmas' 1397.

509 'Biometria' (*Justiça Eleitoral*) <https://www.justicaeleitoral.jus.br/biometria/> accessed 23 January 2023; Interestingly, voting machines were originally introduced in France in 1969 in order to prevent voter fraud. However, as no improvement was detected, they stopped using them

As we can see, paper-based voting security in most Western nations is extremely lax and relies heavily on the expectation that there is little incentive to cheat and that therefore wide-scale cheating will not occur. If something goes wrong the other political parties are expected to find and expose it, as they have the incentive to do so. Such instances, however, are very rare. The parties concerned almost never seriously dispute an election outcome, and thus citizens do not doubt its validity. If political parties did start to engage in such disputes, we would have all of the problems that developing countries have with elections. All it takes to disrupt this entire, allegedly robust and fool-proof system is an accusation, precisely because the system is not 100% technically secure.

We have seen how this has played out in the USA recently, first with the 2016 claims that Russia stole the presidential election in favour of Trump, and then the 2020 claims that vote harvesting and the involvement of NGOs in providing election infrastructure effectively rigged the Presidential election. It is not coincidental that this contention over security has occurred during a heavily contested period of political upheaval.

Electoral disruption is far from impossible to achieve even in paper-based systems. Long lines and inadequate polling stations may be used to intentionally discourage people in some areas from casting their ballots. Likewise, poor practices such as extreme early advance voting, unguarded ballot drop boxes and vote harvesting (in which canvassers can pick up ballots directly from voters) are all easy to abuse. It would be simple for a vote harvester to submit a ballot on behalf of a recently deceased, very ill or mentally incapacitated person, or even on behalf of a person who has stated their intention not to vote. Since voting is anonymous and because people do not always remember if they voted or not, it can be very hard to track such practices down, even if it is politically feasible to do so. This is all the more likely to occur in an atmosphere where the person committing vote fraud believes that they are doing *the right thing* by doing so (e.g. casting a vote in what they believe are the interests of the mentally incapacitated person and/or saving the country from the grave threat posed by 'the other side'). When one looks for security flaws with paper-based voting, it turns out, they are there.

Unfortunately, simply applying digital technology to this fraught electoral process doesn't seem to help much. While digital security measures have helped to purge

---

(Susan Collard and Elodie Fabre, 'Electronic Voting in the French Legislative Elections of 2012' in Dimitrios Zisiss and Dimitrios Lekkas (eds) *Design, Development and Use of Secure Electronic Voting Systems* (IGI Global 2014) 176).

duplicate and false registrations in many countries,[510] they haven't resolved electoral security issues. For example, in the Ghanaian elections of 2012, 'machines were more likely to fail where no observers were present, and...machine failure was correlated with over-voting.'[511] It would be feasible to break machines, or even to falsely claim they broke, in districts where it is expected that votes will disproportionately go against one. Such equipment failures have also occurred in other elections, such as the Nigerian presidential election of 2015 and the Kenyan elections of 2013.[512]

Indeed, in Kenya, where biometric voter registration and digital transmission of local results to a central tabulation centre were supposed to reduce electoral fraud,[513] it was announced only a few days before the 2017 election that more than one-quarter of polling stations would be unable to transmit results as they lacked reliable internet access. That the signal at these stations really was so unreliable is disputed.[514] More troublingly, the opposition (which had been among the most avid proponents of Kenya's digital system) rejected the election results that it produced, claiming the system had been rigged.[515] It certainly didn't help that one of the key people in charge of implementing the online system was murdered a week before the election.[516]

According to close observers, 'Kenyan politics is intensely competitive and won on the slimmest margins'.[517] I believe this is the major component driving cheating and instability, rather than paper versus digital participation, which as we can see, does not unto itself ever resolve this fundamental issue. As long as one creates a bottleneck to power, it will always be vulnerable to cheating, especially in very unequal societies where there is necessarily a lot at stake.

---

510 Cheeseman, Lynch and Willis, 'Digital Dilemmas' 1405–1406; Nwogu Emeka Reginald 'Mobile Secure E-Voting'.
511 Cheeseman, Lynch & Willis, 'Digital Dilemmas' 1402.
512 Cheeseman, Lynch & Willis, 'Digital Dilemmas' 1406.
513 Nanjala Nyabola, *Digital Democracy: Analogue Politics: How the Internet Era is Transforming Politics in Kenya* (Zed Books 2018) 28.
514 Nyabola, *Digital Democracy: Analogue Politics* 188.
515 Nyabola, *Digital Democracy: Analogue Politics* 191.
516 Nyabola, *Digital Democracy: Analogue Politics* 183; Tamerra Griffin, 'He was Meant to Secure an Election: He Turned Up Dead' *BuzzFeed* (5 October 2017) <https://www.buzzfeednews.com/article/tamerragriffin/kenya-chris-msando-murder>.
517 Nyabola, *Digital Democracy: Analogue Politics* 169.

7.1.2.2 The Myth of Vote Secrecy and Security

Regardless of the electoral system used, we have always had to make a choice between absolute secrecy and absolute security. It is possible to have pretty good vote secrecy and pretty good vote security simultaneously, but not absolute security and secrecy. Indeed, privacy and security are two logically opposed things (one requires clarity, the other obscurity). A choice therefore must be made.

If a country uses untraceable ballot papers, as e.g. in Ireland, once a vote is cast, there is no way to later verify that it was cast by a certain person or to remove it if a person fraudulently voted (because we cannot identify their ballot amongst all the other ballots). In other countries, like the UK,[518] it is possible to track ballots back to the person who cast them, because they each have a serial number that can be matched up to the ballot's 'stub' in the record book that indicates the person that ballot was given to (similar to matching a cheque to the cheque book).[519] Ballots and stubs are kept in storage for a set period of time and then destroyed.

Both systems have points of vulnerability. Because secrecy is not absolute under the British system, it would be perfectly possible to gain access to the ballots before they are destroyed and draw up blacklists of people who e.g. vote Communist, etc. It has been alleged that this system may have been used to identify and then surveil those who voted for such parties in the past.[520] Because security is not absolute under the other system, it is possible to impersonate someone, say a nonvoter (chronic non-voters rarely start voting), especially where other methods like postal voting and drop-off boxes are used.

Skewing elections does not even necessarily require large numbers of people to be involved in vote fraud, because often people are limited to voting within districts, where a few hundred votes can determine the fate of the district. While it

---

518 This system is also used in Singapore ('How is my Vote still Secret if the Ballot Paper has a Serial Number on It?' (*Government of Singapore*, August 2015) <https://www.gov.sg/article/how-is-my-vote-still-secret-if-the-ballot-paper-has-a-serial-number-on-it> accessed 23 January 2023) and other Commonwealth countries ((*ACE Electoral Knowledge Network*) <https://aceproject.org/electoral-advice/archive/questions/replies/912993749/mobile_conversation_view> accessed 23 January 2023).

519 Select Committee on Home Affairs, *Fourth Report (1997–1998)*, Section E, Subsection 103–104 <https://publications.parliament.uk/pa/cm199798/cmselect/cmhaff/768/76807.htm>; UK Law Commission, *Research Paper: Manner of Voting in UK Elections*, paras 1.39–1.54 <https://www.lawcom.gov.uk/app/uploads/2015/03/Electoral-Law_Manner-of-Voting_Research.pdf>; The Representation of the People Act 1983 refers to this practice in Art 66. Subsection 2(2)(a), Art. 19(1)(c) and Art. 47.

520 Gordon Winter, *Inside BOSS, South Africa's Secret Police: An Ex-Spy's Dramatic and Shocking Exposé* (Penguin 1981) 417–421.

would be hard to cast millions of false votes without being detected (and it would be hard to do this electronically as well), a few hundred or even thousand are certainly possible.

Western nations love to praise their own voting procedures, but mistakes are inevitably made. In one election I observed, an entire ballot box went temporarily missing. Since the box was found and no one made accusations of foul play, the issue eventually settled. But all it would have taken would be for someone to make such an accusation, and in a more fraught atmosphere perhaps they would have.

According to philosopher Niklas Luhmann, trust is based on assessment of risks, and a decision whether or not to accept those, while confidence neglects the possibility of disappointment, not only because this case is rare, but also because there is not really a choice.[521] For example, few people worry much about the ramifications of aliens landing, because there isn't much they could do about it anyway. Up until now in most Western countries, this has been our attitude towards paper elections – we just haven't really thought about it too much. We think of it as justified trust, but really, it's just blind confidence, generated by a lack of complaints.

Digital technology is so relevant not because it allows us to count votes faster or have a little more convenience, but because it enables a system change that prevents decision bottlenecks (like all-important elections) from forming. With no power to capture in a system of continuous mass participation from ideation to voting to implementation, the incentive to cheat is dramatically decreased (Fig. 7.3). This is the true significance of digital democracy. This is why I outlined my concept of Fuller Democracy in the introduction and why I believe that this is the shape that digital democracy should take.

While we do need to have reasonable verification procedures so that we can process what has happened, this is not the only factor in security and it neither ultimately causes nor prevents cheating on its own. Thus, such measures are necessary, but not sufficient. One cannot work against strong incentives simply with rules and procedures – one needs to attack the root cause of the incentive. However, once that is achieved, one does need to have a reasonable technical security system in place, and this is what we turn our attention to now.

---

521 Niklas Luhmann, 'Familiarity, Confidence, Trust: Problems and Alternatives' in Diego Gambetta (ed) *Trust: Making and Breaking of Cooperative Relations* (Basil Blackwell 1988) 94–108; Jacobs and Pieters, 'Electronic Voting in the Netherlands' 138–140.

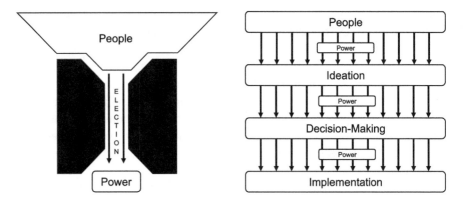

Fig. 7.3: How Power is Channelled in Electoral vs. Direct Democracy.

7.2 How Internet Voting Technically Works

Many internet voting systems make use of what is known as public key security. For example, in Estonia, voters use an ID card inserted into a smart reader and a PIN (PIN1), or their Mobile ID which uses a special SIM Card with security certificates, to identify themselves. The system verifies the voter's eligibility,[522] much as an election official would check that a voter is on the voters' list at a physical polling station. If the voter is eligible, the screen displays the list of candidates in their district to them. The voter casts their ballot by selecting a candidate and entering another PIN (PIN2). The vote is then sent to the server[523] which verifies that PIN1 and PIN2 match up, and thus that the vote was cast by the same PIN holder as the person who signed in.[524]

This type of system is also used to sign documents digitally, and to use financial services and other government services in Estonia. PIN1 gains the user access

---

522 Kristjan Vassil, 'Introduction' in Mihkel Solvak and Kristjan Vassil (eds), *E-voting in Estonia: Technological Diffusion and other Developments over Ten Years, 2005–2015* (Johan Skytte Institute of Political Studies, University of Tartu 2016) 7.

523 Kristjan Vassil, 'The Estonian e-government Ecosystem' in Mihkel Solvak and Kristjan Vassil (eds), *E-voting in Estonia: Technological Diffusion and other Developments over Ten Years, 2005–2015* (Johan Skytte Institute of Political Studies, University of Tartu 2016) 17 et seq.

524 Guido Shryen and Eliot Rich, 'Security in Large-Scale Internet Elections: A Retrospective Analysis of Elections in Estonia, The Netherlands, and Switzerland' (2010) 4(4) IEEE Transactions on Information Forensics and Security 729–744.

to the system (authentication) and establishes the session, while PIN2 is used to authorize an action (transaction), e. g. signing, transferring money, etc.[525]

The 'ballot' itself is processed using similar principles to postal voting. There, the voter generally places their ballot into a blank envelope that is placed inside a signed envelope. When this is received by election officials, they strike the name of the voter off the list (as having voted) and remove the inner envelope from the outer envelope. The inner envelope is then placed in an urn or other container to be counted later. This double envelope system seeks to preserve security and anonymity.

Digital ballots work in similar fashion. The ballot goes inside of a blank (digital) 'envelope' which goes inside a named envelope and it is the outer, named envelope that is checked against the voter rolls when it is received and then discarded so that only anonymous votes remain.[526]

This can occur via what is known as a **blind signature.** Offline, a blind signature is when you put a document (e. g. a ballot) into a carbon-lined envelope and an official signs it (for example, when I present the envelope and my ID) through the envelope, without opening it and seeing the contents. This allows for security and secrecy, documenting that the content has been received as it was presented. Even when the envelope has been removed, the ballot inside has still been verified. It is possible to perform the same function digitally, by combining the ballot with a random 'blinding factor' and signing it digitally.

Most online voting systems also shuffle the votes received before they are counted. In other words, they are mixed up, in much the same way lottery tickets are mixed in a drum, before they are counted in order to preserve secrecy (called **a mix-net**).

The results, which, of course, do not need to be manually counted, but are instead instantly available, are decrypted by unlocking them with a key that has been separated and distributed among stakeholders (e. g. political parties).[527] The process is often certified and time-stamped at each stage. In Estonia, it is filmed so that it can be audited later,[528] and subject to observation by party and international observers. Some online voting systems are also now open-source, in-

---

525 Shryen and Rich, 'Security in Large-Scale Internet Elections' 732; Vassil, 'The Estonian e-government Ecosystem' 17.

526 'E-democracy and Open Data' (*Enterprise Estonia*) <https://e-estonia.com/solutions/e-governance/e-democracy/> accessed 23 January 2023.

527 Shryen and Rich, 'Security in Large-Scale Internet Elections' 733; Polys also uses these distributed keys, whereby only a certain percentage of the key is necessary to unlock the vote, preventing a single party from 'holding the election hostage' be refusing to use their key.

528 'E-democracy and Open Data' (*Enterprise Estonia*).

cluding the Estonian system and Assembly Voting. This allows any member of the public to check the code for security weaknesses.

Many online voting systems also seek to provide what it known as individual verification and universal verification. **Individual verification** means that the voter can check if their vote has been registered by the counting system as they have cast it. So, for example, if a voter cast their ballot for the Green Party, they can check that the ballot has been received as being cast for the Green Party. In Estonia, the voter receives an on-screen confirmation that their vote has been cast when they finish the process,[529] along with a QR code. Voters can then use another device (e. g. a mobile phone) to read the QR code and verify that their vote has been received for the intended candidate or party. Verification must be done from another device, because if the original device was compromised, the verification process from that device would also likely be compromised.[530] Thus far, few Estonians have utilized this process – just 5 % verified their vote in the 2019 general election.[531]

Universal verification means that the entire process can be verified, generally by keeping a record of it on the blockchain, often referred to as a 'publicly-available digital bulletin board'. Any information that goes on a blockchain becomes public and cannot be altered without leaving a record of the alteration. The data displayed in this bulletin board is encrypted (so that e. g. it is not possible to know how someone voted). Some have called this a 'fingerprint' of each vote, rather than the vote itself.[532] However, one can apply checks to this encrypted information to check its veracity without having to decrypt it (using what is known as homomorphic encryption and zero-knowledge proofs).[533] These are methods of checking that data is accurate without having to see it, like a science experiment in which a scientist may not be able to see a particle, but can nonetheless detect its presence by observing its effect on other things. While some systems already claim to utilize universal verification that preserves secrecy, verifying that this verification truly exists in robust form has proven more elusive.[534]

---

529 Shryen and Rich, 'Security in Large-Scale Internet Elections' 733.

530 Mihkel Solvak, 'Verification and Trust' in Mihkel Solvak and Kristjan Vassil (eds), *E-voting in Estonia: Technological Diffusion and other Developments over Ten Years, 2005–2015* (Johan Skytte Institute of Political Studies, University of Tartu 2016) 127, 127–130.

531 Piret Ehin, Mihkel Solvak, Jan Willemson and Priit Vinkel, 'Internet Voting in Estonia 2005–2019: Evidence from Eleven Elections' (2022) 39(4) Government Information Quarterly.

532 Jacobs and Pieters, 'Electronic Voting in the Netherlands' 130.

533 'Black Box Voting vs End-to-End Verifiable Voting' (*Assembly Voting*, 19 April 2022) <https://assemblyvoting.com/blog/black-box-voting-vs-e-2-e-verifiable-voting/> accessed 24 January 2023.

534 See e. g. Atte Juvonen, 'A Framework for Comparing the Security of Voting Schemes' (Masters Thesis, University of Helsinki 2019) 79.

In addition to the various options described above, the security of online votes is often monitored using a method also applied to paper voting – scanning for irregularities, such as unusually high numbers of votes or voting at irregular times. SkyVote, for example, monitors voting continuously, so that they can intervene immediately if one of the typical actions that would indicate possible fraud is detected. The software also has the capacity to filter out VPN users and IP addresses from countries deemed a high risk as the origin point of hacker attacks.[535]

It is also possible to think of introducing even more stringent levels of identification security, such as three-factor authentication which includes '(1) something one knows (PIN), (2) something one has (smartcard), (3) something one is (biometric fingerprint)'[536] that one could apply to the process.

While blockchain and verification processes can be slow,[537] criticisms of digital voting systems are, upon investigation, often less severe than one would think. For example, one scholarly article criticizing blockchain voting did so on the basis that people might be unable to vote digitally because they could lose their passcode (no different than losing one's polling card, and one always has the option to vote offline, anyway) or that if the majority of users (voters) were to collude they could alter the system (not an issue in a democracy which is based on majority rule).[538]

As this indicates, security around internet voting in elections is still in a state of experimentation and continuing development without a clear consensus on how this is to best be achieved. Still there are many exciting and promising developments.

7.3 Overlooked Security Threats

Quite a lot of literature, and certainly lay debate, focuses on the second-tier security threats posed by external hackers or a system malfunction, and fail to pay sufficient attention to perhaps slightly less obvious, but far more serious, threats.

---

535 Interview with Vito Crimi, former Member of the Italian Senate and Deputy Minister of the Interior (3 March 2022).
536 Kimbi and Zlotnikova 'A Secure Model for Remote Electronic Voting' 104.
537 'Moscow Voters Debate: Did Blockchain-Based Online Voting Undermine the Opposition?' *Current Time* (24 September 2021) <https://en.currenttime.tv/a/moscow-voters-debate-did-blockchain-based-online-voting-undermine-russia-s-opposition-/31476383.html>.
538 Sunoo Park, Michael Specter, Neha Narula and Ronald L. Rivest, 'Going from Bad to Worse: From Internet Voting to Blockchain Voting' (2021) 7(1) Journal of Cybersecurity.

7.3.1 The Inside Job

Outside attacks from hackers would likely have the most *disruptive* impact on on-line voting, as hackers often like to publicly take credit for their work. This could affect confidence in the system, regardless of the veracity of such claims.

The biggest real threat, however, comes from the **system administrators** themselves who can access and possibly change data. One of the ways to deal with this is to have oversight over the system conducted by a randomly-selected and constantly changing group of people (much like election observers operate).

Another major threat is presented by the **intelligence services**, in particular, the nation's *own* secret service (internal military coups are, after all, quite common) or that of a larger and more powerful country, which may support one faction in a smaller country over another. The internet, after all was developed by the US military, and the real identity of the inventor of blockchain remains a mystery. There is thus a quite alarming lack of accountability and transparency at the centre of all things digital that rarely gets the attention it deserves. The US government (currently the world's most powerful) develops and monitors many encryption standards, and there is a notable level of cooperation between digital poster-child Estonia and current or former US military associates. For example, Estonia uses KSI blockchain developed by Guardtime, which is also used by NATO, the US Department of Defense, and Lockheed Martin (a military contractor). Guard-time's CEO was in the US military, and its CTO worked for the US Ministry of Defence.[539] NATO's Cooperative Cyber Defence Center of Excellence (not part of the military structure) is also based in Estonia.[540] While these loose associations aren't proof of anything, this is exactly the point. It is the unknown unknowns that are such pesky and seemingly irresolvable security concerns, precisely because one can never be quite sure of what is going on or definitely allay one's suspicions. However, as this demonstrates, it's not the people who get caught in the act who are the issue – it's the people who *don't* get caught who are the real threat. And it is the military and security services of this world who have those kinds of capabilities.

This raises a few considerations. The first is that security services are unlikely to interfere online in any way they couldn't achieve on paper (or, failing that, with

---

539 Roger Peverelli and Reggy de Feniks, 'Guardtime: The World's Largest Blockchain Company' (*Digital Insurance Agenda*, 24 April 2017) <digitalinsuranceagenda.com> accessed 17 February 2023; 'Factsheet: KSI Blockchain in Estonia' (*E-Estonia*) <https://e-estonia.com/wp-content/uploads/2019sept_faq-ksi-blockchain-1-1.pdf> accessed 24 January 2023.
540 'Factsheet: Cyber Security' (*E-Estonia*) <https://e-estonia.com/wp-content/uploads/cyber-security-factsheet-aug2022.pdf> accessed 26 February 2023

force), so their internet dominance doesn't, of itself, necessarily change the long-running dynamics at play in global politics.

The second is that, given the resources at the disposal of large militaries and secret services, it is not terribly likely that a civilian system would succeed in thwarting them on a technical level. This is ultimately why focusing too much on technical solutions, rather than social ones, is something of a waste. The most secretive, hierarchical and forceful parts of any system will always prove the strongest at this game. Rather than trying to make each aspect of the operation impenetrable, one should focus on making system capture fruitless (destroying opportunity and incentive) and ensuring that there is nothing permanent and stable for them to win control over. This is why democracy needs to be a fluid, ever-changing process without clear centres of power (e.g. elected officials who make all the decisions).

7.3.2 Vote Secrecy and the Security Arms Race

On a fundamental level, security concerns around online voting can be resolved in one of three ways:

1. the online infrastructure is deemed satisfactorily secure by the population, parties and election officials, whether or not this is actually true ('confidence')
2. democracy becomes a far less controlled process, and voting is complemented by other activities such as ideation, debate and the ability to easily re-vote, making it harder to maintain fraudulent results and substantially decreasing the incentive to commit electoral fraud (one eliminates the 'hot gate' leaving those who would hack the system with no incentive or opportunity to cheat)
3. the requirements on ballot secrecy are lowered (which makes the system completely technically secure, just not socially secure)

As we have seen, the first option is the one that we already accept most of the time. As long as no one complains, we don't look under the hood, and everything appears to be going smoothly, regardless of whether or not this is truly the case.

The second option involves implementing a more robust democracy, one that doesn't just come down to results on election day. This makes it impossible to control the process, because there are too many people involved too much of the time *to be controlled*. This is my preferred solution and it depends on mobilizing people in an impactful manner through the methods outlined in this book.

The third option, which we turn to here, is certainly the most controversial. However, there are some points that speak for it.

The first is that secret ballots were preceded by a time when voters were required to physically visit a polling place and publicly proclaim who they were voting for to all present. This certainly exposed them to immediate intimidation and bribery – no one wanted to be waylaid riding back to the farm and beaten by the opposing side's supporters. The physical danger posed by one's vote becoming public knowledge is, however, significantly lessened in an online environment.

The second point that speaks for lowering secrecy requirements is that, as we saw in Chapter 2 in relation to the Obama campaign, most politicians already know a great deal about their voters and likely outcomes. In other nations (e.g. Ireland), while some guesswork is involved, parties are remarkably accurate at identifying who voted for them. In addition, voting booths are less controlled, generally being a slightly-partitioned round table rather than the traditional curtained off booth familiar from television.

The third point is that in many countries that are internally stable, fewer and fewer people seem to care if anyone knows how they voted. In two Russian surveys that prompted respondents to name a negative consequence of internet voting only 9 and 14% respectively named the potential lack of anonymity.[541] Many people across the world intentionally share their political views online and even post photos of themselves with their filled-out ballots. At the same time, in those countries where civil unrest or recent armed conflict *has* made people more wary of revealing their voting intentions, this is often because they are being intimidated by paramilitaries. These threats only work because voters are frightened that parties will find out how they voted *anyway*, regardless of the ostensible secrecy that seems to be in place. In other words, in those nations where people are not worried about reprisals, they don't value their vote secrecy very much since it doesn't seem to serve much of a purpose to them (there's no threat, so they don't need protection), and in those nations where people *do* fear reprisals, they often don't trust that the secrecy rules are truly being followed or are enough to protect them. The really existing social conditions are again much more relevant than formal rules.

This is not to say that people are right to abandon their voting privacy or that the compulsion to share has become a permanent feature of society, but it does show that in many countries there is currently little demand for iron-clad, eternal vote secrecy from the public, and we should re-evaluate how we think of privacy and secrecy, particularly the level of guaranteed privacy that is necessary, rather than blindly continue to do things a certain way.

---

541 Valeria Babayan and A.V. Turobov, 'Not Unique, not Universal: Risk Perception and Acceptance of Online Voting Technology by Russian Citizens' (2021) 6 Monitoring of Public Opinion: Economic and Social Changes 319, 330.

This is particularly relevant because one of the concerns with online voting is that even if online voting can be done securely and secretly, it may be possible to figure out how someone voted at a later point due to advances in computing technology.

Most platforms, including online voting platforms, encrypt their data, which means that information is encoded in a difficult mathematical problem. Only those who have the key can 'unlock' the message quickly. Others must try to break the encryption, which takes a great deal of time and effort – too much to make it worthwhile. However, as computers become more powerful, they are more easily able to break *formerly* secure encryption. Twenty years from now, we will likely be able to break the codes of today. Thus, hackers could see how someone voted many years ago, provided, of course, that we fail to delete the voting record once the period for disputing the result has elapsed. The problem is thus easily resolved by simply taking this action, which, as we saw above, is done with paper-balloting in Britain for similar reasons after the window for disputes has expired.

That being said, other breakthroughs may pose additional risks.

Quantum computers (still a work in progress), for example, are more powerful than conventional computers and have been developed in order to perform functions that conventional computers cannot. A classic computer uses bits, which each have a value of 0 or 1, and essentially processes these bits in long chains, e.g.: 01000100 01000101 01001101 01001111 01000011 01010010 01000001 01000011 01011001. It's just a long electric circuit, whereby each bit has to be on (1) or off (0) for the computer to work.

Quantum computing, by contrast, can operate on the basis of uncertainty. It can keep calculating even if it is unknown whether or not each quantum bit (qubit) is on or off. This means it can work with multiple unknown variables. Completing these kinds of operations requires holding the qubit in a suspended state (called superposition) where it represents all of its possible configurations, and not letting it lapse into certainty (called decoherence).

This is no easy task – it requires the qubit to be kept at absolute zero and free of electrical interference. As this is very difficult to maintain, some people believe we may never have high-functioning quantum computers. But if we do, the retroactive effects on our privacy will be considerable, because quantum computers can quickly perform factoring (breaking numbers down into prime numbers) a common basis for encryption today. According to some sources, '[t]here are rumours that intelligence agencies across the world are already stockpiling vast amounts of encrypted data in the hope that they'll soon have access to a quantum computer that can crack it.'[542]

Robust encryption methods based on lattice and isogeny-based math are being developed partly in anticipation of quantum computing.[543] However, if quantum computers, due to their technical requirements, are never available to the general public, it would lead to a very asymmetrical situation in which perhaps only the military and large corporations own such superior devices. It is hard to say how this would affect the issue of encryption (in all its applications) over time.

7.3.3 Vote Coercion

In most developed countries it is difficult to directly coerce someone into voting a certain way, particularly with explicit, physical threats. Even tracking down and firing employees over their voting record would likely prove to be more effort than it is worth to any given employer.

Where protective laws exist and are reasonably enforced (such as labour laws), it is far more effective to simply *socially* pressure people to vote in a certain way. For example, in the run up to the 1988 Canadian federal election, many companies encouraged their workers to vote for the pro-NAFTA party with the argument that the company (and thus all of its employees) would otherwise suffer. Likewise, before the 2016 US Presidential election, many American companies encouraged, in some cases even portrayed it as self-understood, that their employees would vote for Hillary Clinton. In the run up to the 2020 US Presidential election, one CEO even went a step further and sent a mass email to *customers* telling them to vote for Joe Biden and accusing them of being selfish if they failed to do so.[544] Considering the kind of behaviour that is already rife, if remote voting were allowed, one can easily imagine a work or social party where everyone is encouraged to cast their vote together under the blithe assumption that all present are already politically aligned, and that to admit to voting for another party would

---

542 Amit Katwala, 'Quantum Computing and Quantum Supremacy Explained' *Wired* (5 March 2020) <https://www.wired.co.uk/article/quantum-computing-explained>.

543 Alessandro Curioni, 'How Quantum-Safe Cryptography will Ensure a Secure Computing Future' (*World Economic Forum*, 6 July 2022) <https://www.weforum.org/agenda/2022/07/how-quantum-safe-cryptography-will-ensure-a-secure-computing-future/>.

544 Chip Cutter, 'Expensify CEO Urges Customers to Vote Against Trump' *Wall Street Journal* (23 October 2020) <https://www.wsj.com/articles/expensify-ceo-urges-customers-to-vote-against-trump-11603489825>; David Barrett 'Protect Democracy: Vote for Biden' (October 2020) <https://community.expensify.com/discussion/7632/protect-democracy-vote-for-biden> accessed 24 January 2023.

cause one to become a social outcast. Under these circumstances one could imagine workers going along with the group in order to avoid social censure.

The technical solution to this problem is to give remote voters the option of recasting their ballots at any point before voting closes. In this way, even if a voter were to be pressured by e.g. their colleagues to cast their vote at a 'work voting party' they could cancel that vote and resubmit it with their preferred candidate as soon as they left the office. The same could be said if a candidate came to a voter's home (common in some countries that practice door-to-door canvassing) and pressured them into voting for their party on the spot. In Estonia, vote re-casting as a method of preventing coercion is aided by the fact that vote verification is only available for 30 minutes after a ballot is cast, making it difficult for voters to 'prove' their vote to someone else, either in exchange for money or as a proof of social loyalty. No one could be sure the voter wouldn't collect their reward and keep switching their vote (theoretically they could collect from every party this way), so the incentive to attempt coercion vastly diminishes.

Again, the only country where we have statistics on how this works in real life is Estonia. There, only about 1–2% of voters cancel and re-cast their ballot in any given election,[545] and many of these likely to do so because they are testing the system or are genuinely undecisive about who to vote for (30% of votes that are recast are submitted within 10 minutes of the original vote and 50% within 12 hours).[546] Thus, there is no reason to believe that there is any significant level of vote coercion in the classical sense.

However, it must be said here that there is a big difference between social pressure that forces one to do something one is seriously opposed to (e.g. voting for candidate A whom one absolutely detests) and social pressure to do something one has no strong feelings about (e.g. to vote for candidate A when one is not particularly committed to any candidate and may otherwise not have voted). In the latter scenario, people are far less likely to recast their votes, and this is probably where social pressure could be most effective in 'gently' coercing votes.

Of course, this same pressure has always existed offline – people have always discussed their political decisions with family and friends, and often even travel to the polling station together. If voters were being more easily 'gently coerced' in the digital era, we would expect to see voter turnout increase and/or the outcomes of elections to change dramatically, which we have so far, not yet seen. Still the pos-

---

545 Taavi Unt, Mihkel Solvak and Kristjan Vassil, 'Does Internet Voting make Elections less Social? Group Voting Patterns in Estonian e-voting Log Files (2013–2015)' (2017) 12(5) PLoS ONE.

546 Taavi Unt, Mihkel Solvak and Kristjan Vassil, 'E-vote Log Files 2013–2015' in Mihkel Solvak and Kristjan Vassil (eds), *E-voting in Estonia: Technological Diffusion and other Developments over Ten Years, 2005–2015* (Johan Skytte Institute of Political Studies, University of Tartu 2016) 71, 83.

sibility for 'gentle' social coercion and parties pressuring voters to vote for them 'right now' are concerns, and another reason to pursue more in-depth democracy that doesn't let everything hinge on one point in time and that severely reduces the capacity of others to mobilize their influence.

A final issue regarding coercion concerns vulnerable voters, particularly people with dementia. It is a known practice (sometimes known as 'granny harvesting') to solicit votes from nursing home residents and other vulnerable people. As we saw above, as many as 50 – 70 % of nursing home residents suffer from dementia, often severely.

People with dementia usually retain their voting rights, although when virtually all voting was done in voting booths, it was obviously more difficult for those with progressed dementia to vote. Thus, the issue somewhat regulated itself – if someone was still capable of forming a decision on voting than they were also likely to possess the capacity to make arrangements to cast their ballot at the polling station.

This has changed since the advent of remote voting – not just internet voting, but postal voting and drop-off voting as well. Nothing could be easier than casting ballots in bulk for nursing home residents with advanced dementia remotely (whether postal or digital), and the nature of their disease is unfortunately conducive to covering up the wrongdoing. At the same time, stripping people with dementia of their right to vote is also very serious and many people who suffer mild dementia are still capable of voting. This is a thorny issue considering the aging population in many countries, and any system of regulation could potentially be abused to try to exclude older voters (especially if they disproportionately vote for another party), in much the same manner as some parties try to reduce polling stations in areas where the residents vote disproportionately for other parties.

7.4 Security in Other Forms of Online Democracy

While absolute technical security combined with absolute privacy may not be any more possible to achieve than it has been on paper, it should be noted that many e-voting systems at least have robust mechanisms in place. Many other instances of online democracy use very low levels of security – some none at all. As we saw in Chapter 4, this can make participation more accessible and easy for people to use (no logging in).

However, due to low security in some participatory processes, it is hard to tell if results have been manipulated. It is quite possible that some people may log-in using different emails or IP addresses in order to cast multiple votes. If a high level of security cannot be guaranteed, it is hard to see why authorities should regard outcomes as binding. Thus, failing to implement reasonable security can become an excuse to ignore outcomes.

7.5 Privacy

A downside of moving both service provision and democracy online is that it can result in less privacy. For example, in Estonia, police can access residents' health and tax information. This is mitigated by the fact that they must have a reason for doing so, the entire transaction is digitally documented, and residents can see who has accessed their information.[547] The data cannot be copied (merely used) and data exchange is encrypted. In addition, this is subject to 24/7 monitoring by the Information System Authority.[548] However, once data is collected, some leaks are likely inevitable. In 2020, public Irish health data was leaked, for example. The only way to prevent leaks with absolute certainty is not to collect data – but data is simply too useful for that.

The vast data collected today can also have ramifications for democracy if votes are not deleted within a certain time period. Approaches to this question of privacy have changed over time. Previously Rousseau, used by M5S, kept a record of votes, but SkyVote, currently used by the movement, resets once the votes have been counted.[549] M5S also switched to a split system, where voter data is stored and managed in a separate system (Odoo – an open-source Belgian software) and only imported into SkyVote when a vote is about to occur.[550] Unlike

---

547 'Factsheet: X-Road' (*Riigi Infosüsteemi Amet*) <https://e-estonia.com/wp-content/uploads/2020mar-facts-a4-v02-x-road.pdf> accessed 24 January 2023; 'Data Tracker' (*Riigi Infosüsteemi Amet*) <https://www.ria.ee/riigi-infosusteem/inimkeskne-andmehaldus/andmejalgija> accessed 26 February 2023.

548 'Factsheet: Cyber Security' (*E-Estonia*).

549 'Mr. SkyVote: "Our Voting Model is the Opposite of Rousseau"' *Breaking Latest News* (17 June 2021) <https://www.breakinglatest.news/health/mr-skyvote-our-voting-model-is-the-opposite-of-rousseau/>.

550 'M5S, dopo Rousseau il Movimento sceglie due piattaforme: SkyVote Cloud per il voto online e Odoo per i dati degli iscritti' *La Repubblica* (15 June 2021) <https://www.repubblica.it/politica/2021/06/15/news/m5s_dopo_rousseau_plattaforma_skyvote_assemblea_gruppi_parlamentari-306204842/>; Sebastiano Messina, 'M5S e l'addio di Casaleggio, la penosa fine di un imbroglio spacciato per democrazia' *La Repubblica* (6 June 2021) <https://www.repubblica.it/politica/2021/06/06/news/m5s_rousseau_davide_casaleggio-304409994/>; Riccardo Ferrazza, 'SkyVote, l'alternativa a Rousseau che nel 2020 ha moltiplicato gli utili' *Il Sole 24 Ore* (2 July 2021) <https://www.ilsole24ore.com/art/skyvote-l-alternativa-rosseau-che-2020-ha-moltiplicato-utili-AEqgdRU?refresh_ce=1>.

Rousseau, which started in close conjunction with the M5S movement, SkyVote is a private business without any connection to the party, creating a level of distance between the political movement and voting apparatus.[551] Which approach works best remains to be seen.

However, it does open up a further-going line of thought regarding data retention. As we pointed out in Chapter 2, the more information someone has about a person or a group of people, the easier it becomes for them to manipulate them, particularly if one has the resources to facilitate this. This can lead to rather duplicitous uses of 'online democracy'. For example, a government may not run a Covid consultation in order to better respond to the public's wishes; they may run it with the intention of figuring out which messaging will make the public more acquiescent to a pre-decided policy. Unfortunately, this is exactly how a lot of engagement software *is marketed* – as a way to get people to *accept* decisions, rather than truly take part in making them. Indeed, this is often what 'building trust' is taken to mean. As we saw above, the Obama campaign tracked so much information about voters, *precisely* so that they could try to target people with the right message to acquire their vote. Similarly, many people believe that surveilling people and monitoring their behaviour is superior to direct participation. If a researcher asks a voter how many times they went to the park, they may give the researcher an incorrect answer, but if the researcher geotags them, they can learn the truth by monitoring the voter.

This all fails to acknowledge that politics is about forming a will and making free choices, not trying to figure out what voters subconsciously want in a sort of enlightened despotism. The latter fails utterly to build accountability and is an attempt to conduct politics without politics. This again, is why it is so important to ensure that digital democracy unfolds in an emancipatory fashion in order to prevent the reams of data made available by technology from being used in these manipulative, asymmetrical ways.

7.6 Conclusions on Security

Despite the well-founded theoretical concerns, thus far, there have been few actual cases of serious technical security breaches around digital participation. This is despite the fact that many nations have implemented pilots, local online voting (e.g. Canada) or online voting for ex-pats.

---

551 'M5S, dopo Rousseau il Movimento sceglie due piattaforme' *La Repubblica.*

Pakistan used a vote tabulation system which officials allege crashed during the 2018 election, but this is disputed by its creators.[552] In Ontario, Canada due to a miscommunication between provider Dominion and a subcontractor, bandwidth was throttled in 43 municipalities during local elections in 2018.[553] Because the voting page could not be loaded and some municipalities had no paper back-up system, the voting period had to be extended, in some cases by 24 hours.[554] As it turned out, no one was particularly put out by this. After all, one could easily be prevented from voting in person due to inclement weather in Canada, in which case one *doesn't* get another opportunity to cast one's vote. Municipal officials in Ontario, even those directly affected by the issue, reported themselves unfazed by it. When researchers questioned them, many pointed out that there were issues with all methods of voting and that they had also experienced difficulty with mail-in ballots in the past.[555]

A recent study of voting machines in India was also unable to unearth evidence of fraud occurring in real life, regardless of whether the machines used paper trails or not. This study is interesting because it was able to detect a marginal and unexpected change in voter behaviour – that the number of spoiled ballots drastically declined (by over 90 %) and the votes in favour of fringe candidates increased (likely because voters were unable to spoil their ballots, they voted for fringe candidates instead, as a form of protest).[556] Since the study was able to detect minor variations in voting behaviour, it likely would have found evidence of voter fraud had it been there.

Nothing will ever make elections run on any system that is completely secure. It's possible to rig elections, the incentive to do so is very high and the risks are fairly low. These are the important factors. Many people erroneously believe that simply making laws prevents people from engaging in behaviour such as corruption. This is untrue. Even in nations where corruption is punishable by execution, there is

---

552 Amir Wasim, 'RTS Controversy Likely to haunt ECP, Nadra for a Long Time' *Dawn* (2 August 2018) <https://www.dawn.com/news/1424394>.
553 Aleksander Essex, Anthony Cardillo and Nicholas Akinyokun, *Online Voting in Ontario's Municipal Elections: A Conflict of Legal Principles and Technology?* (Whisper Lab Research Report, Western University 2020) <https://whisperlab.org/ontario-online.pdf>.
554 Helen A. Hayes, Nicole Goodman, R. Michael McGregor, Zachary Spicer and Scott Pruysers, 'The Effect of Exogenous Shocks on the Administration of Online Voting: Evidence from Ontario, Canada' (International Joint Conference on Electronic Voting 2022) *Lecture Notes in Computer Science, Vol. 13553* (Springer 2022) 70, 73.
555 Hayes et al., 'Exogenous Shocks' 82.
556 Zuheir Desai and Alexander Lee, 'Technology and Protest: The Political Effects of Electronic Voting in India' (2021) 9(2) Political Science Research and Methods 398–413.

still corruption, because the incentives to be corrupt are there. It is impossible to regulate against a very strong incentive, so to make democracy secure, we have to reduce the scope for vote-locking, that is locking in a vote following an election or referendum for a sustained period of time.

That being said, security remains a highly contested space around online participation and both technical and social security measures are underutilized.

Chapter 8
The Feedback Loop

The most neglected part of nearly all digital democracy processes is the connection between input and output, that is between participants expressing a preference and then something resulting from that expression. This is the so-called 'feedback loop'. This is critical, because as we have seen above, most people do not participate for the sake of 'being involved'. They only make time for something that has *a point*.

The 'feedback loop' doesn't just refer to informing people about the collected data or decisions made (although that is part of it); it is about creating a self-reinforcing system. If you have ever used a microphone that was too close to the amplifier, you have heard feedback – a loop that constantly amplifies the sound from the microphone and projects it out the speaker, where it is picked up by the microphone again and fed back into the amplifier. While this is irritating when it comes to sound systems, this kind of self-amplifying loop is what democracy needs: decisions that lead to actions that lead to more decisions and so on.

The lynchpin of this entire process is implementation. Just as every decision of parliament must be executed, so too, every decision made online, whether it be a referendum or participatory budgeting, must also be executed in the real world. Digital democracy can itself serve as a way to pressure for implementation, because it often creates a transparent view of what people want. In situations where there is a high level of participation and a clear majority in favour of a decision, it is hard to see why it should not be implemented.

However, too often, civil servants and politicians are pressured to comply with buzzwords like 'engagement' without having thought through what that means or why citizens would want to 'engage'. This leads to two kinds of implementation difficulties – the first is with the process itself, which often fails to define why exactly citizens are participating. The second is in failing to produce concrete outcomes. In a successful project, citizens should be able to point to something in their lives and say (whether they agree with it or not), 'that happened because of a consultation, participatory budget, vote, etc.' When this fails to happen, citizens can quickly lose interest in the process and refuse to take part again. One can only be associated with a 'window-dressing' level of democracy that does not deliver results for so long before it tarnishes one's reputation completely, and this is a real risk for advocates of digital democracy today. In order to avoid this, digital democracy must serve a substantive purpose and not be a veneer on pre-decided outcomes. This is particularly important when deciding on the scope of a project.

https://doi.org/10.1515/9783110794465-012

8.1 Don't Use Digital Democracy to Do What You Were Going To Do Anyway

Possibly one of the most harmful things that organizers do is to view digital democracy as a 'crowdsourcing' exercise that lets them pick and choose projects that align with pre-existing plans. Not only do authorities tend to use it this way, academics and activists sometimes encourage officials to use online consultation to solicit ideas in order to pick through them and select the ones they like. Participants also expect this to happen (for example, in the Finnish experiment on Road Traffic, participants expressed the idea that the civil servants would take onboard those comments that aligned with what they wanted to do anyway and ignore others).[557] Participants in the Lethbridge CIP and Okotoks 2080 expressed the same sentiment, stating that what they were doing was likely pointless, 'since the council will do what it wants to do anyway' with several comments complaining that officials rarely took them seriously at face to face meetings, either.[558] While expressing the wish to continue the consultation process in the future, participants also wanted to be told how the consultation impacted on the final decisions, or as they put it: 'some assurance that our opinion counts and it's not just a paper exercise to appease the masses'.

Using digital democracy to provide a cover for pre-existing plans makes taking part pointless, and as we discussed in Chapter 3, likely has an even more discouraging impact on the most vulnerable citizens who have the least time to waste. Because digital democracy often necessitates some expenditure of resources, using it this way is a waste of everyone's time and money, and it obscures accountability for the ultimate decision. *If* you have already decided upon what you are going to do – just do it and take responsibility for it. Do not use democracy or 'engagement' as a cover.

---

557 Tanja Aitamurto, Hélène Landemore and Jorge Saldivar Galli, 'Unmasking the Crowd: Participants' Motivation Factors, Expectations, and Profile in a Crowdsourced Law Reform' (2017) 20(8) Information, Communication and Society 1239–1260.
558 Comment on Okotoks Ethelo <https://okotoks-2080.ethelo.net/page/collective-results> accessed 20 September 2022.

8.2 Also Don't Use Digital Democracy For What You *Should* Have Done Anyway

In Iceland, basic infrastructure projects like street lighting were eventually removed from participatory budgeting, as they were viewed as a basic service that citizens weren't particularly interested in negotiating over. In the United States, participants have at times complained that PB is used to fund basic necessities, like school bathrooms or street lighting, which should be provided in any event.[559] The residents of Lethbridge were also confounded at the parts of the Lethbridge CIP consultation that dealt with basic electricity and water infrastructure.

Don't use digital democracy (or any 'democracy') to ask people if they would like to continue to receive basic services that no one has ever put into question. At best this is confusing and, at worst, can be used as a cover for manipulation as people are pressured to choose between things that are all absolutely vital. Only put these life necessities into question if you are also willing to open up the other side of the equation and e. g. allow citizens to raise taxes, etc., as this broader decision-making power is necessary to truly deal with basic infrastructure provision.

8.3 There Really Does have to be Something at Stake

Between these two poles (of putting nothing important on the table and confronting citizens with choices so basic as to not truly be choices) there lies a middle ground where something *is* genuinely at stake, but citizens are not being manipulated into giving up things understood to be integral to the social contract.

Organizers often make one of several common mistakes in trying to negotiate this space.

One is simply to drastically limit the scale of projects to a point where no one really finds them interesting. One of the key reasons behind the decline and eventual suspension of PB in some Brazilian cities is that its financial importance dramatically decreased. This was (among other reasons) partly due to the federal government limiting municipal discretion over funds, and partly because the World Cup was hosted in Brazil around this time, leading to a large sum of money

---

559 Carolina Johnson, 'Engaging Democracy: An Institutional Theory of Participatory Budgeting' (DPhil Thesis, University of Washington 2017) 91.

being spent on capital investment projects that were managed top-down, side-lining PB in importance for many years.[560]

Another is to simply act differently than the results of the exercise would suggest one should do. Representatives routinely undermine participatory budgets when they allocate their additional funds to complete projects that surfaced via PB but did not gain the votes of the participants.[561] In other cases, no discernible difference is made by citizen participation. The Lethbridge CIP, for example, an extremely lengthy and detailed consultation, with a high level of interested and thoughtful engagement, is a case in point. Based on all available public information, no relation between the outcomes of the consultation (how people voted) and the ultimate actions of the city council could be determined.[562] An extremely charitable reading of documents could suggest that funding for some projects may have been *slightly* delayed in favour of others, but this impact (if it even exists) is minimal, and funding was approved for many of the consultation's least popular options, such as the Henderson Ice Centre Upgrade (41% approval), the SAAG Facility Enhancement (31% approval), the Galt No. 6 Mine Interpretive Park (40% approval) and the Nikka Yuko Japanese Garden Pathway (36% approval).[563] No clear relationship between the online consultation and these ultimate outcomes is discernible, much less obvious, as it should be.

It is common, and not entirely farfetched, for organizers to defend such decisions with the argument that not enough people take part in consultations to be representative of the population as a whole. After all, there are 100,000 people in Lethbridge and only a few thousand took part in the online consultation. Other forms of participation like PB in Chicago, Paris and New York might add to this that because they allow minors and residents not normally entitled to vote in elections to participate, the results cannot be legally binding. This is precisely why such practices, while they seek to 'celebrate democracy' actually devalue the entire concept of democratic citizenship. If the voting outcome isn't ultimately respected than each individual voter also hasn't been respected – it's

---

560 Rebecca Abers, Igor Brandão, Robin King and Daniely Votto, 'Porto Alegre: Participatory Budgeting and the Challenge of Sustaining Transformative Change' (2018) World Resources Report Case Study, World Resources Institute 13–14.
561 Colin O'Connor, *Gotham Gazette* <https://www.gothamgazette.com/govermnent/5946-participatory-budget>.
562 'City of Lethbridge 2022–2031 Capital Improvement Programme' (*City of Lethbridge*) Section D <https://www.lethbridge.ca/City-Government/Financial-Documents/Documents/CIP/2022-2031CIPFinal.pdf> accessed 24 January 2023.
563 'City Council approves 2022–2031 CIP Recommendations' (*City of Lethbridge*, 1 June 2021); 'City of Lethbridge 2022–2031 Capital Improvement Programme' 4 and 80 et seq.

easy to encourage all people, whether citizens or not, to vote when you have no intention of taking their vote seriously.

This is a vicious cycle, because as long as nothing is truly at stake, few people participate, and as long as few people participate, organizers can claim they are not representative of the population as a whole and ignore them. There is then great head-scratching as to why people are so hostile (usually the ambitious, higher-income people) and apathetic (usually more vulnerable people) to 'opportunities' to 'engage'.

This also negatively affects the attitudes of people who do participate. Every time a project is not implemented (without a truly good reason), it reduces the accountability of participants. When people know that an authority will come along and change things to what they want them to be anyway, they may as well enjoy the rush of acting like a rebellious teenager and calling a boat 'Boaty McBoatface' as British voters did when asked to name a research vessel via online poll in 2016.[564] There is no such thing as a functioning democracy without accountability, because there is no way for people to discover their own boundaries without accountability.

The only way out of this quandary is to at some point start making binding decisions, even if they are somewhat less than ideal from a representation point of view. This sends the message that participating has an impact and that if one wants to get one's way, one had better take part. This is exactly the message we give to voters at every election. We do not swoop in and change the results of elections in order to help out people who did not vote, or adjust the outcome to be what we believe it 'would have been' if every single person had voted. We must create *opportunity* for people to participate, but also *accountability* for their choices, including the choice not to take part. Everyone must learn to use their own reason and to take responsibility for doing so, rather than remaining dependent. This, according to Kant, was the meaning of the Enlightenment.[565]

That being said, finding something worthwhile to vote on can be a serious challenge for local authorities, as they are restricted by many programmes and laws set at a higher level of government. This is why local democracy alone is not the ideal vehicle for digital democracy. It simply comes with too many constraints from higher levels of government that frustrate everyone. Activists who extol the virtues of local democracy above all else therefore pursue the wrong strategy.

564 Hannah Ellis-Petersen, 'Boaty McBoatface wins poll to name polar research vessel' *Guardian* (17 April 2016).
565 Immanuel Kant, 'Was ist Aufklärung?' *Berlinische Monatsschrift* (December 1784).

However, there are still things one can do to ameliorate this situation. One way to make things more meaningful is to focus on a few major projects. These are higher-impact and often have the potential to generate more cost-savings over time than many short-term cosmetic projects would. These longer-term, more impactful projects are also often preferred by voters but not necessarily by politicians. For example, building a health clinic, which is expensive and time-consuming, is likely a far better use of resources than a campaign telling people to eat more healthily. Establishing cooperation between higher and municipal levels of government helps to ensure that the reasonably large projects that are desired by the public can be completed and people don't feel like they are simply fiddling around the edges.

Some researchers believe this was a factor in the decline of participatory budgeting in Brazil where voters often selected projects that took substantial time and effort to complete. Elected politicians were reluctant to commit themselves to these projects as the completion date could stretch beyond their term. Thus, they risked going to a lot of effort to initiate a project that their political successor could then take credit for.[566] This complex is itself an illustration of *avoiding* problems (another politician taking credit for one's work) rather than addressing them (mounting one's own campaign to point out what one did and having some faith in constituents' ability to see this). It is a risk to truly implement democracy, but if one is not prepared to take that risk, the entire exercise becomes futile. When problems are avoided rather than addressed, they tend to snowball.

8.4 Finish What You Start

Even in those cases where organizers do commit to implementing policies or projects that people have voted for, completion rates often vary.

In Icelandic PB, results are regarded as binding by authorities and, over the course of the years, have only in very rare cases been unable to be implemented.[567] According to Róbert Bjarnason, the head of Citizens Foundation, if an idea that was voted on was not implemented, the person who submitted it would simply let the

---

566 Carla Bezerra and Murilo de Oliveira Junquiera, 'Why has Participatory Budgeting Adoption Declined in Brazil?' (114th Annual Meeting and Exhibition of the American Political Science Association, Boston, 30 August – 2 September, 2018).
567 Eiríkur Búi Halldórsson, Project Manager – My Neighborhood, City of Reykjavik Human Rights and Democracy Office, Personal communication to author (8 November 2022).

public know that it had not been completed. This would create pressure that authorities would be bound to deal with.[568]

Completion rates of PB projects in Porto Alegre started off high before declining. Between 1994 and 2004, 82 % of the 5,556 projects decided upon using PB were completed during this same time (ca. 414 a year), whereas between 2005 and 2016 only 42 % of the 3,712 projects decided upon were completed during this time (ca. 129 a year).[569] According to sources familiar with the government, the failure to complete projects was not due to a lack of resources: projects were being completed – just not those projects that had been decided via PB.[570]

By 2013, Recife (another Brazilian city which had started PB in 1993) had a backlog of 1,045 projects that had been approved by PB, but had not even begun to be implemented. Thus, when a new party came to power in 2013, it picked 320 of these projects to complete and turned PB into a non-binding consultation.[571]

A third Brazilian city, Belo Horizonte decreased the resources decided upon via PB and introduced more stringent criteria for a proposal to be eligible, leading to fewer proposals being passed. Nonetheless, by 2018, 441 projects passed via PB had never been completed. Some of these projects stemmed from decisions made as long ago as 2001. Completing all the outstanding projects 'would account for 9 % of the total budget ($2.9 billion USD)'.[572] Thirty-three of these 441 overdue projects were, by 2018, being executed, but the rest were still in the public bidding process, project drafting stage or 'pending judicial and expropriation cases'.[573]

Failing to have impact *does* have an impact – just not a good one. The failure to implement previous decisions made via online PB in Belo Horizonte was:

> a major cause of public disenchantment with the process. The most popularly supported project (voted for by 48,000 citizens) in the 2008 ePB had still not been enacted in 2011 when the third ePB took place and remained unimplemented at the time of the 2013 ePB. Faced with

---

568 Personal communication from Róbert Bjarnason, President Citizens Foundation, to author (8 November 2022).

569 Abers et al., 'Porto Alegre' 4.

570 Tarson Nuñez, 'From a Role Model to a Crisis' in Nelson Dias (ed) *Hope for Democracy: 30 Years of Participatory Budgeting Worldwide* (Epopeia Records, Oficina 2018) 517, 522.

571 Bezerra and Oliveira Junquiera, 'Why has Participatory Budgeting Adoption Declined In Brazil?' 10.

572 Bezerra and Oliveira Junquiera, 'Why has Participatory Budgeting Adoption Declined in Brazil?' 12.

573 Bezerra and Oliveira Junquiera, 'Why has Participatory Budgeting Adoption Declined in Brazil?' 12.

this record of decisions voted for and then not implemented, it was hardly surprising that citizens felt less motivated to vote.[574]

Delays and cancellations of PB-decided projects have also been reported in Chicago (partly due to understaffing in the city),[575] as well as in New York, where it has led to some previous participants becoming discouraged with the process.[576] One researcher who investigated PB in North America and the UK, also noted that implementation was where 'the quality and quantity of public engagement drops'.[577]

Paris PB attempts to implement projects within two years of them winning a vote, although this goal is not always met and implementation has at times been spotty. Sometimes, a project also has to be modified or abandoned for technical reasons.[578]

In Lisbon, 162 projects have been approved by PB since 2008 with 98 of them having been implemented so far (ca. 60 %). PB in Lisbon is also regarded as binding, with it usually taking 2–3 years to implement a project. Some, however, have taken up to 8 years to implement and on occasion projects have proven impossible to implement due to technical difficulties which were not caught at the technical review stage.[579]

While public administrators who used Decidim (for a wider range of activity) agreed that it increased transparency and helped with organization and ideation, they were rather more blasé on whether it increased citizens' ability to make decisions.[580] Although Decidim includes a module that can theoretically track execution quite tightly,[581] the proposals and actions are generally vague, including many

---

574 Stephen Coleman and Rafael Cardoso Sampaio, 'Sustaining a Democratic Innovation: A Study of Three E-Participatory Budgets in Belo Horizonte' (2016) Information, Communication and Society 10–11.

575 Anna Clark, 'Is Participatory Budgeting Real Democracy?: Politics People's Choice Style in Chicago' *Next City* (28 April 2014) <https://nextcity.org/features/is-participatory-budgeting-real-democracy-chicago>.

576 Aryeh Gelfand, 'Participatory Budget Community Meeting' *The Wave* (25 November 2016) <rockawave.com/articles/participatory-budget-community-meeting/>.

577 Johnson, 'Engaging Democracy' 65 et seq.

578 Estela Brahimllari, *Multi-Layered Participatory Budgeting: The Case of Low-Income Neighbourhoods in Paris* (FrancoAngeli 2020) 81.

579 Interviews with officials.

580 Rosa Borge, Joan Balcells and Albert Padró-Solanet, 'Democratic Disruption or Continuity? Analysis of the Decidim Platform in Catalan Municipalities' (2022) American Behavioural Scientist 8.

581 'Pla d'Actuació Municipal 2016–2019: Seguiment Actuacions' (*Decidim Barcelona*) <https://www.decidim.barcelona/processes/pam/f/8/> accessed 25 January 2023.

'campaigns', 'promotions, 'thinkings' and 'evaluations', so that, despite often high levels of implementation, the level of effective action isn't immediately apparent to the casual observer. Some researchers have reported that, despite its wide functionality, Decidim has mainly been used for a 'managerial model of e-governance'.[582]

Follow-through on commitments is one of the most difficult and under-rated aspects of public administration, business and indeed, of life in general. One should, of course, not blindly finish things that have lost their relevancy through an intervening event. However, it is worth remembering that turning an idea into reality is far more difficult than just coming up with the idea in the first place, and this part of the process is often under-recognized, while other aspects, like ideation and crowdsourcing are over-celebrated with predictable results – a great many ideas are generated and too few are ever actually implemented.

The most concerning aspect of all of this is that the above figures are from some of the world's most successful projects and all are still rather good rates of implementation compared to the many other instances where the outcomes of digital democracy, be that ideation, consultation or something else, simply aren't actioned at all. There are various obstacles here: vague proposals from citizens (why structuring this is so important), resistance from other departments, or even just lack of staff resources.[583]

It is important to allocate the time and resources to implementing decisions, rather than just continuing to gather more information. It is also a good idea to try to estimate the organizing entity's capacity for completion. One quick way to increase that capacity is to stop completing projects people voted against. By refraining from doing those things people *don't* like, one gains the time and resources to do what they *do* like.

8.5 Smart Contracts as a Method of Implementation

Smart contracts are a method for instantly executing or fulfilling a contract when the conditions of that contract have been met (rather than this depending on the parties concerned undertaking a further 'implementation act'). Smart contracts mainly have applications for finance. For example, if one agrees to sell a commodity when the price hits a certain level, ownership could be automatically transferred once this condition is fulfilled. As this indicates, smart contracts work

---

582 Borge, Balcells and Padró-Solanet, 'Democratic Disruption or Continuity?' 9.
583 Interviews (2022).

best when all components of the contract are online, and often the object or money to be transferred is placed into escrow pending execution.

Another possible use of smart contracts is in determining when an obligation has been fulfilled. For example, a freelance worker may submit work to a contractor who disagrees that the work meets the contractual requirements. In this case, the decision could be submitted to a jury of freelancers and contractors who would decide if the work meets the contractually agreed criteria by online vote. The money in question would then automatically be transferred to the winning party.

One could contemplate using such methods to automatically allocate budget to projects decided on via digital democracy, or to decide if projects have been correctly implemented and can be struck from the list of outstanding obligations. This would prevent organizers from making one-sided (possibly biased) decisions about when these obligations are fulfilled.

8.6 Gather Data on Implementation and Publicize that Data

As we saw in Chapter 4, gathering and structuring information is an important part of any process – when this fails, the whole process deteriorates and this passes all the way down the line into implementation.

In Porto Alegre, PB was initially accompanied by renewed budgetary transparency which made all spending (and project completion) easier to track.[584] Data collection has, however, since fallen off and there is no public method for tracking projects. An internet site which was to allow this was either never completed,[585] or was completed but fell into disuse early on.[586] In addition, the process via which citizens were provided with budgetary information deteriorated. Prior to 2004, public officials engaged in information sessions using actual budgetary documents, but after 2004, this changed to being a short PowerPoint presentation that did not provide participants with access to the underlying numbers. In 1995, when participants were asked if the information and renderings of accounts by municipal officials were satisfactory, 80.7% of respondents responded affirmatively. By 2000, only 63.8% did so and by 2009 this had decreased further to 40.1%.[587]

In American PB, the proposals put to vote are sometimes quite different than those suggested during the ideation phase, likely due to the budget delegate proc-

---

584 Abers, et al., 'Porto Alegre' 11.
585 Abers et al., 'Porto Alegre' 12.
586 Nuñez, 'From a Role Model to a Crisis' 525.
587 Nuñez, 'From a Role Model to a Crisis' 525.

ess,[588] which at times has been so closed off as to not even allow researchers to attend as observers.[589] This makes it difficult for anyone to track projects through ideation and voting to implementation, and to know if the projects being voted on and implemented are really what citizens want.

Collecting information throughout the process is an additional cost in terms of time and investment, but making savings here is a false economy. Without this information the entire project becomes a waste, sometimes creating more problems than it answers.

Fortunately, it is often possible to just keep using the digital tool of your choice to collect this data, even over longer periods. The city of Lisbon simply posts the status of each PB project on its website, along with before-and-after photos, where appropriate. For example, a decision to upgrade crosswalks included numerous labelled photos of the crosswalks in question before and after the works had been completed.[590] The Scottish Parliament has also used Your Priorities (software from Citizens Foundation) to collect information from people about how legislation is impacting them and to try to determine whether it is achieving its goal (e. g. on how an increase to free childcare hours is working out for people). Digital tools also help to pre-sort this feedback, e. g. according to geographic area, cutting down on the time-consuming nature of such work.[591]

Although tracking the project life-cycle generates more work, the effort is worth it. One of the most common requests in both Okotoks 2080 and Lethbridge CIP was for more information, including information on whether proposals were ultimately approved and implemented. One person stated in the feedback section of the Lethbridge CIP that they would like to see if projects came in over- or under-budget in the end. Another who used the petition site Manabalss in Latvia told us that one of the best things about it was that the organization kept those who had signed the petition informed of the progress of the issue they were petitioning for. For example, they received an email notification if a public hearing on the issue had been scheduled. This enabled the signatories to participate in events they may otherwise have missed, and allowed them to track the progress of the petition

---

588 Clark, 'Is Participatory Budgeting Real Democracy?'

589 Daniel Williams and Don Waisanen, *Real Money, Real Power? The Challenges with Participatory Budgeting in New York City* (Palgrave MacMillan 2020) 13.

590 'Projectos Vencedores: Mobilidade para Todos em Benfica' (*Lisboa Participa, Câmara Municipal de Lisboa*) <https://op.lisboaparticipa.pt/projetos-vencedores/6048eb500b405d5c803c6ff5/570fa466f41ec1c4356c3dc0> accessed 25 January 2023.

591 Interview with Alistair Stoddart, Senior Participation Specialist, Participation and Communities Team, The Scottish Parliament (11 March 2022).

and be involved in it, beyond just seeing if the necessary number of votes had been collected.[592]

However one chooses to communicate outcomes, the data around them needs to be collected in the first place and it is important to incorporate this as an intrinsic part of the process. It is, after all, impossible to report information one does not have.

8.7 Feedback Isn't After the Process, It's Part of the Process

Public officials who report a high degree of success and satisfaction with digital democracy often incorporate feedback into their process. For example, Citizen Space (by Delib) provides consultations which have an explicit three-part feedback section, 'We Asked – You Said – We Did'. Essex County Council in England uses this to give the public concrete examples of how consultation feedback has been incorporated into public policy. This provides specific information about the number of respondents who agreed with certain points in the proposed policy, as well as the specific alterations that would be made, e.g. 'The public have reiterated how important hard copy book stock is for them – an ambition we have always supported. We will make it clearer in the Plan that our ambition to keep our stock up to date and appealing includes hard copy as much as electronic resources.'[593] Others, such as Dun Laoghaire-Rathdown County Council in Dublin, do not utilize this function, simply stating 'we received X number of consultations' and 'DLR has reviewed all of the comments and feedback'.[594] Such failures to make use of the opportunity to reconnect with citizens following a consultation not only prevents healthy communication and information, but can contribute to suspicion and apathy.

Some officials strove for even better, faster communication with their constituents. For example, in PB in Iceland, public officials must notify members of the public if their proposal cannot be included for voting because it is infeasible. Citizens Foundation already automatically generates an email to complete this task, whereby the administrator only has to fill in a few details and send it. However, it would be even easier to have a conversation with the person concerned within

---

592 Interview with Inete Ielīte, Chair of the Board, Women's NGOs Cooperation Network (11 March 2022).

593 'Everyone's Library Service 2022–2026 Survey' (*Essex County Council*) <https://consultations.essex.gov.uk/rci/libraries-survey/> accessed 25 January 2023.

594 See e.g. 'Traffic and Road Safety: Taney Road to N11 Active Travel Route' (*DLR County Council*) <https://dlrcoco.citizenspace.com/transportation/taney-road-to-n11-active-travel-route/> accessed 25 January 2023.

the PB portal (with the portal generating a record of the conversation). Communication with the public would be thus even quicker than the back and forth of emails which could take several days and require more effort on the part of both parties.[595] Officials in Iceland confirm that their interaction with the public does alter the kind of projects that are implemented, pointing to examples like the installation of 'jumping pillows' (ground-level inflatable trampolines) as something the city would unlikely have come up with without the initiative from the public.[596]

Researchers of Paris PB have recommended creating a monitoring page for project completion, as well as sending a newsletter out once a year informing people of project completion with photos.[597] This type of communication helps to create a cycle of participation in which citizens and residents are constantly reminded that there is a good reason to take part, as well as providing a trigger for renewed conversation and debate.

8.8 Conclusions on the Feedback Loop

One of the biggest benefits of digital democracy is that it makes everything, including implementation, much easier to trace. Previously, this traceability was almost impossible.

For example, Brazil held national public policy conferences between 2003 and 2011 that involved about 7 million people (5% of all Brazilian adults). The largest was likely the National Conference on Health in 2011, which involved about 600,000 people. Participation mainly occurred at municipal meetings (i. e. at thousands of meetings with hundreds of participants each). Despite the impressive numbers of people involved, researchers found it challenging to trace the impact of these conferences on policy outcomes and had to use the indirect method of trying to see if laws and policies passed at a later point matched the content of recommendations made at the conferences. While they found that in some cases legislation was 'congruent' with conference recommendations, this was generally in a minority of cases (sometimes a small minority),[598] and whether this was directly

---

595 Interview Eiríkur Búi Halldórsson.

596 Interview Eiríkur Búi Halldórsson.

597 William Arhip-Paterson, Ari Brodach and Titouan Tence, 'Budget Participatif de Paris: Etude de la répétition du vote numérique à deux éditions consécutives' Rapport pour la Ville de Paris (May 2018) 6.

598 Thamy Pogrebinschi and David Samuels, 'The Impact of Participatory Democracy Evidence from Brazil's National Public Policy Conferences' (2014) Comparative Politics 313–332.

attributable to the conference was unclear (sometimes the issue had received a lot of press coverage or was the subject of a high-profile court case, which may also have motivated legislators).

Digital democracy gives organizers the opportunity to show people that their decisions are, in fact, impacting and leading policy in a far more causal relationship. Of course, this means that failures also become obvious, and some forms of public participation have been stopped precisely because it was making these failures too noticeable.[599] This continues the cycle of problem avoidance that we have referred to many times and which is the root issue of so much of the 'crisis of democracy' we experience today. Even where public officials don't intend to obscure policy failures, most 'public engagement' still occurs in an atmosphere where there is no clear idea of why the public is even being engaged and no plan with what to do with the information that is collected. All too often, organizers get excited about what they *could* do with the information collected, without being realistic about what they *will* do.

Failure to generate a feedback loop is not the only reason participation sometimes winds down, but it is certainly an important one. To give one cautionary tale: the White House petition platform, launched under President Obama, was initially celebrated. Obama, after all, was young, in-touch with the digital age and committed to transparency. However, while the White House did diligently respond to the petitions, these responses tended to simply reiterate pre-existing policy, failed to show petitioners that they led to change and thus fell into disuse.[600]

Having a good feedback loop is imperative for addressing societal issues. Almost any disadvantaged person will tell you that their reasons for not participating in an activity is that 'it won't change anything'. 'Democratic' activity that doesn't offer the chance or hope of thorough-going change is therefore likely to continue to attract only those participants who are happy to have their say without seeing the necessity of a direct, significant impact.

599 Brian Wampler and Benjamin Goldfrank, *The Rise, Spread and Decline of Brazil's Participatory Budgeting: The Arc of a Democratic Innovation* (Palgrave MacMillan 2022) 140.
600 The archives can be viewed here: <https://petitions.obamawhitehouse.archives.gov/>.

Chapter 9
Challenges

We have already addressed many challenges for digital democracy throughout this book. As we saw, some of these were red herrings, like fears of click-button voting or exaggerated versions of the digital divide. But there are some that are often overlooked, and they are, once again, often social rather than technical in nature. For example, the functionality of available tools tends to be vastly **underutilized.** In other words, public officials pay for or develop tools and then fail to fully use their functionality, resulting in inefficiency and, sometimes, disappointment.

Low participation rates also present a problem for legitimacy. The vast communication campaigns necessary to let citizens and residents know they can participate in a timely fashion are rarely in place. When authorities reach out to interest groups and NGOs to promote participation, they save money, but tend to bias their results. These issues can and should be addressed, but it takes effort to do so and requires a much higher degree of professionalization and commitment to such practices.

Digital democracy and other offline participatory practices also frequently struggle with a **loss of momentum.** Projects either fail to achieve anything that inspires continuing participation or wind down because the person who championed them within the administration leaves their role without having anchored processes within the official framework and ensured that more than one person is conversant with them.[601]

However, although these are all serious challenges for digital democracy, perhaps the most serious challenges are psychological in nature. As we saw with the Dark Triad above, when people relentlessly channel their own psychological needs into a process, this inevitably degrades that process. Today, virtually all activists, writers, academics and politicians feel justified in viewing democracy merely as a vehicle for achieving their own personal aims, and as a result they crush the process under the weight of their own ever-changing expectations. These overblown expectations, hysterical demands and self-righteous efforts to impose one's own will on the entire world under the guise of democracy are often yet another manifestation of the Dark Triad traits mentioned above, and like the Dark Triad, they are best avoided.

---

601 Interviews (2022).

https://doi.org/10.1515/9783110794465-013

9.1 Overblown Expectations

Debate over digital democracy tends to veer between promises of utopianism and relentless criticism of anything that falls short of that utopianism. For example, a common argument made against democracy (of all forms) today is that people are too stupid, impulsive and uninformed to make decisions for their lives without extreme forms of control, but when well-informed people take part in digital democracy and become irate at being condescended to, this is also condemned, and they are dismissed as being 'the usual suspects' and overly 'privileged' due to their higher levels of education and prosperity. This leaves us with a simultaneous belief that people are ignorant *and* anger at people who are not ignorant, but for that 'privileged'. There is simply no winning under this hypercritical worldview.

This unrealistic level of criticism tends to go into overdrive the moment any aspect of democracy becomes even moderately successful. The treatment received by M5S and Podemos, both unexpectedly successful parties, demonstrates this.

M5S explicitly conceived of itself as being a non-ideological movement, something one would expect to have been welcomed in a world where fears of hyperpartisanship and polarization abound. This cross-spectrum appeal was more than just a statement of intent and was actually reflected in the movement's support, which included Eurosceptics, Conservatives, left-wing voters, moderate voters and many former non-voters.[602] M5S thus achieved two things that many commenters claim to want for democracy: it built a broad coalition of voters originating from a wide spectrum of beliefs and ideological positions, and it reinvigorated non-voters to participate in the political process. However, rather than being welcomed as working against polarization and apathy, M5S was constantly criticized for not aligning neatly under simplistic ideological categories pre-determined by political scientists, and incessantly condemned for being 'populist'.[603]

Both M5S and Podemos were also harshly criticized for the way they facilitated online participation.

Academics complained, for example, that the party leadership could set the timing of online votes and frame questions, putting forward their own case without alternative viewpoints being given an explicit airing in the original setting of

---

602 Eric Turner, 'The 5 Star Movement and its Discontents: A Tale of Blogging, Comedy, Electoral Success and Tensions' (2013) 5(2) Interface: A Journal for and about Social Movements 178, 201–202, relying on Roberto Biorcio and Paolo Di Natale, *Politica a 5 Stelle. Idee, Storia e Strategie del Movimento di Grillo* (Feltrinelli 2013).
603 E.g. Catherine Fieschi, *Populocracy: The Tyranny of Authenticity and the Rise of Populism* (Agenda Publishing 2019).

the question.[604] However, it would be counterproductive for party leaders not to put forward a strong case for their preferred measures or to launch a discussion that deviates from the general party orientation (for example, it would be quite odd for a leftist party to include anti-union arguments in its platform proposals for the sake of 'neutral debate'.).

Podemos and M5S *are* political parties that contest elections, not disinterested facilitators. When leaders pose questions, they are asking the members to endorse their position. What was different, compared to conventional parties, was that they committed to not proceeding with policies that failed to receive that endorsement, and they established a mechanism for measuring this. This can be understood as an effort to prevent corruption within the party (anti-corruption efforts being a major theme for both parties) not to end the concept of party leadership immediately and entirely. Of course, who provides the information does influence the outcome, but as long as we accept agonistic pluralism, we accept that proposers are not presenting 'objective' 'one truth' information, but rather laying out their case and hoping that people rally to them rather than tear them down.

Academics also criticized M5S for the manner in which it allowed members to propose legislation, regionally, nationally and Europe-wide.

This was deemed flawed, because most legislation continued to be proposed by elected representatives and only a small proportion of bills formally tabled by M5S originated with non-elected members. It has also been criticized because only the most popular ad hoc member proposals make it through the process, as opposed to central party proposals which do not need this validation. This process has also been criticized because the multiple online forums that deal with legislation are 'filled with hundreds of bills of law drafts uploaded by elected representatives', and while any member can comment on the drafts put forward by representatives, the program does not allow for back-and-forth inline commenting, which means that it is difficult for a discussion to develop between members.[605]

However, M5S allows (or at least did allow during this time) anyone to stand as a candidate, subject to an open members' vote. Furthermore, each representative was limited to two terms of office, so the distinction between representative and average member was far less significant than in other parties. Finally, M5S held forums to develop the main tenets of party policy, so the policies put forward by central party leadership were not themselves divorced from member input.

---

604 Marco Deseriis and Davide Vittori 'The Impact of Online Participation Platforms on the Internal Democracy of Two Southern European Parties: Podemos and the Five Star Movement' (2019) 13 International Journal of Communication 5696–5714.

605 Deseriis and Vittori 'Impact of Online Participation Platforms' 5700.

The ability of members to propose legislation at any time, came *in addition* to all of these other possibilities. That such initiatives would have to go through the process before being put forward as potentially Europe-wide law seems reasonable.

At the same time, every time it did let its members vote on something (e. g. a coalition agreement) M5S was subjected to an intense barrage of national and international vitriol for failing to recognize that such decisions were 'too important' for democracy and that they should be made by party leadership rather than the general membership. This created an irrational double standard which no party or movement could withstand, but which continued relentlessly across the commentary on the subject. Indeed, one of the authors who criticized the lack of inline commenting on legislation on Rousseau (the platform used by M5S at the time), accepted that other software like pol.is and Loomio also prevent direct replies in the service of preventing trolling and flame wars.[606]

While M5S and former M5S members I have spoken to would also have liked to have even more scope to participate, they joined the movement because it gave them significantly more than any other party. The people working at Rousseau were also quite proud of the considerable functionality they managed to achieve with a small team that had to keep the system up, running and secure for an entire nation under great scrutiny. They were not sitting on a great deal of surplus capacity to enable even greater participation and simply failing to allow it. The only thing remarkable here is that this level of mass participation, unprecedented at any other time in modern history, and only recently made technically feasible, worked at all for any length of time. What only a few years ago was routinely dismissed as 'impossible' is now – just as routinely – cast aside for not being perfect enough.

Most of the criticism of M5S and Podemos amounts to an argument for an infeasible level of structurelessness and a criticism that while these parties substantially reduced barriers to participation while still working within the representative system, they did not immediately annihilate all of them.

Scrutinizing these processes is, of course, helpful, and they should not be exempt from criticism or improvement, but loading them with magical thinking that is then disappointed when results that never could have occurred failed to materialize is not.

Even under a well-run democracy with minimum distortions and corruption, we will all still have plenty of problems. However, even achieving that requires us to work with realistic expectations.

---

606 Marco Deseriis, 'Reducing the Burden of Decision in Digital Democracy Applications: A Comparative Analysis of Six Decision-Making Software' (2021) Science, Technology and Human Values 1, 10 – 12.

9.2 The Democracy 'Industry'

As mentioned above, it is hard to overstate the damage that extreme wealth inequality does to democracy, as it eradicates the relative material equality between citizens that is necessary for a method of government based on legal equality (as democracy is) to survive.

However, this increasing wealth inequality can also erode democracy in more direct ways. As tax loopholes that benefit the very wealthy are not closed and they thus avoid paying,[607] States – deprived of public funds – increasingly look for ways to outsource their responsibilities, thereby removing more and more areas of policy from public control. This is often criticized when the State outsources contracts to private companies, but it can also happen with NGOs. And NGOs, like companies, are good at maintaining their sources of revenue.

For example, NGOs began to provide some of the services approved by PB in Brazil. Naturally enough they then began to encourage those who benefitted from those services to vote for their projects in PB in order to maintain their revenue stream. This turned something that was supposed to be a public exercise into a more private process with people competing for money to stay in business.[608] It also allegedly led to the government prioritizing projects where they could find a corporate or NGO partner that could help carry the organizational and financial burden of the project 'rather than to programs the communities preferred.'[609] This essentially gives NGOs, especially those who can provide matching funds from large donors, a veto over public life.

However, destructive as this already is, the problem gets much worse.

Some well-financed NGOs have come to believe that they should *run* democracy and that State officials should outsource the *process* of democratic decision-making *to them*. Such organizations often claim a great deal of expertise that they do not, in fact, possess and tend to advocate highly controlled processes, such as citizens' assemblies, manipulative consultations or tightly controlled forms of PB. These organizations and 'experts' range from well-meaning amateurs (such as those described in Caroline Lee's *Do-It-Yourself Democracy*)[610] to more mercenary processes.

---

607 See e.g. Gabriel Zucman, *The Hidden Wealth of Nations: The Scourge of Tax Havens* (University of Chicago Press 2015).
608 Abers et al., 'Porto Alegre' 14.
609 Abers et al., 'Porto Alegre' 16.
610 Caroline Lee, *Do-It-Yourself Democracy: The Rise of the Public Engagement Industry* (Oxford University Press 2015).

We saw the examples of People Powered and Public Agenda above, but other organizations are also involved here, such as DemocracyNext (funded by the Rockefeller Foundation, Open Society Foundation, One Project, and the National Endowment for Democracy).[611] DemocracyNext, which is currently seeking to hire a COO on a €100,000 salary also works with the Berggruen Institute to embed citizens' assemblies in the European Union.[612]

The citizens' assembly is a method of citizen 'engagement' that invites a very small number of randomly-selected people (ca. 100–500) to deliberate a matter interspersed with hand-picked expert presentations. These expert presentations guide the selected citizens with 'carefully-vetted' information and help them to make 'the hard choices'. Associates of DemocracyNext (and similar organizations) often flirt with or outright advocate making binding decisions via these tiny assemblies[613] – in other words disenfranchising 99.99 % of the population, who will need to wait their turn (possibly forever) to be selected to participate in one of these prestigious assemblies. Citizens' assembly advocates justify this extreme tactic with the necessity of fighting oligarchs. But it is in the interests of the politically active super-wealthy who intentionally use their resources (rather than democratic institutions) to alter society (colloquially referred to as oligarchs), and *only* of oligarchs, to disenfranchise the vast majority of people – and the people funding DemocracyNext *are* oligarchs (see Fig. 9.1).

---

611 Details available on Democracy Next's Open Collective Account: <https://opencollective.com/one-project>. One Project donated over $54k on 28 October 2022; NED donated over $100k on 12 October 2022 <https://opencollective.com/national-endowment-for-democracy>; Open Society gave over $225k <https://opencollective.com/open-society-foundations> and the Rockefeller Foundation gave almost $278k <https://opencollective.com/the-rockefeller-foundation> accessed 25 January 2023.

612 'Terms of Reference, Chief Operations Officer' (*DemocracyNext*) <https://demnext.org/wp-content/uploads/2022/11/democracynext-terms-of-reference-coo.pdf> accessed 11 March 2023; the Berggruen Institute also gave DemocracyNext 900 EUR for a presentation delivered in August 2022 <https://opencollective.com/democracynext/orders/624274> accessed 11 March 2023; co-operation with Berggruen detailed on <www.demnext.org> accessed 28 November 2022 (since removed).

613 See e.g. Nathan Gardels, 'Another Kind of Democratic Future' (*Noema/Berggruen Institute*, 13 May 2022) accessed 19 March 2023; Tweet from DemocracyNext's CEO Claudia Chwalisz 'Should we Replace Voting with a Lottery? Hint: Yes' (7 September 2022) <https://twitter.com/ClaudiaChwalisz/status/1567397860903161856?t=slJU5dbPRKWu94dvnlKY4Q&s=03>.

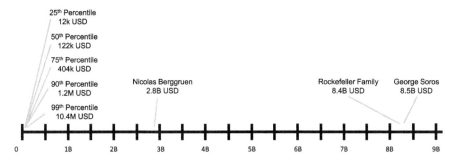

Fig. 9.1: Wealth Comparison – General Population vs. Personal Wealth of Selected Billionaires

DemocracyNext's CEO previously worked at Populus Ltd (a market research firm now part of Yonder Consulting), and at Policy Network.

According to its website, Yonder currently focuses on things like, 'How do you get the nation to eat healthy?' a project they undertook in the interests of a company that sells a fruit and yogurt snack. The campaign, which worked from the premise that turning fruit into puree is very bad for you, included making little faux-authentic poems like:

> There once was a man who loved berries
> From strawberries to raspberries to cherries,
> He flew into a craze when they were turned into purees
> So he kept them chunky and put them in our pots
> And we aren't poets...sorry![614]

The inclusion of these little rhymes here may seem spurious at first glance, but it is highly relevant because it is approximately the level of 'insight' such civil society organizations now bring to bear on democracy, musing on the big topics like what painting their year would be, if years were paintings,[615] and creating gifs of themselves next to their own inspirational quotes as people sometimes do for particularly well-known spiritual leaders, like the Dalai Lama.

Policy Network bills itself as 'the international ideas exchange for progressives', although its many articles would indicate a decidedly more centre-left approach. It has received funding from Lord Sainsbury (one of the most generous do-

---

614 'Oh my Fruity Goodness: How Do You Get the Nation to Eat Healthy?' (*Yonder Consulting*) <https://yonderconsulting.com/case-study/ohmyfruitygoodness/> accessed 25 January 2023.

615 Claudia Chwalisz, 'An Expansive Year' (*Medium*, 11 January 2023) <https://medium.com/@claudiachwalisz/2022-an-expansive-year-4dfd6f6fb0a4> accessed 18 February 2023.

nors to the Remain campaign during Brexit)[616] and features articles on its page such as 'What could a Labour government do to undo Brexit?'.[617] This mindset – *how to get people to do something* (answer: with marketing) – drives an enormous part of the democracy industry and we can see these funded organizations hiring people to try to turn democracy into little more than (what they believe to be) a clever marketing campaign.

This phenomenon of billionaire-sponsored dilettantism is not limited to democracy proper. It also affects the medical field,[618] the legal system,[619] research in general,[620] and media and journalism.[621] Having 'ideas' about society is now what is called a 'pay to play' scenario. You need to put up money in order to participate in the public conversation. For example, the Berggruen Institute is a 'knowledge partner' of the New York Times Athens Democracy Forum[622] as well as a 'Strategic Partner' of the organizers[623] (and got four speakers associated with it on the conference's agenda). NewDemocracy, which receives a large proportion of its funding from the foundation of Australian investor Luca Belgiorno-Nettis as well as from Google Australia, co-sponsors a journal on the topic.[624]

These organizations flood the discourse about democracy, pushing out all other voices in media, conferences, and frequently even in the academic world, where researchers must now often procure funding from the very wealthy in order to keep their jobs (much as the tobacco industry once funded research

---

616 'Our Supporters' (*Policy Network*) <https://policynetwork.progressivebritain.org/work/> accessed January 2023; Sam Harrison, 'Cambridge Chancellor Donated £8 million to EU Remain Campaign' *Varsity* (26 August 2016) <https://www.varsity.co.uk/news/10588> accessed 18 February 2023.

617 Richard Rose, 'What Could a Labour Government Do To Undo Brexit?' (*Policy Network Opinions*, 24 July 2020) <https://policynetwork.progressivebritain.org/opinions/blogs/what-could-labour-government-do-undo-brexit/> accessed 25 January 2023.

618 See e.g. Linsey McGoey, *No Such Thing as a Free Gift: The Gates Foundation and the Price of Philanthropy* (Verso 2016).

619 See e.g. Gaëtan Cliquennois, *European Human Rights Justice and Privatisation: The Growing Influence of Foreign Private Funds* (Cambridge University Press 2020).

620 See e.g. Daniel W. Drezner, *The Ideas Industry: How Pessimists, Partisans and Plutocrats are Transforming the Marketplace of Ideas* (Oxford University Press 2017).

621 Anand Giridharadas, *Winners Take All: The Elite Charade of Changing the World* (Knopf 2018).

622 'Partners' (*Athens Democracy Forum*) <https://www.athensdemocracyforum.com/partner-with-us/partners/> accessed 26 February 2023.

623 'Who We Work With' (*The Democracy and Culture Foundation*) <https://www.democracyculturefoundation.org/who-we-work-with/> accessed 26 February 2023.

624 'Sponsors' (*Journal of Deliberative Democracy*) <https://delibdemjournal.org/site/about/> accessed 26 February 2023; 'Supporters and Funding' <https://www.newdemocracy.com.au/funding/> (*newDemocracy*) accessed 26 February 2023; 'Transfield Holdings' <https://transfield.com.au/> accessed 26 February 2023.

into smoking). Rather than focusing on things we could actually be doing, we instead run after chimera after chimera that will magically 'fix' everything and get the public to acquiesce to the wished for policy, whether that is eating a certain kind of yogurt or accepting a certain kind of health policy.

As this indicates, the kind of 'democracy' promoted by such organizations is often extremely manipulative. For example, Involve is a British organization that bills itself as *the* 'UK's public participation charity, on a mission to put people at the heart of decision-making'.[625]

One of its more recent engagements has been on 'impact investing', that is, exactly what we have briefly spoken of in this section – using money to change laws, social practices, or the physical landscape while making money in the process (to engage, in other words, in exactly the kind of social engineering that participants in the Albertan Ethelo consultations were so upset about).

According to Involve's webpage:

> The Impact Investing Institute challenges the common myth that investing with impact means sacrificing financial returns…We will be delivering a series of Community Cuppas in the North of Tyne area – one of the place-based pilot areas identified by the Impact Investing Institute – where we will ask members of local communities about who should be involved in decision-making in local impact investing and which principles/criteria should underpin such community engagement…. Our aim is to create a framework that is responsive to the needs of institutional investors, is non-prescriptive in nature, and offers a menu of different options to reflect the diversity of institutional investing structures.[626]

The Impact Investment Institute is supported by: HSBC, Blackrock, Credit Suisse, Columbia Threadneedle, BNY Mellon, Federated Hermes and Triodos Bank, among others (some of the wealthiest investors and investment banks in the world).[627]

One has to ask why community engagement is working so hard to convince residents that 'impact investors' are going to help their community *and* make a lot of money doing so. Furthermore, one needs to ask why *any kind* of public en-

---

625 'About' (*Involve*) <https://involve.org.uk/about> accessed 26 March 2023.

626 'How can Institutional Investors Bring in Community Engagement into Impact Investing' (*Involve*)   <https://involve.org.uk/our-work/our-projects/embedding-good-practice/how-can-institutional-investors-bring-community> accessed 26 January 2023.

627 'Our Supporters' (*Impact Investing Institute*) <https://www.impactinvest.org.uk/our-supporters-2/> accessed 26 January 2023. Credit Suisse has been involved in multiple financial crises, partly as a result of having entangled itself with too many fraudulent businesses over the years.

gagement is being conducted at the behest of private investors.[628] This is, at best, market research, *not* democracy. In a democracy, business is *subordinate* to the collective will. It is not a competitor to the government or able to undertake sovereign acts. That is *the definition* of oligarchy or plutocracy ('rule by the few' or 'rule by the rich'; respectively – but also somewhat redundantly).

By methods like these, oligarchs are using 'pro-democracy' NGOs to literally redefine their own usurpation of political power as 'democracy' and 'citizen engagement'. There are extreme dangers in this complete boundarylessness which has no checks and balances, but instead insists on 'collaboration' in which participants are told that their interests and those of billionaires seeking to invest in their communities at a return align, and that there is no need for agonistic debate since it is all about 'an economy that works for all', 'building mixed investor and community coalitions', 'work[ing] with investors to address...challenges' and 'deliver projects which both improve people's lives, contribute to local economic resilience and generate an appropriate risk-adjusted financial return.'[629] Far from enabling community participation, this is a thinly-veiled way for the very wealthy to insert themselves at yet another layer of the political process. Investment funds and banks don't *have* a vote. They don't *exist* democratically. In a democracy, there is literally *nothing* these entities can do without the permission of 'the people', whereas the government can do almost *anything* to them. They can be expropriated tomorrow if the people desire such an action, because in a democracy 'the people' hold power. Yet this is the kind of activity 'democracy NGOs' are arranging.

Similarly, the 'People's Assembly for Nature' part of the 'People's Plan for Nature' is 'powered by' not any actual people, but the World Wildlife Fund, the Royal Society for the Protection of Birds and the National Trust in 'a unique collaboration with the UK public to protect and restore nature in the UK'.[630] Of course, every law and regulation about protecting and restoring nature in the UK is only passed on the authority of 'the UK public' which as a result, does not really need private organizations (all of whom are already committed to their own programmes), to condescend to 'collaborate' with them. However, this role reversal where *the public* is invited to cooperate with private entities is increasingly common.

---

628 Involve's webpage refers to this project as 'embedding good practice' ('How can Institutional Investors Bring in Community Engagement' (*Involve*)).

629 'Place-based Impact Investing' (*Impact Investing Institute*) <https://www.impactinvest.org.uk/project/place-based-impact-investing/> accessed 26 January 2023.

630 'People's Assembly for Nature' (*People's Plan for Nature*) <https://peoplesplanfornature.org/peoples-assembly-nature> accessed 26 January 2023.

The People's Assembly for Nature is essentially a vehicle for pro-environment propaganda, complete with a one-sided advisory board.[631] It receives funding from the Samworth Foundation, which already has its own extensive climate change policy,[632] and the Esmee Fairbairn Foundation, which is also pre-committed to various environmental policies.[633] Indeed, all participants randomly selected to be part of the Assembly are required to adhere to a travel policy (which strongly encourages participants to take public transportation to reach the venue and to obtain permission to fly)[634] and its strict catering policy,[635] although they do receive £800 (a substantial amount of money in Britain) for their trouble.[636] Despite this generous offer, organizers had to send out 300 invites per person ultimately selected to participate.[637] The point here is not whether or not we agree with the goals pursued by any of these organizations. The issue is that we are now seeking to label heavily slanted processes as 'innovations in democracy'.

Organizations like Involve have brought the demand for intensely manipulative events like these on themselves by claiming that they can deliver the required results, that they can *get people* to do the things they should want to do. That they can, in other words, get rid of the messy and annoying politics of politics.

This 'democracy industry' whose fauxperts promise to deliver all the 'right' answers that their sponsors are looking for, often limits the 'solutions' possible for participants to choose from. If we look at the Irish Citizens' Assembly on Ageing (citizens' assemblies in Ireland were started with money from Atlantic Philanthropies, but are now financed by tax), we can see how participants are often put in a position where their only real choice to deal with an issue is to tax themselves.

631 'Who is in the Advisory Group?' (*People's Plan for Nature*) <https://peoplesplanfornature.org/who-advisory-group> accessed 26 January 2023.

632 'Funder Commitment on Climate Change' (*Samworth Foundation*) <https://web.archive.org/web/20220629150407/https://www.samworthfoundation.org.uk/about-us-2/funder-commitment-on-climate-change-2> accessed 28 January 2023.

633 'Our Natural World' (*Esmee Fairbairn Foundation*) <https://esmeefairbairn.org.uk/our-aims/our-natural-world/> accessed 26 January 2023.

634 'People's Assembly for Nature: Travel Policy' (*People's Plan for Nature*) <https://peoplesplanfornature.org/sites/default/files/2022-11/People%27s%20Assembly%20for%20Nature%20-%20Travel%20Policy.pdf> accessed 26 January 2023.

635 'People's Assembly for Nature: Catering Sustainability Policy' (*People's Plan for Nature*) <https://peoplesplanfornature.org/sites/default/files/2022-11/People%27s%20Assembly%20for%20Nature%20-%20Catering%20Policy_0.pdf> accessed 26 January 2023.

636 'Frequently Asked Questions' (*People's Plan for Nature*) <https://peoplesplanfornature.org/frequently-asked-questions> accessed 26 January 2023.

637 'Frequently Asked Questions' (*People's Plan for Nature*) <https://peoplesplanfornature.org/frequently-asked-questions> accessed 26 January 2023.

For example, one question asked participants: "Where do you believe overall funding for care of older people should come from?"

Four options were presented:

- Option 1: General taxation (income tax, VAT, indirect taxes, property taxes etc);
- Option 2: Compulsory social insurance payment– an earmarked tax for all workers linked to labour market participation– not unlike the current PRSI mechanism to fund long-term/social care for older people;
- Option 3: Long-term/ social care private insurance (privately funded by the insured);
- Option 4: Cost sharing arrangements for users of all services (including for example, home care)– e. g. co-payments, a charge on assets (similar to the fair deal scheme).[638]

Participants 'decided' for option 2 – a compulsory social insurance payment. Options like 'close tax loopholes', 'raise corporation tax', or 'introduce tax-free personal savings schemes' were not included. In this case, the original wording of the question spoke of *additional* funding, but participants got this changed to *overall* funding, indicating that they were trying to preclude tax raises on the general population – the obvious intent of the original question. However, this didn't really resolve the issue or address where future shortfalls would come from. This was especially problematic as in the previous two questions participants had resolved to spend more money on care for older persons. Thus, the process ended with a resolution to spend more money and an apparent indirect (and thus extremely unclear) acquiescence that that additional money would come from a compulsory social insurance payment, which would presumably need to be increased.

A similar assembly, again run by Involve in the UK, voted to raise tax on all those over the age of 40 to finance social care.[639] Because this assembly was run for the House of Commons, this policy actually got as far as being floated in the

---

638 Citizens Assembly, *Second Report and Recommendations of the Citizens' Assembly: How we best Respond to the Challenges and Opportunities of an Aging Population* (December 2017) 24 <https://2016-2018.citizensassembly.ie/en/How-we-best-respond-to-challenges-and-opportunities-of-an-age ing-population/Final-Report-on-how-we-best-respond-to-the-challenges-and-opportunities-of-an-age ing-population/Final-Report-on-Older-People-Incl-Appendix-A-D.pdf> accessed 18 February 2023.
639 Involve, *Citizens Assembly on Social Care: Recommendations for Funding Adult Social Care* (June 2018) 16 <https://oecd-opsi.org/wp-content/uploads/2019/02/Citizens-Assembly-on-Social-Care-Recommendations-for-funding-social-care_2.pdf> accessed 18 February 2023.

press[640] (it did not survive the night on social media). As usual, participants had been asked to choose from a number of options to raise tax on themselves (e.g. income tax, VAT, council tax, inheritance tax).

Participants spontaneously suggested other options during the process such as: 'including a "wealth tax", "sugar / junk food tax", "clamping down on tax avoidance", and revisiting "overall priorities on where general taxation is spent". Members were also interested in ways that companies could contribute through tax, including through higher National Insurance contributions or a compulsory social responsibility tax.'[641] However, these errant thoughts of participants are not the things that get voted on. Citizens' assemblies (and other forms of 'engagement') are used to funnel opinion into pre-decided channels (how would you like to tax yourselves?) rather than reflecting the spectrum of actual opinion. To top things off, a recent French citizens' assembly on euthanasia discouraged its participants from trying to become experts themselves on the matter at hand or continuing to look for information, encouraging them instead to make a decision based on the information provided by organizers.[642]

Not only is this all manipulative, the 'democracy industry' uses citizens' assemblies and other controlled processes to starve governments of input from other sources. The content presented here is but a tiny sliver of this complex into which wealthy foundations pour tens of millions of dollars every single year, side-lining people and government. The fact that this, and not emancipatory democracy, is being pushed as 'democratic innovation' is one of the greatest, if not *the* greatest, threat to democracy today.

9.3 Manipulation by Officials or Government

Unfortunately, private foundations are not the only actors that engage in manipulative practices. These are often all too common in government as well.

Many things that are called 'public participation', 'public engagement' and even 'democracy' today, fall under the categories of Non-Participation and Tokenism defined by Arnstein. In particular, many exercises and organizations have as their goal to give people the *feeling* that they have *been heard* or to get citizens to

---

640 Alex Matthews-King 'Over 40s Should Pay New Tax to Fund Creaking Social Care, MPs Say' *Independent* (27 June 2018) <https://www.independent.co.uk/news/health/social-care-tax-over-40s-retirement-pension-nursing-home-meals-a8418171.html> accessed 26 January 2023.
641 *Citizens' Assembly on Social Care* 17.
642 Hugh Pope, 'How Non-Expertise Becomes a Strength' (*DemocracyNext*, January 2023) <https://demnext.substack.com/p/how-non-expertise-becomes-a-strength> accessed 26 January 2023.

trust government. These are often the only two goals public participation has. But, as discussed above, democracy is the opposite of trust; it is about scrutinizing, and officials should be happy when participants catch a mistake or register their objections before a project begins.

Officials are also often guilty of using 'democratic innovation' to avoid politics.

To give an example of this kind of evasive practice in the digital space, let's look at an Ethelo consultation in London, Ontario. In this case, council staff were required to make a Climate Emergency Action Plan, but were daunted by this task, as according to them, 'the climate emergency' is 'complex and polarizing'. In an effort to side-step the politics of politics, they decided to 'turn the engagement into a game' by presenting 'participants with twenty greenhouse gas reduction actions that the city could take, like energy efficiency upgrades, a green bin program, and new cycling infrastructure. Then, using a sliding scale, participants decided how much they personally thought the City should prioritize each action over the next 10 years'. However, whatever they chose, it had to result in reducing greenhouse gas emissions by at least one million tonnes by 2030.[643]

Of course, by framing things this way, it is unlikely that anyone who opposed making carbon cuts or who doubted there was a climate emergency took part, as these were not options one could express. The ads for the consultation included videos telling Londoners that climate change would cause more severe flooding, driving up their insurance rates, as well as causing Lyme disease and West Nile virus. An animation indicated that the people of London would also run out of coffee and chocolate while other food became more expensive, and promised Londoners that things would get more difficult for them if they did not take strong, collective action.

London is one of the fastest growing cities in Canada with half of all immigration coming directly from overseas. Despite this, London's carbon emissions have been dropping.[644] London is thus in a similar situation to Okotoks; also growing quickly, with officials under pressure to undertake climate action. In Okotoks, this consultation was more open and participants voiced their dissatisfaction with rapid growth as well as plans to reduce living standards, especially around housing. London, by contrast, did not give participants the opportunity to express such views. As they acknowledged, the topic was polarizing, so they excluded that

---

643 'Gaming the System to Fight Climate Change: London, Canada' (*Ethelo*) <https://ethelo.com/case-studies-directory/london-climate-case-study/> accessed 26 January 2023.

644 This official video claims that London's carbon emissions were 380,000 tonnes lower than in the base year 1990: <https://getinvolved.london.ca/climate/widgets/81531/videos/6540> accessed 12 March 2023.

polarization from the consultation, which they aptly referred to as 'gaming the system'.

Organizers also seem to have overly generously weighted votes, with many proposals that attracted a high number of neutral votes, and many seemingly with as many opposing as supporting votes, still enjoying over 60% *support*.[645] This inflation of agreement is all too common when officials are determined to get the results they need, and it has a very detrimental effect.

Every time you use democracy as window-dressing and avoid confrontation, you delegitimize democracy as an idea.

Experts seem easily able to identify this problem of co-optation when it comes to other countries. For example, participatory budgeting has been used in some parts of China as a form of 'orderly' citizen participation. Indeed, Article 27 of the Chinese Constitution states, 'All state organs and state employees must rely on the support of the people, stay engaged with them, listen to their opinions and suggestions, accept their oversight, and work hard to serve them'. This managerial view of politics is similar to many Western activists' and academics' views of democracy.

Indeed, there is a striking overlap between the Communist Party of China (CPC) and Western government here on citizen participation, with China doing things like:

- creating online portals where citizens can contact mayors with questions and concerns
- working with business and government officials to set prices for utilities and transportation (called participatory pricing)
- evaluating the work of government departments online

When Chinese officials vet projects for feasibility or limit participation, it is seen as controlling, rather than simply part of the process, even though some of the sums available through PB in China number in the tens of millions of yuan and turnout can be very high (in one PB that covered several large housing estates (ca. 1500 households), turnout was 62%).

Authors argue that in the case of China, PB is used to 'ensure ideological conformity, political stability and strengthening the legitimacy of the CPC'. However,

---

645 London Climate Action Plan Simulator (*Ethelo*) 21, 35, 37 and 38 <https://blog.ethelo.org/hubfs/Case%20Study%20Reports/London-report.pdf>.

this is exactly the argument that many advocates make for democracy 'innovations' like PB and citizens' assemblies today. Their goal is also to get people to accept 'hard choices' and 'trust' authority. In China, and in the West, this is a strategy for aligning 'the people' to the ruler's goals under the banner of achieving harmony and consensus. When the people are not aligned to the ruling classes' goals, be that a political party, like the CPC, or wealthy oligarchs, there is 'division' which is 'harmful'. The object of participation has become to erase that division.[646]

In Western countries, this is often expressed as an attempt to get citizens to acquiesce in policy they would otherwise not tolerate using sufficiently 'subtle tools' that give citizens 'the right context and framing' so that they 'can think themselves collectively towards a better understanding of problems and more effective collective solutions'. Participation understood this way, is a superior alternative to 'nudge theory' which also attempts to get people to change their behaviour by giving them a 'nudge' (trying to manipulate people into undertaking an action with subconscious enticements (e.g. giving someone a smaller plate in the hopes that they will eat less)). Manipulation is necessary because, 'the public would not accept the level of intervention that is needed to affect large-scale change across numerous policy areas'. But practitioners hope to get them to put up with such change, anyway, 'Because citizens are expected to justify their perspectives and preferences in public, there is a strong motivation to constrain self-interest and to consider the public good.' This will have a 'moralising effect', and work to eliminate 'irrational preferences based on false empirical beliefs, morally repugnant preferences that no one is willing to advance in the public arena and narrowly self-interested preferences.'[647]

Again, this overlooks the subjective nature of policy and beliefs – to many people having women fight in the armed forces has been considered morally repugnant (because they believe it would be wrong for a man to kill a woman and that allowing women to fight puts them in an impossible moral quandary), as has intermarriage between people of different cultures or religion. Most people who oppose gay marriage and abortion do so because they consider these things morally repugnant. There is no reason the dominant morality of any culture is more 'rational' or 'superior' or that any particular counterculture morality is. As we said in the beginning, democracy is a means for examining issues, *not* for im-

---

646 Yuan Li, Yanjun Zhu and Catherine Owen, 'Participatory Budgeting and the Party: Generating 'Citizens Orderly Participation' through Party-Building in Shanghai' (2022) Journal of Chinese Governance.

647 Peter John, Graham Smith and Gerry Stoker, 'Nudge Nudge, Think Think: Two Strategies for Changing Civic Behaviour' (2009) The Political Quarterly 4 and 8 – 9.

posing pre-decided beliefs. If you only do things to get your way, people will sense that and distrust the process. So avoid the temptation to try to manipulate them.

9.4 Crusading Amateurs

We've spoken about citizens' assembly advocates and the damage they have done to democracy, but they are not the only ones. The most damage to democracy is likely perpetrated by extreme social justice warriors. When organizers are allowed to insist that their personal whims and *beliefs* be catered to as part of the process, it simply delegitimizes the process. For example, People Powered (behind much of PB in NYC), writing in an article about itself, explicitly rejected the 'traditional criteria' of expertise and 'hegemonic academic research practices' and committed to different kinds of 'knowledges'.[648] People Powered selects its board based on demographic criteria rather than expert achievement as this is 'defying' 'both norms of neoliberal colorblindness and checklist definitions of diversity' and serves to 'destabilize traditional hierarchies of knowledge'.[649] Members engage in a kind of kindergarten show-and-tell 'such as bringing an object of meaning to share with new members, help participants to grapple with their own subjectivities, situate one another's positionalities' and avoid 'fetishiz[ing] productivity'.[650]

This level of poorly reasoned existential philosophy is then apparently somehow connected to a PB exercise that decides over the banalities of school bathrooms and streetlighting. In this way, something that would in the normal course of things inherently reduce polarization, ('let's drop this argument and get on with where we want to put the bathroom'), loads pointless polarization onto it ('if we go with where the plumber says we should put the bathroom are we not just privileging traditional ways of knowing and upholding colonialist hierarchies of knowledge production?')

Without a scientific method, there is no way to construct a bow and arrow, weave cloth, understand the medicinal properties of plants or create family structures (as humans have done worldwide for many thousands of years). There is also *no way* out of oppression, there is *no way* to determine fairness, there is *no way* for masses of free and equal citizens to cooperate with each other. Instead, one falls

---

648 Carolin Hagelskamp, Celina Su, Karla Valverde Viesca and Tarson Nuñez, 'Organizing a Transnational Solidarity for Social Change through Participatory Practices: The Case of People Powered – Global Hub for Participatory Democracy' (2021) American Journal of Community Psychology 298, 300 and 301.

649 Hagelskamp et al., 'Organizing a Transnational Solidarity' 299.

650 Hagelskamp et al., 'Organizing a Transnational Solidarity' 302.

into a tangled mass of endless self-contradiction and infantilized, dependent behaviour.

People Powered describes itself as 'deliberately not neutral, but value-driven'.[651] But democracy is not their private playground and they are not entitled to treat it as a vehicle for their own values at the expense of others who are *equally entitled* to participate. Requiring everyone to pre-agree on political goals is *the opposite* of democracy. One can work as a lobbyist or a pressure group (although this is bad enough) to achieve one's preferred values, but certainly one should not be running the democratic exercise *itself* on this basis. Attitudes like these have put millions of people, including many moderate liberals and conservatives, completely off the idea of participatory democracy. And People Powered are hardly alone in this.[652]

Presenting democracy as a kind of amateur-hour event for motivational speakers to say whatever pops into their heads (generally the latest ill-considered fad) has caused countless educated, informed citizens to question if democracy is truly the best form of government. *If* democracy is the end of logic and reason where hard work and merit are not rewarded, decisions are not scrutinized, accountability loses all meaning, whole categories of opinion and belief and traditional ways of life are dismissed as illegitimate, and people must spend their days engaged in Cultural Revolution-style struggle sessions, one should not be surprised if many people begin to think that dictatorship and authoritarianism may not be as bad as they sound.

And while many crusading amateurs view themselves as 'progressive' this is not always the case. Many cyberwarriors also feel entitled to say whatever comes into their heads with no thought for the consequences.[653] Continuously playing to their own self-image as societal outcasts, unfairly punished for their nonconformist brilliance, cyber-activists also often live in a realm where 'groundbreaking' democratic theory tends to consist of 500 words of fact-free, hastily-written blog based on what they can remember from high school history. Their own

---

651 Hagelskamp et al., 'Organizing a Transnational Solidarity' 303.

652 See e.g. Microsoft democracy 'experts' here: Adam J. Hecktman, 'Participatory Budgeting: Decision-Making by Residents' (*Microsoft*, 26 August 2016) <https://blogs.microsoft.com/chicago/2016/08/26/participatory-budgeting-decision-making-by-residents/> accessed 26 January 2023 and here 'I'm Divya Siddarth' <https://www.divyasiddarth.in/> accessed 26 January 2023.

653 See Balaji Srinivasan, *The Network State*, available at <https://thenetworkstate.com/?s=03> as but one example of this.

alleged 'bad-assness' is a perpetual stand-by of conversation and clearly as necessary to their self-identity as saintliness is to social justice warriors.[654]

Stay away from people who want to play amateur hour. They feel no sense of responsibility to constituents or organizers, and rarely have a thorough grounding in
any subject matter.

It is hard enough to create fair processes without someone on board obviously
and offensively trying to make those processes unfair, because they believe they
have unique access to holy truths.

9.5 The Iron Law of Oligarchy

As the ability of the well-funded to monopolize 'democratic innovation' for their
own ends makes apparent, power is a self-centralizing force. Very small advantages and levels of unfairness inevitably accumulate to form greater levels of advantage and unfairness over time. The game Monopoly was invented in order to illustrate this principle on an economic level – and if you have ever played a game of
Monopoly, you will know how players who are able to gain small advantages near
the beginning of the game, can easily turn these into great ones and drive others
off the stage.

Democracy always needs to work against this natural accumulation, continuously breaking up centres of power. One of the most common mistakes people
make is to habitually underestimate the amount of work one has to do to overcome
the natural formation of oligarchy, and we can see this playing out again and
again.

While several things eventually went wrong with PB in Brazil, one of its key
flaws was that it maintained a privileged position for budget delegates. This allowed delegates to amplify their own power, and they used this initial minor advantage to erode the rules that had made PB meaningful.

Originally, any one person could only serve as a budget delegate twice, but this
restriction was dropped in 2008. Soon after, a new rule was issued that to be elected to the highest deliberative body, a person had to have at least 2 years' prior experience as a delegate and have attended 60% of all meetings. These filters favoured incumbents and slowed down turnover, with the highest levels of

654 See e. g. <https://seed.sourceforge.net/ld_k5_article_004.html> cited in Nicolás Mendoza, 'Liquid
Separation: Three Fundamental Dimensions within LiquidFeedback and other Voting Technologies'
(2015) 7(2) Journal of E-Democracy and Open Government 45, 47.

participation tending to be occupied by people who had been re-elected numerous times.[655] Thus, a system that was supposed to enable spontaneous participation from every person, created its own caste. This is why it is so important to reduce and eliminate such positions of privilege at every opportunity. Those who inhabit them will always reassert themselves and attempt to abolish democracy, which becomes too irritating and work-intensive for them. This *exact issue* also surfaced within the Five Star Movement in Italy. Originally M5S also limited members to serving two terms as elected officials. However, as the two terms of many officials neared their end, they worked (successfully) to overturn these limits for local positions, splitting the party in the process.[656]

In Brazil, neighbourhood assemblies became an optional part of PB, and additional rules ensured that participation in the budget delegate process became much more formalized, with different 'sides' representing pre-decided agendas rather than debating spontaneously. Because they essentially made a career out of being budget delegates and needed to retain their power, many people at the upper echelons of Porto Alegre's PB system started to align with city politicians rather than the constituents they were supposed to be representing. While in 1995, 50.7% of participants said that councillors and delegates always answered their demands and consultations, by 2015, this had decreased to 28.3%.[657]

Liquid democracy hasn't fared any better. One researcher who made the effort to track down use cases discovered that most of the communities who pushed for liquid democracy significantly throttled their own use of the platform. The researchers reported that the people they interviewed were often embarrassed to admit that they had never used LiquidFeedback (the Pirate Party's preferred digital platform) to make any actual decisions, but rather merely for question-and-answer sessions. If an issue put forward on the LiquidFeedback platform enjoyed a high level of support, it was put on the agenda for the next in-person assembly. As the researchers put it, this amounted to using an online platform billed as revolutionarily returning power to the people for nothing more than 'floating ideas'. The researchers also spoke to Martin Haase, an academic who at one point held the most proxy votes on LiquidFeedback. He explained that the Party Congress wanted to have the final say on all decisions and thus did not want to use LiquidFeedback for these purposes. As the researchers observed, there is 'a fascinating inversion

655 Tarson Nuñez, 'From a Role Model to a Crisis' in Nelson Dias (ed) *Hope for Democracy: 30 Years of Participatory Budgeting Worldwide* (Epopeia Records, Oficina 2018) 517, 528.
656 Interviews with M5S and former M5S members.
657 Nuñez, 'From a Role Model to a Crisis' 527.

between how the proponents of the platform portray its purpose and the way it is actually used'.[658]

9.6 Conclusions on Challenges

The biggest challenge for digital democracy (or indeed any democracy) is that there is a significant sector of society that simply doesn't want it. Instead, the preference is for a managerial style of politics that refuses to acknowledge the possibility of differing interests and real conflict. Instead, participation is purely demonstrative.

It is interesting to note that as the managerial concept of political participation has been further and further imposed on society, polarization and frustration have grown exponentially. This is because democracy is a method of channelling political energy, thought, agreement and disagreement in a manner that produces knowledge and accountability. If politics is a river, democracy is a waterwheel. Seeking to cut this off with managerial-style methods is like creating a dam instead, a dam which will eventually give way, because the materials do not exist to create a dam capable of coping with the kind of energy political life produces.

In some sense, the challenges enumerated in this chapter are the easiest thing in the world to deal with, since they are completely subjective and require only that the people involved be a little more humble and a little less selfish. This, as democracy itself, is a choice anyone can make at any time.

---

[658] Mendoza, 'Liquid Separation' 55.

Chapter 10
Conclusions

This book has contradicted many conventional beliefs about digital democracy – but they are just that – beliefs. Things people want to be true, but aren't. Their advocates are continuously frustrated by these beliefs not working out, but don't change their theory to fit reality. Above all, they continuously search for the answer to problems in other people (people with fringe beliefs, 'misinformation') or with inanimate technology.

Almost all discourse on democracy today is based on the self-understood premise that the object of 'participation' and 'engagement' is to *get* people to do something or feel something. This is usually accompanied by the belief that conflict, unhappiness and irreconcilable interests can somehow be made to disappear, that the object of democracy is a harmonious existence where everyone realizes that 'we all want the same thing'.

This is a radical, extreme, new interpretation of democracy, which, despite the fact that the word democracy means 'people power' entirely ignores the question of power and aims instead at depoliticizing politics. The challenge of democracy is to figure out what people want and implement it – not to *change* what people want to 'the right thing' or to put a veneer of 'engagement' on whatever decisions have already been made. This is *oppressive* not emancipatory, and continuing to do it leads to more oppression, *never* to emancipation. Democracy depends not on achieving certain objectives, but on creating institutions such as those outlined throughout this book.

I have mentioned a few digital democracy tools throughout these pages, mainly for illustrative purposes. However, even if every tool mentioned in this book eventually disappears the underlying principles will *always* remain the same. There will never be a time in which it is not important to have clear communication or the best data possible. There will never be an instance in which it is not vital to carefully consider how votes are counted in order to accurately express the democratic will. There will also never come a time in which manipulation and the Iron Law of Oligarchy cease to exert their force. It is thus imperative to always work to move democracy forward and upward on the measurement scales we analysed at the beginning of this book, to constantly seek to have more people take part at a higher level of decision-making and to reinforce accountability and the feedback loop.

It is also important to remember that democracy *is* class politics. It is the preferred ruling method of the middle class. The poor want socialism and the rich want aristocracy. Recently, we have seen some try to turn democracy into a

https://doi.org/10.1515/9783110794465-014

rich-poor method of government, whereby the rich rule, but 'give back' to the permanently marginalized, sometimes through small-scale 'democracy' innovations. Every year, this makes more poor people and fewer rich people. When the middle rules, under a democracy, it tries to make as many people as possible middle-class, generally by taxing the very rich and using this money to fund social programmes that prevent people from becoming very poor. Under a well-functioning democracy, every year, more and more people become middle-class. This idea may not appeal to everyone, but I believe it is far better than the alternative, which is a rich-poor feudalism punctuated by very occasional socialist revolts – how humans have existed for the majority of known history.

However, if a sufficient number of municipal offices, political parties, academics and – above all – people start to implement these principles that underlie a virtuous cycle of democratic participation, if we harness the advances in technology (and are neither scared nor blinded by them) and if we celebrate democratic successes (rather than allowing ourselves to be held to unrealistic and unfair standards), then we cannot only overcome entropy, but break the constraints identified by Rousseau and Robert Michels and institute a scalable digital democracy where people aren't just 'heard' or 'get a voice' but they are in power.

Bibliography

Named Authors

Abers, R, I Brandão, R King and D Votto, 'Porto Alegre: Participatory Budgeting and the Challenge of Sustaining Transformative Change' (2018) World Resources Report Case Study, World Resources Institute <https://files.wri.org/d8/s3fs-public/wrr-case-study-porto-alegre_1.pdf>

Agbesi, S, F Tehiru, and A Osei-Owusu, 'Investigating the Feasibility of Implementing E-Voting System in Ghana' (2014) 10(1) International Journal of Innovation and Scientific Research 218

Agrawal, S, S Mani, A Jain and K Ganesan, 'State of Electricity Access in India, Insights from the India Residential Energy Survey (IRES 2020)' (*Council on Energy, Environment and Water, October 2020*) <https://www.ceew.in/publications/state-electricity-access-india>

Ahrens, M, 'Smoke Alarms in US Home Fires' (*National Fire Protection Association*, February 2021) <https://www.nfpa.org/-/media/Files/News-and-Research/Fire-statistics-and-reports/Detection-and-signaling/ossmokealarms.pdf>

Aitamurto, T and J Saldivar, 'Motivating Participation in Crowdsourced Policymaking: The Interplay of Epistemic and Interactive Aspects' (2017) 1(CSCW) Proceedings of the ACM on Human-Computer Interaction <doi.org/10.1145/3134653>.

Aitamurto, T, H Landemore and J Saldivar Galli, 'Unmasking the crowd: Participants' Motivation Factors, Expectations, and Profile in a Crowdsourced Law Reform' (2017) 20(8) Information, Communication and Society 1239

Akintaro, S, 'Top 10 Internet Service Providers in Nigeria Offering Unlimited Data Plans as of January 2023' *Nairametrics* (January 2023)

Allegretti, G, 'Common Patterns in Coping with Under-Representation in Participatory Processes: Evidence from a Mutual Learning Space for Portuguese Local Authorities (LAs)' (2021) 34(5) Innovation: The European Journal of Social Science Research 729

Andrews, K, 'The Dark Triad sums up psychopaths, but the light triad defines saints' *ABC News* (15 May 2019) <https://www.abc.net.au/news/science/2019-05-16/psychopaths-narcissm-the-dark-triad-fascinate-us-the-light-triad/11093104>

Ang, C, 'These are the Countries where Internet Access is Lowest' (World Economic Forum, 17 August 2020) <https://www.weforum.org/agenda/2020/08/internet-users-usage-countries-change-demographics/>

Aragón, P, A Kaltenbrunner, A Calleja-López, A Pereira, A Monterde, XE Barandiaran and V Gómez, 'Deliberative Platform Design: The Case Study of the Online Discussions in Decidim Barcelona' (2017) International Conference on Social Informatics 277

Arhip-Paterson, W and A Brodach, 'Budget participatif de Paris: Analyse des votants papiers et de leurs practiques', Rapport pour la Ville de Paris (December 2018)

Arhip-Paterson, W, 'Budget participatif de Paris: Les comportements des participants numériques dans la durée', Rapport pour la Ville de Paris (April 2019)

Arhip-Paterson, W, 'Budget participatif de Paris: Tendances dans la participation' Rapport pour la Ville de Paris (February 2019)

Arhip-Paterson, W, 'Wear and Tear: Civil Servants Grueling Implementation of Paris Participatory Budgeting (2014–2020)' (2022) COSTAction Working Paper No. 16/2022

Arhip-Paterson, W, A Brodach and T Tence, 'Budget Participatif de Paris: Etude de la répétition du vote numérique à deux éditions consécutives' Rapport pour la Ville de Paris (May 2018)

Ash, L, 'London, France's Sixth Biggest City' *BBC News* (30 May 2012) <https://www.bbc.com/news/magazine-18234930>

Aung, J, 'How to Leverage AI in Community Engagement' (*CitizenLab*, 15 June 2022) <https://www.citizenlab.co/blog/civic-engagement/how-to-leverage-ai-in-community-engagement%ef%bf%bc/> accessed 22 January 2023

Babayan, V and AV Turobov, 'Not Unique, not Universal: Risk Perception and Acceptance of Online Voting Technology by Russian Citizens' (2021) 6 Monitoring of Public Opinion: Economic and Social Changes 319

Baron, S, 'Internet Voting – What New Zealand can Learn from International Trials & Errors', (B.A. Paper, Victoria University of Wellington 2012) <https://www.academia.edu/5426756/Internet_Voting_What_New_Zealand_Can_Learn_From_International_Trials_and_Errors>

Barrett, D, 'Protect Democracy: Vote for Biden' (October 2020) <https://community.expensify.com/discussion/7632/protect-democracy-vote-for-biden> accessed 24 January 2023

Bartlett, R and M Deseriis, 'Loomio and the Problem of Deliberation' *Open Democracy* (2 December 2016) <https://www.opendemocracy.net/en/digitaliberties/loomio-and-problem-of-deliberation/>

Behrends, S, S Geisler, K Kott and M Ziebach, 'Internetzugang, Datenreport 2021' (*Bundeszentrale für politische Bildung*, 10 March 2021) <https://www.bpb.de/kurz-knapp/zahlen-und-fakten/datenreport-2021/private-haushalte-einkommen-und-konsum/329906/internetnutzung/>

Berti Arnoaldi Veli, F, 'Digital Signature for Referendums: Italy in Pole Position in Europe' (*Cloud Signature Consortium*, 31 August 2021) <https://cloudsignatureconsortium.org/digital-signature-for-referendums-italy-in-pole-position-in-europe/>

Bezerra, CP and O Junquiera, 'Why has Participatory Budgeting adoption declined in Brazil?' (114th Annual Meeting & Exhibition of the American Political Science Association, Boston, August 30 – September 2, 2018)

Boghossian, H, *"I Have Nothing to Hide": And 20 Other Myths about Surveillance and Privacy* (Beacon Press 2021)

Borge, R, J Balcells and A Padró-Solanet, 'Democratic Disruption or Continuity? Analysis of the Decidim Platform in Catalan Municipalities' (2022) American Behavioural Scientist

Borge, R, J Brugué and D Duenas-Cide, 'Technology and Democracy: The Who and How in Decision-making: The Cases of Estonia and Catalonia' (2022) 31(3) El Profesional de la Información

Brahimllari, E, *Multi-Layered Participatory Budgeting: The Case of Low-Income Neighbourhoods in Paris* (FrancoAngeli 2020)

Brand, D, 'Queens' 14 Council Districts may Lose Participatory Budgeting for Second Year in a Row' *Queens Daily Eagle* (19 October 2020) <https://queenseagle.com/all/queens-may-lose-participatory-budgeting-for-second-year-in-a-row>

Cabannes, Y and B Lipietz 'Revisiting the Democratic Promise of Participatory Budgeting in Light of Competing Political, Good Governance and Technocratic Logics' (2018) 30(1) Environment and Urbanization 67

Cabannes, Y, 'Participatory Budgeting: Conceptual Framework and its Contribution to Urban Governance and the Millennium Development Goals' (August 2004) UN HABITAT, Urban Management Programme, Working Paper No. 140

Chartier, G, 'Pirate Constitutions and Workplace Democracy' (2010) 18 Annual Review of Law and Ethics, 449

Cheeseman, N, G Lynch and J Willis, 'Digital Dilemmas: The Unintended Consequences of Election Technology' (2018) 25(8) Democratization 1397

Chen, C-H, C-L Liu, BPH Hui and M-L Chung, 'Does Education Background Affect Digital Equal Opportunity and the Political Participation of Sustainable Digital Citizens? A Taiwan Case' (2020) 12(4) Sustainability, Article 1359.

Chwalisz, C, 'An Expansive Year' (*Medium*, 11 January 2023) <https://medium.com/@claudiachwalisz/2022-an-expansive-year-4dfd6f6fb0a4> accessed 18 February 2023

Ciornei, I and E Østergaard-Nielsen, I, 'Transnational Turnout: Determinants of Emigrant Voting in Home Country Elections' (2020) 78 Political Geography

Clark, A, 'Is Participatory Budgeting Real Democracy?: Politics People's Choice Style in Chicago' *Next City* (28 April 2014) <https://nextcity.org/features/is-participatory-budgeting-real-democracy-chicago>

Cliquennois, G, *European Human Rights Justice and Privatisation: The Growing Influence of Foreign Private Funds* (Cambridge University Press 2020)

Coi, G and A Hernandez-Morales, 'Living Cities: European Cities' Big Cash Handover' *Politico* (21 April 2022) <https://www.politico.eu/article/europe-big-city-cash-handover/>

Coleman, S and R Cardoso Sampaio, 'Sustaining a Democratic Innovation: A Study of Three E-Participatory Budgets in Belo Horizonte' 2016 Information, Communication and Society

Collard, S and E Fabre 'Electronic Voting in the French Legislative Elections of 2012' in Dimitrios Zisiss and Dimitrios Lekkas (eds) *Design, Development and Use of Secure Electronic Voting Systems* (IGI Global 2014).

Copeland, L, 'Blacks Feel Auto Industry's Pain: It was Road to Middle Class' *USA Today/ABC News* (21 January 2009) <https://abcnews.go.com/Business/story?id=6694808&page=1>

Creamer, J, EA Shrider, K Burns and F Chen, 'Poverty in the United States 2021: Current Population Reports' (*United States Census Bureau*, September 2022) <https://www.census.gov/content/dam/Census/library/publications/2022/demo/p60-277.pdf>

Curioni, A, 'How Quantum-Safe Cryptography will Ensure a Secure Computing Future' (*World Economic Forum*, 6 July 2022) <https://www.weforum.org/agenda/2022/07/how-quantum-safe-cryptography-will-ensure-a-secure-computing-future/>.

Cutter, C, 'Expensify CEO Urges Customers to Vote Against Trump' *Wall Street Journal* (23 October 2020) <https://www.wsj.com/articles/expensify-ceo-urges-customers-to-vote-against-trump-11603489825>

Daramy, A, 'Why Gambians Won't Stop Voting with Marbles' *BBC* (1 December 2021) <https://www.bbc.com/news/world-africa-59476637>

Davidson, S, 'Digital Inclusion Evidence Review 2018' (*Age UK*, November 2018) <https://www.ageuk.org.uk/globalassets/age-uk/documents/reports-and-publications/age_uk_digital_inclusion_evidence_review_2018.pdf>

Davis, N, 'This is What Martin Luther Tells Us About Today's Technological Disruption' (*World Economic Forum*, 31 October 2017) <https://www.weforum.org/agenda/2017/10/what-we-can-learn-from-martin-luther-about-todays-technological-disruption/>

Desai, Z and A Lee, 'Technology and Protest: The Political Effects of Electronic Voting in India' (2021) 9(2) Political Science Research and Methods 398

Deseriis, M and D Vittori 'The impact of online participation platforms on the internal democracy of two Southern European parties: Podemos and the Five Star Movement' (2019) 13 International Journal of Communication 5696

Deseriis, M, 'Digital Movement Parties: A Comparative Analysis of the Technopolitical Cultures and the Participation Platforms of the Movimento 5 Stelle and the Piratenpartei' (2020) 23(12) Information, Communication and Society 1770

Deseriis, M, 'Direct Parliamentarism: An Analysis of the Political Values Embedded in Rousseau, the 'Operating System' of the Five Star Movement' (2017) 9(2) eJournal of EDemocracy and Open Government 60

Deseriis, M, 'Reducing the Burden of Decision in Digital Democracy Applications: A Comparative Analysis of Six Decision-Making Software' (2021) Science, Technology and Human Values

Drezner, DW, *The Ideas Industry: How Pessimists, Partisans and Plutocrats are transforming the Marketplace of Ideas* (Oxford University Press 2017)

Driskell, J, 'An Atlas of Self-Reliance: The Negro Motorists' Green Book [1937 – 1964]' (National Museum of American History, Behring Center, 30 July 2015) <https://americanhistory.si.edu/blog/negro-motorists-green-book>

Dubner, SJ, 'Mothers and the Model T' (Freakonomics, 4 December 2009) <https://freakonomics.com/2009/12/mothers-and-the-model-t/>

Eason, B, '$120 million in the requests and $40 million in the bank. How an obscure theory helped prioritize the Colorado budget' *The Colorado Sun* (28 May 2019) <https://coloradosun.com/2019/05/28/quadratic-voting-colorado-house-budget/>

Ehin, P, M Solvak, J Willemson and P Vinkel, 'Internet Voting in Estonia 2005 – 2019: Evidence from Eleven Elections' (2022) 39(4) Government Information Quarterly

Ellis-Petersen, H, 'Boaty McBoatface wins poll to name polar research vessel' *Guardian* (17 April 2016)

Essex, A, A Cardillo and N Akinyokun, 'Online Voting in Ontario's Municipal Elections: A Conflict of Legal Principles and Technology?' (Whisper Lab Research Report, Western University 2020) <https://whisperlab.org/ontario-online.pdf>

Faniran, S and K Olaniyan, 'Strengthening Democratic Practice in Nigeria: A Case for E-Voting' (ICE Gov Conference 2011) 337

Ferrazza, R, 'SkyVote, l'alternativa a Rosseau che nel 2020 ha moltiplicato gli utili' *Il Sole 24 Ore* (2 July 2021) <https://www.ilsole24ore.com/art/skyvote-l-alternativa-rosseau-che-2020-ha-moltiplicato-utili-AEqgdRU?refresh_ce=1>

Fieschi, C, *Populocracy: The Tyranny of Authenticity and the Rise of Populism* (Agenda Publishing 2019)

Ford, B, 'Delegative Democracy' (2002) Unpublished paper. Available at http://www.brynosaurus.com/deleg/deleg.pdf

Ford, B, 'Delegative Democracy Revisited' Blog post available at https://bford.github.io/2014/11/16/deleg.html.

Forenbacher, I, S Husnjak, I Cvitić and I Jovović, 'Determinants of Mobile Phone Ownership in Nigeria' (2019) 43(7) Telecommunications Policy, Article 101812

Francis-Devine, B, 'Poverty in the UK: Statistics' (*House of Commons Library*, 29 September 2022) <https://commonslibrary.parliament.uk/research-briefings/sn07096/>.

Freeman, J, 'The Tyranny of Structurelessness' (1972) 17 Berkeley Journal of Sociology 151

Fryth, L, B Batinic and PK Jonason, 'Social media use and personality: Beyond Self-reports and Trait-level Assessments' (2023) 202 Personality and Individual Differences, Article 111960

Fuller, R, 'A Call to Re-Embrace our Privacy' *Los Angeles Review of Books* (31 August 2021)

Fuller, R, *Beasts and Gods: How Democracy Changed Its Meaning and Lost Its Purpose* (Zed/Bloomsbury 2015)

Fuller, R, *In Defence of Democracy* (Polity 2019)

Fuller, R, 'Digital Democracy: Past, Present and Future' in Matt Qvortrup and Daniela Vancic (eds), *Complementary Democracy: The Art of Deliberative Listening* (De Gruyter 2022) 115

Fuller, R, 'Power before People: The Global Crisis of the Faux Democracy Industry and Its Consequences' (Eastern Economics Association Annual Conference, 26 February 2021)

Fuller, R, *2022 Digital Democracy Report* (Solonian Democracy Institute 2022)

Gardels, N 'Another Kind of Democratic Future' (*Noema/Berggruen Institute*, 13 May 2022) accessed 19 March 2023.

Gakunga, M, 'Kenya Lauded for Achieving 75 % Electricity Access Rate' (*COMESA*, 9 June 2021) <https://www.comesa.int/kenya-lauded-for-achieving-75-electricity-access-rate/>

Gelfand, A, 'Participatory Budget Community Meeting' *The Wave* (25 November 2016) <rockawave.com/articles/participatory-budget-community-meeting/>

Geringer-Sameth, E, 'Civic Engagement Commission to Launch Citywide Participatory Budgeting after Pandemic Delay' *Gotham Gazette* (1 May 2022) <https://www.gothamgazette.com/city/11269-nyc-civic-engagement-commission-participatory-budgeting>

Germann, M, 'Internet Voting Increases Expatriate Voter Turnout' (2021) 38(2) Government Information Quarterly

Gilens, M & BI Page, 'Testing Theories of American Politics: Elites, Interest Groups and Average Citizens' (2014) 12(3) Perspectives on Politics 564

Giridharadas, A, *Winners Take All: The Elite Charade of Changing the World* (Knopf 2018)

Glaeser, EL, M Resseger and K Tobio, 'Urban Inequality' WP-2008–10 (Harvard Kennedy School, Taubman Center for State and Local Government) <https://www.hks.harvard.edu/sites/default/files/centers/taubman/files/glaeser_08_inequality.pdf>

Goldenberg, S, 'Mayoral Hopefuls Roast Council Pork' *New York Post* (9 July 2013) <https://nypost.com/2013/07/09/mayoral-hopefuls-roast-council-pork/>.

Goodman, N, 'Online Voting in the City of Markham: Patterns and Trends, 2003–2018' (November 2019) <https://pub-markham.escribemeetings.com/filestream.ashx?DocumentId=19612>

Greenwald, G, 'Nonvoters are Not Privileged. They are Disproportionately Lower-Income, Nonwhite and Dissatisfied with the Two Parties' *The Intercept* (9 April 2020) <https://theintercept.com/2020/04/09/nonvoters-are-not-privileged-they-are-largely-lower-income-non-white-and-dissatisfied-with-the-two-parties/>

Griffin, T, 'He was Meant to Secure an Election: He Turned Up Dead' *BuzzFeed* (5 October 2017) <https://www.buzzfeednews.com/article/tamerragriffin/kenya-chris-msando-murder>

Guinier, L, *The Tyranny of the Majority: Fundamental Fairness in Representative Democracy* (Free Press 1994)

Gurdus, L, 'Boeing CEO: Over 80 % of the world has never taken a flight. We're leveraging that for growth' *CNBC* (7 December 2017) <https://www.cnbc.com/2017/12/07/boeing-ceo-80-percent-of-people-never-flown-for-us-that-means-growth.html>

Hagelskamp, C, C Su, K Valverde Viesca and T Nuñez, 'Organizing a Transnational Solidarity for Social Change through Participatory Practices: The Case of People Powered – Global Hub for Participatory Democracy' (2021) American Journal of Community Psychology

Hagelskamp, C, Silliman, R, Godfrey, EB, and Schleifer, D, 'Shifting Priorities: Participatory Budgeting in New York City is Associated with Increased Investments in Schools, Street and Traffic Improvements, and Public Housing' (2020) 42(2) New Political Science 171

Harrison, S, 'Cambridge Chancellor Donated £8 million to EU Remain Campaign' *Varsity* (26 August 2016) <https://www.varsity.co.uk/news/10588> accessed 18 February 2023

Hayes, HA, N Goodman, RM McGregor, Z Spicer and S Pruysers, 'The Effect of Exogenous Shocks on the Administration of Online Voting: Evidence from Ontario, Canada' (International Joint Conference on Electronic Voting 2022) Lecture Notes in Computer Science, Vol. 13553 (Springer 2022) 70

Hecktman, AJ, 'Participatory Budgeting: Decision-Making by Residents' (Microsoft, 26 August 2016) <https://blogs.microsoft.com/chicago/2016/08/26/participatory-budgeting-decision-making-by-residents/> accessed 26 January 2023

Holmes, H and G Burgess, 'Pay the wi-fi or Feed the Children: Coronavirus has Intensified the UK's Digital Divide' (University of Cambridge) <https://www.cam.ac.uk/stories/digitaldivide>

Honig, B, *Political Theory and the Displacement of Politics* (Cornell University Press 1993)

Hubacher, S, 'Neuchâtel: the New E-Voting Hub' (*Swiss Post*, 25 August 2020) <https://www.post.ch/en/about-us/news/2020/neuchatel-the-new-e-voting-hub>

Jacobs, B and W Pieters 'Electronic Voting in the Netherlands: From early Adoption to early Abolishment' (2009) Foundations of Security Analysis and Design 121

John, P, G Smith and G Stoker, 'Nudge Nudge, Think Think: Two Strategies for Changing Civic Behaviour' (2009) The Political Quarterly

Johnson, C, 'Engaging Democracy: An Institutional Theory of Participatory Budgeting' (DPhil Thesis, University of Washington 2017)

Johnston, N, *2016 Overseas Citizen Population* (Federal Voting Assistance Programme, September 2018) <https://www.fvap.gov/uploads/FVAP/Reports/FVAP-2016-OCPA-FINAL-Report.pdf>

Juvonen, A, 'A Framework for Comparing the Security of Voting Schemes' (Masters Thesis, University of Helsinki 2019)

Kant, I, 'Was ist Aufklärung?' *Berlinische Monatsschrift* (December 1784).

Kasdan, A and L Cattell, *A People's Budget: A Research and Evaluation Report on the Pilot Year of Participatory Budgeting in New York City* (The Urban Justice Center and PBNYC Research Team 2012)

Kasdan, A, Lindsay Cattell and Pat Convey, *A People's Budget: A Research and Evaluation Report on Participatory Budgeting in New York City, Year 2* (Urban Justice Center 2013).

Katwala, A, 'Quantum Computing and Quantum Supremacy Explained' *Wired* (5 March 2020) <https://www.wired.co.uk/article/quantum-computing-explained>

Kaufman, SB, 'The Light Triad vs Dark Triad of Personality' *Scientific American* (19 March 2019) <https://blogs.scientificamerican.com/beautiful-minds/the-light-triad-vs-dark-triad-of-personality/>

Kemp, S, 'Digital 2021, Nigeria' (*DataReportal*, 11 February 2021) <https://datareportal.com/reports/digital-2021-nigeria>

Kemp, S, 'Digital 2021: France' (*DataReportal*, 10 February 2022) <https://datareportal.com/reports/digital-2021-france>

Kennedy, R, AE Sokhey, C Abernathy, KM Esterling, DMJ Lazer, A Lee, W Minozzi and M Neblo, 'Demographics and (Equal?) Voice: Assessing Participation in Online Deliberative Sessions' (2020) 69(1) Political Studies

Kersting, N, 'Online Participation: From 'Invited' to 'Invented' Spaces' 6(4) International Journal of Electronic Governance 270

Kimbi, S and I Zlotnikova 'A Secure Model for Remote Electronic Voting: A Case of Tanzania' (2014) 3(4) Advances in Computer Science: An International Journal 95

Kircaburun, K and MD Griffiths, 'The dark side of internet: Preliminary Evidence for the Associations of Dark Personality Traits with Specific Online Activities and Problematic Internet Use' (2018) 7(4) Journal of Behavioural Addictions, 993

Klippenstein, K and L Fang, 'Truth Cops: Leaked Documents Outline DHS's Plans to Police Disinformation' *The Intercept* (31 October 2022) <https://theintercept.com/2022/10/31/social-media-disinformation-dhs/>

Krimmer, R, D Duenas-Cid and I Krivonosova, 'New Methodology for Calculating Cost-Efficiency of Different Ways of Voting: Is Internet Voting Cheaper?' (2021) 41(1) Public Money and Management 17

Krugman, P, 'Why Do the Rich have so much Power?' *New York Times* (1 July 2020)

Kuo, L, 'Kenya's National Electrification Campaign is Taking Less than Half the Time it Took America' *Quartz* (16 January 2017) <https://qz.com/africa/882938/kenya-is-rolling-out-its-national-electricity-program-in-half-the-time-it-took-america/>

Lalwani, V, 'Why has the Modi Government's Plan to make Food Grain more Accessible not Taken Off?' *Quartz* (7 July 2021) <https://qz.com/india/2030281/why-modis-one-nation-one-ration-for-india-hasnt-taken-off/>

Lee, C, *Do-It-Yourself Democracy: The Rise of the Public Engagement Industry* (Oxford University Press 2015)

Lerner, J and D Secondo, 'By the People, For the People: Participatory Budgeting from the Bottom Up in North America' (2012) 8(2) Journal of Public Deliberation, Article 2

Lerner, J, *Making Democracy Fun: How Game Design can Empower Citizens and Transform Politics* (MIT Press 2014)

Li, Y, Y Zhu and C Owen, 'Participatory budgeting and the party: Generating 'citizens orderly participation' through party-building in Shanghai' (2022) Journal of Chinese Governance 56.

London, S and M Engel, *Immigration: Who Should we Welcome, What Should We Do?* (National Issues Forums Institute 2020)

Luhmann, N, 'Familiarity, Confidence, Trust: Problems and Alternatives' in Diego Gambetta (ed) *Trust: Making and Breaking of Cooperative Relations* (Oxford 1988) 94

MacGuill, D, 'We now have more female TDs than ever before – but do we really have gender quotas to thank?' *The Journal* (1 March 2016) <http://www.thejournal.ie/women-in-32nd-dail-election-2016-2630150-Mar2016/>

Mair, P, *Ruling the Void: The Hollowing of Western Democracy* (Verso 2013)

Matsusaka, J, *Let the People Rule: How Direct Democracy can Meet the Populist Challenge* (Princeton University Press 2020)

Matthews-King, A 'Over 40s Should Pay New Tax to Fund Creaking Social Care, A, MPs Say' *Independent* (27 June 2018) <https://www.independent.co.uk/news/health/social-care-tax-over-40s-retirement-pension-nursing-home-meals-a8418171.html> accessed 26 January 2023

McGoey, L, *No Such Thing as a Free Gift: The Gates Foundation and the Price of Philanthropy* (Verso 2016)

McIntosh, J, 'Who are Italy's Two Leading Populist Parties: Five Star Movement and the League?' *Deutsche Welle* (6 March 2018) <https://www.dw.com/en/who-are-italys-two-leading-populist-parties-five-star-movement-and-the-league/a-42838238>

McNicoll, T, 'Mapped: Expats Kick Off French Legislative Elections with Online Voting' *France 24* (27 May 2022) <https://www.france24.com/en/france/20220527-mapped-expats-kick-off-french-legislative-elections-with-online-voting>

Mearian, L, 'Utah county moves to expand mobile voting through blockchain' *ComputerWorld* (21 October 2019) <https://www.computerworld.com/article/3446836/utah-county-moves-to-expand-mobile-voting-through-blockchain.html>

Megill, C, 'Pol.is in Taiwan' (*Medium*, 25 May 2016) <https://blog.pol.is/pol-is-in-taiwan-da7570d372b5>

Mendez, F and U Serdült, 'What drives fidelity to internet voting? Evidence from the roll–out of internet voting in Switzerland' (2017) 34(3) Government Information Quarterly 511

Mendoza, N, 'Liquid Separation: Three Fundamental Dimensions within LiquidFeedback and other Voting Technologies' (2015) 7(2) Journal of E-Democracy and Open Government 45

Mercier, H, *Not Born Yesterday: The Science of Who We Trust and What We Believe* (Princeton University Press 2020).

Messina, S, 'M5S e l'addio di Casaleggio, la penosa fine di un imbroglio spacciato per democrazia' *La Repubblica* (6 June 2021) <https://www.repubblica.it/politica/2021/06/06/news/m5s_rousseau_davide_casaleggio-304409994/>

Michels, R, *Political Parties: A Sociological Study of the Oligarchical Tendency of Modern Democracy* (Verlag Werner Klinkhardt 1911)

Miscoiu, S and S Gherghina 'Poorly designed deliberation: explaining the banlieues' non-involvement in the Great Debate' (2021) 34(5) Innovation: The European Journal of Social Science Research 694

Mokre, M and T Ehs, 'If no Vote, at least Voice? The Potential and Limits of Deliberative Procedures for the Creation of a more Inclusive Democracy' (2021) 34(5) Innovation: The European Journal of Social Science Research 712

Montesquieu, C, *The Spirit of Laws, Volume 1* (Thomas Nugent tr, first published 1748/1752, Batoche Books 2001)

Moreau, É and W Arhip-Paterson, 'Budget participatif de Paris: Qui sont les Parisiens qui y participants?' (2018) No. 123 Atelier Parisiene de Urbanisme <https://www.apur.org/sites/default/files/documents/publication/etudes/note_123_budget_participatif.pdf>

Mouffe, C, 'Deliberative Democracy or Agonistic Pluralism' (2000) Institute for Advanced Studies, Vienna

Neblo, MA, KM Esterling and DMJ Lazer, *Politics with the People: Building a Directly Representative Democracy* (Cambridge University Press 2018).

Neblo, MA, KM Esterling, R Kennedy, D Lazer and AE Sokhey 'Who Wants to Deliberate and Why?' (15 September 2019) HKS Working Paper No. RWP09 – 027

Nez, H, 'Les budgets participatifs européens peinent à lutter contre la ségrégation' (2013) 74 Mouvements 123

Noveck, BS, *Smart Citizens, Smarter State: The Technologies of Expertise and the Future of Governing* (Harvard University Press 2015)

Ntwayame, L, 'A Conceptual Model for Designing and Implementation of Secure and Trustable Remote Electronic Voting within the Developing World' (MSc, Botswana International University of Science and Technology 2018)

Nuñez, T, 'From a Role Model to a Crisis' in Nelson Dias (ed) *Hope for Democracy: 30 Years of Participatory Budgeting Worldwide* (Epopeia Records, Oficina 2018)

Nyabola, N, *Digital Democracy: Analogue Politics: How the Internet Era is Transforming Politics in Kenya* (Zed Books 2018)

Nylen, WR, 'The Making of a Loyal Opposition: The Workers' Party (PT) and the Consolidation of Democracy in Brazil' in Peter R. Kingstone and Timothy J Power (eds), *Democratic Brazil: Actors, Institutions and Processes* (University of Pittsburgh Press 2000)

O'Connor, C, *Gotham Gazette* <https://www.gothamgazette.com/govermnent/5946-participatory-budget>

O'Neill, A, 'Voter Turnout in US Presidential Elections by Age 1964 – 2020' (*Statista*, 21 June 2022) <https://www.statista.com/statistics/1096299/voter-turnout-presidential-elections-by-age-historical/>

Opinko, D, '"Oki" Signs with Indigenous Art to be Displayed across Lethbridge' *Lethbridge News Now* (28 September 2022) <https://lethbridgenewsnow.com/2022/09/28/oki-signs-with-indigenous-art-to-be-displayed-across-lethbridge/>.

Orr, A, *Direct Democracy Manifesto: Politics for the 21st Century* <http://www.kulanu-nahlit.org/English. htm#mozTocId192120>.

Ostwald, M, *From Popular Sovereignty to the Sovereignty of Law: Law, Society and Politics in Fifth-Century Athens* (University of California Press 1986).

Pape, M and J Lerner, 'Budgeting for Equity: How Can Participatory Budgeting Advance Equity in the United States' (2016) 12(2) Journal of Deliberative Democracy, Article 9

Park, S, M Specter, N Narula and RL Rivest, 'Going from Bad to Worse: From Internet Voting to Blockchain Voting' (2021) 7(1) Journal of Cybersecurity.

Paul, E, 'The Cost of Internet Data in Nigeria is Increasing, but it is Not Really Obvious' *Techpoint Africa* (23 June 2020) <https://techpoint.africa/2020/06/23/internet-data-nigeria-increased/>

Paulhus, DL and KM Williams, 'The Dark Triad of Personality: Narcissism, Machiavellianism and Psychopathy' (2002) 36(6) Journal of Research and Personality 556

Pearce, N, 'Juncture Interview: Bonnie Honig' *IPPR* (6 March 2013) <https://www.ippr.org/juncture/juncture-interview-bonnie-honig>

Peixoto, T, 'E-Participatory Budgeting: E-Democracy from Theory to Success?' (2008) Zurich University, E-Democracy Center Working Paper

Peixoto, T, 'Unequal Participation: Open Government's Unresolved Dilemma' (*DemocracySpot*, February 2013) <https://democracyspot.net/2013/02/>

Peixoto, T, P Spada, J Mellon and FM Sjoberg, 'Effects of the Internet on Participation: Study of a Public Policy Referendum in Brazil' (2015) World Bank Policy Research Working Paper 7204

Petitpas, A, JM Jaquet and P Sciarini, 'Does E-Voting Matter for Turnout, and to Whom?' (2020) 71(4) Electoral Studies

Peverelli, R and R de Feniks, 'Guardtime: the World's Largest Blockchain Company' (*Digital Insurance Agenda*, 24 April 2017) <digitalinsuranceagenda.com> accessed 17 February 2023

Piketty, T, *Capital in the 21st Century* (Harvard University Press 2017)

Piscopo, JM, 'How Women Vote: Separating Myth from Reality' (*Smithsonian Magazine*, 6 October 2020) <https://www.smithsonianmag.com/history/how-have-women-voted-suffrage-180975979/>

Pogrebinschi, T and D Samuels, 'The Impact of Participatory Democracy Evidence from Brazil's National Public Policy Conferences' (2014) Comparative Politics 313

Pope, H, 'How Non-Expertise Becomes a Strength' (*DemocracyNext*, January 2023) <https://demnext. substack.com/p/how-non-expertise-becomes-a-strength> accessed 26 January 2023

Prewitt, M and P Healy, *The Handbook for Radical Local Democracy v2.0* (RadicalXChange Foundation) <https://www.radicalxchange.org/media/papers/The_Handbook_for_Radical_Local_Democracy. pdf> accessed 22 January 2023.

Pukas, A, 'Lebanese across the globe: How the country's international community came to be' *Arab News* (4 May 2018) <https://www.arabnews.com/node/1296211/middle-east>

Putnam, RD, *Bowling Alone: The Collapse and Revival of American Community* (Simon and Schuster 2000)

Qvortrup, M *A Comparative Study of Referendums: Government by the People* (2nd edn, Manchester University Press 2005)

Rajagopal, D and A Sharma, 'Canada's Anti-Trust Tribunal Clears C$20 billion Rogers-Shaw Deal' *Reuters* (30 December 2022) <https://www.reuters.com/markets/deals/canada-competition-tribunal-approves-c20-bln-rogers-shaw-merger-2022-12-30/>

Reginald, NE, 'Mobile, Secure E – Voting Architecture for the Nigerian Electoral System' (2015) 17(2) IOSR Journal of Computer Engineering 27

Renault-Tinacci, M and W Arhip-Paterson, *Implications des Associations dans le democratie participative: le cas du budget participatif parisien* (Institut national de la jeunesse et de l'éducation Populaire, September 2020) <https://injep.fr/wp-content/uploads/2020/09/IAS38_democratie-participative.pdf>

Ribble, B, 'PBNYC: The Challenges and Opportunities of Scale' (Harvard Ash Center, *Medium*, 7 December 2016) <https://medium.com/challenges-to-democracy/pbnyc-the-challenges-and-opportunities-of-scale-951dabeae8d>

Roger, P, 'Legislative elections: First round kicks off for French citizens abroad, with flawed online Voting' *Le Monde* (4 June 2022) <https://www.lemonde.fr/en/politics/article/2022/06/04/legislative-elections-first-round-kicks-off-for-french-citizens-abroad-with-flawed-online-voting_5985648_5.html>

Rogers, EM, *Diffusion of Innovations* (5th edn, Free Press 2003).

Rogier, G and P Velotti, 'Narcissistic Implications in Gambling Disorder: The Mediating Role of Emotion Dysregulation' (2018) 34 Journal of Gambling Studies 1241

Rose, R, 'What Could a Labour Government Do To Undo Brexit?' (*Policy Network Opinions*, 24 July 2020) <https://policynetwork.progressivebritain.org/opinions/blogs/what-could-labour-government-do-undo-brexit/> accessed 25 January 2023.

Roser, M, 'Literacy Rate in England and the UK since 1580' (*Our World in Data*) <https://ourworldindata.org/literacy#historical-change-in-literacy> accessed 25 February 2023

Roser, M and Ortiz-Ospina, E, 'Literacy' (*Our World in Data*, 20 September 2018) https://ourworldindata.org/literacy accessed 19 March 2023

Rousseau, J, *The Social Contract and Discourses* (G.D.H. Cole tr, E.P. Dutton & Co 1913)

Savitch-Lew, A, 'Factcheck: Has Councilmember Perkins Ever Participated in Participatory Budgeting?' *City Limits* (25 September 2017)

Schattschneider, E, *Party Government: American Government in Action* (Taylor & Francis Group 2004)

Schwartz, EI, 'Direct Democracy: Are you ready for the Democracy Channel?' *Wired* (1 January 1994) <www.wired.com/1994/01/e-dem/>

Schwartz, PM, 'The Computer in German and American Constitutional Law: Towards and American Right of Informational Self-Determination' (1989) 37 American Journal of Comparative Law, 676

Serdült, U and M Germann, 'Internet Voting for Expatriates: The Swiss Case' (2014) 6(2) eJournal of eDemocracy and Open Government 197

Serdült, U, 'Switzerland' in Matt Qvortrup (ed) *Referendums Around the World* (Palgrave Macmillan 2018)

Serdült, U, M Germann, F Mendez, A Portenier and C Wellig, 'Fifteen Years of Internet Voting in Switzerland: History, Governance and Use' in Luis Teran & Andreas Meier (eds), *Second International Conference on eDemocracy & eGovernment (ICEDEG)* (2015)

Serdült, U, M Germann, M Harris, F Mendez and A Portenier 'Who are the Internet Voters' in E. Tambouris et al. (eds), *Electronic Government and Electronic Participation* (IOS Press 2015)

Severns, M, 'Top Dem Strategists Launch Secret Money Group to Rebrand Party' *Politico* (29 April 2019) <https://www.politico.com/story/2019/04/29/democrats-money-future-majority-1291388>

Shryen, G and E Rich, 'Security in Large-Scale Internet Elections: A Retrospective Analysis of Elections in Estonia, The Netherlands, and Switzerland' (2010) 4(4) IEEE Transactions on Information Forensics and Security 729

Simitis, S, 'Reviewing Privacy in an Information Society' (1987) 135(3) University of Pennsylvania Law Review 710

Smith, G, *Democratic Innovations: Designing Institutions for Citizen Participation* (Cambridge University Press 2009).

Solvak, M, '"Stickiness" of eVoting' in Mihkel Solvak and Kristjan Vassil (eds), *E-voting in Estonia: Technological Diffusion and other Developments over Ten Years, 2005–2015* (Johan Skytte Institute of Political Studies, University of Tartu 2016)

Solvak, M, 'Mobilization' in Mihkel Solvak and Kristjan Vassil (eds), *E-voting in Estonia: Technological Diffusion and other Developments over Ten Years, 2005–2015* (Johan Skytte Institute of Political Studies, University of Tartu 2016)

Solvak, M, 'Verification and Trust' in Mihkel Solvak and Kristjan Vassil (eds), *E-voting in Estonia: Technological Diffusion and other Developments over Ten Years, 2005–2015* (Johan Skytte Institute of Political Studies, University of Tartu, 2016)

Souza, C, 'Participatory Budgeting in Brazilian Cities: Limits and Possibilities in Building Democratic Institutions' (2001) 13(1) Environment and Urbanization 159

Srinivasan, B, *The Network State*, available at <https://thenetworkstate.com/?s=03>

Staveley, E, *Greek and Roman Voting and Elections* (Thames and Hudson, 1972)

Stefanello, V, 'Italy Gets Closer to Referendum Decriminalizing Cannabis' *EurActiv* (17 September 2021) <https://www.euractiv.com/section/politics/short_news/italy-gets-closer-to-referendum-de criminalising-cannabis/>

Stéphan, N, '48.7 million voters registered for the 2022 presidential election' INSEE Focus No. 264, (Institute National de le Statistique et des Etudes economiques, 24 March 2022), <https://www.insee.fr/en/statistiques/6327287>

Su, C, 'Beyond Inclusion: Critical Race Theory and Participatory Budgeting' (2017) CUNY Graduate Center

Surian, A, 'Foreword' in Estela Brahimllari, *Multi-Layered Participatory Budgeting: The Case of Low-Income Neighbourhoods in Paris* (FrancoAngeli 2020)

Surowiecki, J, *The Wisdom of Crowds* (Anchor Books 2005)

Szczepańska, A, M Zagroba and K Pietrzyk, 'Participatory Budgeting as a Method for Improving Public Spaces in Major Polish Cities' (2022) 162 Social Indicators Research 231

Taber, CS and MR Lodge, 'Motivated Skepticism in the Evaluation of Political Beliefs' (50) American Journal of Political Science (2006) 755

Thomson-DeVeaux, A and M Conroy, 'Women won the Right to Vote 100 Years Ago. They Didn't Start Voting Differently from Men until 1980' (*FiveThirtyEight*, 19 August 2020) <https://five thirtyeight.com/features/women-won-the-right-to-vote-100-years-ago-they-didnt-start-voting-dif ferently-from-men-until-1980/>.

Turner, E, 'The 5 Star Movement and its Discontents: A Tale of Blogging, Comedy, Electoral Success and Tensions' (2013) 5(2) Interface: A Journal for and about Social Movements 178

Uberoi, E, *Turnout at Elections* (House of Commons Library, 26 August 2021) <https://assets-learning.parliament.uk/uploads/2021/12/Turnout-at-Elections.pdf>

Unt, T, M Solvak and K Vassil, 'Does Internet Voting make Elections less Social? Group Voting Patterns in Estonian e-voting Log Files (2013–2015)' (2017) 12(5) PLoS ONE

Unt, T, M Solvak and K Vassil, 'E-vote Log Files 2013–2015' in Mihkel Solvak and Kristjan Vassil (eds), *E-voting in Estonia: Technological Diffusion and other Developments over Ten Years, 2005–2015* (Johan Skytte Institute of Political Studies, University of Tartu 2016) 71

Vancic, D, 'First Ever Online Collection of Signatures sets Italy Up for Referendum on Euthanasia' (*Democracy International*, 10 September 2021) <https://www.democracy.community/stories/first-ever-online-collection-signatures-sets-italy-referendum-euthanasia>

Vassil, K and M Solvak, 'Diffusion of E-Voting in Estonia' in Mihkel Solvak and Kristjan Vassil (eds), *E-voting in Estonia: Technological Diffusion and other Developments over Ten Years, 2005 – 2015* (Johan Skytte Institute of Political Studies, University of Tartu 2016).

Vassil, K, 'Political Neutrality of E-Voting' in Mihkel Solvak and Kristjan Vassil (eds), *E-voting in Estonia: Technological Diffusion and other Developments over Ten Years, 2005 – 2015* (Johan Skytte Institute of Political Studies, University of Tartu 2016) 142

Vassil, K, 'The Estonian e-government ecosystem' in Mihkel Solvak and Kristjan Vassil (eds), *E-voting in Estonia: Technological Diffusion and other Developments over Ten Years, 2005 – 2015* (Johan Skytte Institute of Political Studies, University of Tartu 2016)

Vassil, K, M Solvak and P Vinkel, 'The Diffusion of Internet Voting: Usage Patterns of Internet Voting in Estonia between 2005 and 2015' (2016) 33(3) Government Information Quarterly

Vevea, B, 'What Would You Do With A Million Dollars? Whether Participatory Budgeting Is Worth The Effort' *WBEZ* (9 December 2017) <https://www.wbez.org/stories/what-would-you-do-with-a-million-dollars-whether-participatory-budgeting-is-worth-the-effort/ac8a69e6-8ad0-44bd-adb7-30de877601c6>.

Vittles, P, 'Let's Think Deeply about Citizens' Assemblies & Citizens' Juries' (*Medium*, 15 November 2020) <https://paulvittles.medium.com/lets-think-deeply-about-citizens-assemblies-citizens-juries-2038daa37b8d>

Wampler, B, 'Citizen Participation and Participatory Institutions in Brazil' in *The People Shall Govern: Public Participation Beyond Slogans, Deliberations of the International Conference on Public Participation 2012* (Gauteng Legislature 2012) 88

Wampler, B and B Goldfrank, *The Rise, Spread and Decline of Brazil's Participatory Budgeting: The Arc of a Democratic Innovation* (Palgrave MacMillan 2022)

Wasim, A, 'RTS Controversy likely to haunt ECP, Nadra for a long time' *Dawn* (2 August 2018) <https://www.dawn.com/news/1424394>

West, RF, RJ Meserve and K Stanovich, 'Cognitive Sophistication does not Attenuate the Bias Blind Spot' 103(3) Journal of Personality and Social Psychology (2012) 506

Williams, D and D Waisanen, *Real Money, Real Power? The Challenges with Participatory Budgeting in New York City* (Palgrave MacMillan 2020)

Winter, G, *Inside BOSS, South Africa's Secret Police: An Ex-Spy's Dramatic and Shocking Exposé* (Penguin 1981)

Woodhouse, T, 'Advancing Meaningful Connectivity: Towards Active and Participatory Digital Societies' (*Alliance for Affordable Internet*, 2022) <https://a4ai.org/wp-content/uploads/2022/02/FullreportFINAL.pdf>.

Zuboff, S, *The Age of Surveillance Capitalism: The Fight for a Human Future at the New Frontier of Power* (Public Affairs 2019)

Zucman, G, *The Hidden Wealth of Nations: The Scourge of Tax Havens* (University of Chicago Press 2015)

Online Sources and Organizational Sources

AACOM, 'Climbing the Ladder: A Look at Sherry R. Arnstein' <https://www.aacom.org/become-a-doc
tor/financial-aid-and-scholarships/sherry-r-arnstein-minority-scholarship/sherry-arnstein-biogra
phy>

ACE Electoral Knowledge Network <https://aceproject.org/electoral-advice/archive/questions/replies/
912993749/mobile_conversation_view> accessed 23 January 2023

AFP, 'Cosmonaut Votes on Putin's Reforms from ISS' *The Moscow Times* (30 June 2020) <www.themo
scowtimes.com/2020/06/30/russian-cosmonaut-votes-on-putins-reforms-from-iss-a70742>
accessed 1 February 2023

Alliance for Affordable Internet, 'Advancing Meaningful Connectivity: Towards Active and
Participatory Digital Societies' (28 February 2022) <https://a4ai.org/research/advancing-mean
ingful-connectivity-towards-active-and-participatory-digital-societies/>.

ARD/ZDF, 'ARD/ZDF-Onlinestudie 2022: Mediale Inhalte verstärken Internetnutzung' (10 November
2022) <https://www.ard-zdf-onlinestudie.de/ardzdf-onlinestudie/pressemitteilung/>

Assembly Voting, 'Assembly Pre-Election' <https://assemblyvoting.com/products/pre-election/>

Assembly Voting, 'Black Box Voting vs End-to-End Verifiable Voting' (19 April 2022) <https://assem
blyvoting.com/blog/black-box-voting-vs-e-2-e-verifiable-voting/> accessed 24 January 2023

Assembly Voting, 'Flexible Conference System: From Hybrid Model to 100% Digital Party Congress',
(22 May 2021) <https://assemblyvoting.com/customer-stories/flexible-conference-system-from-hy
brid-model-to-100-digital-party-congress/>

Assembly Voting, 'How the Danish Society of Engineers Navigates Complex Elections with Assembly
Voting' (20 May 2022) <https://assemblyvoting.com/customer-stories/how-the-danish-society-of-
engineers-navigates-complex-elections-with-assembly-voting/>

Athens Democracy Forum, 'Partners' https://www.athensdemocracyforum.com/partner-with-us/part
ners/ accessed 26 February 2023.

Atlas Mundial dos Orçamentos Participativos (OFICINA) <http://www.oficina.org.pt/atlas.html>

Bloomberg, 'Bloomberg Billionaires Index' (11 February 2023) <https://www.bloomberg.com/billion
aires/profiles/pierre-m-omidyar/> accessed 11 February 2023

Breaking Latest News, 'Mr. SkyVote: "Our Voting Model is the Opposite of Rousseau"' (17 June 2021)
<https://www.breakinglatest.news/health/mr-skyvote-our-voting-model-is-the-opposite-of-rous
seau/>

Central Statistics Office, 'Census of Population 2016 – Profile 9, Health, Disability and Carers'
<https://www.cso.ie/en/releasesandpublications/ep/p-cp9hdc/p8hdc/p9d/>

Central Statistics Office, 'Population and Migration Estimates, April 2017' (28 September 2017)
<https://www.cso.ie/en/csolatestnews/póessreleases/2017pressreleases/populationandmi
grationestimatesapril2017/>.

Chicago's Participatory Budgeting Project (*Participedia*) <https://participedia.net/case/43>

CitizenLab, 'Automated Text Analysis Tool' <https://www.citizenlab.co/platform-features/insights>
accessed 22 January 2023

City of Lethbridge, 'City Council approves 2022–2031 CIP Recommendations' (1 June 2021)

City of Lethbridge, 'City of Lethbridge 2022–2031 Capital Improvement Programme' <https://www.
lethbridge.ca/City-Government/Financial-Documents/Documents/CIP/2022-2031CIPFinal.pdf>
accessed 24 January 2023

City of Lethbridge, 'City of Lethbridge Capital Budget' <https://lethbridgecipbudget.ethelo.net/page/
Community%20Group%20Projects> accessed 16 February 2023

City of Lethbridge, 'City of Lethbridge Capital Budget' <https://lethbridgecipbudget.ethelo.net/page/welcome> accessed 16 February 2023

City of Lethbridge, 'City of Lethbridge: Indigenous Placemaking Strategy and Public Realm Audit' (13 April 2022).

City of Lethbridge, 'Lethbridge Census Online, 2019 Census Results' <https://www.lethbridge.ca/City-Government/Census/Documents/2019%20Final%20Census%20Report.pdf>

City of Lethbridge, 'Mayors and Councillors' <https://www.lethbridge.ca/City-Government/City-Council/Pages/default.aspx> accessed 22 December 2022.

Civica, 'Insights from our over 70s' https://www.civica.com/en-gb/campaign-library-uk/2020/a-word-from-the-wise/insights-from-our-over70s/

Claudia Chwalisz tweet (7 September 2022) https://twitter.com/ClaudiaChwalisz/status/1567397860903161856?t=slJU5dbPRKWu94dvnlKY4Q&s=03

Cleveland Clinic, 'Mild Cognitive Impairment' (18 March 2019) <https://my.clevelandclinic.org/health/diseases/17990-mild-cognitive-impairment>

COFRA Holding, 'Working, Investing and Giving Together' <https://www.cofraholding.com/en/family/> accessed 17 January 2023

Connectivity Technology Blog, 'Paris Metro is Now 100% Covered with LTE' (July 22 2020) <https://www.connectivity.technology/2020/07/paris-metro-is-now-100-covered-with-lte.html>

Current Time, 'Moscow Voters Debate: Did Blockchain-Based Online Voting Undermine the Opposition?' (24 September 2021) <https://en.currenttime.tv/a/moscow-voters-debate-did-blockchain-based-online-voting-undermine-russia-s-opposition-/31476383.html> accessed 1 February 2023

Cybernetica, 'X-Road as Created by Cybernetica' (2 November 2021) <https://cyber.ee/resources/case-studies/x-road-as-created-by-cybernetica/> accessed 26 February 2023.

Decidim Barcelona, 'Pla d'Actuació Municipal 2016–2019: Seguiment Actuacions' <https://www.decidim.barcelona/processes/pam/f/8/> accessed 25 January 2023

Delib, 'Citizen Space for Hamilton City Council New Zealand' https://www.delib.net/citizen_space/resources/citizen-space-for-statutory-consultation

Democracy Next, 'Terms of Reference, Chief Operations Officer' <https://demnext.org/wp-content/uploads/2022/11/democracynext-terms-of-reference-coo.pdf> accessed 11 March 2023

Demoex, 'Information about Demoex' <http://demoex.se/en/>

Department for Communities and Local Government, 'English Housing Survey, Smoke Alarms in English Homes Report 2014–2015' (July 2016) <https://assets.publishing.service.gov.uk/government/uploads/system/uploads/attachment_data/file/539096/Smoke_Alarms_in_English_Homes_Full_Report.pdf>.

Department of Foreign Affairs, Irish Abroad Unit, 'Irish Emigration Patterns and Citizens Abroad' (20 June 2017) <https://www.dfa.ie/media/dfa/alldfawebsitemedia/newspress/publications/ministersbrief-june2017/1-Global-Irish-in-Numbers.pdf>

Der Spiegel, 'Offline in Deutschland: Mehrere Millionen Bürger leben ohne Internet' (5 April 2022) <https://www.spiegel.de/netzwelt/web/internetnutzung-in-deutschland-mehrere-millionen-buerger-leben-offline-a-fc4b289d-a6bc-488c-837d-912bdd5263e3>

Discuto, 'Überarbeitung Umweltzeichen Tourismus – Überblick/Ausblick/Anhang' <www.discuto.io/en/informationsseite/ueberarbeitung-umweltzeichen-tourismus-ueberblick-ausblick-anhang>

DLR County Council, 'Traffic and Road Safety: Taney Road to N11 Active Travel Route' <https://dlrco.citizenspace.com/transportation/taney-road-to-n11-active-travel-route/> accessed 25 January 2023

E-Estonia, 'Factsheet: Cyber Security' <https://e-estonia.com/wp-content/uploads/cyber-security-fact sheet-aug2022.pdf> accessed 26 February 2023

E-Estonia, 'Factsheet: KSI Blockchain in Estonia' <https://e-estonia.com/wp-content/uploads/2019sept_ faq-ksi-blockchain-1-1.pdf> accessed 24 January 2023

E-Governance Academy, 'E-Governance Factsheet' <https://e-estonia.com/wp-content/uploads/e-gover nance-factsheet-aug2022.pdf>

E-Governance Academy, 'Factsheet: E-Governance' <https://e-estonia.com/wp-content/uploads/e-gover nance-factsheet-sep2021.pdf> accessed 11 January 2023

Economic Times, 'India to have 900 Million Active Internet Users by 2025, says Report' (3 June 2021) <https://economictimes.indiatimes.com/tech/technology/india-to-have-900-million-active-internet-users-by-2025-says-report/articleshow/83200683.cms?from=mdr>

Elections Canada, 'Estimation of Voter Turnout by Age Group and Gender at the 2019 General Election' <https://www.elections.ca/content.aspx?section=res&dir=rec/eval/pes2019/vtsa2&docu ment=p1&lang=e>

Elections Canada, 'FAQs on Voting' <https://www.elections.ca/content.aspx?section=vot&dir=faq&docu ment=faqvoting&lang=e#a4> accessed 23 January 2023

Elections Saskatchewan, 'Vouching' <https://www.elections.sk.ca/what-we-do/glossary/vouching/> accessed 23 January 2023

Enterprise Estonia, 'E-democracy and Open Data' <https://e-estonia.com/solutions/e-governance/e-de mocracy/> accessed 23 January 2023

Esmee Fairbairn Foundation, 'Our Natural World' <https://esmeefairbairn.org.uk/our-aims/our-natu ral-world/> accessed 26 January 2023

Essex County Council, 'Everyone' <https://consultations.essex.gov.uk/rci/libraries-survey/> accessed 25 January 2023

Ethelo, 'Gaming the System to Fight Climate Change: London, Canada' <https://ethelo.com/case-stud ies-directory/london-climate-case-study/> accessed 26 January 2023

Ethelo, 'London Climate Action Plan Simulator' <https://blog.ethelo.org/hubfs/Case%20Study%20Re ports/London-report.pdf>

Ethelo, 'Okotoks 2080' <https://okotoks-2080.ethelo.net/page/collective-results> accessed 16 February 2023

EUROStat, 'Households with internet access, 2010 and 2016 (as % of all households)' <https://ec.euro pa.eu/eurostat/statistics-explained/index.php?title=File:Households_with_internet_access,_2010_ and_2016_(as_%25_of_all_households)_F2.png>

Ford Foundation, Database search for the Center for Investigative Reporting <https://www.for dfoundation.org/work/our-grants/awarded-grants/grants-database/?q=Center%20for%20Inves tigative%20Reporting&p=1>, accessed 12 February 2023

Get Involved London, 'Climate Emergency Action Plan: Trouble with Bubbles' <https://getinvolved.lon don.ca/climate/widgets/81531/videos/6540> accessed 26 January 2023

Government of Singapore, 'How is my Vote still Secret if the Ballot Paper has a Serial Number on It?' (August 2015) <https://www.gov.sg/article/how-is-my-vote-still-secret-if-the-ballot-paper-has-a-serial-number-on-it> accessed 23 January 2023

Harmony Labs 'Mission' <https://www.harmonylabs.org/mission> accessed 22 February 2023

Harmony Labs 'People' <https://www.harmonylabs.org/people> accessed 22 February 2023

Harmony Labs 'Projects' <https://www.harmonylabs.org/projects> accessed 22 February 2023

Health in Aging Foundation, 'Nursing Homes' (October 2020) <https://www.healthinaging.org/age-friendly-healthcare-you/care-settings/nursing-homes>

Il Fatto Quotidiano, 'Referendum cannabis, in tres giorni 333mila sottoscrizioni. E da oggi si può firmare anche senza identità digitale: ecco come' (14 September 2021) <https://www.ilfattoquoti diano.it/2021/09/14/referendum-cannabis-in-tre-giorni-333mila-sottoscrizioni-e-da-oggi-si-puo-fir mare-anche-senza-identita-digitale-ecco-come/6320391/>

Impact Investing Institute, 'Our Supporters' <https://www.impactinvest.org.uk/our-supporters-2/> accessed 26 January 2023

Impact Investing Institute, 'Place-based Impact Investing' <https://www.impactinvest.org.uk/project/ place-based-impact-investing/> accessed 26 January 2023

Involve 'About' https://involve.org.uk/about accessed 26 March 2023

Involve, 'Citizens Assembly on Social Care: Recommendations for Funding Adult Social Care' (June 2018) <https://oecd-opsi.org/wp-content/uploads/2019/02/Citizens-Assembly-on-Social-Care-Rec ommendations-for-funding-social-care_2.pdf> accessed 18 February 2023

Involve, 'How can Institutional Investors Bring in Community Engagement into Impact Investing' <https://involve.org.uk/our-work/our-projects/embedding-good-practice/how-can-institutional-in vestors-bring-community> accessed 26 January 2023

Irish Citizens' Assembly, 'Second Report and Recommendations of the Citizens' Assembly: How we best Respond to the Challenges and Opportunities of an Aging Population' (December 2017) <https://2016 – 2018.citizensassembly.ie/en/How-we-best-respond-to-challenges-and-opportunities-of-an-ageing-population/Final-Report-on-how-we-best-respond-to-the-challenges-and-opportunities-of-an-ageing-population/Final-Report-on-Older-People-Incl-Appendix-A-D.pdf> accessed 18 February 2023.

Journal of Deliberative Democracy, 'Sponsors' <https://delibdemjournal.org/site/about/> accessed 26 February 2023

Justiça Eleitoral, 'Biometria' <https://www.justicaeleitoral.jus.br/biometria/> accessed 23 January 2023

Krat-id, 'AI "kratt" strategy' <https://e-estonia.com/wp-content/uploads/2020-april-facts-ai-strategy. pdf> accessed 11 January 2023

La Repubblica, 'M5S, dopo Rousseau il Movimento sceglie due piattaforme: SkyVote Cloud per il voto online e Odoo per i dati degli iscritti' (15 June 2021) <https://www.repubblica.it/politica/ 2021/06/15/news/m5s_dopo_rousseau_piattaforma_skyvote_assemblea_gruppi_parlamentari-306204842/>

Latin American Economic Outlook 2010 (OECD 2009)

Legislative Assembly of Alberta, 'Members' <https://www.assembly.ab.ca/members/members-of-the-legislative-assembly> accessed 22 December 2022

Lisboa Participa, Câmara Municipal de Lisboa <op.lisboaparticipa.pt/> accessed 18 January 2023.

Lisboa Participa, Câmara Municipal de Lisboa, '#2 Cricao de Caminho Pedonal com a Apoio para Bicecletas' <https://op.lisboaparticipa.pt/propostas/604f388a6a7c8600a9eba5bb> accessed 18 January 2023

Lisboa Participa, Câmara Municipal de Lisboa, 'Edicões Anteriores' <https://op.lisboaparticipa.pt/ edicoes-anteriores> accessed 17 January 2023

Lisboa Participa, Câmara Municipal de Lisboa, 'Perguntas Frequentas' <https://op.lisboaparticipa.pt/ faqs> accessed 17 January 2023

Lisboa Participa, Câmara Municipal de Lisboa, 'Projectos Vencedores: Mobilidade para Todos em Benfica' <https://op.lisboaparticipa.pt/projetos-vencedores/6048eb500b405d5c803c6ff5/570fa466 f41ec1c4356c3dc0> accessed 25 January 2023

MacArthur Foundation, 'Grant Search: Public Integrity' <https://www.macfound.org/grants/?q=center +for+public+integrity> accessed 12 February 2023

Mayor's Office of Immigrant Affairs, 'State of our Immigrant City: Annual Report for Calendar Year 2020' https://www1.nyc.gov/assets/immigrants/downloads/pdf/MOIA-Annual-Report-for-2020.pdf

'Monster Grown Ventures LLC' (*Open Corporates*) https://opencorporates.com/companies/us_de/4603076 accessed 25 March 2023

National Equity Atlas, 'Car Access' <https://nationalequityatlas.org/indicators/Car_access#/>

New York City Council, 'PB NYC Rulebook' <https://www.participatorybudgeting.org/wp-content/up loads/2016/10/PBNYC2016_2017-Rulebook_PBP.pdf>

New York City, Independent Budget Office, 'Understanding New York City' <https://www.ibo.nyc.ny.us/iboreports/IBOCBG.pdf>

newDemocracy, 'Supporters and Funding' accessed 26 February 2023

NYC Civic Engagement Commission 'The People's Money' <https://www.participate.nyc.gov/processes/Citywidepb/f/304/proposals/2507?page=2> accessed 18 January 2023

NYC Civic Engagement Commission, 'The People' <https://www.participate.nyc.gov/processes/Cit ywidepb/f/304/proposals/2353> accessed 11 February 2023

NYC Civic Engagement Commission, 'The People's Money' <https://www.participate.nyc.gov/proc esses/Citywidepb/f/303/> accessed 18 January 2023

NYU, 'New Research on Participatory Budgeting Highlights Community Priorities in Public Spending' (22 July 2020) <https://www.nyu.edu/about/news-publications/news/2020/july/new-research-on-participatory-budgeting-highlights-community-pri.html> accessed 17 January 2023

OECD 2001, 'Understanding the Digital Divide' <https://www.oecd.org/digital/ieconomy/1888451.pdf>

Ofcom, 'Communications Market Report 2021' (22 July 2021) <https://www.ofcom.org.uk/__data/as sets/pdf_file/0011/222401/communications-market-report-2021.pdf>

Office for National Statistics, 'Internet Access – Households and Individuals: 2020' (7 August 2020) https://www.gov.uk/government/statistics/internet-access-households-and-individuals-2020

Open Collective Account, Democracy Next <https://opencollective.com/democracynext> accessed 26 March 2023.

OneProject.org, Form 990-PF (2015) available at 'Non-Profit Explorer' (*ProPublica*) <https://projects.pro publica.org/nonprofits/display_990/463259572/12_2017_prefixes_45-46%2F463259572_201512_990PF_2017120715013752> accessed 25 March 2023

OneProject.org, Form 990-PF (2019) available at 'Non-Profit Explorer' (*ProPublica*) <https://projects.pro publica.org/nonprofits/organizations/463259572/202043219349102909/full> accessed 25 March 2023

Paris, 'Budget Participatif 2023: Deposez vos Idées' <https://www.paris.fr/pages/budget-participatif-de posez-vos-idees-22902> accessed 21 February 2023

People Powered, 'Funding' <https://www.peoplepowered.org/funding> accessed 17 January 2023

People Powered, 'Partners: Funders' <https://www.peoplepowered.org/about/partners> accessed 17 January 2023

People's Plan for Nature, 'Frequently Asked Questions' <https://peoplesplanfornature.org/frequently-asked-questions> accessed 26 January 2023

People's Plan for Nature, 'People' <https://peoplesplanfornature.org/peoples-assembly-nature> accessed 26 January 2023

People's Plan for Nature, 'People' <https://peoplesplanfornature.org/sites/default/files/2022-11/People %27s%20Assembly%20for%20Nature%20-%20Catering%20Policy_0.pdf> accessed 26 January 2023

People's Plan for Nature, 'People' <https://peoplesplanfornature.org/sites/default/files/2022-11/People %27s%20Assembly%20for%20Nature%20-%20Travel%20Policy.pdf> accessed 26 January 2023

People's Plan for Nature, 'Who is in the Advisory Group?' <https://peoplesplanfornature.org/who-advisory-group> accessed 26 January 2023

Pew Research Center, 'An Examination of the 2016 Electorate Based on Validated Voters' (9 August 2018) <https://www.pewresearch.org/politics/2018/08/09/an-examination-of-the-2016-electorate-based-on-validated-voters/>

Pew Research Center, 'Internet/Broadband Fact Sheet' (7 April 2021) <https://www.pewresearch.org/internet/fact-sheet/internet-broadband/>

Piratar Kosningakerfi, 'Issues to Discuss' https://x.piratar.is/polity/1/topics/ accessed 22 March 2023

Policy Network, 'Our Supporters' <https://policynetwork.progressivebritain.org/work/> accessed January 2023

Polys, 'APSS Council Member Election 2019' <https://ru.polys.me/success-stories/election-of-apss-board-members> accessed 11 January 2023

Polys, 'Large Scale Elections at RANEPA' <https://ru.polys.me/success-stories/elections-at-ranepa> accessed 11 January 2023

Polys, 'Online Election of the Director of the Federal Scientific Research Center of the Russian Academy of Sciences' <https://ru.polys.me/success-stories/online-election-of-the-director-of-frsc-ras> accessed 11 January 2023

Polys, 'Voting for "Sailor of the Year"' <https://ru.polys.me/success-stories/voting-for-seafarer-of-the-year>

Polys, 'Voting in the Primaries in the Yabloko Party' <https://ru.polys.me/success-stories/yabloko-party-primaries> accessed 11 January 2023

Project Isizwe, 'Our Work' <https://www.projectisizwe.org/our-work/> accessed 21 February 2022

ProPublica, 'Steal Our Stories' <https://www.propublica.org/steal-our-stories/> accessed 12 Feb 2023

Public Agenda, 'Our Institutional Supporters' <https://www.publicagenda.org/about/our-funders/> accessed 17 January 2023

RATP Group, 'Pour une ville plein de vie' https://ratpgroup.com/fr/notre-contribution/pour-une-ville-pleine-de-vie/

Reboot Democracy <https://www.rebootdem.com/> accessed 22 February 2023

Riigi Infosüsteemi Amet, 'Data Tracker' <https://www.ria.ee/riigi-infosusteem/inimkeskne-andme haldus/andmejalgija> accessed 26 February 2023

Riigi Infosüsteemi Amet, 'Factsheet: X-Road' <https://e-estonia.com/wp-content/uploads/2020mar-facts-a4-v02-x-road.pdf> accessed 24 January 2023

RTE, 'Spain's Far-Left Leader Wins Confidence Vote After Luxury Home Purchase' (28 May 2018)

Samworth Foundation, 'Funder Commitment on Climate Change' <https://web.archive.org/web/20220629150407/https://www.samworthfoundation.org.uk/about-us-2/funder-commitment-on-climate-change-2> accessed 28 January 2023

Scottish Parliament, Participation and Communications Team, 'Fireworks and Pyrotechnics Articles (Scotland) Bill: Digital Engagement: Summary of Online Forum Submissions to Support the Criminal Justice Committee's Scrutiny of the Bill' (March 2022) <https://www.parliament.scot/-/media/files/committees/criminal-justice-committee/fireworks-bill-engagement-summary.pdf>

Select Committee on Home Affairs, Fourth Report (1997–1998) <https://publications.parliament.uk/pa/cm199798/cmselect/cmhaff/768/76807.htm>

Smart Dublin <www.smartdublin.ie> accessed 18 January 2023.

Social Metrics Commission, 'Measuring Poverty 2020: A Report of the Social Metrics Commission' (2020) <https://socialmetricscommission.org.uk/wp-content/uploads/2020/06/Measuring-Poverty-2020-Web.pdf>

Solonian Democracy Institute, 'Building Trust & Breaking Down Complexity: The Past, Present & Future of Participatory Budgeting: Interview with Tarson Nuñez' (24 November 2021) <www.so lonian-institute.com/post/building-trust-breaking-down-complexity-the-past-present-future-of-par ticipatory-budgeting>

Solonian Democracy Institute, 'Interview with Patricia Namakula: Democracy and Digitalization: A Ugandan Perspective' (16 September 2022) <https://www.solonian-institute.com/post/digital-de mocracy-a-ugandan-perspective>

Statistics Canada, 'Access to the Internet in Canada, 2020' (31 May 2021) <https://www150.statcan.gc. ca/n1/daily-quotidien/210531/dq210531d-eng.htm>

Statistics Canada, 'Census Profile 2016 Census, London' <https://www12.statcan.gc.ca/census-recense ment/2016/dp-pd/prof/details/page.cfm?Geo1=CMACA&Code1=555&Geo2=PR&Code2=35&Data= Count&SearchText=london>

Statistics Canada, 'Census Profile, 2016 Census, Lethbridge' <https://www12.statcan.gc.ca/census-re censement/2016/dp-pd/prof/details/page.cfm?Geo1=POPC&Code1=0467&SearchText=Lethbridge> accessed 18 February 2023

The Democracy and Culture Foundation, 'Who We Work With' https://www.democracycultur efoundation.org/who-we-work-with/ accessed 26 February 2023

Transfield Holdings, 'Transfield Holdings' <https://transfield.com.au/> accessed 26 February 2023.

Trevor Noah – It's My Culture, 'Zambia Loves Escalators – Just Don't be Gay' (5 November 2018) <https://www.youtube.com/watch?v=L3SIdXPtB0M> accessed 21 January 2023.

Tribunal Superior Eleitoral, 'Biometrics' <https://www.tse.jus.br/eleitor/justificativa-eleitoral/con sequencias-para-quem-nao-justificar> accessed 23 January 2023

UK Law Commission, 'Research Paper: Manner of Voting in UK Elections' <https://www.lawcom.gov. uk/app/uploads/2015/03/Electoral-Law_Manner-of-Voting_Research.pdf>

UNDP, 'Human Development Index' <https://hdr.undp.org/data-center/human-development-index> accessed 20 November 2022

UNICEF, 'Nearly one third of Nigerian children do not have enough water to meet their daily needs – UNICEF' (22 March 2021) <https://www.unicef.org/nigeria/press-releases/nearly-one-third-niger ian-children-do-not-have-enough-water-meet-their-daily-needs>

UNICEF, 'WASH Situation in Mozambique' https://www.unicef.org/mozambique/en/water-sanitation-and-hygiene-wash accessed 22 March 2023

UNICEF, 'Water, Sanitation and Hygiene – Kenya' <https://www.unicef.org/kenya/water-sanitation-and-hygiene> accessed 12 January 2023

Unique Identification Authority of India, Government of India, 'Aadhaar: A Unique Identity for the People' <https://uidai.gov.in/images/Aadhaar_Brochure_July_22.pdf> accessed 11 January 2023

United States Census Bureau, '2020 Presidential Election Voting and Registration Tables Now Available' (29 April 2021) <https://www.census.gov/newsroom/press-releases/2021/2020-presi dential-election-voting-and-registration-tables-now-available.html>

United States Census Bureau, 'New York City' <https://www.census.gov/quickfacts/new yorkcitynewyork>

United States Securities and Exchange Commission, 'Document SG 13/A' <https://www.sec.gov/Ar chives/edgar/data/1326801/000119312514040883/d672846dsc13ga.htm> accessed 25 February 2023

Urban Institute, 'Annual Report 2021' <https://www.urban.org/sites/default/files/2022-10/2021%20Fi nancial%20Report.pdf>

US Department of Agriculture, 'Racial and Ethnic Minorities, Economic Research Service' (13 October 2020) <https://www.ers.usda.gov/data-products/chart-gallery/gallery/chart-detail/?chartId=99538>

World Bank, 'Gini Index' <https://data.worldbank.org/indicator/SI.POV.GINI> accessed December 21 2022

World Bank, 'Individuals using the Internet (% of population) France' <https://data.worldbank.org/indicator/IT.NET.USER.ZS?locations=FR> accessed 28 December 2022

World Bank, 'Nigeria to Improve Electricity Access and Services to Citizens' (5 February 2021) <https://www.worldbank.org/en/news/press-release/2021/02/05/nigeria-to-improve-electricity-access-and-services-to-citizens>

Yonder Consulting, 'Oh my Fruity Goodness: How Do You Get the Nation to Eat Healthy?' https://yonderconsulting.com/case-study/ohmyfruitygoodness/ accessed 25 January 2023.

Zencity, 'Community-Based Insights for Better City Management' <https://zencity.io/zencity-for-cities/> accessed 22 January 2023

Zencity, 'Data Snapshot, The Housing Crisis in the UK: An Analysis of Resident Discourse' <https://zencity.wpenginepowered.com/wp-content/uploads/2022/10/Data-Report-The-Housing-Crisis-in-the-UK.pdf> accessed 22 January 2023

Interviews & Emails

Bjarnason, Róbert. Emails to Roslyn Fuller, 8 November 2022 and 11 January 2023

Britt, Lori. Interview. Conducted by Roslyn Fuller 11 March 2022

Búi Halldórsson, Eiríkur. Interview. Conducted by Roslyn Fuller, 22 March 2022

Búi Halldórsson, Eiríkur. Email to Roslyn Fuller, 8 November 2022

Casaleggio, Davide. Interview. Conducted by Roslyn Fuller, 15 September 2020

Crimi, Vito. Interview. Conducted by Roslyn Fuller, 3 March 2022

Ielīte, Inete. Interview. Conducted by Roslyn Fuller, 11 March 2022

Neblo, Michael. Interview. Conducted by Roslyn Fuller 1 April 2022

Stoddart, Alistair. Interview. Conducted by Roslyn Fuller, 11 March 2022

Index

Note: References in *italic* and **bold** refer to figures and tables. References followed by "n" refer to notes.

https://doi.org/10.1515/9783110794465-016